Children's Worlds and
Children's Language

New Babylon

Studies in the Social Sciences

47

Mouton de Gruyter · Berlin · New York · Amsterdam

Children's Worlds and Children's Language

Edited by

Jenny Cook-Gumperz
William A. Corsaro
Jürgen Streeck

Mouton de Gruyter · Berlin · New York · Amsterdam

Mouton de Gruyter (formerly Mouton, The Hague)
is a Division of Walter de Gruyter & Co., Berlin.

Library of Congress Cataloging in Publication Data

Children's worlds and children's language.

(New Babylon, studies in the social sciences ; 47)
Includes bibliographies and index.
1. Socialization. 2. Children-Language. 3. Social inter-
action in children. 4. Interpersonal communication in children.
i. Cook-Gumperz, Jenny. ii. Corsaro, William A. iii. Streeck,
Juergen. iv. Series.
HQ783.C543   1986   303.3'2   86-24213
ISBN 0-89925-089-0 (alk. paper)

CIP-Kurztitelaufnahme der Deutschen Bibliothek

Children's worlds and children's language / ed. by Jenny Cook-
Gumperz ... — Berlin ; New York ; Amsterdam : Mouton de
Gruyter, 1986.
(New Babylon ; 47)
ISBN 3-11-010681-7
NE: Cook-Gumperz, Jenny [Hrsg.]; GT

Printed on acid free paper

Typesetting: Arthur Collignon GmbH, Berlin. Printing: Gerike GmbH, Berlin. —
Binding: Dieter Mikolai, Berlin.   Printed in Germany.

Preface

When I finally compiled the index for *Children's Worlds and Children's Language* (hastily, so the book could go into print), a six-year enterprise was coming to an end. It began in 1980 when we were invited to organize the subsection „Language, Socialization, Children's Worlds, and Social-Structural Settings" at the 10th World Congress of Sociology. Ten papers in this book were originally given at that conference in Mexico City in the summer of 1982. Those of us who were there thank our sponsors. We feel more grateful, however, to our Mexican hosts who made us feel welcome and at ease, while their own country was suffering from its worst economic crisis. We owe thanks also to Fritz Schütze; as organizer of the Sociolinguistics Research Council he devoted years of his life to make everything comfortable for us. To the people at Mouton de Gruyter's I want to say that working with them has been a pleasure. Not only are they *echte* professionals; what is more: they are fun. As editors, finally, we would like to let the authors know that we sincerely appreciate their patience.

Six years — that is almost half of a childhood. Children were born during these six years to some of the authors, and we dedicate this book to them. While they are growing up, acquiring social competence through routinely interacting with their peers, we keep wondering whether our view of childhood will be meaningful to them when they reach our age and look at this book to find out about the theory behind their parents' way of bringing them up.

West Berlin, September 1986 Jürgen Streeck

Contents

List of Contributors

Manfred Auwärter
Tübingen
(W. Germany)

Michael Bamberg
Shanghai
(People's Republic of China)

Nancy Budwig
Shanghai
(People's Republic of China)

Luigia Camaioni
Rome
(Italy)

Herman Coenen
Tilburg
(The Netherlands)

Jenny Cook-Gumperz
Berkeley
(USA)

William A. Corsaro
Bloomington
(USA)

Gerard M. Duveen
London
(Great Britain)

Susan Ervin-Tripp
Berkeley
(USA)

Gary Alan Fine
Minneapolis
(USA)

David W. Gegeo
Honolulu
(USA)

Kurt Kreppner
W. Berlin
(W. Germany)

Max Miller
München
(W. Germany)

Sibylle Paulsen
W. Berlin
(W. Germany)

Yvonne Schütze
W. Berlin
(W. Germany)

Maureen M. Shields
London
(Great Britain)

Michael T. Siegert
Dhaka
(Bangladesh)

Amy Strage
Berkeley
(USA)

Jürgen Streeck
W. Berlin
(W. Germany)

Jürgen Weissenborn
Nijmegen
(The Netherlands)

Karen Ann Watson-Gegeo
Honolulu
(USA)

Anthony J. Wootton
York
(Great Britain)

Introduction

Jenny Cook-Gumperz and William A. Corsaro

> "Sticks and stones may break my bones,
> but words can never hurt me"

1. Language in Children's Worlds

Most of us, at some time during our childhood have sought by means of this familiar chant or similar magical incantations to stave off the increasing realization of the power of the language of others over ourselves and our self-presentation. The awareness that language has a special power arises most dramatically in childhood through children's games and perhaps most indelibly through taunts and teasing routines where even the gestures of "make-up-and-be-friends" do not always eradicate the hurtful words from our minds or restore our self-esteem. The understanding that language has a power to affect us or to change the behavior of others toward us, develops in early childhood. As adults we often assume that in children's interaction the power of language itself can be displaced by the direct intervention of physical action. Such an assumption is based on our observations that although language often operates as a means of achieving satisfactory outcomes to activities and as a strategy for control, direct action often appears to be the ultimate arbiter of disputes and arrangements in children's worlds. There are, however, many times when young children experiment with language (e. g., verbal games, jokes and rhymes) that show an intrinsic rhetorical satisfaction in the exercises of language as an end in itself. It is through these games and routines that we are reminded that children begin life with an exclusively oral culture. Although much of the research on language development has not focused on this fact, language is initially a completely oral experience for children, and continues throughout childhood with many of the mnemonic devices of traditional oral cultures (Opie and Opie, 1959, 1969; Harré, 1978).

Our perspective in this collection of studies is on children's worlds and the role that language plays within them. We emphasize the fact that social experience is shaped for and by children in their acts of speech. The social worlds within which children live their daily lives are created and maintained by them through the use of child-specific communicative means. We are focusing upon language not simply as a grammatical skill, but as a set of speech strategies which children use to structure social action and to control and effect communication. Reflexively these speech strategies give rise to social knowledge which helps to form a social identity for the child.

Initially, children acquire language as part of a dialogue between self and others; a spoken dialogue that develops from children's earliest experiences with their mothers (see Ryan, 1974; Snow, 1977). Research has considered how children can effect the transition from non-speech to early speech through games and play activities (see Bruner, 1975; Ratner and Bruner, 1978). However, the interface of further language development with social development, once the child has begun to speak is as of yet uncharted territory. This is an area which must be explored in order to put children's social development into a balanced perspective.

Communicative competence is more than the cultural ability to select the appropriate linguistic forms for the social context. Human spoken communication is a far more complex process in which various systems of meaning and expression must be brought into alignment. In face-to-face interaction speech is always embedded in a web of 'embodied' meanings and tacit understandings. In recent work researchers from various theoretical perspectives have shown that orderliness and mutual understanding in the flow of talk is achieved through the participants' joint reliance on rule-systems for the performance and sequencing of verbal activities and nonverbal cues which facilitate speaker-exchange. The social situation of talk does not provide a prepatterned set of procedural rules, but is itself generated as a product of verbal interaction which is at the same time interpreted by reference to it. This fact attests the inherent complexity of human speech in action and its reflexive ties to the ongoing construction of social worlds.

Given the complexity of adult communication any study of children's communicative competence should perhaps begin by asking some basic questions about how children can be seen to be acquiring speech-in-action which is both the product and guide of particular social outcomes. The key to the pragmatic realization of speech may not lie in children's appropriate use of any particular speech act, but in the ways in which speech acts are sequenced across time to perform ongoing, joint activities which have for children and for adults a demonstrable and realizable structure.

It is within children's worlds that language as speech practice takes on it own particular importance. Many developmental psychologists, following Piaget, have suggested that there are two key periods of rapid change in childhood. The first occurs between four and six years when the closely structured world of adult and child gives way to the world of ritual action and self-presentation (see Harré, 1974). The second occurs toward the 12th and 13th year when the content of children's worlds changes into one in which peer structures established in the earlier years play a much larger role in the development of individual social identity. But how language learning links with the development of such phases of social competence and how social rules and speech practices interact in children's experiences are questions that have not received consistent study.

Our aim in this volume is to address this gap in the literature and to bring together studies across the full range of childhood from early infancy through adolescence. These studies, while sharing a common perspective toward the study of children's language and social development, employ a range of methodologies including quasi-experiments, clinical interviewing, ethnography, and discourse analysis (see chapter 1). All the studies view social and linguistic development throughout childhood as forming a single continuum. Therefore, the central theme of this volume is essentially *language socialization*.

2. Language Socialization

By language socialization we do not wish to evaluate children's language ability by the standards of adult competency. By denoting the theme of this collection as *children's worlds and children's language* we are attempting to take the child's perspective on the uses of language in social life. The study of children's socialization has too often been dominated by the view that childhood is only a transition period before reaching adult status. Conversely it has been argued that children live their lives in a separate world with its own stock of knowledge, relevances, meanings and appropriateness rules. Social situations created by children as well as the interpersonal relations which they entertain are 'culturally different' from the adult world rather than being incomplete versions thereof (see Corsaro, 1985; Goodwin, 1980, 1982). But it is incorrect to argue that a culture of childhood — shared by all children — exists alongside of but separate from the adult world. Some elements of peer culture, such as children's games and lore, may indeed be acquired solely within children's groups and be transmitted from child to child beyond the influence of adults (see Opie and Opie, 1959, 1969). Nevertheless, the majority of elements of peer culture originate from children's perceptions of and reactions to the adult world (see Corsaro, 1985). It is in the gradual development of children's discourse strategies and social skills across the entire period of childhood that we can best see this interaction between children's reactions to the adult world and the requirements of that world taking shape for children. It is this process that we are calling language socialization.

Since the term, language socialization, is rarely used it is necessary to make explicit our understanding of the idea. By socialization we mean the growth of social understanding and of the capabilities for the maintenance of social relations that develop throughout childhood. Childhood is an apprenticeship that is variously defined (in different societies and eras) as the period necessary for the replacement of society's personnel and the reproduction of its social structure. Through variations in the definition of this period one can trace the development of an ideology of childhood (Ariès, 1962). The history of the individual disciplines' involvement in the study of this social reproduction process has made the term socialization one which begs almost as many questions as it provides theoretical frameworks with possible answers. Therefore, it is necessary to begin any work that is concerned with these processes with some discussion of the concept.

The first mention of the term 'socialization' is in the Oxford Dictionary of 1828 where it is defined as "to render social, to make fit for living in society". An awareness of socialization as a problem for a theory of society was first developed at the end of the last century (see Giddings, 1897; Ross, 1896). Durkheim's conception of *conscience collective* (1893) and of the "penetration of the social into the individual" (1912) was a cornerstone for the development of socialization theory. As a full fledged theoretical construct, however, 'socialization' did not exist until 1939 — 40 when it emerged almost simultaneously within the three areas of anthropology, psychology, and sociology (Danziger, 1971). The earliest use of the term from a sociological perspective was in a text by Ogburn and Nimkoff where socialization was described as "the process whereby the individual is converted into the person". The term also implied "the active intervention in the life of the individual by social agents who seek to mould him/her" (Danziger 1971: 4).

There has always been a theoretical ambivalence at the core of the usage of the term "socialization". This ambivalence is between the unfolding of the biological patterning of the individual under pressure of the environment and the assumption that growing persons are shaped by, or can shape their own social futures. As Danziger (1971: 17) suggests "socialization bears the marks of its historical orgins; on one level this can be seen as a persistent tendency to emphasize the permanent plasticity of the human response and to deny the existence of irreversible structural changes in human development". But at the same time "socialization research has continued to show the influence of what might be called the ideology of social engineering". The study of socialization has focused upon the adaption of individuals to particular life styles and social roles which are already prepared for their entry. Brim (1966) in work on socialization through the life cycle states that "the function of socialization is to transform the human raw material of society into good working members". The procedures by which this process takes place provide for the construction of a research paradigm which takes as given the structuring of any social system and looks only at integral replacement as the major problem. The paradigm that developed was a linkage of functionalist sociology with neobehaviorist psychology. This linkage produced a basic ideology of socialization in which the emphasis is upon adaption as the shaping of the individual to the constraints of the group and the pressure upon the group in its turn to perform appropriately within the social system. When the Freudian theory of personality was adopted to account for the social development of the individual psyche and the 'internalization' of social norms, values, and role-expectations (see Parsons and Bales, 1955), and the psyche was described as a reflection of the social value system, the functionalist cycle was complete. The perennial conflict and polarity between biological nature (drives) and the society's demands which was so characteristic of Freud's thinking was harmonized in favor of a view of the individual as fully integrated into the social system.

Socialization became established within a functionalist paradigm in which the normative pressure of society upon the individual resulted in the acquisition of social roles and the successful internalization of the value system. This paradigm was attacked as providing an over-socialized conception of man (Wrong, 1961), but the flight from the use of this concept is perhaps more recent. For example, in a collection of studies focussing on the perspective of the 'integration of the child into a social world' Richards (1974: 5—6) argues that the term socialization:

> has tended to become the property of psychologists who adopt a neo-behaviorist approach to the study of development. . . . As I have already indicated, the analysis of human social development requires both an adequate notion of what a society is and of a biological individual, as well as of the ways in which an individual lives in his social and environmental space. These are lacking in the neo-behaviorist tradition, where socialization is seen as a psychological process of learning and of the training of the individual. It is regarded as something that has to be imposed on the child — the child does not become social but is made social by the conscious efforts of various members of society. . . . Such concerns have led to a brand of sociology which has over-emphasised the adaption of individuals to particular styles of life and social roles and has underemphasised the process by which the individual is to take part in any social life. Adapting to a new job has been put on a par with the process of becoming a social human being. The term socialization has been used to describe both these processes and in doing so has become trivialized.

We would like to suggest that it is possible to untrivialize the study of socialization, but focusing explicitly upon the language based activities and processes by which children construct a social world through interaction with others.

3. An Interpretive Approach to Language Socialization

Our approach to childhood socialization is essentially interpretive. From an interpretive perspective the child is viewed as beginning life as a social being within an already defined social network. In short, the child is seen as a discoverer of a world endowed with meaning. The views of cognitive developmentalists like Piaget provide a good starting point for this perspective. However, the interpretive view goes a step further in arguing that the child's own actions are part of reciprocal interactions, even if they take place within power relationships with more mature persons. Children help to shape their own learning experience by their interactive responses. Moreover, their interpretive search is essentially built around their developing control of speech and language as the centralized communication system. How much the developing biological individual or the social group to which the child is a member contribute to the child's development, while seen as important in language development studies, is not a relevant issue for the interpretive approach. We see socialization as an interpersonal activity of 'becoming' rather than an unfolding of a biologically based plan or an imprinting of social structure on the person.

As such a process of becoming, socialization begins at the very earliest stages of life through the communicative process that develops at birth between the mother and child. The complexities of such early communication are a growing area of study (see Bullowa, 1980). Central to an understanding of social development are the communicative uses of language as acts of speaking and conversation in the life of the socializing members. Moreover, it is through these verbal and communicative processes as conversational exchanges that social action itself is constituted. Methodologically, the growth of new understandings and techniques in the analysis of discourse and conversation have provided increased possibilities for clarifying the processes by which language as speaking practice becomes a critical force in its own right (as opposed to just a medium for transmission of social cultural information). It is this perspective that enables us, in this volume, to consider our explorations in the growth of children's worlds as language socialization.

4. Language Socialization: Reproduction or Transmission of Social Knowledge?

We began by describing an inherent ambivalence at the core of socialization studies between the biological and the environmental (the given and the learned) and how we have been able to use a new understanding of the nature of the social process to show that this was essentially a false opposition. The biological bases are transformed by the intrinsically interactive character of human life from its very beginning. However, there still remains a dilemma for socialization studies to distinguish between the character of the learning that takes place throughout the life cycle in the acquisition of new social skills and the process of becoming a competent member of the society from first entry. The former process has been traditionally defined as horizontal transmission of culture (or enculturation) where information and learning is passed between members of a generation. The term socialization was kept for the transmission of culture across generations, or what we have been referring to as the reproduction of the social order. However, this distinction became blurred in the development of what Richards (1974) has referred to as the psychological take-over of the study of socialization.

We suggest that a restatement of this distinction is necessary. In order to do so there is a need to distinguish between two perspectives on the process of socialization; one, a linear transmission model and a second, a social reproductive model. The transmission model is characterized by a linear view of development in which the assumption is made that the child must pass through a transition from a purely biological being through a period of childhood into a socially competent membership in a social group and in a set of social institutions. In this view the period of childhood is often seen as a set of developmental stages in which skills and identities are acquired in preparation for adult life.

The linear model assumes that age, to an important extent, determines membership in specific social institutions (e. g., family, school and occupation) which form societal environments through which the socializing individual moves or is moved. From a sociological perspective the linear model is derived from a Durkheimian view of the social structure in which modern societies cohere through the independent functioning of differentiated institutions and the society as a whole is integrated through processes of competition and co-operation, exchange and commitment to overarching values. In this view childhood is the period during which the basic skills of co-operation, exchange and moral values are acquired through progressive experience in different institutional settings.

In many studies of children's social development, moral development, and language acquisition in the 1950s and 1960s this linear view of progressive development was established (see, for example, chapters by Bandura, Jenkins, and Kohlberg in Goslin, 1969). This linear view, in which development is seen as a series of progressive stages that are exclusive though cumulative, depends upon a transmission model in which it is assumed that the child has to be made into a social being.

The reproductive model, on the other hand, assumes that the child will, to a certain extent, be interactively responsible for constructing social activities from the beginnings of life. Central to this view of socialization is the belief that in children's communication with others, language provides a sociocognitive apparatus for the child and others to use. Speech and conversation become the most critical tool for the construction of the social world, because it is through the use of language that social action is generated. In this respect, socialization can be seen as the simultaneous production and reproduction of the social order through individuals' interactions and acts of speech (see Bourdieu and Passeron, 1977; Giddens, 1981).

In the reproductive model the biological child enters into a social nexus and through self-generated interaction with others builds up a social understanding which becomes a developing core of social knowledge on which he/she builds throughout the life course. From this perspective, the phases of development are supportive of each other and not exclusive.

This view of the child as an active constructor of a socially meaningful and cognitively apprehensible world has support from both developmental psychologists and sociologists. The tradition in children's developmental studies began with constructivist theorists, like Piaget, G. H. Mead, and Vygotsky, who argue that children acquire skills and knowledge through interaction with the environment. However, if children do indeed construct social knowledge and acquire interactive skills by acting on the environment, then there is a need to examine these actions within their social contexts, that is within the lifeworlds of children.

Thus, the reproductive model extends the constructivist view by specifically focusing upon the language and speech-dependent micro-processes through which interaction takes place and is stored for future use. Central to the distinction between transmission and reproductive models is the perspective which is taken on the character of social knowledge. The crux of the problem of socialization, as we see it, is between the view of social growth as a linear progression of stages or as a productive-reproductive complex. In the reproductive view we can, through the study of the micro-social process and language practices, explore the growth of children's worlds and how these worlds are eventually transformed into adult knowledge and practices. Thus, from the interpretive perspective children eventually reproduce a social world, which to paraphrase Vygotsky, contains within it the knowledge of generations.

References

Aries, Philippe
    1962   *Centuries of Childhood* (New York: Knopf).
Brim, Orville
    1966   *Socialization After Childhood* (New York: Wiley).
Bordieu, Pierre and Jean Claude Passeron
    1977   *Reproduction in Education, Society and Culture* (London and Beverly Hills: Sage).
Bruner, Jerome
    1975   "The ontongenesis of speech acts," *Journal of Child Language* 2: 1 – 20.
Bullowa, Margaret
    1980   *Before Speech* (New York: Cambridge University Press).
Corsaro, William A.
    1985   *Friendship and Peer Culture in the Early Years* (Norwood, N. J.: Ablex).
Danziger, Kurt
    1971   *Socialization* (Middlesex: Penguin).
Durkheim, Emile
    1893   *De La Division Du Travail Social* (Paris: Alcan).
    1912   *Les Formes Elementaires De La Vie Religieuse* (Paris: Alcan).
Giddens, Anthony
    1981   *A Contemporary Critique of Historical Materialism* (Berkeley: University of California Press).
Giddings, F. P.
    1897   *The Theory of Socialization* (New York: Macmillian).
Goodwin, Marjorie Harness
    1980   "He-said-she-said: Formal cultural procedures for the construction of a gossip dispute activity," *American Ethnologist* 7: 674 – 695.

1982 "Processes of dispute management among urban black children," *American Ethnologist* 9: 76–96.

Goslin, David (ed.)
1969 *Handbook of Socialization Theory and Research* (New York: Rand-McNally).

Harré, Rom
1974 "The conditions for a social psychology of childhood", *The Integration of a Child into a Social World*, edited by Martin P. Richards (New York: Cambridge university Press), 245–262.

Opie, Iona and Opie, Peter
1959 *The Lore and Language of School Children* (Oxford: Oxford University Press).
1969 *Children's Games in Street and Playground* (Oxford: Oxford University Press).

Parsons, Talcott and Bales, Robert F.
1955 *Family, Socialization, and Interaction Process* (Glencoe, Ill.: Free Press).

Ratner, Nancy and Bruner, Jerome
1978 "Games, social exchange and the acquisition of language," *Journal of Child Language* 5: 391–401.

Richards, Martin P. (ed.)
1974 *The Integration of a Child into a Social World* (New York: Cambridge University Press).

Ross, E. A.
1896 "Social control," *American Journal of Sociology* 1.

Ryan, Joanna
1974 "Early language development: Towards a communicational analysis," *The Integration of a Child into a Social World*, edited by Martin P. Richards (New York: Cambridge University Press), 185–214.

Snow, Catherine
1977 "The development of conversation between mothers and babies," *Journal of Child Language* 4: 1–22.

Wrong, Denis
1966 "The oversocialized conception of man in modern sociology," *American Sociological Review* 26: 183–193.

Issues in Theory and Method
of Studying Children's Worlds

Studying Children's Worlds: Methodological Issues

William A. Corsaro and Jürgen Streeck

1. Introduction

Over the last several years we have witnessed the emergence of a holistic approach to the study of children's language acquisition and socialization. Linguistic models which narrowly defined language development as the growth of the ability to produce increasingly complex and grammatically correct sentences have gradually been replaced by frameworks which seek to link the child's growing mastery of language both to the development of socio-cognitive skills and to the interactive structures of social activities in which the child takes part. The data-base of studies informed by this new theoretical orientation has correspondingly been enlarged so as to document not only the child's 'output' but the ways in which the child's linguistic utterances are shaped by the interactive circumstances in which they are produced.

The complexities of interaction — its focused, reciprocal, collaborative, and cross-modal nature, its sequential unfolding in real time and the need for participants to adjust to local constraints imposed by situational properties as well as to the perspectives held by co-participants — all require skills that go beyond the production of meaningful or well-formed utterances. Thus, children must learn to enlist the attention of others, to wait and take their turn, and to design their utterances so as to meet their partners' informational needs and levels of understanding. The study of language acquisition should therefore be viewed as a part of the study of the development of interactive abilities.

One of the consequences of this new interactionist approach to children's language has been an increasing cooperation between pragmatic-oriented researchers of child discourse (Ervin-Tripp and Mitchell-Kernan, 1977; Garvey, 1984; Ochs and Schieffelin, 1979), sociolinguists and anthropologists who investigate children's language use and socialization in its ethnographic context (Heath, 1983; Ochs and Schieffelin, 1984; cf. also Cook-Gumperz, this volume, and the introduction by Cook-Gumperz and Corsaro), and researchers of cognitive development working in the tradition of Piaget (1932), Kohlberg (1969) and Selman (1980), who are interested in the child's shift from egocentric to sociocentric thinking, role-taking, and cognition in the social domain (cf. Damon, 1977; Glick and Clarke-Stewart, 1978; Turiel, 1978; Youniss, 1977). Despite the fact, however, that these different approaches address a single subject matter, the development of interactional competence, their articulation into a unified methodology and research-paradigm proves difficult. Researchers in the cognitive tradition have largely relied on clinical interviewing (Piaget, 1926) to elicit children's conceptions of, e. g., justice, social rules, and social relations at different developmental stages. The relationship between verbal representations of the social world and interactional competence, however, is problematic; it is not clear, for example, if verbal accounts are organized at the same conceptual level as the scripts and schemata of interpretation underlying actual performances in situations of joint activity (cf. Auwärter and Kirsch, 1984). Mental substrata of interactional competence do not directly surface in overt performances. In order to bridge the gap between cognition and interaction in developmental research, it is necessary to approach documents of interaction scenes from a developmental perspective and pinpoint structural features of communication with children that mediate the internalization of the "machinery" (Sacks, Schegloff and Jefferson, 1974) of face-to-face communication (cf. Bruner, 1975).

To support the claim that social interaction "is an essential part of the developmental process itself and [that] structures of interaction determine the acquisition of specific abilities" (Auwärter and Kirsch, 1984: 167; cf. also Damon, 1984), researchers have recently found it useful to adopt the concept of "microgenesis" developed by Soviet psychologists (cf. Wertsch and Stone, 1978) as well as Vygotsky's similar notion of the "zone of proximal development" (Vygotsky, 1978; cf. Budwig, Strage and Bamberg, this volume). According to Vygotsky, cognitive growth is characterized by successions from "inter-psychological" to "intra-psychological" (mental) functioning. The "zone of proximal development" is "the distance between the actual developmental level as determined by independent problem solving and the level of potential development as determined through problem-solving under adult guidance or in collaboration with peers" (Vygotsky 1978: 86).

The German sociologist Overmann (whose works has, to some extent, been influential to the German contributions to this volume) has outlined a comparable conception of the "structure of interaction in socialization" and suggested that the structure of parent-child interaction provides the child with experiences which transcend his interpration capacities and thereby stimulate his cognitive development. In a dialectic process the child is then enabled to successively assign meaning patterns to interaction sequences. "A sociological theory of socialization must accordingly analyze the specific structural features constituting interaction in socialization" (Oevermann et al. 1976: 372−373).

In line with this new theoretical orientation, the large number of research studies in children's language and social cognition that have been conducted over the last several years show a noticeable movement away from strict experimental and hypothesis-testing methods to more naturalistic and interpretive approaches. However, this shift is not only the result of the discovery of limitations of traditional methods when studying young children (most especially experiments, cf. Bronfenbrenner, 1979), but also reflects a recognition of our lack of knowledge of children's worlds and peer cultures. Children are not passive receivers, processors, and storers of social and linguistic information but use their growing mastery of language and interactional strategies to actively construct a social world around themselves. Children's worlds are endowed with their own rules, rituals, and principles of conflict resolution and, depending upon the roles children are given within a society, not always easily accessible to adults. Besides our own memories of childhood we have little first-hand ethnographic information on the worlds children live in (but cf. Corsaro, 1985; Goodwin, 1982; Schwartzman, 1979), even though it is now a widely shared belief that peer-interaction may be a decisive context for the child's linguistic and socio-cognitive development in a variety of domains (Damon, 1977). It is therefore not satisfactory to conceive of children's language use and life-worlds as merely more primitive versions of adult social functioning; some of the children's complex interactive strategies may be solely linked to specific organizational principles of peer-cultures and thus be given up later in life without being replaced by equivalent, though more intricate, structures of interaction. Research studies which provide information on consistent features of children's life-worlds are therefore essential for the development of theory in childhood socialization which captures the perspective of the child and the importance of peer interaction and culture for the developmental process. (The substantive relevance of this new methodological orientation is attested, for example, by findings that young children may in fact have a much greater mastery of socio-cognitive skills and develop an aptitude at sociocentric thinking at an earlier age than has previously been assumed on the basis of results gained from experiments or clinical interviews; cf. Shields and Duveen, this volume.)

This volume contains papers which illustrate the shift away from more traditional methods. The papers range from quasi-experimental and interview studies to naturalistic observation and detailed micro-ethnographies of children's worlds. Overall, the studies in this volume reflect the attempt by many contemporary researchers to develop methodological strategies which either:

(1) identify consistent trends and stages in children's development of social knowledge and communicative skills while not overlooking the importance of social contextual factors; or

(2) discover and document stable features of children's worlds while at the same time attempting to link or articulate these features with children's developing conceptual knowledge and communicative abilities.

2. Methods for Identifying Consistent Trends in Children's Social Development

Several of the researchers who have contributed to the present volume employ methods which are most useful for identifying trends and stages in children's development of social skills and knowledge. The research procedures in these studies are similar to, but differ in important respects from more traditional hypothesis-testing approaches (experiments, surveys, and clinical interviewing). The methods are similar in that they involve a focus on specific social skills or concepts, as well as the use of procedures to elicit performances by children which manifest these skills or concepts. Once such data are generated, researchers attempt to identify specific patterns or variations in the children's performances by age or in some cases gender, social class or culture. For some of the studies in this volume the researchers do not employ elicitation procedures, they rely instead on direct observation of children at different points in time. In these cases, however, the primary emphasis is still on the identification of developmental patterns of specific social skills or types of social knowledge.

Although these studies try to maintain some of the advantages of more traditional approaches, they also differ from such methods in at least two important respects. First, while they build on a critical examination of previous theory they primarily seek to identify developmental trends and are, therefore, interested in generating theory rather than in testing specific operational hypotheses. There is a shared belief that existing theories (e. g., Piagetian Structuralism, Social Learning Theory, etc.) cannot, without substantial refinement, capture the complexities of children's social development. The identification of specific trends in the development of social skills and knowledge is seen as an important step toward a more comprehensive theory. Secondly, since there is less emphasis on statistical testing of specific hypotheses, the researchers are free to focus on aspects of the data other than just task performance (cf. Streeck, this volume). The researchers in this volume pay careful attention to the fact that children's development of social skills and concepts is always embedded in social context (i. e., the children's everyday life-worlds). As a result, the way children perceive an elicitation task, the processes or strategies they employ in dealing with the task, and their eventual performance *are all seen as data* which may be useful for better understanding the developmental process. In this respect the research in this volume which focuses on trends in children's development of communicative skills and social knowledge is generally in line with Vygotsky's (1978) dialectical alternative to traditional experimentation.

The studies which focus on trends or patterns in children's social development involve three general methodological procedures: quasi-experimentation, interviews, and direct observation. Weissenborn and Auwärter employ quasi-experimental procedures in their research. These studies can be seen as quasi-experiments in that an elicitation task is employed to generate specific performances by children of different age or social class groups. However, in all cases the children's perception of the task is carefully considered and the data are analyzed to generate rather than test theoretical propositions. In a series of quasi-experimental studies Weissenborn has investigated the development of the ability to negotiate common frames of reference in dyadic communication. Children had to perform a range of spatial tasks in a setting in which they were completely dependent on the verbal mode of communication.

Auwärter's research on children's construction of fictional playframes involves quasi-experimental methods to analyze data which were collected in a natural setting. Unlike Weissenborn, Auwärter is interested in communicative strategies which children employ in spontaneous play rather than under pre-established cognitive demands. As a result Auwärter placed few restrictions on the children's behaviors in data collection. Auwärter and Weissenborn both document developmental patterns in communicative behavior. For Auwärter the emphasis is placed on identifying developmental stages in children's use of communicative strategies; dimensions of data-analysis (scope of validity of speech acts and identity adopted by the speaker) were accordingly formulated in advance.

Three of the studies in this volume (Shields and Duveen, Siegert, and Miller) involve the use of the inverview method. In the cases of Shields and Duveen and Miller, however, the researchers' use of interviews is quite different from the clinical interviewing method frequently employed in work on children's development of social cognition. While a great deal of research on children's social cognition has examined children's understanding of specific social concepts like friendship, morality, and positive justice (cf. Damon, 1977), the aim of the research of Shields and Duveen is to explore children's concepts of general features of persons and the interpersonal world.

Compared to previous research, Shields' and Duveen's use of the interview method has several advantages: the questions they asked of the children were, for the most part, straightforward requests for information (e. g., after displaying a picture of a farmer, cow, tractor and a tree the researchers asked: Which of these eats? Which of them goes to sleep at night? etc.). The questions were not hypothetical. They did not demand that the children envision an event and then reflect on and evaluate it in terms of some set of social characteristics. Questions of the type asked by Shields and Duveen, we believe, access the children's understanding of social reality better than the elicitation of judgments about ambiguous and reified social concepts and relations. Additionally, the simplicity of their interview methods enabled the researchers to study the social concepts of preschool children (3;6 to 5;6 years of age). Children this young are rarely included in research on social cognition, and when they are included preschoolers often score at the lowest levels of the stage models of sociocognitive development. A major problem with such research is that it is surely erroneous to argue that children lack a certain type of social knowledge because the task used to elicit this knowledge may be beyond their cognitive processing abilities (i.e., the requirement to envision and reflect upon hypothetical social events). Shields and Duveen avoid this problem and their results demonstrate that children under six have substantial knowledge of basic social characteristics of humans.

Although Miller's article on moral development involves the questioning of children about a hypothetical moral dilemma, it differs both theoretically and methodologically from previous research in this area. For Miller moral development is best investigated by focusing on children's acquisition of the linguistic and discourse skills of moral argumentation. Miller sees moral argumentation as a complex type of communicative behavior which arises when two or more parties have contradictory views regarding what is 'right or wrong'. As a result Miller's methodology involves presenting a moral dilemma to small groups of children of differing ages. The children were asked to discuss the dilemma and come to an agreement regarding a solution. The researcher then challenges these initial solutions in an attempt to generate more complex argumentation among the children and possibly to get them to shift to a higher perspective where they can envision the elements of an opposing view to their collective position.

Miller's data collection procedures involve both peer and adult-child interaction. In this way Miller is able to break down, to a large degree, the asymmetrical nature of clinical interviewing research (cf. Siegert, this volume) by including peer discussions, while at the same time as an adult researcher he challenges and encourages the children to go beyond their intitial attempts at a collective solution to the problem.

Siegert's paper is a carefully documented methodological critique of the clinical interviewing method for studying children's development of social competence. We can add little to Siegert's excellent discussion of the inherent paradox of using the clinical interview method (an asymmetrical adult-child interactive context) to attain information about knowledge and behavior that arises in egalitarian situations (friendship and communicative processes with peers). Siegert's work is important in that it reminds us of a central feature of most methods used to study children's social development. Such research often involves adult contacts with children and children's worlds. We ask children questions, we have them perform tasks, and we observe and record their behavior in natural settings. In every case children must determine what we are doing and what we want them to do. In these circumstances children will always ask themselves and each other what it is we adults want. Why are adults asking these questions? Why do adults want us to perform these tasks? Why are adults watching us? In some cases the cognitive and communicative processes children employ in attempting to answer questions such as these (i. e., in trying to "make sense" of the researcher's methods) may have little to do with the cognitive and communicative processes the researcher wishes to understand and document. More importantly, in some research the children's attempts to make sense of experimental tasks or hypothetical dilemmas may be more demanding cognitively than the processes and knowledge such methods are designed to measure. This is one of the main themes of Siegert's argument, and it is a problem which cannot be easily dismissed in future research on children's social development.

The studies by Camaioni, Budwig, Strage and Bamberg, and Ervin-Tripp are based on observation in natural — rather than experimental — settings. They are all designed as longitudinal studies aiming at the documentation of developmental trends in children's acquisition and use of linguistic competence. The studies share an interesting methodological feature in that they all concentrate on *shifts* in the child' use of prelinguistic and linguistic forms, that is, on transitions from one developmental stage to another. Whereas Camaioni analyzes processes at the juncture between the pre-linguistic and linguistic stages, Budwig, Strage and Bamberg focus on the transition from adult-supported to child-administered sequences of interaction among peers. Ervin-Tripp shows that extra-linguistic 'scaffolding' structures also operate in second-language acquisition.

The studies illustrate that new developmental stages are only reached after the child has been sufficiently involved in specifically structured interactional environments and that, therefore, interaction is indeed a *part of* cognitive development. In addition, these studies demonstrate that such intensive longitudinal studies in natural settings help us to understand better *how* the interactive styles of mother-child dyads may be a reflection of the everyday routines in their particular social worlds. Additional case studies of this type may help us pinpoint the overall relations among such factors as family structure, the nature and scheduling of everyday activities, cultural conceptions of children and the mother's role in language development.

In the long run, however, it will not be sufficient to cite data from Western middle-class parent-child interaction to document the role of interactional 'scaffolding' structures in child development. These structures may be related to social-structural features such as the existence of a rather clear-cut boundary between the adult world on the one hand and more or less play-oriented interactive contexts for children on the other and to the fact that parents appear to be increasingly concerned about playing an active role in their children's linguistic development. The frequent use of question-answer formats and decontextualizing naming practices in middle-class parents' communication with children across Western societies (cf. Corsaro, 1977; Heath, 1983), for example, seems to serve as an exercise in "pre-school literacy" (Heath and Thomas, 1982) and to be historically linked to the growing influence of schooling and classroom modes of interaction on socialization patterns inside the family (cf. Scollon and Scollon, 1981). These patterns differ sharply from what has been reported on children raised in other cultures or lower classes in Western societies (cf. Ochs and Schieffelin, 1984).

Overall, the sparse findings from cross-cultural research seem to indicate that there is as much variation in patterns of interacting with children as there is in other aspects of culture. To account for these variations, it will be necessary to link adult-child interaction patterns to culturally held beliefs and attitudes regarding the nature of language learning (cf. Watson-Gegeo and Gegeo, this volume) as well as to the place of the young child in the attention patterns organizing family and community interaction. It will be interesting to discuss, in the light of cross-cultural data on caregiver-child

interaction, whether one can formulate universal principles underlying the overt variety and what effects variation has on sequences
in the development of linguistic and socio-cognitive skills.

3. Methods for Discovering Stable
Features of Children's Worlds

In several of the studies in this volume the researchers employ
methods which aim at the discovery and documentation of meaningful organizational features of the social worlds within which children
interact. Rather than focusing on trends or stages in children's
development of communicative skills and social knowledge, the
researchers in these studies attempt to enter directly into children's
worlds and to establish how the development of social competence
is embedded in social contexts. Here there is an emphasis on how
children acquire, use, and refine social knowledge and discourse
skills in their everyday interactions with peers and adults and on the
communicative procedures by which they structure the interpersonal
world around them.

These studies can be classified into one of two general types. The
first type consists in studies which involve direct observation of
children's development and use of specific communicative skills.
The data base of these studies consists mostly in audiovisual recordings of naturally occurring interactive events. These data are then
intensively examined to discover how specific communicative processes are embedded in and shape children's everyday lifes. (The
studies of Wootton and Fine fall into this group; the papers by
Auwärter, Budwig, Strage and Bamberg, and Camaioni that we
have discussed above also address the role of language in the
shaping of children's day-to-day interaction, but clearly from the
point of view of development.)

A second group involves micro-ethnographic case studies of
children's worlds at various ages within different institutions. Although these studies also focus on children's development of communicative skills, they are broader in scale than those in the first
group. Instead of focusing in depth on particular discourse skills
or types of social knowledge, there is an attempt to discover what
it is like 'to be a child' at certain points in the developmental

procoess. With such ethnographic information in hand these researchers go on to specify how developing skills and knowledge are
related to the range of stable routine events making up children's
worlds. The micro-ethnographic studies of this type in the present
volume (Coenen, Corsaro, Schütze, Kreppner and Paulsen, Streeck
and Watson-Gegeo and Gegeo) cover a variety of children's experiences within institutions such as the school, the family and the
adolescent peer-group, and they display interrelationships between
these small life-worlds of children and the wider socio-cultural
context.

Turning first to studies which focus on specific communicative
skills we can begin with Wootton's article on the invocation of rules
in adult-child interaction. To discover how rules are evoked in the
process of constructing different types of social relations Wootton
takes the approach that has emerged in the work of conversational
analysts. He begins with the important finding that rules are seldom
explicitly invoked in adult-child interaction. This finding is in line
with other research on children's exposure to social norms (cf.
Corsaro, 1979; but cf. also Schieffelin, 1979) as well as work on
children's exposure to grammatical rules (cf. Brown, 1973). Wootton
then proceeds to carefully examine the few cases where rules are
explicitly evoked to specify *how* and to what ends this is done. In his
analysis, he discovers two distinct forms of linguistic organization in
the evocation of rules and examines how such forms are sequentially
placed in the flow of interactive events. Wootton's micro-analysis
reveals that, rather than initiating a lesson on morality and proper
conduct, parental invocation of rules serves to maintain a smooth
flow of interaction by closing the side-sequence (Jefferson, 1972)
which had been initiated by the child's unfavourable behavior. It
suggests that studies of children's practices and repertoires of actions
for dealing with occasions where social rules are relevant (e. g., the
occurrence of misdeeds) can lead to a better understanding of the
emergence of children's knowledge about rules.

In his article on the social organization of adolescent gossip,
Fine, like Wootton, presents a detailed analysis of a small number
of segments of naturally occurring interaction. Fine's approach,
however, differs significantly from conversational analysis in that
he is more concerned with *what* is being said, where and by whom,
than with *how* it is being said. Being concerned with social consensus
in talk, Fine continually links patterns in the actual discourse to

background information about the participants (e. g., their relationship to one another and to characters in the gossip, details of particular interactive events, etc.). In this sense Fine's analysis is less concerned with conversational structure than with the ways in which a stable conversational routine is embedded in adolescent culture.

The contrast between the approaches of Fine and Wottoon is an interesting one. They both tell us something about the role of discourse and talk in children's worlds: for Wootton the important issues reside in the organization of the discourse itself; he relates the linguistic display of sociocultural knowledge (i. e., rules) to its role in that organization. This interest in conversational organization is reflected in the method of sequential analysis adopted by Wootton. For Fine, on the other hand, discourse analysis must always be supplemented with additional ethnographic information about the participants, topic, and interactive setting because he sees discourse as a *reflection of* more general cultural patterns and social relationships. In contrast to the chapters by Wootton and Fine, the remaining papers in this section are all ethnographic micro-analyses focussing on types of interactive events in children's worlds. The studies cover the socialization process from infancy through adolescence and represent several cultural groups (Melanesian, German, Italian and American children). The ethnographies explore adult-child and peer interaction in a wide range of social settings.

The study by Watson-Gegeo and Gegeo on interaction processes between caregivers and young children in several Melanesian (Kwara´ae) villages in the Solomon Islands reveals parallels between the child's acquisition of language and his/her acquisition of social values, especially in the domain of interpersonal relations. Values are both explicitly taught and implicitly structure adult-child interaction; the authors have used a combination of ethnographic research techniques and discourse analysis to capture these interconnections. Watson-Gegeo and Gegeo's data collection procedures include participant observation over an extended period of time, in-depth interviewing, and audio recordings, and they yield a detailed set of diverse materials: audio recorded interactive events, detailed field notes which capture background cultural knowledge (which are also supplemented by Gegeo's knowledge as a member of Kwar'ae culture), and parents' interpretations of specific events and general views on child socialization.

In their analysis Watson-Gegeo and Gegeo make excellent use of these rich materials. They blend the micro-analyses of specific events with detailed descriptive accounts of the culture and individual interpretations of a number of the participants in the study. The result is an example of what the authors refer to as an "interpretive account" of early socialization in Kwar'ae society. In addition, Watson-Gegeo and Gegeo compare their results with those from similar studies in other cultures and develop the significance of their work for theoretical statements regarding cross-cultural variation in early socialization processes.

The study by Watson-Gegeo and Gegeo is interesting also because, linking language socialization to the teaching of values, they make an attempt to relate micro-patterns of interaction with children to the way in which the child is gradually integrated into the society's macro-structure. The shape of childhood socialization and the type of integration of the child into society varies considerably across cultures and depends, among other things, upon the position children of different ages are afforded within the social structure. The ways in which patterns of caretaker-child interaction are organized are not only related to the need of endowing the child with social competences. Parent-child interaction is also a medium of reproduction of inherently differentiated social systems. The type of solidarity, cooperation, and stratification at the macro-level of the social system bears upon the modes of reciprocity encountered and enacted by the child in both asymmetrical (authoritarian) and symmetrical (egalitarian) situations of communication. Modes of reciprocity, in turn, bear upon the shaping of the child's social competencies. It does make a difference whether children have a voice in village council-meetings or are regarded as more or less irrational 'animals' before they reach a certain level of linguistic fluency (as Ochs, 1982 has reported from Western Samoa). The existence of separate and bounded peer-groups or initiatory grades, the involvement of different biological and/or classificatory kinspeople in the socialization of the child, as well as the introduction of formal schooling all figure as factors in the shaping of the child's interactive experiences and the patterning of language socialization.

The exact nature of the relationship between societal macro-structures and the micro-patterns of face-to-face interaction, however, is an open-ended issue currently much discussed in sociological theory (cf. Collins, 1981; Gumperz and Cook-Gumperz, 1982;

Knorr-Cettina and Cicourel, 1981; Schegloff, forthcoming). One attempt to link social structure and parent-child interaction is Bateson's (1949) study of Balinese character formation in which he suggested that the "anti-cumulative" rhythms of the mother's behavior towards her child may endow the latter with self-regulating, plateau-like, behavioral mechanisms which in turn help sustain the "steady state" of the Balinese social system.

Bateson's system-theory approach to interaction and social organization is part of the theoretical background of the research on early socialization conducted by Schütze, Kreppner and Paulsen. The authors focus on the social construction of the sibling relationship between first and second children. This research is groundbreaking simply for the extensive data collected in this relatively unexplored area. The research report is based on a two year longitudinal study of 16 families (father, mother, first born child less than 3 1/2 years old, and newborn second child) in West Berlin. Data collection involved the video recording of routine interactive events as well as extended biographical interviews with the parents at different stages of the field work.

Schütze, Kreppner and Paulsen's paper is a report of findings from preliminary data analysis. The analysis procedure combines deductive and inductive analytic methods in the micro-analysis of the audiovisual materials. The authors isolate recurrent interaction patterns in their data which are illustrated in the specification of a three-phase process in the social construction of the sibling relationship. The first phase of the process, establishing contact between the children and introducing the older child to his/her new position in the family, is demonstrated by interpretive micro-analyses of exemplary interactive scenes. The interpretations involve different levels of analysis. The authors move from surface level descriptions of specific features of the event to a comparison of these features with those of other events within and outside the particular family, and finally to a more general comparative consideration of interaction patterns on the basis of assumptions derived from systems theory. The authors refer to this method of analysis as "iterative heuristics" because it involves the generation of hypotheses from the movement back and forth between interpretations of patterns in the data and initial theoretical assumptions.

Recently, there has been an increasing awareness of the role of micro-processes of interaction in children's social development. The ways in which children use their bodies to achieve involvement and orderliness in their interaction with others, to show and elicit attention, are issues which are presently receiving attention from researchers in child development (Brazelton, Koslowski and Main, 1974; Bullowa, 1979; Trevarthen, 1979). Most of these studies focus on interaction patterns involving pre-linguistic infants. In contrast, Coenen in his contribution to this volume reconstructs how he learned to use his body in ways that enabled him to enter, share, and take part in the world of a group of deaf children. He wanted to find out how the body or "corporeality, in its various aspects of perspective and expressive functioning, can be seen at work in the development and structuring of interactive situations". Coenen provides a phenomenological explication of experiences made while reflecting on the intentional use of the body as a communicative medium; for the deaf, the sharing of experience and meaning evolves from the joint tuning of body configurations.

Like Watson-Gegeo and Gegeo and Corsaro (see below) Co-enen's use of participant observation required a careful and patient period of field entry. But for Coenen the process of acceptance or what he terms "incorporation" into the world of the children he studied was itself a phenomenological experience. And this process of incorporation comprises the core of Coenen's findings. Before presenting these findings to the reader Coenen notes that the reduc-tion of the results into some set of disctinct propositions would, even if possible, be unsuitable. Rather than summarizing the results, Coenen presents a recounting of the research process itself. In this way the analysis follows "the lines of a flowing argumentation in which, through the means of relevant citations of field notes and adequate concepts built up in the analytic process, a synthetic insight is evoked pertaining to the field under study. It presents a structure that has its plausibility with respect to the world of experience at stake." In studying the social worlds of young children phenomenological approaches such as Coenen's are perhaps the adequate way of capturing basic communicative and interactive processes from the child's perspective.

Streeck in his analysis of brief sequences of children's interaction in a 'peer-teaching' setting also focuses on aspects of nonverbal behavior; he proposes that in order to reveal social-organizational implications of talk it is often useful, and sometimes necessary, to study it within its 'embodied' local environment (cf. Streeck, 1983,

1984). Streeck analyzes some of the ways in which a group of children administers a situated social system; taking into account features of body-posture and gaze, he reconstructs how pragmatic aspects of task-related speech are constrained by properties of peer-relations such as gender and relative rank. His main argument is that the group's social system is not a fixed entity; rather, social categories and statuses are resources which can variably be used for 'political' purposes. The children continuously struggle to maintain and re-equilibrate the status quo of their egalitarian relations, and they agree on and sustain a range of states of the system to meet the diverse demands of the situation. Reciprocity thus emerges as an ongoing accomplishment of situated interactive practices.

In his article Corsaro describes some basic routines in the peer culture of nursery school children in the United States and Italy. Corsaro argues that a frequent developmental pattern for preschool children is the children's exposure to social knowledge and communicative demands in everyday interactions with adults which raise problems, confusions and uncertainities which then are later reproduced and readdressed in play routines making up peer culture. These routines offer children the opportunity to gain control over and actively deal with problems, confusions and concerns jointly or communally with peers.

Although Corsaro's methods rely heavily on the audiovisual recording of natural events, he has argued that such recording and micro-analysis should be part of conventional ethnography to cope with the methodological problems of this new technology (cf. Corsaro, 1982). For example, since audiovisual recording produces much richer and more detailed records of interactive events than field notes, Corsaro argues that there is a tendency to overinterpret the data. Researchers sometimes fail to take the information processing capacities and limitations of individuals into account in their analyses. Corsaro argues that the information processing capacities of individuals participating in interaction may be more limited than those of researchers when reviewing and interpreting an audiovisual record of the event after the fact (cf. also Cicourel, 1979). Furthermore, without background information on the participants and setting the meaning of the recorded events can be easily distorted. This problem is especially acute when studying young children because researchers naturally tend to interpret the data from an adult rather than child perspective. Thus, Corsaro's research demonstrates the importance of directly entering and becoming part of children's worlds for theory development in the area of childhood socialization.

Conclusion

We have noted above that there has recently been a movement away from traditional experimental and interview methods of hypothesis-testing in research on children's linguistic, communicative and socio-cognitive development. There is a growing recognition of the numerous and highly complex interconnections between the acquisition of conceptual schemata representing recurrent types of social events, the development of linguistic skills necessary to become an active participant in social life and create social worlds shared with other children, and the modes of reciprocity organizing interactive sequences at successive developmental stages. In term of theorizing, this recognition yields more and more attempts to frame research problems in ways which entail orientations or trends emerging in other than one's own immediate disciplines. Methodologically, we find a tendency to place greater emphasis on the microscopic analysis of data-fragments from interactional episodes in 'natural' social situations. Finally, the results from research conducted in this new fashion clearly indicate that a reconsideration of findings generated within previous frameworks (relating, for example, to the age at which different social concepts and strategies are acquired) is necessary.

We have argued that the studies in this volume are in line with this trend and that they can be classified into one of two types. The first includes quasi-experimental, interview and observational studies which emphasize the identification of consistent patterns in children's development of communicative skills and social knowledge while paying careful attention to how features of social context can affect development. The second type includes studies involving naturalistic observation and micro-ethnography where the focus is on discovering and describing stable features of children's life-worlds. It is clear that these two approaches are complementary. Data from ethnographic studies which reveal children's values, concerns, communicative styles and behavioral routines can be of great value in the design of quasi-experimental and interview studies in more structured settings. Likewise, findings from quasi-experimental and interview studies can yield important data on developmental trends in children's social cognition which may aid ethnographers in their attempts to link features of peer culture with children's acquisition of social skills and knowledge.

In the future there is a need for both types of research to become more comparative in nature. Individual comparisons of children by age must be supplemented by group comparisons by age (peer subcultures), gender, and social class. There is also a clear need for more cross-cultural research, especially for studies of children from non-Western societies. The "social constitution hypothesis" (Miller, 1980) which is at the core of the new trend, i.e., the assumption that mental competences are the outcome of the child's participation in increasingly complex interaction formats, can, in the long run, only be validated on the basis of comparative data. Cross-cultural research, in this domain as in others, must address itself to the issue of the units of social organization and analysis that can appropriately be selected for comparison. The interpretive nature of social interaction forces us to take into account culturally defined categories of events, episodes, and interaction roles; these categories are also acquired by children through their gradual immersion into their parent culture. If we want to find evidence for the ways in which culturally patterned interaction routines shape children's competence through performance, then we must also be able to define *functional* standards of comparison between interaction contexts across social classes or cultures. This issue of task-related functional equivalence of contexts or 'ecological validity' also applies to the generalizability of children's performance under experimental conditions to their performance in natural, everyday life situations (cf. Cole, Hood and McDermott, 1982).

For the reader, the contributions to this volume also provide an opportunity to compare different traditions in studies of child development. To us, the differences between the US-American and German traditions appear to be of particular interest. The American approach is largely marked by a careful consideration of the ethnographic details of the data-base and a certain hesitance to relate these to universalistically oriented theoretical models of society, language, and development; the trend in recent German social sciences, in contrast, has been to move down from predefined, embracing models of society as communicative action (most prominently represented by the work of Habermas, 1970, 1981) to tests of their viability in empirical research on documented scenes of social life. But it appears as though here, too, we are faced with a gradual convergence of research strategies which results in what may be called, borrowing Peirce's (1957) term, "abductive reasoning".

Overall, if the diversity and innovation of the methods employed in the studies in this volume are an indication of future developments, then we can expect to know much more about children's worlds and childhood socialization in the next few years.

References

Auwärter, Manfred and Edit Kirsch
  1984   "Zur Ontogenese der sozialen Interaktion. Eine strukturtheo-
             retische Analyse", in: Wolfgang Edelstein and Jürgen Ha-
             bermas (eds.), *Soziale Interaktion und soziales Verstehen*,
             (Frankfurt/Main: Suhrkamp), 167 – 219.
Bateson, Gregory
  1949   "Bali: The Value System of a Steady State", in: Meyer Fortes
             (ed.), *Social Structure: Studies Presented to A. R. Radcliffe-
             Brown*, (Oxford: Clarendon), 35 – 53.
Brazelton, T. Berry, Koslowski, Barbara, and Main, Mary
  1974   "The origins of reciprocity: the early mother-infant interac-
             tion", in: Michael Lewis & Leonard A. Rosenblum (eds.), *The
             effect of the infant on its caregiver*, (New York: John Wiley),
             49 – 76.
Bronfenbrenner, Urie
  1979   *The Ecology of Human Development*, (Cambridge, Mass.: Har-
             vard University Press).
Brown, Roger
  1973   *A First Language: The Early Stages*, (Cambridge, Mass.: Har-
             vard University Press).
Bruner, Jerome
  1975   "The Ontogenesis of Speech Acts". *Journal of Child Language*
             2, 1 – 20.
Bullowa, Margaret (ed.)
  1979   *Before speech: The beginnings of interpersonal communication*,
             (Cambridge: Cambridge Univ. Press).
Cicourel, Aaron V.
  1979   "Field Research: The Need for Stronger Theory and More

Control over the Data Base". In: W. Smizerk, M. Miller & E. Fuhrmann (eds.), *Contemporary Issues in Theory: A Meta-Sociological Perspective*. (West Port, Conn.: Greenwood).

Cole, Michael, Lois Hood and Ray P. McDermott
1982   "Concepts of ecological validity: Their differing implications for comparative cognitive research". *Quarterly Newsletter of the Laboratory of Comparative Human Cognition 2(2)*, 19 – 26.

Collins, Randall
1981   "On the Microfoundations of Macrosociology". *American Journal of Sociology, 86*, 984 – 1014.

Corsaro, William A.
1977   "The clarification request as a feature of adult interactive styles with children". *Language in Society, 6*, 183 – 207.
1979   "Sociolinguistic Patterns in Adult-Child Interaction". In: Elinor Ochs and Bambi B. Schieffelin (eds.), *Developmental Pragmatics*. (New York: Academic Press), 373 – 390.
1982   "Something Old and Something New: The Importance of Prior Ethnography in the Collection and Analysis of Audiovisual Data". *Sociological Methods and Research, 11*, 145 – 166.
1985   *Friendship and Peer Culture in the Early Years*. (Norwood, N. J.: Ablex).

Damon, William
1977   *The Social World of the Child*. San Francisco: Jossey-Bass.
1982   "Zur Entwicklung der sozialen Kognition des Kindes. Zwei Zugänge zum Verständnis von sozialer Kognition." In: Wolfgang Edelstein and Monika Keller (eds.), *Perspektivität und Interpretation*. (Frankfurt/Main: Suhrkamp), 110 – 145.
1984   "Struktur, Veränderlichkeit und Prozeß in der sozialkognitiven Entwicklung des Kindes." In: Wolfgang Edelstein and Jürgen Habermas (eds.), *Soziale Interaktion und soziales Verstehen*. (Frankfurt/Main: Suhrkamp), 63 – 112.

Ervin-Tripp, Susan and Claudia Mitchell-Kernan (eds.)
1977   *Child Discourse*. (New York: Academic Press).

Garvey, Catherine
1984   *Children's Talk*. (Oxford: Fontana).

Glick, Joseph and K. Allison Clarke-Stewart (eds.)
1978   *The Development of Social Understanding*. (New York: Gardner Press, Inc.).

Goodwin, Marjorie Harness
1982   "Processes of Dispute Management among Urban Black Children". *American Ethnologist, 9*, 76 – 96.

Gumperz, John J. and Jenny Cook-Gumperz
1982   "Introduction: Language and the Communication of Social

Identity". In: John Gumperz (ed.), *Language and Social Identity*. (New York: Cambridge University Press), 1 – 22.

Habermas, Jürgen
1970   "Toward a Theory of Communicative Competence". In: Hans-Peter Dreitzel (ed.), *Recent Sociology, Vol. 2.* (London: Macmillan), 114 – 149.
1981   *Theorie des kommunikativen Handelns.* 2 vols. (Frankfurt/ Main: Suhrkamp).

Heath, Shirley B.
1983   *Ways with Words. Language, Life and Work in Communities and Classrooms.* (Cambridge: Cambridge University Press).

Heath, Shirley B. and Charlene Thomas
1982   *The Achievement of Preschool Literacy for Mother and Child.* Paper presented for the University of Victoria Symposium on Children's Responses to a Literate Environment.

Jefferson, Gail
1972   "Side Sequences". In: David Sudnow (ed.), *Studies in Social Interaction.* (New York: The Free Press), 294 – 337.

Knorr-Cettina, Karin and Aaron V. Cicourel (eds.)
1981   *Advances in Social Theory and Methodology. Towards an Integration of Micro- and Macro-Sociologies.* (Boston and London: Routledge and Kegan Paul).

Kohlberg, Lawrence
1969   "Stage and Sequence: The Cognitive-Developmental Approach to Socialization". In: David A. Goslin (ed.), *Handbook of Socialization Theory and Research.* (Chicago: Rand McNally & Co.), 347 – 480.

Miller, Max
1980   "Sprachliche Sozialisation". In: Klaus Hurrelmann and Dieter Ulich (eds.), *Handbuch der Sozialisationsforschung.* (Weinheim: Beltz), 649 – 668.

Ochs, Elinor
1982   "Talking to Children in Western Samoa". *Language in Society, 11*, 77 – 104.

Ochs, Elinor and Bambi B. Schieffelin (eds.)
1979   *Developmental Pragmatics.* (New York: Academic Press).
1984   "Three Developmental Stories and their Implications". In: Richard A. Shweder and Robert LeVine (eds.). *Culture Theory. Essays in Mind, Self and Emotions.* (Cambridge: Cambridge University Press).

Oevermann, Ulrich et al.
1976   "Beobachtungen zur Struktur der sozialisatorischen Interaktion". In: Manfred Auwärter, Edit Kirsch and Manfred

Schröder (eds.), *Seminar: Kommunikation, Interaktion, Identität.* (Frankfurt/Main: Suhrkamp), 371—403.

Peirce, Charles Sanders
1957   *Essays in the Philosophy of Science.* (New York: The Liberal Arts Press).

Piaget, Jean
1932   *Le Jugement Moral chez l'Enfant.* (Paris: Presses Universitaires de France).
1968   *Le Langage et la Pensée chez l'Enfant.* 7. Edition. (Neuchâtel: Delachaux et Niestlé).

Sacks, Harvey, Emanuel A. Schegloff & Gail Jefferson
1974   "A Simplest Systematics for the Organization of Turn-Taking for Conversation". *Language, 50,* 4, 696—735.

Schieffelin, Bambi B.
1979   "Getting it Together: An Ethnographic Approach to the Study of the Development of Communicative Competence". In: Elinor Ochs and Bambi B. Schieffelin (eds.), *Developmental Pragmatics.* (New York: Academic Press), 73—102.

Schegloff, Emanuel A.
forthcoming   "Between Macro and Micro: Contexts and Other Connections." To appear in B. Giesen, R. Munch and N. Smelser (eds.), *The Micro-Macro Link.* (Berkeley and Los Angeles: University of California Press).

Schwartzman, Helen
1979   *Transformations: The Anthropology of Children's Play.* (New - York: Plenum).

Scollon, Ron and Susan Scollon
1981   *Narrative, Literacy, and Face in Interethnic Communication.* (Norwood, N. J.: Ablex).

Selman, Robert L.
1980   *The Growth of Interpersonal Understanding.* (New York: Academic Press).

Streeck, Jürgen
1983   *Social Order in Child Communication. A Study in Microethnography.* Pragmatics and Beyond, 4. (Amsterdam: Benjamins, B. V.).
1984   "Embodied Contexts, Transcontextuals and the Timing of Speech Acts", *Journal of Pragmatics, 8,* 113—137.

Trevarthen, Collin
1979   "Communication and cooperation in early infancy: a description of primary intersubjectivity". In: Margaret Bullowa (ed.), *Before speech: The beginning of interpersonal communication.* (Cambridge: Cambridge University Press), 321—348.

Turiel, Elliot
  1978   "The Development of Concepts of Social Structure: Social Convention". In: Joseph Glick and K. Alison Clarke-Stewart (eds.), *The Development of Social Understanding*. (New York: Gardner Press), 25−108.

Vygotsky, Lev
  1978   *Mind in Society*. (Cambridge, Mass.: M. I. T. Press).

Wertsch, James V. and C. A. Stone
  1978   "Microgenesis as a Tool for Developmental Analysis". *The Quarterly Newsletter of the Laboratory of Comparative Human Cognition, 1*, 1, 8−10.

Younniss, James
  1977   "Socialization and Social Knowledge". In: Rainer Silbereisen (ed.), *Soziale Kognition*. (Berlin: Technische Universität Berlin), 3−22.

Caught in a Web of Words: Some Considerations on Language Socialization and Language Acquisition.[1]

Jenny Cook-Gumperz

> "The word, handing on the experience of generations as this is incorporated in language ... Language which incorporates the experience of generations or, more broadly speaking of mankind, is included in the process of the child's development from the first months of life."
>
> A. R. Luria and
> F. Ia. Yudovitch.

1. Socialization and the transmission of knowledge

The transmission of knowledge across successive human generations constitutes the central issue in any theory of socialization; an issue to which there can be a variety of solutions. We owe our awareness of the importance of language in this process to Mead and Vygotsky who in contemporaneous but unrelated work in the 1930's both saw words and therefore language itself, as the fundamental social reproductive agents. However, their perspectives have only recently begun to be incorporated into studies of language development. Moreover the question of the actual mechanism through which this transmission takes place, that is, the components of language in which the "social genes" are carried, is the subject of much debate. Findings in child language acquisition from the past two decades have provided a great deal of detailed information on the development of grammatical skills but the question of how language assists the child to become a full fledged member of society has not received any systematic attention. To answer this question we need to consider language acquisition as part of a more general theory of socialization; it is toward this goal that the papers in this volume are moving.

This chapter explores the reasoning necessary to develop an approach to the study of language that could perhaps form the basis for an interpretive theory of socialization and provide a model for the actual process of transmission. It has been argued recently that it is in learning to seek for and provide meaning through verbal actions, that the child gains personhood (Kaye 1983). The emergence of subjectivity, that is the development of the individual as a cultural person, is seen as intrinsically a linguistic process and one in which concerns in language development are beginning to come together with interpretive theory (Shotter, 1974, 1978; Lock, 1978). Such a view places the concept of human agency at the very center of any process of socialization. (Giddens, 1979). It stresses the role of the child as an active human agent with the rapidly developing ability to look for, recognise and use socially meaningful communication.

Placing human agency in such a central position makes the transmission of socio-cultural knowledge, not simply an instrumental matter, but a creative process. Children's efforts to make sense of the communicative environment that surrounds them from the initial stages of life, involve both learning to understand interpersonal relations and a growing realization of the inescapable normativeness of language as a system of shared meanings. The power of language lies in its ability to influence and control others (Cook-Gumperz, 1981). The more traditional approach to the problem of the transmission of socio-cultural knowledge, by contrast, viewed the child's acquisition of an adult socio-normative system as a gradual process of adaptation to the "correct" forms of adult practices. Appropriate language use was seen as only one component of these practices.

Vygotsky's position that the acquisition of a semantic system of words and concepts provides a readymade entry into the adult world, can be seen as a key to this creative approach to children's language and social learning. It suggests that there is a linguistic base on which children can build further social knowledge through their own communicative experience. His statement that "the history of the process of internalisation of social speech is also the history of the socialization of the children's practical intellect" (1978: 23) suggests such a new departure. From this view both language learning and the transmission of social knowledge are seen as cognitively organised in ways specific to children's own social activities; thus raising the possibility of looking at the child as an innovative language learner, who both works within and modifies the knowledge base. In this perspective the child becomes a "practical reasoner" building on the reflexive understanding of the social world through exercise of linguistically related abilities. These abilities are founded on the knowledge that language symbols are reciprocally meaningful (Cook-Gumperz, 1975).

Thus, metaphorically, language acts as a web of words which supports the child's earliest attempts to construct socially acceptable communicative exchanges. Not only are children enmeshed in language from their initial entry into life; even their earliest acts of communication are mediated through language (Bullowa, 1979). By attempting to communicate and later to talk they achieve shared and situated understandings with others, understandings that are sustained by "the elasticity of the web of words". By this I mean that since what is done or said in everyday life is always subject during the course of on-going interaction to multiple interpretations, this fact allows children to be accredited the status of a purposeful communicator. Whatever the syntactic limits on their language processing, both the assumption of social agency and that of purposeful intent underlying all talk, tends to give the child's verbal acts a sense of contextual appropriateness. Thus, we might say that the web not only sustains children's attempts at communication, but also offers a safety net through which the apprentice speaker gains both the good graces and attention of others in order to have opportunities for correction or repetition of their message. It is also on this basis that the "polite fiction" of childhood rests, the fiction by virtue of which children are treated as if they had conversational and social understanding far in advance of their apparent grammatical capabilities. This is an assumption of competence that only gradually becomes realised in the course of further development. (Dunn and Kendrick, 1983: Schütze, Kreppner and Paulsen, this vol.)

The metaphoric image of the child "caught in a web of words" gives us, moreover, some sense of the moral imperative that Durkheim suggests underlies all socialization. That is, that children have no choice but to be social beings; and thus, to inherit the language of their community. From their entry into the world at birth, they are a part of an inter-personal network of communication and social understandings. As part of this network, the semantic and syntactic resources of language create possibilities for children to appear to possess more knowledge of the world than may be the case. The conventions which are encoded within each community's language system lends to children's communications an appearance of social competency in advance of their full socio-cognitive understanding. Thus the realisation that this network is linguistically and socio-linguistically created and sustained, potentially provides the study of children's activities with an interpretive model of the process of social production and reproduction. But a social perspective on language socialization involves more than the addition of social information to existing linguistic concerns. It requires a rethinking of basic social developmental process and reformulation of what is involved in language use. Before discussing the form this new approach might take, we must look briefly at the major directions research in child language has taken.

2. Toward a constructivist view of language

With the growth of modern linguistic theory in the 1960's the interest in acquisition as a linguistic process greatly expanded. However, the exploration of the relationship between the child's verbal development and other aspects of the child's social life became even further from the centre of concern. This has primarily meant that language study has given little or no consideration to the developing child as a communicator, but rather focused almost exclusively on the nature of the grammar that is revealed in the child's different developmental stages of acquisition. As Deutsch has pointed out in a recent review of the history of child language study:

> "the classical problem of child language research that has received changing emphasis throughout the history of this field [is] what are the basic developmental mechanisms that move the child from one level of linguistic functioning to the next one? Does the child himself play the main role in the acquisition of his/her mother tongue or is the process and product of language acquisition mainly shaped by the social environment of the child?"   (1980: 1)

Thus whether the child is an active participant in the construction of language is historically an issue which has been of importance but is one which has been pushed to one side because of the focus on developmental variations of syntactic rule systems. Deutsch goes on to say that much of the early debate centered around whether language learning was the result of a passive repetition of language given in the environment or whether it was an active cognitive process in which the child constructed a linguistic system from available elements. Pointing to early research by Stern (1928) which suggests that language acquisition should be seen as a convergent process, he suggests that there is a constant interaction between children's own constructive work on language and their interaction with the environment.

However while over the past 20 years research has focused on grammatical competence and its potentially innate unfolding, this psycho-biological concern has overshadowed the implications of the earlier more socio-cognitive, constructivist perspective. It is only recently that interest in the child's own constructive work on language has again surfaced and along with this, a renewed interest in the role of the environment in this process. Now the classical problem of child language can be restated as involving larger issues of continuity in the learning process, and as the way in which the child moves from immature communication to mature communication. Since the study of grammatical development did not yield sufficient explanation for the process of maturation (Ingelby, 1980), a different approach to language learning which focuses on the child as increasingly competent communicator was seen as needed. From a developmental perspective it is obvious that while children by the age of seven or so can reach a stage of adequate approximation to adult grammar their socio-cognitive abilities and social interactional skills are far from adult maturity. Clearly, other mechanisms than grammatical skills are at work in the acquisition of communicative competence, and it becomes necessary to look at the child as more than an apprentice grammarian (Keenan, 1974; Ryan, 1974). It was in the search for a model of the child as a social communicator that attention came to focus upon insights into the theory of speech acts and therefore on speech rather than language as the form of intentional social action. A very brief overview of the recent history of child language research, in the past two decades, will give us some idea as to why the perspective of language as a socially constructive skill has been so neglected.

3. Language acquisition studies

3.1. Early grammatical development

Research of the 60's to early 70's was most effectively summarised in Roger Brown's "A First Language" (1973). The goal was to explain the achievement of full adult grammatical competence and to explore the underlying strategies by which children accomplished this task. In this way children's acquisition of language provided linguistic enquiry with a natural experimental context, serving to test assumptions about the psychological bases of current models of grammar, although as Brown pointed out, psycholinguistics, the parent discipline to child language, lagged approximately five years behind linguistic theory. The specific challenge for child language studies was to construct a grammar of child language which could provide adequately for the regularity and variability observed in the studies of children's speaking and so provide a universal that is a context-independent description of children's acquisition processes. Most studies concentrated on the speech of middle class English speaking children. Where other languages were studied the goal was accounting for the differences in acquisition processes so as to test the universality of grammatical descriptions.

3.2. The cognitive bases of acquisition

More recently an alternative, more cognitively-oriented approach based on comparative studies of learning in different language environments has emerged. While continuing the concern with possible universal order of developmental stages the main interest was to use acquisition studies as a way of gaining insight into learning heuristics and children's cognitive abilities (Slobin, 1973, 1978). The comparative thrust of this work in child language provided a valuable corrective to the overreliance on acquisition theory developed from English. While the impetus has been the search for universals, both of language and of cognitive development, the increasing sophistication of grammatical models and the large data-base of these comparative studies have gone a long way toward providing a strong model of grammar learning in the child's early years. By looking at children's ability to abstract grammatical categories as prototypes or icons from the linguistic input it is becoming possible to construct a theory of the way in which grammar encodes relationships within the real world and, thus, has a powerful potential for the study of cognition. (Slobin, 1984).

3.3. Speech act analysis

It was in answer to this dilemma of grammatical versus communicative competence that speech act analysis seemed to provide a useful and radical departure from previous research on acquisition. The speech act approach is useful because it focuses attention on intentionality and emphasises the child as a purposeful communicator. It seemed radical because the shift of emphasis from utterance meaning to the speaker's or utterer's meaning (Searle, 1969) provided guidelines for the way in which the context of the social environment could be seen directly to influence and shape interpretation of the child's speech.

Work on childrens' spontaneous naturally occurring speech was able to show that from early in life children have a communicative goal toward the achievement of which they use all their limited verbal resources, both syntactic and semantic. As Bruner has recently argued, the origin of the motivation for language acquisition begins essentially before speech:

> "during the second half of the first year, the infant begins to make a distinction between the extrinsic or message function of his communicative acts and their affiliative or regulatory function — that aspect of communication that has to do with maintaining a transactional relationship with another. This, of course, is a crucial distinction for the mastery of speech acts"   (1980: 43).

Here Bruner is suggesting that the move into speech and language is built on the child's ability to distinguish between the linguistic form and content and the social function of a message within a specific communicative context.

An early study of children's uses of speech acts showed that they could indeed distinguish between different interactional contexts of hearers and alter their message form accordingly (Gelman and Shatz, 1977). In this can be seen one of the attractions of the speech act model for the study of child language, the power of the distinction between context-free propositional content and the context-bound, or context-dependent interpretation of intent. For this model provides a means to build the child's increasing syntactic control of language, which has been demonstrated in the previous decade of studies, into a theory of communication which may help to explain the essential steps from immature to mature speech. It allows the exploration of the way in which the developing syntactic control is mapped onto contextually supported communicative intent (Ryan, 1974).

For many researchers in child language such a theory seemed to make both practical as well as theoretical sense, for so much of the construction of children's messages was a collaborative enterprise between the child and the adult. A new impetus was given to studies of naturally occuring conversational speech between mothers and their children and between children themselves which would move further in looking at the creation of meaning in actual social contexts (McTear, 1985). It was found that the most commonly used speech acts in conversations seemed to be requests of various degrees of definiteness, directions and commands, and forms of promises and persuasion (Ervin-Tripp, 1977; Garvey, 1983). These concerns with the encoding of speech acts as strings of utterances which have a particular meaning within the context refocused attention on the contribution of the social context to the process of meaning. As the work on speech acts grew, so did a concern not only with the developmental progression of language knowledge in the child, but also with the child's understanding of the speech events in which acquisition takes place as an essential part of the child's language experience (Ervin-Tripp and Mitchell-Kernan, 1977). Moreover, focus on the child's communicative intent uncovered many situations where children stretch to the limits their syntactic knowledge in order to convey more than they can say. The realisation of the social power of language in the child's life can be seen as a very positive stimulus toward communicative growth (Halliday, 1975).

3.4. Problems in speech act analysis

The influence of speech act studies on our present understanding of language socialization and why the promises of this early programme have not been fulfilled can best be assessed if we examine some problems in recent research. Firstly, children, because of their contextual dependence in many interpretive situations, are less likely to be troubled by apparent logical gaps or non-sequiturs in the semantic argument. This is not so, however, for research coders. In a recent example Dore drew attention to this problem in attempting to do an exhaustive speech act coding of the performative utterances of children during play sessions in nursery school (Dore, 1977). He noticed that the children's situated judgements of the outcome of speech acts were not in agreement with the coders' interpretation of the linguistic message and its illocutionary force. He comments:

> "in general, it seems clear that utterances which we have been calling non-sequiturs are related to the situation and the overall discourse, if not to the local sequence" (Dore 1977: 158).

From this comment it seems that children's notions of the range of context to which the presuppositions of any single speech act apply differ from the adult's non-situated judgement. Moreover, children are less likely to lexicalise intermediate steps in an argument, thus leaving the range of presuppositions that the listener and respondent needs to rely upon imprecise or difficult to recover. Such imprecision does not bother other child respondents, particularly when they are involved in activities together since their needs can be answered from the context. Dore gives examples from children's games of the kinds of question-answer pairs that illustrate such gaps of inferencing:

> Q: Are you finding us a book?
> A: We're going to catch the sheriff.

A further example of an answer implies contextual knowledge

> Q: He's trying to run away, so let's catch up with him, shall we?
> A: Oh them sheriff ... I found the sheriff (1977: 159).

In these examples Dore suggests information presupposed in the question is not reflected in the response. Children seem to rely on contextual information dependent on implicit understanding of the goals of the games and which is embedded in natural units of interaction (Cook-Gumperz and Corsaro, 1977). This contextual information appears to make the chain of reasoning used by the linguist redundant for the child's understanding and response in action.

Secondly, what appears to an adult to be an utterance founded on a complex expression of intent may not have to the child utterer such a complex derivation. As Ervin-Tripp has pointed out, in cases of frequently used idiomatic phrases the child may be reproducing the phrase without control over the full range of intent. She suggests

that English-speaking children may learn the phrase *Can I have ...*
as a request idiom when they are otherwise incapable of producing
modal verbs. Likewise, Bates' comments:

> "It is possible that in this way children may learn several direct, idio-
> matic mapping rules for various portions of a performative, without
> analysing or understanding the internal syntactic structure of such
> idioms. [Thus] a child could acquire a fairly good repertoire of such
> idiomatic direct mappings without having the flexible direct conscious
> control over the [outcomes]"   (1976: 292).

In this sense the child could be taken as meaning more then she
can actually say, that is, have the syntactic resources to manipulate
in other textual contexts. Ervin-Tripp (1977) gives other examples
of the textual and contextual dependence of children's uses of
performatives, especially modals, and indirect requests. It seems
that one of the problems of speech act analysis with children's
language is that of the analyst's over-interpretation of intent most
especially when speech acts are used formulaically in specific contexts and are then interpreted by adults as generalised codings of
intent. Here serious assumptions that affect validity arise which the
speech act model cannot solve.

Thirdly, we can see some of the weaknesses in the application of
speech act theory when research concerns are with wider issues of
socialization. Although using the speech act model allows the analyst to find out a great deal of information about the relationship
between grammatical encodings and norms of language use, any
judgement of speaker's intent requires the analyst to draw on
"knowledge of the world" which is implicit in the theory. Without
some guide as to how to interpret the context and the speaker's
relationship to it, such knowledge may need to be encyclopedic.
Noting this Bates' has commented:

> "A grammar generating all possible hints, seductions, and persuasions
> would require a 'human nature' component, an encyclopedia of motives,
> habits, quirks, irritations, and preferences of all potential listeners. This
> is clearly the point where the boundary between linguistic knowledge
> and world knowledge breaks down"   (1976: 293).

To speak of world knowledge as an abstract ideal-typical representation, as Bates does, does not enable us to link linguistic encoding
of intent to any reasoning about real life or real situations. Thus,
the model of reasoning which underlies speech act analysis may

provide linguistic insights, but it generates many conflicts with real life events and activities in which children might engage. It becomes necessary to see how the participants' understanding of the social context becomes essential to the linguistic message. The problem for study is how children draw on their own knowledge of the world to do things with words and how their perceptions of social setting or context shapes the outcomes of the verbal exchanges. However, this difficulty is perhaps inherent to all speech act theory.

In a recent critique of speech act theory Streeck (1980) has shown that theoretically problems of interpretation of context should be taken care of in Searle's "principle of expressibility" which states that in properly formulated speech acts the performance in context of the act is all that is necessary for understanding and explication of the intended illocutionary force of any utterance. Searle states:

> "for every possible speech act there is a possible sentence or set of sentences the literal utterance of which in a particular context would constitute a performance of that speech act"   (1969: 19).

Since this principle is central to the study of speech acts, it is also crucial in the study of speech act acquisition. The fact that the child's syntactic knowledge is far from complete makes its application difficult and dependent on other contextual information besides that available in the linguistic message itself and so the analysis of actual interactional exchanges by speech act coding is likely to violate the conditions of the principle. As Wells (1981) and Ochs and Schieffelin (1979) have shown, in making a speech act analysis of children's language, researchers have become aware of the complex relationship between the social function of an utterance, its linguistic form and the social context. While an analytic coding frame can be interpreted by the coders with only a minimum of contextual information, in order to understand the speakers' actions it is necessary to have some additional knowledge of their understanding of the context of interaction. That is, speech acts must be seen as occurring within activities that have a social meaning for the participants (Levinson 1981). How the participants' knowledge of the setting, of the actor's knowledge and of the goal of the activity are all socially and linguistically coded and communicated has become the most necessary direction that a socialization perspective on child language must take (Cook-Gumperz and Gumperz, 1978). It is not knowledge of the world but knowledge of activities in the world, that is, of the participant's own conception of the social activity of which speaking is a guiding part, that we need to seek.

4. An interpretive approach to language socialization

We can now see why, given the development of child language as a major area of enquiry, there has been so little interest, until very recently, in language socialization. Part of the problem lies in the fact that the study of language socialization must involve a view of language which is interactive and constitutive of social action. Such a view is not available from a linguistic standpoint. It would need more than just the enriching of language acquisition studies with knowledge of the social context, background or values of mothers and parents; or with the addition to linguistic variables of some cultural characteristics of the society in which interactants live. To create an adequate theory of language socialization both linguistic and social knowledge must be seen to focus on the social transmission process and the linguistic means through which social knowledge is reproduced.

In order to deal in a more socially realistic way with the issues of the participants' uses of language to achieve social goals, it is necessary to move toward a broader conception of speech in action by taking discourse as the prime unit of analysis. By discourse is meant the whole interactional sequence of speech in context and the situated judgements of interpretation and effectiveness that make up its outcome in social action. Such an approach has been recommended by Bruner as part of the pragmatic study of children's language acquisition. He suggests that a weakness inherent in most child language research is continuing to rely upon a sentence-based view of linguistic processing, while at the same time attempting to study language interactively within discourse frames. He comments:

> "in so far as pragmatics is concerned with context, presupposition, deixis, and the like, its proper data base is discourse and its rules will be discourse rules. Yet most linguistic description is based not upon discourse or conversational exchange, but upon sentence parts, the products of grammatical analysis. We tend therefore to formulate our discourse related rules in terms of sentence based grammatical concepts

that were constructed to be as discourse independent as possible"
(Bruner 1980: 40).

Here is the crux of the problem for any analysis of language which
concerns itself with the pragmatic study of discourse: the inadequacy
of the syntactic processing model to take care of the range of
implicature that is part of any linguistic reasoning based on natural
language. Linguistic rules, as context-free abstractions from an
everyday performance reality, are not able to provide us with the
categories we seek to understand the situated activity of speaking.
To quote Bruner again:

> "Pragmatics for all its linguistic predigree probably can never be exclusi-
> vely a linguistic concern. It is too rooted in principles of human action
> and interaction. As Fillmore (1977) puts it: 'whenever we pick up a
> word or phrase, we automatically drag along with it the larger context
> or framework in terms of which the word or phrase we have chosen
> has an interpretation' −. The 'context or framework' is most certainly
> broader than language" (1980: 41).

From a sentence- or utterance-focused perspective, specification of
what the larger context is proves to be a major problem which
linguistic analysis by itself can not solve. However, from a socio-
interpretive perspective it is exactly this knowledge of how the social
activity of speaking is linguistically coded that we must seek in
looking at the pragmatic purpose of an utterance in context. That
is, while grammatical rules and social knowledge are part of a
common reality, the same descriptive categories will not serve to
account for both. By looking at the child's development of grammar
or speech acts, even in different social contexts, we are not solving
the problem of the child as a developing social person. To explore
how the interactive process of speaking is situated within the social
constructive occurrence of any activity we must look directly at
social uses of linguistic knowledge and how linguistic knowledge
serves to convey social information.

   This statement takes us back full circle to the beginning of this
chapter where the coming together of interpretive social analysis
with the study of children's acquisition of speaking practices was
discussed; from this perspective we can see that any attempt to have
a discourse-based study of acquisition must go beyond much of
the sentence-based perspective which has dominated the past two
decades of research. While building upon the psycholinguist's devel-

opmental findings we must move toward formulating problems in terms of which language practices will be constitutive of social reality, rather than from the position of social information being used to remedy the particular problems or gaps in the linguistic chain of reasoning, or where the social reality addressed was an ideal-typical construction of world knowledge contained within a speech act lexicon.

Finally, let us look at an approach to child language which might be able to form a basis for language socialization studies. Bruner has suggested that a constructivist's approach calls for a child-centered notion of language acquisition, using discourse and situated language in use as the prime units. However, while such a direction would be both socially and pragmatically more valid, the primary focus needs, from the socialization perspective, to be on the social organisation of speaking, and it is to do this that we need to look at three basic principles that have begun to emerge in the study of child language in context.

5. Three principles of language socialization

5.1. The child's dialogic achievement of language

Firstly, the essential basis of study must be that the child's social achievement of language acquisition rests upon a dialogic model of communication. The child's earliest understanding of the matrix of social relationships is founded upon a communicative dialogue with a caretaker/mother through which experience is shaped into meaningful acts. In discussing this central principle of dialogic communication Bruner has pointed out that conventionalisation of communication between the mother/parent and child is as early in life 'as crying'; and is a 'transactional process of convention-making' in which the mother responds to the child's intentions and provides a frame into which further communication is fitted. A similar view of the centrality of dialogic communication, even at the prespeech level, is discussed by Schütze, Kreppner and Paulsen (this volume) and by Kaye in his studies of the development of personhood (1983). In this way, what Schütze, Kreppner and Paulsen call the 'as-if counterfactual' refers even to the very beginnings of life, and is seen to be instrumental in establishing this essential dialogic principle.

From a rather different and more philosophical perspective Habermas (1973) has argued for the dialogic basis of all communication, in contrast to the monologic model which is the basis of linguistic reasoning and inference. Some discussion of Habermas' perspective is given in Miller's study of the development of moral discourse in this volume. Once we begin to see dialogic communication as fundamental to the growth of linguistic skills we come to place the analytic emphasis clearly on discourse as the relevant unit of speech.

5.2. Language acquisition as socio-cognitive strategies

A second principle of both an interpretive and a constructivist approach to children's linguistic development is that language presents the child with a cognitive challenge. The child both recognises patterns of relationships within the linguistic signals received and develops hypotheses for further production. Language forms, for the child, an internal problem space (Karmiloff-Smith, 1979) within which the child works to construct a linguistic system out of available input and of experimentation within the communicative relationship. To see the child as a hypothesis forming and hypothesis testing communicator provides a more child-focused view of the linguistic acquisition process. How far this hypothesis testing process also applies to the child's learning of situational or contextual coding of social activities, as I suggested earlier, becomes clearer by looking at some recent research by reported by Peters (1983).

Peters, in a study of acquisition strategies, suggests that the language learning child's perception of the segmentation of streams of talk into units may not be the same developmentally as that suggested a priori by the grammatical model. That is, the child's way of unitising language may give a saliency to elements of structure in relationships that differ from those described in a model of grammar. She suggests that children work to segment, analyse and reanalyse the available linguistic input and thus to generate hypotheses which form the basis for building up the knowledge of linguistic regularities. In the following example of on-the-spot analysis of linguistic input two children work to communicate dialogically and, in the situated urgency of their communication, they discover new grammatical regularity as part of the contextually embedded activity of interpretation of each other's meaning and intention. Peters', quoting from the research of Iwamura, comments:

"A complex example of reanalysis comes from Iwamura's study of the speech of two 3 year-old girls, Suzi and Nani, who were recorded daily (five days a week) as they talked to each other in the back seat of a car on their way to and from nursery school. In order to better communicate with each other the girls often struggled valiantly with constructing a particular sentence and in the process they sometimes produced evidence about analysis in progress. A particularly intriguing example involves what Iwamura calls the "unpacking" of the catenative 'wanna'. In this instance Suzi (3.8) has suggested that Nani (3.5) pretend that Nani's shawl was a poncho, but Nani did not want to do this:

1. S: Just pretend to have a poncho.
2. N: No, I wan' to. No I don' wanna. I wanna be it, a shawl.
3. S: Sha'
4. N: I wan' it to be a shawl. I n'
5. S: Sha' sha'
6. N: (shouts) No, I say it myself (giggles)   (1980: 44)

The reanalysis allowed Nani, in line 4, to break "wanna" into "want to" so that she could insert it into the sequence. Nani's difficulty in negating is here clearly related to her limited understanding of lexical boundaries and her need to resegment the items under the pressure of communicative needs. As Iwamura points out:

"'wanna' is hard to analyse, not only because it tends to occur as a unit in American English, but also because it can be analysed in two ways: in the case of wanna Nani had probably used it for a long time in such sentences as 'I wanna cookie' and 'I wanna come too'. She would have had to learn the difference between wanna meaning 'want a' and wanna meaning 'want to' before she could approach the construction of want + NP + VP" [44]

which she is able to end up reproducing here. In other words the input to language acquisition is not just words or constructs as such but situated utterances which must be further worked on to provide language regularities.

We can see that as children extract patterns from their language experience they develop hypotheses to govern future similarities or differences of linguistic forms within different language-discourse environments. These hypotheses both unify, simplify and consolidate previous experience, as Karmiloff-Smith suggests:

"thus freeing the representational processing space for other developments ... [the child] uses metaprocedures to organise her own procedures into a system of options" (1979: 240).

The process of consolidating and the systematising of options enables children to gain increasing predictive control over their language and its social organisational occurrence in dialogue.

5.3 The social organisation of language: language as an external problem space

The third principle of the social interpretive view of language socialization must consider not only how language operates as an internal cognitive domain or problem space in which the child builds up a linguistic rule system, but also whether a similar model might be appropriate to describe the developmental acquisition of social knowledge. Our question is then: how do social rules and regularities expressed socio-linguistically become part of the child's organised cognitive domain, what we will call the language-as-an-external-problem-space principle. How can we discover some of the socio-cognitive or interpretive procedures which are constitutive of socially organised reality (Cicourel 1974, 1978); Corsaro 1985)? While language knowledge and social knowledge are part of the same organisational structure, learnt at the same time by the child, abstracted and derived from the same reality, these two domains of activity are, in analysis, kept apart and treated as if they are part of two different systems of knowledge. As we have tried to show in the foregoing arguments such a separation provides linguists with context-free rules which do not always make sense within the developmental maturation of children but which linguistically remain useful. Shatz reflects this position in commenting:

> "The tasks of acquiring social and syntactic knowledge are seen as being mainly simultaneous, primarily because the facts suggest that much of both are learned over the same time period in development" (33).

She goes on to say that

> "there is no necessary temporal relationship between them. Nor is there any reason to suppose that the acquisition of one facilitates the acquisition of the other. Obviously, learning how to use one's language appropriately in social situations may be closely tied to social knowledge but it is the acquisition of syntax that is our concern and not pragmatic development" (1980: 33).

So that what we have described as an essential interlocking of social and linguistic knowledge does not appear as such from Shatz's linguistic viewpoint. From the interpretive standpoint reflected in this book, the relationship of language learning and language socialization needs to be reversed. Ultimately, language and social rules are expressions of the same phenomena, but the paths through which these are learnt, the rules for learning the rules, deviate from their common beginnings.

5.4 The study of language socialization as children's situated activity

Children's language socialization occurs as part of the continuing history of conversational exchanges that make up daily life. It has recently been pointed out that:

> "it is not hard to see why one should look at conversation for insight into pragmatic phenomena for conversation is clearly the prototypical kind of language usage, the form in which we are all first exposed to language — the matrix of language or language acquisition" (Levinson 1983: 284).

Studies of children's conversations, therefore, can give more than additional social information on the contexts of learning, they can provide evidence of the ways in which interpersonal interaction structures the language learning environment for the child (Ochs and Schieffelin, 1981; Wells, 1981). It is from such conversational exchanges that we gain insight into the very social organisation of reality provided for and by children themselves (Cook-Gumperz, 1985). For the linguist, the existence of social regularities or social rules adds predictive control over the variation of what is seen as a single continuum of the "social context", and so provides a fuller description of the child's language learning opportunities. But to those interested in how language development mediates children's acquisition of social knowledge, the child's perception of differing social categories of context is all important. If we accept that language provides socially constitutive knowledge, we need to locate sociolinguistic regularities used for generating social understanding in interactional performance. The analytic problem that we have identified above, remains: what are the "social genes" of language? As we have shown, study of child language, even from a discourse or interactional perspective, has still focused on the acquisition of linguistic forms, but not yet on the maturation of the social person. We must look for the kind of evidence that could begin to show us how children's perception of situations is shaped by the development of their communicative skills. How, from the time of early language learning onwards, can we identify a changing socio-cognitive understanding occurring in synchrony with linguistic maturation? To answer these queries we need to find social categories within the performance of language as speaking practices.

We begin from the perspective outlined in Cook-Gumperz and Gumperz (1978): the contextual presuppositions in terms of which speakers and hearers interpret what they hear are renegotiated in the course of conversation. In this negotiation process children initially rely both on background knowledge, acquired as part of their interactional history, and on their understandings of contextualisation conventions. These conventions govern the use of verbal cues by means of which they categorise what occurs as part of any particular activity type. An initial assessment takes the form of an hypothesis which is then confirmed or changed during the course of the interaction. So social context cannot be considered as a set of fixed rules but as a set of guiding principles for organising further interactional particulars and to fulfill or change expectations of social outcomes. The inputs for the hypothesis confirming or rejecting view of context comes from both linguistic and social sources. To the extent that contextualisation conventions rely upon verbal signs they work by principles that differ from context-independent linguistic rules. Gumperz' states that

> "although it is true that conversations are governed by general organising principles, these principles operate differently from all or none, categorical, grammatical rules. Conversational principles do not determine what can or cannot be said or understood but rather act as guidelines or standards of evaluations which, when violated, give rise to the implicatures on which interpretation of what is intended rests" (1984: 279).

In other words conversations are governed by a logic which differs essentially from the context-free logic underlying the abstract linguistic system. It is on the process of conversational inference in which the decision-making of conversational interpretation rests. In the operation of this process conversationalists make situated judgements about the progress of interaction and of its effectiveness in achieving communicative ends.

It is this interpretive process which guides children's acquisition of language within the conversational context, and which gives them the basis for the situated understanding of social processes. For it is by such means that interactional histories are developed on which children draw for their background social knowledge. Research on children's language socialization from this perspective must of course vary from the studies discussed above in that it focuses upon conversation as the central unit of acquisition so that developmental understanding of children's processes of acquisition must build on a theory of conversational interpretive understanding. To do this we must get away from apriori adult assumptions of what a speaker means or intends and look at the interactive process of conversational negotiation by which children seek to achieve their own communicative goals and by which they demonstrate empirically how they have understood the message. Gumperz points out that this process of negotiation builds on verbal conventions that are often not directly lexicalised. He goes on to suggest that

> "when we look at problems of understanding from a participant's perspective we can see that what is to be explained is how processing strategies operate. Conversationalists must employ specific strategies to chunk or to segment the stream of talk into information or idea units. These strategies are also used to locate transition relevant points for turn taking, in inferring the contextual presuppositions which guide expectations about what is to be accomplished in an encounter and how to integrate what is said at various points in the exchange into coherent themes. Such a perspective leads us to discover that stylistic and prosodic cues not ordinarily covered in sentence level linguistic analysis are crucial for conversational understanding. These performance features form the bases for contextualisation conventions that retrieve schematic information and make it available as an input into the interpretive process" (Gumperz 1984: 278).

This capacity to contextualise and thus to intergrate what is heard with what is already known is governed by cognitive abilities which share many of the characteristics of grammatical abilities in that they are conventional in nature, learned as part of the language acquisition process, and are employed automatically, that is, without conscious reflection. However, and this is an important qualification, they are part of a transitory auditory medium and so are difficult to report on or to recall for post hoc analysis. Furthermore contextualisation cues channel and organise the progress of the interaction and so constrain and shape the information flow. It is in these ways that analysis of conversational discourse must differ from the practices of sentence-based grammar. In order to illustrate this new direction of analysis more fully I will briefly explore two examples of children's conversational interaction where the analysis of the contextualisation cues provides us with essential information.

I have chosen sequences of tape-recordings of children at play in a home and a nursery school that, from the longer event in the full transcript, can be considered to be self-contained, naturally occurring episodes, that is, the phase of activity begins and ends with the short sequence we have selected. However, we realize in the analysis that the history of the interaction is, of course, much longer and the episode I analyze is embedded within a longer period of interaction.

The first example takes place in a nursery school. The children, a boy and a girl about three and a half years old, Jeff and Mandy, often play together and have a close school specific relationship. Jeff and Mandy have been playing mother and father in the play-house earlier in the morning. The game has finished and they have gone their separate ways to get their morning snack and do other things. When observed, Mandy was playing with some toy animals — horses, cows, sheep, a zebra — on a rug. Jeff goes over to Mandy, stands behind her while she is kneeling on the rug moving the animals around making them do various things. After standing for a while he says:

1. J: Let's go to bed honey let's go to bed.
2. M: (after a pause) No I'm playing with these animals ...
3.   The animals are going to bed ...
4. J: Honey, it's nighttime let's go to bed.
5. M: Yes It's nighttime the animals are sleepy ...
6.   They're all going to bed. Horse is going to bed.

J stands for some time watching M playing with the animals, putting them on their sides, neither speaks, then J walks away.

Jeff's initial remark is made in a slightly higher than normal pitch, with rising intonation contour on each phrase and slight lengthening of the phrase final words. Mandy does not pick up on Jeff's tone of voice but replies in her own game talk mode, which is just a slightly more "sing-song" version of her normal voice and she continues not to respond to Jeff's voice cue. Jeff is clearly alluding to the previous game by adopting the rhythm and prosody of that game, and, by implication, asking Mandy to resume the

game. Mandy either did not understand him or chose not to cooperate; most likely the latter, since she uses the suggestion of Jeff's
remarks, but puts them to use in playing a game of her own.

In trying to persuade Mandy to change her game, Jeff has
presented his case not with a lexicalised statement but by the way
he contextualises his message, that is, by using a change of voice
tone to mark the change of context. Both his voice tone and his
remarks signal that he wants to resume playing "mothers and
fathers". In a sense, he "acts out" the character of "the Daddy" in
his attempt to be persuasive, by directly using a Daddy-type request
as if already in the game. To an adult hearer it might seem that his
communicative failure is in not announcing his request explicitly to
Mandy by giving her the additional information it seems she would
need to understand his other utterances. Also to an adult Jeff's
remarks, made as they are without any preamble or prerequest
sequences, seem "out of context", breaking into and failing to
acknowledge the event that Mandy is now engaged in. An adult
reply to Jeff could easily be a reproach. Mandy, however, does not
react as if Jeff's request were at all out of place, or badly timed, it
seems she is just busy doing something else. She uses the idea of
"going to bed" as if it applied to the development of the plot of in
her own game. Jeff's attempt to be more persuasive merely results
in repetition, plus an elaboration on the first remark. He does not
find an alternate strategy to establish any further arguments for
persuasion, rather he relies on a prosodic switch into the character
of Daddy/husband and the giving of some scene-setting comment,
which he lexicalises as "it's nighttime".

Our next example involves two three-year old girls, Lucy and
Sophie, who are regular playmates. Here Lucy and Sophie are
playing a game of 'mothers and babies' while Lucy's mother, in the
same room is busy arranging some clothes in a closet and the
children are trying on clothes that have been put aside.

1. M: Well you're getting dressed up in all my clothes now, are you?
2. L: (imitating baby talk) natcha natcha, dika dika ...
3. M: Wait a minute. This box ... I'm stacking up to keep, allright?
4. L: Right
5. M: You can play with those things over there
6. L: Natcha natcha ...
7. M: Leave it alone
8. S: sota ... sota ...

 9. L: natcha ... natcha ...
10. S: No ... No ...
11. L: natcha, natcha ... Mummy. Mummy ... that my pillow
12. M: Wait a minute
13. S: No. she doesn't mean you ... I mean ...
14. L: natcha natcha ...
15. S: (to M) I'm putting this for Lucy, out there.
16. M: Alright Sophie
17. L: natcha natcha ... what are you doing mama?
18. M: I'm still sorting through all these things.
19. L: No. I mean dattie
20. M: You mean Sophie's you're mummy?
21. L: Yea.

In this episode the mother, while busy at her own task of organising, overhears the children's talk and following the conversational rule of third-person listenership, assumes that any mention of 'mummy or mamma' refers to herself, even though the voice quality is still that of the baby talk. The children indignantly correct her since they know that the voice quality contextualises these talk sequences as part of the in-character game talk. From an adult perspective we might say that Lucy failed to signal that this was an in-game sequence and that she was not talking to the mother herself. Similarly, from an adult perspective, Jeff might be seen as having failed to communicate to Mandy that he wanted to continue with the previous game although it is clear that Mandy and Jeff both understand what he wants and that she rejects his idea.

The problem in these two examples is not the children's lack of knowledge but a difference in contextualisation strategies by which the talk activity sequence is signalled. Children's contextualisation can vary from the adult expectation and so lead to differential recognition of the communicative work being done by similar semantic and syntactic sequences. This realisation shows us that children learn their sociolinguistic strategies on their own terms, through the practice of setting and achieving their own communicative goals within activities which they to some extent define themselves. The notion of activity then serves as a framing device to limit the degrees of freedom in the search for interpretation of any referential items, any gestural/kinesic schema and any novel semantic/lexical utterances. This contextual information is both coded as a form of semantic information and signalled as part of the interaction process. The signalling of context makes this information available to the participants in the on-going situation as a potentially sharable cognitive construct, which frames the range of possible interpretations both in terms of the relevance of any presuppositions and as guides to further action.

While these two examples might appear to be very small, fleeting instances, they do indicate a much larger issue that involves child-adult communication. What I am suggesting here is that in order to understand the socio-cognitive consequences of language learning we must ask not only what context is involved, in terms of the preceding utterances or of the activity taking place, but most importantly, how the context is perceived by the speaker and listener. This point is as valid for adult, as it is for children's, communication (Gumperz, 1982). For the perceived context becomes a part of the communicative activity itself and is recognised as such by participants. This is expecially apparent in situations of conversational misunderstanding or repair, as shown in the example from Iwamura. In these ways activity becomes a bridging concept that accounts for both knowledge of social rules, that is, how social action is perceived and practiced by actors, and how this knowledge is signalled linguistically in discourse. Thus activity is at one and the same time a linguistic and a social concept. By focusing on the acquisition of activity as a socio-cognitive construct, which can be ethnographically observed in varied situations and developmentally seen to change as the child's network of relationships expands, we have a key to an interpretive approach to language socialization. This key, as part of an ethnographically-based discourse study of children's socio-cultural and linguistic experience, may help to provide the beginnings of an answer to the issue of the transmission of inter-generational knowledge through language itself.

Note

1. The title of this paper is adapted from that of a recent book about the making of the Oxford English dictionary: *"Caught in the Web of Words": James Murray and the Oxford English Dictionary*, by E. Murray, Oxford 1981: Oxford University Press.

References

Bates, Elizabeth
    1976   *Language and Context: the acquisition of pragmatics*. Academic Press: London and New York.

Brown, Roger
    1973   *A First Language*. Harvard University press, Cambridge, Mass.

Bruner, Jerome
    1980   The pragmatics of acquisition. In W. Deutsch ed. *The Child's Construction of Language*. Academic Press, London and New - York.

Bullowa, Margret
    1979   *Before Speech: the beginning of interpersonal communication*. Cambridge University Press, Cambridge and New York.

Cicourel, Aaron V.
    1974   *Cognitive Sociology*. Penguin Books, London.
    1978   Language and society: cognitive, cultural and linguistic aspects of language in use. In *Sozialwissenschaftliche Annalen*, Band 2, Physica, Vienna.

Cook-Gumperz, Jenny
    1975   The child as a practical reasoner in Mary Sanches & Ben Blount eds. *Socio-cultural dimensions of language use*. Academic Press. New York and London.
    1981   Persuasive talk; the social organization of children's talk. in Judith Green & Cynthia Wallat eds. *Ethnography and Language in Educational Settings*. Ablex Publishing. Norwood N. J.
    1985   Keeping it together: text and context in childrens' language socialization. In James Alatis & Deborah Tannen eds. *Linguistics and Language in Context: the interdependence of theory, data and application*. Georgetown University Press, Washington D. C.

Cook-Gumperz, Jenny & Corsaro, William
    1977   Socio-ecological constraints on children's communicative strategies. *Sociology*, vol. 11 411 – 434.

Cook-Gumperz, Jenny & Gumperz, John J.
    1978   Context in children's speech. In Natalie Waterson and Catherine Snow eds. *The development of communication: social and pragmatic factors in language acquisition*. John Wiley: London.

Corsaro, William
    1985   *Peer Culture in the Early Years*. Ablex publishing corporation. Norwood N. J.

Deutsch, Werner
1980   Introduction to *The Child's Construction of Language.* Academic Press. London and New York.

Dore, John
1977   "Oh them Sherrif": pragmatic analysis of children's responses. In Susan Ervin-Tripp & Claudia Mitchell-Kernan eds. *Child Discourse.* Academic Press, London and New York.

Dunn, Judy & Kendrick, Carol
1982   *Siblings: love, envy and understanding.* Grant McIntyre: London.

Ervin-Tripp, Susan
1977   Wait for me, roller skate. In Susan Ervin-Tripp & Claudia Mitchell-Kernan eds. *Child Discourse.* Academic Press London and New York.

Ervin-Tripp S. & Mitchell-Kernan C.
1977   *Child Discourse.* Academic Press, London and New York.

Fillmore, Charles
1977   The case for case reopened. In Peter Cole & Jerry Saddock eds. *Syntax and Semantics*, vol. 8. Academic Press, New York and London.

Garvey, Catherine
1983   *Children's Talk.* Harvard University Press. Cambridge Mass.

Gelman, Rochelle & Shatz, Marilyn
1977   Appropriate speech adjustment: the operation of conversational constraints on the talk of 2 year olds. In Michael Lewis and Lewis Rosenblum eds. *Interaction, Conversation and the Development of Language.* John Wiley: New York.

Giddens, Anthony
1979   *Central Problems in Social Theory: action, structure and contradiction in social analysis.* Campus books, University of California Press Berkeley and Los Angeles.

Gumperz, John J.
1982   *Discourse Strategies.* Cambridge University Press Cambridge and New York.

1984   Communicative competence revisted. In Deborah Shiffrin ed. *Meaning, Form and Use in Context.* Georgetown University Press. Washington D. C.

Habermas, Jürgen
1970   Towards a theory of communicative competence in Hans-Pieter Dreitzel ed. *Recent sociology 2.* Macmillian: London.

Halliday, Michael
1975   *Learning How To Mean: explorations in the development of language.* Edward Arnold. London.

Ingleby, David
    1980   Review of Action, Gesture and Symbol, ed. by Andrew Lock.
            In *European Journal of social psychology* vol 10 pp 319−328.
Iwamura, Susan
    1980   *The Verbal Games of Pre-school Children.* Croom Helm: London.
Karmiloff-Smith, Annette
    1979   *A Functional Approach to Child Language: a study of detirminers and reference.* Cambridge University Press, Cambridge and New York.
Kaye, Kenneth
    1982   *The Mental and Social Life of Babies: how parents create persons.* University of Chicago Press, Chicago.
Keenan-Ochs, Eleanor
    1974   Conversational competence in children. In *Journal of Child Language* vol 1 p. 130−185.
Levinson, Stephen
    1981   Some pre-observations on the modelling of dialogue. In Jenny Cook-Gumperz, ed. Special issue *Discourse Processes* vol 4 no 2 pp 51−74.
    1983   *Pragmatics.* Cambridge University Press, Cambridge and New York.
Lock, Andrew
    1978   Introduction: *Action, Gesture and Symbol: the emergence of language.* Academic Press: New York.
Luria, A. V. & Yudovitch, F. Ia
    1959   *Speech and the development of mental processes in the Child.* Translated by Brian Simon. Staples Press. London.
MacTear, Michael
    1985   *Children's Conversations.* Basil Blackwell Books Oxford and New York.
Ochs, Elinor & Schieffelin, Bambi
    1979   *Developmental Pragmatics.* Academic Press, London and New-York.
    1981   *Acquiring Conversational Competence.* Routledge and Kegan Paul, London and Boston.
Peters, Ann
    1983   *The Units of Language Acquisition.* Cambridge University Press: Cambridge and New York.
Searle, John
    1969   *Speech Acts.* Cambridge University Press: Cambridge and New York.
Shotter, John
    1974   The development of personal powers in Martin Richards ed.

64   *Cook-Gumperz*

The Intergration of the Child into a Social World. Cambridge University Press: Cambridge and New York.

1978   The cultural context of communication studies: theoretical and methodological issues. In Andrew Lock ed. *Action, Gesture and Symbol.* Academic Press, London and New York.

Shatz, Marilyn

1980   Learning the rules of the game: four views of the relationship between grammar acquisition and social interaction. In Werner Deutsch ed. *The Child's Construction of Language.* Academic Press, London and New York.

Slobin, Dan I.

1973   Cognitive prerequistes for the development of grammar. In Charles Ferguson and Dan I. Slobin eds. *Studies of child language development.* Holt Rienhardt and Winston: New - York.

1978   Suggested universals in the ontogenisis of grammar. In Vera Honsa & Mary. J. Hardman-de-Bautista eds. *Papers on Linguistics and Child Language: Ruth Hirsch Weir memorial volume.* Mouton, Berlin.

1984   *The child as a Linguistic Icon-Maker.* Technical report 14. Program in Cognitive Science, University of California, Berkeley.

Streeck, Jürgen

1980   Speech acts in interaction: critique of Searle. In Hugh Mehan ed. Special issue of *Discourse Processes* vol 3 no 2 pp 133 — 154.

Stern, Carlotta & Stern, Wilhelm

1928   *Die Kindersprache.* Barth, Leipzig.

Vygotsky, Lev. S.

1978   *Mind in Society: the development of higher psychological processes.* Michael Cole, Vera John-Steiner, Sylvia Scribner and Ellen Souberman, eds. Harvard University Press, Cambridge Mass.

Wells, Gordon et al.

1981   *Learning Through Interaction: the study of language development.* Cambridge University Press, Cambridge and New York.

The Preschool Years

The chapters in this section focus on children's early years within the family. The chapters cover a wide range of features of children's worlds, encompassing mother-child interaction in infancy, sibling relationships and children's first entry into peer relations. In chapter 3 Camaioni presents an analysis of early language acquisition which stresses the importance of mother-child play during infancy. Camaioni extends Bruner's (1975) conception that early language development is preceded by firmly patterned prelinguistic mother-child interaction formats by demonstrating that it is not interactive formats *per se*, but rather *conventionalized* interaction patterns which serve as frames for the acquisition of first words. Such patterns include games that involve a structured exchange of activity roles (e. g., Peekaboo). Camaioni's findings demonstrate the importance of the mother's role as communicator and context-builder in the child's first steps toward speech. The child's first words are often uttered, as Camaioni's study shows, in the course of such conventional games. Camaioni develops the importance of this finding by reference to the fact that these interactive fomats entail unique form-function relationships and thus have a built-in "scaffolding" structure which facilitates the early development of the lexical component of language. Finally, in line with the main theme of this volume we can see, given Camaioni's naturalistic and longitudinal method, precisely how mother-child conventional games and the language learning which results are embedded in the everyday lifes of young children.

While Camaioni exhibits the mother's role in "scaffolding" conventionalized and reciprocal interaction formats which facilitate the child's transition form the prelinguistic to the linguistic stage, Budwig, Strage and Bamberg (chapter 4) focus on the caregiver's role in establishing and safeguarding interactions among peers. The transition from adult-structured to independently organized interaction is a crucial one in children's life-worlds. Budwig, Strage and Bamberg demonstrate that this transition often begins within the home setting with the aid of the mother prior to the child's entrance into day care or nursery school settings. The authors' longitudinal study of two mother-child dyads in the home demonstrates how children are gradually instigated by their mothers to construct self-organizing frames of joint play which eventually operate without the support system provided by the caretakers. Budwig, Strage and Bamberg identify a number of strategies by which mothers help their children to enlist the attention of peers, to join in on activities which involve a differentiation of roles, and to maintain a shared focus of attention. Using Vygotsky's notion of the zone of proximal development, the authors suggest that each new achievement in the acquisition of concepts and communicative strategies must, before it is internalized as a mental substratum, be present in the social or interpersonal sphere. In this way Budwig, Strage and Bamberg demonstrate how Vygotsky's notion of internalization occurs within the everyday worlds of mothers and their children.

In chapter 5 Watson-Gegeo and Gegeo's study of interactive processes between caregivers and young children in several villages of West Kwar'ae, Malaita in the Solomon Islands reveals parallels between the children's acquisition of language and their acquisition of social values. In Kwar'ae values are both explicitly taught and implicitly structure adult-child interaction. Watson-Gegeo and Gegeo's study is important because it sheds light on an area, cultural variation in early socialization and language development, where there is growing theoretical interest but little empirical research. It has, for example, been argued (see Ochs and Schieffelin, 1984) that the socialization orientation of Western societies is to center socio-communicative situations around the child and to structure them according to his/her needs and level of competence, while the reverse is often the case for non-Western societies. While Camaioni's (this volume) findings are in line with this position, Watson-Gegeo and Gegeo argue that the Kwar'ae show a tendency to use both orientations and this tendency is a result of their "practical" theory of socialization. For the Kwar'ae the overall goal is to adapt the child to the situation. However, the Kwar'ae believe this goal is best reached by beginning at the child's level. In sum, Watson-Gegeo and Gegeo's study demonstrates how cultural beliefs regarding the nature of childhood and children have dramatic effects on features of children's life-worlds, which in turn influence early language acquisition and children's development of interactive skills and social knowledge.

In chapter 6 Schütze, Kreppner and Paulsen address a much neglected issue in childhood socialization, the social construction of sibling relations. In their longitudinal study of sixteen families from different social class backgrounds in West Berlin, the authors investigate the transition from the triad to the tetrad (i. e., from the one child to the two child family). The authors argue that this crucial transition in children's worlds is achieved through the parents' behaving (counterfactually) "as if" the relationship between the first and second child already existed at the moment of the second child's birth. This contention is supported and demonstrated in examples from the authors' observational data and parallels results from studies on language acquisition which show that parents behave *as if* the child were already capable of language and social action in early interactive routines. In fact, this chapter nicely complements the earlier chapters by Camaioni and Watson-Gegeo and Gegeo by demonstrating how the mother is able to re-establish and extend basic interactive formats and routines first constructed with the older child to now meet the demands of the second child while at the same time including the older child in such a way that he/she comes to recognize his/her new position in the family network.

Wootton's analysis of how children are exposed to social and moral rules in chapter 7 is similar to the other chapters in this section in that he argues that the acquisition of rules (be they linguistic, social or moral) is often indirect and results from children's everyday participation in discourse events with caretakers and peers. According to Wootton the way in which a rule is invoked in discourse can be seen as a technique through which members of a society can display their recognizable engagement in particular social practices. Wootton notes that rules are regularly oriented to in his data, but most often without overt formulation. However, Wootton argues that the non-formulation of a rule does not prevent members of society from organizing their actions as if a rule existed. In his analysis, Wootton discovers two distinct forms of linguistic organization in the evocation of rules, and he examines how such forms are sequentially placed in the flow of interactive events. Wootton's results suggest that studies of how children deal with occasions in their everyday lifes where social rules are relevant (e. g., the occurrence of misdeeds) can lead to a better understanding of the emergence of children's knowledge about rules.

References

Bruner, Jerome
   1975   "The Ontogenesis of Speech Acts," *Journal of Child Language*,
             2, 1—20.
Ochs, Elinor and Schieffelin, Bambi B.
   1984   "Language Acquisition and Socialization: Three Developmen-
             tal Stories and Their Implications", *Culture Theory: Essays in
             Mind, Self and Emotion*, edited by Richard A. Shweder and
             Robert Le Vine (Cambridge: Cambridge University Press).

From Early Interaction Patterns To Language Acquisition: Which Continuity?

Luigia Camaioni

1. Introduction

In the light of recent research (cf. Freedle and Lewis, 1977; Richards, 1977) a continuity has been postulated between pre-linguistic communication and subsequent language acquisition in which this continuity is defined in social and interactive terms rather than in cognitive terms. More specifically, the aim of this research was to identify a continuity, and consequently an at least partial derivation of the second from the first, between pre-linguistic categories such as the child-adult interactive patterns and subsequent linguistic categories displayed by the child. One such attempt has so far run into serious difficulty and some of the researchers involved have spoken explicitly of the failure of research based on explaining language acquisition in interactionist terms (Richards, 1977; Kaye, 1979).

In particular, Marilyn Shatz, at the end of a chapter on communication development claims that:

"With regard to the question of the relation between language and communication development, we have seen an explosion of work that has carefully described early interactive patterns between infants and their caretakers. Yet, any real evidence that patterns of interaction developed in the early months or even the first year of life have any direct bearing on the speed or order of language acquisition still is lacking" (1983: 877).

Since Shatz' point of view is that communicative development and language have partially independent courses in the early years of life, an interesting starting point could be an analysis of the characteristics that Shatz considers to define conventional communication systems and particularly the language system. This analysis would indeed appear to be a necessary prerequisite to any correct answer to the question "which patterns can justifiably be taken as precursors of which more sophisticated behaviors" (Shatz 1983: 853).

According to Shatz any conventional communication system entails the use of conventional signs, i. e. of signs whose meaning depends on a culturally defined and agreed-upon set of rules. Conventional signs therefore imply some degree of learning on the part of the child.

The language system in particular implies the existence of multiple form-function relationships, which only complicates the language acquisition process since unique form-function pairings would probably make it easier to solve the problem of matching a given sound with a given meaning. This is why Grimshaw (1981) argues that in order to acquire language the child must start off by postulating unique pairings of form and function. Otherwise, at the beginning, he would have no device to allow him to make the correct choice from among many possible alternatives.

Both the features identified by Shatz appear to define also those sequences of child-adult (usually the mother) interaction called "social games" or "routine game formats" (Ratner and Bruner, 1978). These consist of conventional games or routines, which are characterized by a set of culturally defined and agreed-upon rules, and also contain unique form-function relationships (e. g. *give* always marks the function of asking for an object and *thank you* that of receiving it in the "Give and Take" game).

It is thus not the social interaction *per se* nor the mastery of its structural properties (e. g. turn-taking, role differentiation, etc.) that could provide a suitable precursor of later linguistic development, but only those interaction episodes characterized by a conventional structure and by unique form-function relationships.

On this basis it is possible to explain the failure of research attempting to identify a continuity between interactive categories and linguistic categories, which appear weakly related to each other on a theoretical level[1].

2. Early Social Games and Language Acquisition

The link between play and language is not a new one either in philosophy (cf. Wittgenstein, 1958) or in psychology. Piaget in particular (1945) postulated a close connection between symbolic play and language, considering them both as manifestations of the representational capacity emerging at the 6th sensorimotor stage. His hypothesis was verified empirically by subsequent research (cf. Nicholich, 1977; Bates et al., 1979). However, these studies ignored the social nature of children's play and therefore, methodologically speaking, consisted of a unilateral analysis of the data themselves in which the behavior of the playing child was evaluated and the contribution of the adult (who is normally present and actively participating) to the construction of the game episodes was neglected.

Only recently has there been a growing interest in the literature for the nature and development of social games between child and adult (usually the mother), within the framework of a more general interest in the structural and functional aspects of the adult-child interaction (Bruner and Sherwood, 1976; Crawley et al., 1978; Gustafson, Green and West, 1979; Stern, 1974). Daniel Stern (1974) has identified play episodes occurring between mother and child already in the first few months of life which he has defined as "pure interaction" since they appear to be directed towards a completely intrinsic objective (i. e. the pleasure of being together) and lack any utilitarian function. Analysing the interaction between mother-child dyads at child ages of 3, 4 and 6 months, Snow et al. (1979) have identified a category of maternal language, denoted as "talking for fun", which is clearly differentiable in its content and structure from "business oriented" speech. It is characterized by the creation of "situations within which the mother can be most certain that she has in fact effectively communicated with her child" (1979: 286). In other words, "mothers are thus assured that, for the few moments they spend engaged in the game, at least, they and their babies are 'on the same wavelenght', thinking about the same thing, engaged in seeking the same goals, in short, communicating" (1979: 286).

Also Bruner (1975) stresses the importance of the non-instrumental nature of play and of the possibility of actions carried out during it being detached from their normal consequences. In this way "play has the effect of drawing the child's attention to communication itself, and to the structure of the acts in which communication is taking place" (1979: 10).

In their mutual play, adult and child basically work out a restricted and shared set of 'meanings' which could act as referents for gradually more advanced communication signals. The fact that the adult repeatedly produces certain standard action or attention formats allows the child (a) to interpret the adult's actions and signals starting from the positions (privileges of occurrence) they occupy in the routine sequence, and (b) subsequently to reproduce the same actions and signals inside the sequence, usually moving from the use of non-standard signals to the use of standard lexical items. The work of Bruner and colleagues shows how the child's role in play gradually changes from mere spectator to actor; he learns to carry out one or more of the actions involved in the game and also to produce the linguistic marking that accompanies, precedes or completes these actions.

Even though Bruner clearly attempts to produce evidence of a structural continuity between infant's pre-linguistic and linguistic development, the critical point in his approach is that "whereas 'interactional formats' represent adequate interactive categories, the same cannot be said of the linguistic categories (agent-action, action-object, possession, etc.) derived by Bruner from Case Grammar. It is in fact rather difficult to find in the nature of these linguistic categories the *mutuality* of action and attention used to define the interactional formats" (Camaioni et al. 1984: 95).

This means that any attempt to verify a significant relationship between early mastery of the rules and conventions of social interaction and subsequent acquisition of language should adopt linguistic models whose unit of analysis is not the single utterance or word but the *dialogue*, i. e. an interactional unit which takes into account the contribution of at least two interlocutors. In this sense the child's first words cannot be interpreted as nouns in the proper sense (i. e. instantiations of object reference) as far as they appear to be linguistic procedures used to refer to the whole or to aspects of the interactional situations in which they were produced. Moreover these linguistic procedures are seen to correspond quite often to segments of the adult discourse used in the same interactional situations. This amounts to saying that the traditional relationship between form and function or name and referent may be traced back in development to the intersubjective processes of constituting shared objects by which such a relationship was established.

Only on the basis of this early intersubjectivity of highly conventionalized forms of interaction does the child gradually learn to decenter or decontextualize objects from the ongoing forms of interaction of which they were originally an integral part and becomes able to single out particular objects or properties, producing his/her own first meaningful linguistic units in the form of words or sentences.

In this sense we agree with Michael Bamberg's conclusion that

"the meaning of first words cannot be based on some pre-existing, abstract semantic knowledge, but rather has to be seen as being derived from particular forms of interaction in the caregiver-child dyad. Therefore, an a priori differentiation between speech act knowledge, i. e. pragmatic knowledge, and semantic knowledge cannot be inferred; rather, the semantics of first words always have to be considered in pragmatic terms". (1980: 38)

3. Empirical Evidence

Starting off from these theoretical considerations we carried out a longterm longitudinal study of three mother-child dyads which were followed for a 12-month period, from the children's ages of 6 to 18 months. The aim of this research, which is reported in detail elsewhere (cf. Camaioni and Laicardi, 1985), was twofold: (1) to analyze developmental changes in the quality of social games played by mothers and children during normal home activities, (2) to show how the conventional nature of some games and the way mothers use language in them might contribute to the child's early mastery of language.

With respect to methodological choices, it was deemed necessary (a) to collect data in a naturalistic rather than an experimental setting so as to reconstruct the developmental patterns (both interactive and linguistic) peculiar to individual children, and (b) to document analytically a rather large age span stretching from the middle of the first year of life until the middle of the second year, in order to trace the development of prelinguistic interactive patterns to the point where they become linguistic exchanges.

3.1. Subjects and procedure

The three mother-child dyads investigated were homogeneous as regards social class (middle-upper), mother's educational level (high school or college) and children's birth order (first born and only children). The children consisted of one female (S I) and two males

(S II, S III). All the mothers were engaged in an outside professional activity. Both mothers and children were white and Italian speaking.

Thirty-minute observation sessions were carried out every 20 days on the average during a free-play situation in the family environment. The first observation session was preceded by several visits in which the observer went to the child's house to get to know the child, the mother and their environment. All observation sessions were audio and videotaped. Data collection was carried out by three observers, each of whom followed the same mother-child dyad in all observation sessions (14 for each dyad).

3.2. Coding

The categories used in coding the data were as follows: (a) type of mother-child social game; (b) child's role in social game; (c) mother and child's linguistic production during social game. Videotapes were segmented into interaction episodes defined as social games, and a distinction was made between non-conventional games (characterized by the *repetition* of specific behaviors) and conventional games (characterized by the presence of invariant *roles*). Repetition was considered to occur when at least one behavior produced in the previous turn remained unchanged in the following one, even when there were changes in other behavioral components. For instance, one turn could consist of tickling the child's stomach (motor component) at the same time uttering a vocalization (vocal component). The repetition of at least one of the two components, either the motor or the vocal one, in the following turn was the minimum necessary condition for the sequence to be coded as a non-conventional game. In the case in which invariant roles could be identified (e. g., giving-taking, disappearing-reappearing, etc.), their presence was sufficient for the episode to be identified as a conventional game (e. g., exchange of objects, peekaboo). Eighteen different types of social games have been identified, for each of which a detailed description is available:

NON-CONVENTIONAL GAMES
    1. Tactile and/or motoric stimulation
    2. Perceptual stimulation (visual and/or acoustic)
    3. Vocal imitation
    4. Gestural imitation

CONVENTIONAL GAMES
  5. Give and take
  6. Peekaboo
  7. Horsie
  8. Patacake
  9. Bye-bye
 10. Ball
 11. Build-knock down
 12. No
 13. Point and name
 14. Put on-take off, slip on/off, open-shut
 15. Joint book-reading
 16. Question-answer
 17. Linguistic imitation
 18. Other

The child's role in each occurrence of a game has been divided into: (a) *passive*, which consists mainly in looking, smiling, vocalizing and generally displaying excitement and pleasure; (b) *active*, which consists in producing at least one of the behaviors or roles characteristic of the particular game.

Lastly, for each social game episode, a careful recording was made of the mother's linguistic production, as well as of the child's, if any.

4. Results

4.1. Development of mother-child social games

The development of social games as a function of child age was analyzed dividing the 14 observation sessions into two time blocks (6−12 and 13−18 respectively) to each of which a linear trend test was applied (cf. Camaioni and Laicardi, 1985). In all dyads conventional games increased in significant linear fashion between 6 and 12 months of age, while the frequency of non-conventional games over the same age range remained constant. From 6 to 12 months children also became increasingly able to play an active role during games. However, if the child's active participation was differentiated as a function of game type (conventional versus non-conventional), the active role increased significantly only in the case of conventional games. No significant trend was found for the 13 – 18 month period either in the child's role or in game type.

In sum, the important developmental changes in the quality of social games played by mothers and children cooccur in the second half of the first year of life and are related to (a) the transition from non-conventional to mainly conventional games and (b) the transformation of the child's role from passive to active inside social game episodes. It seems useful to interpret this progress as the result of the mother's and child's joint contribution, since it signals both the mother's capacity to represent and respond to the child's growing abilities (suggesting conventional types of game with increasing frequency as the child grows older) and the child's capacity to play his/her own part in the game, its role changing from mere spectator to actor.

4.2. Individual differences in social games and in patterns of language acquisition

Besides these similar developmental trends the three dyads showed consistent differences in some characteristics of social games as well as in mother's style of linguistic production during game episodes. First, there were significant inter-dyad differences in the proportion of total games accounted for by conventional and non-conventional types respectively, and in the distribution of active and passive roles in conventional games. Second, the dyads differed significantly in the mother's capacity for linguistically marking the conventional, rather than the non-conventional, games and for linguistically marking conventional game turns in which the child's participation was active rather than passive. From this pattern of inter-dyad differences Dyad I appears to differ markedly from the other two dyads in the following aspects: (a) in conventional games, the role assumed by the child was more frequently active than passive; (b) the mother chose to mark linguistically the conventional game turns in which the child was active rather than those in which we has passive. On the other hand, dyads II and III resembled each other in the same aspects, i. e. in both dyads the child tended to participate less actively in the game and the mother chose less freqently to linguistically mark the child's active participation.

As far as children's early linguistic development was concerned, all three subjects (S I, S II, S III) produced their first linguistic utterances *only* within conventional game episodes and particularly inside a limited number of different game types (6 for S I and S II, 5 for S III). Moreover, these first words corresponded to the linguistic forms used by the mother to mark certain segments of joint action and/or attention during the same types of game (see Table 1). In some cases the linguistic units produced by the child belonged to types of game frequently played by that particular mother-child dyad (for example, "Question-answer" for S I, "Other" for S II and S III), while this was not true in other cases (for example, "Linguistic imitation" for all three subjects). Table 1 also shows the different rate of language acquisition displayed by the three children. S I produced a number of linguistic utterances nearly three times greater than that of the other two children (57 versus 24 and 21 respectively) and displayed also a higher variety of linguistic forms (12 versus 10 and 8 respectively).

It seems reasonable — as I have tried to argue before — to relate this different rate of language acquisition to the previously analyzed pattern of dyad differences in social games. In fact the linguistically most advanced child (S I) resulted to be the same child whose participation in conventional games was more frequently active than passive and whose mother chose to mark linguistically the child's active participation during conventional games. This means that both the child's capacity to join in the interaction as an active agent and the mother's capacity to use language differently in relation to the type of on-going interaction (conventional versus non-conventional game) and to the type of child's participation (active versus passive) are important factors affecting the course and rate of language acquisition. In particular, the fact that conventional games, unlike non-conventional ones, contain highly stereotyped and routinized roles (give-take, disappear-reappear, build-knock down) enables the child (a) to recognize these reciprocal roles and their underlying contingencies and consequently (b) to actively assume them and to relate their meaning (or parts of their meaning) to the linguistic units produced by the mother when playing these games.

5. Conclusions

In a recent review of research on individual differences in language development, Katherine Nelson reached the following conclusion: "*How* and *why* mothers use language may be as important for the

Table 1 Type and Frequency of Child's Linguistic Utterances per Type of Social Game

Subject I

	%*	NO	PU	DA	CIAO	MAMMA	PO	BUM	DUM	BAVA	TU-TU	BABBO	UNO	Total
Question-answer	22	25	5				2							32
Linguistic imitation	4	1	1	1		2		1	1	1	1	1	1	11
No	14	5												5
Bye-bye	9				4									4
Give-take	9			4										4
Build-knock down	2			1										1
Total		31	6	6	4	2	2	1	1	1	1	1	1	57

Subject II

	%	NO	TAO	VAH-VAH	PAPA'	CACA	DAO	IEH-IEH	MIAO-MIAO	MMM	GNAGNA	Total
Bye-bye	7		7									7
Question-answer	8	2		2						1		5
No	5	5										5
Linguistic imitation	3	1			1	1					1	4
Other	40							1	1			2
Peekaboo	19						1					1
Total		8	7	2	1	1	1	1	1	1	1	24

Subject III

	%	NO	BRR	BAU	MAMMA	PAPA'	NONA	MIAO	OPOP	AAM	Total
Linguistic imitation	3		1	1	2	2				1	7
Other	16	3					2				5
Peekaboo	11		3								3
Book reading	2			3							3
Question-answer	3	1						1	1		3
Total		4	4	4	2	2	2	1	1	1	21

* Percentage frequencies of single games based on total number of conventional games for each dyad.

child's pattern of acquisition as what kind of language they use" (1981: 181, our italics). It seems to me that the results previously discussed allow at least some of the contextual variables possibly affecting the course and rate of early language acquisition to be specified. The relevant variables isolated in this study could be characterized essentially in terms of the extent to which the mother's discourse is *matched* to the child's ongoing activities.

It was hypothesized that the contingency between maternal linguistic production and the child's active participation in conventional game episodes provides the child with the ability to relate specific actions to specific interactive contexts (games) as well as to relate sounds to actions/objects shared within the game.

In the same direction Cross (1978) found that acceleration in the linguistic development of children aged 19 to 33 months (with MLU values between 1.5 and 3.5 morphemes) was associated with a maternal input containing greater proportions of expansions, semantic extensions and "synergistic sequences" (i. e. expansions and extensions that were also repeated or paraphrased within two conversational turns of the original). On the other hand, in the same sample, no significant differences were found between children with normal and accelerated linguistic development for any of the syntactic measures of maternal speech. This led Cross to the conclusion that, while the degree of syntactic simplicity in maternal speech is of only secondary importance, those specific sequences of mother's speech may have the function of freeing the child so that he can concentrate on the formal aspects of the mother's linguistic expressions.

Of course the processes of decontextualization, generalization and abstraction of the communicative message underlying the increase in the number of child's linguistic procedures and their lexical, morphological and syntactic categorization, need to be specifically investigated and tested in future research. The nature of these processes nevertheless remains the same insofar as they do not operate on private cognitive abilities, but on "cognitive transactions" (De Gelder, in press), i. e. on intersubjective procedures for constituting shared meanings.

Note

1. For a more detailed analysis of the reasons behind this failure see Camaioni, de Castro Campos and de Lemos, 1984.

References

Bamberg, Michael
1980　"A fresh look at the relationship between pragmatic and semantic knowledge", *Archivia Psychologica* 133: 23–43.
Bates, Elizabeth, Benigni, Laura, Bretherton, Inge, Camaioni, Luigia and Volterra, Virginia
1979　*The emergence of symbols. Cognition and communication in infancy* (New York: Academic Press).
Bruner, Jerome S.
1975　"The ontogenesis of speech acts", *Journal of Child Language* 2: 1–19.
Bruner, Jerome S. – Sherwood, Virginia
1976　"Early rule structure: the case of peekaboo", *Play: its role in evolution and development*, edited by Jerome S. Bruner, Alison Jolly and Kathy Silva (Harmondsworth: Penguin), 277–285.
Camaioni, Luigia and Laicardi, Caterina
1985　"Early social games and language acquisition", *British Journal of Developmental Psychology* 3: 31–39.
Camaioni, Luigia, de Castro Campos, Maria Fausta and de Lemos, Claudia
1984　"On the failure of the interactionist paradigm in language acquisition: a reevaluation", *Social interaction in individual development*, edited by Willem Doise and Augusto Palmonari (Cambridge: Cambridge University Press), 93–106.
Crawley, Susan, Rogers, Peggy, Friedman, Steven, Iacobbo, Maria, Criticos, Anne, Richardson, Lani and Thompson, Margaret
1978　"Developmental changes in the structure of mother-infant play", *Developmental Psychology* 14: 30–36.
Cross, Tony
1978　"Mother's speech and its association with rate of linguistic development in young children", *The development of communication*, edited by Natalie Waterson and Catherine Snow (New York: Wiley), 199–216.
De Gelder, Beatrice
in press　"Cognitive transactions and objects of beliefs", *On believing. Epistemological and Semiotic Approaches*, edited by Herman Parret (Berlin: de Gruyter).
Freedle, Roy and Lewis, Michael
1977　"Prelinguistic conversation", *Interaction, conversation and the development of language*, edited by Michael Lewis and Leonard Rosenblum (New York: Wiley), 157–185.

Grimshaw, J
1981   "Form, function and the language acquisition device", *The logical problem of language acquisition*, edited by L. Baker and J. J. McCarthy (Cambridge: M. I. T. Press).
Gustafson, Gwen, Green, James and West, Meredith
1979   "The infant's changing role in mother-infant games: the growth of social skills", *Infant Behavior and Development* 2: 301 – 308.
Kaye, Kenneth
1979   "The social context of infant development", *Final report to the Spencer Foundation.*
Nelson, Katherine
1981   "Individual differences in language development: implications for development and language", *Developmental Psychology* 17: 170 – 187.
Nicholich, Lorraine
1977   "Beyond sensorimotor intelligence: assessment of symbolic maturity through analysis of pretend play", *Merril-Palmer-Quarterly* 23: 89 – 99.
Ninio, Anat and Bruner, Jerome
1978   "The achievement and antecedentes of labelling", *Journal of Child Language* 5: 1 – 15.
Piaget, Jean
1945   *La formation du symbole chez l'enfant* (Paris: Delachaux et Niestlé).
Ratner, Nancy and Bruner, Jerome S.
1978   "Games, social exchange and the acquisition of language", *Journal of Child Language* 5: 391 – 401.
Richards, Martin
1977   "Interaction and the concept of development: the biological and the social revisited", *Interaction, conversation and the development of language*, edited by Michael Lewis and Leonard Rosenblum (New York: Wiley), 187 – 206.
Shatz, Marilyn
1983   "Communication", *Handbook of child psychology*, edited by John Flavell and Ellen Markman, vol. III (New York: Wiley) 841 – 885.
Snow, Catherine, De Blauw, Akke and Van Roosmalen, Ghislaine
1979   "Talking and playing with babies: the role of ideologies of child-rearing", *Before speech. The beginning of interpersonal communication*, edited by Margaret Bullowa (Cambridge: Cambridge University Press), 269 – 288.

Stern, Daniel
    1974   "Mother and infant at play: the dyadic interaction involving facial, vocal and gaze behaviors", *The effect of the infant on its caregiver*, edited by Michael Lewis and Leonard Rosemblum (New York: Wiley), 187–213.

Wittgenstein, Ludwig
    1958   *Philosophical investigations* (Oxford: Blackwell).

The Construction of Joint Activities with an Age-Mate: The Transition from Caregiver-Child to Peer Play

Nancy Budwig, Amy Strage and Michael Bamberg

Communicating involves more than the mere exchange of information. To communicate successfully, partners must draw on a base of shared background knowledge, conventions, goals and expectations. And further, the communicative event itself can be characterized as a dynamic process: it is the *product* of an ongoing negotiation between interactants. Partners must work together to establish a mutual focus and negotiate maintenance and termination of activities. The study of processes of collaboratively interpreting and defining the purpose and nature of an ongoing exchange have only recently received the attention of anthropologists, linguists, philosophers and sociologists (c. f. Burke, 1962; Goffman, 1974; Gumperz, 1982; Rommetveit, 1974; Streeck, 1980; Wertsch, 1980). These studies have lent much insight into the dynamic processes of communication in general and the role of language in such interchanges in particular. Given the complexity of negotiating a joint activity, one can ask how it is that children come to be able to establish and sustain activities with others. In this chapter, we will address this question, concerning ourselves more specifically with the issue of how children learn to work out joint activities with their age-mates. We will discuss the extent to which actual interactions between the child and others provide a forum for the acquisition of strategies that can be used in the construction of social activities with a wide variety of others.

Our emphasis on the social setting as an arena for the acquisition of communicative strategies draws heavily upon two constructs initially proposed and discussed by L. S. Vygotsky. We will begin by briefly discussing them before proceeding with our own analysis.

1. Two Aspects of Vygotskian Theory

1.1. The Zone of Proximal Development

Vygotsky defines the zone of proximal development as

> the distance between the actual developmental level as determined by independent problem solving and the level of potential development as determined through problem solving under adult guidance or in collaboration with more capable peers   (1978: 86).

Two key assumptions are embedded in this notion. The first is that any attempt to understand human psychological functioning must account for both the origins and the development of such functions. The second assumption is that social processes play a fundamental role in the origin and development of psychological functioning:

> Any function in the child's cultural development appears twice, or on two planes. First, it appears on the social plane, and then on the psychological plane. First it appears between people as an interpsychological category, and then within the child as an intrapsychological category   (1981: p. 183).

In short, the development of psychological functioning involves a transition from the social or interpsychological plane to the individual or intrapsychological plane of development. The child is provided with a "point of entry" at the interpsychological plane: with the special strategic assistance of more experienced others, the child carries out tasks which he or she does not yet fully understand.

Recently a number of developmental and cognitive psychologists have incorporated this notion in their investigations of a variety of issues such as intelligence testing, memory and problem solving (c. f. Brown & Ferrara, 1985; McLane & Wertsch, 1983; Rogoff & Gardner, 1984; Wertsch, 1979, in press; Wertsch, McNamee, McLane & Budwig, 1980). As McLane and Wertsch (1983: 3) have noted, such research focuses mainly on the interpsychological plane, emphasizing "ways in which the level of potential development is created in social interaction". One exception to this almost exclusive focus on the interpsychological plane of development is the research of Wertsch (Wertsch, 1979) where the *transition* from the interpsychological to intrapsychological functioning is illustrated in detail. Wertsch stresses the gradual nature of this transition.

1.2. The role of language

A second important aspect of Vygotsky's framework is the role attributed to language in organizing human activities. Vygotsky was primarily concerned with the power of language in mediating social interaction.[1] Furthermore, Vygotsky also stressed the importance of language in individuals' activities. Vygotsky claimed that the speech used to regulate *one's own* activities (inner speech) emerges out of developmentally earlier speech activities taking place in *social interaction*.

These two aspects of Vygotsky's theory can be summarized together as follows: individual psychological processes develop out of social experiences, and language plays a critical role in the creation of such functions. Language plays an important role at both the interpsychological and intrapsychological planes of development.

2. Discrepancies in the Assessment of the Child's Skills as a Communicative Partner

Having briefly summarized two aspects of Vygotsky's theory that are central to our analysis, we can now return to the question raised at the outset of this paper: how do children come to construct joint activities with their age-mates? It should be noted that the question here is not whether young children are interested in one another, but rather, whether young children can actually construct activities with one another. This question rests on the assumption that at some early age, children are unable to construct joint activities with age-mates, but that at some later age, they are able to do so successfully. In fact, such an assumption has been well supported by studies of peer interaction. These studies can be divided into two groups: those that examine the interactions of toddler peers, and those which focus on pre-school age children.

A major debate in the literature on toddler-peer interaction centers around whether they can collaborate in joint activities. Those researchers who claim that reciprocity indeed exists between toddler playmates (cf. Becker, 1977; Doyle, Connolly & Rivest, 1980; Mueller & Brenner, 1977; Rubenstein & Howe, 1976) have focused primarily on the peers' *attempts* to coordinate shared frames, rather than on actual success at mutually organizing a joint activity. Bronson (1982) suggests that although toddlers may be interested in their peers, they are still very much dependent on a more experienced communicative partner to help structure joint play activities.

In contrast to the toddler-peer literature, studies of pre-school peers suggest that these slightly older children *can* negotiate mutually organized activities. Pre-school age peers have been credited with a variety of skills necessary for initiating and maintaining joint activities with an age-mate (cf. Corsaro, 1979). Furthermore, they are able to negotiate cooperative activities through the ongoing interpretation of both verbal and non-verbal cues (Cook-Gumperz, 1975, 1976; Cook-Gumperz and Gumperz, 1976; Schwartzman, 1976, 1978). Though successful activities can be coordinated by pre-school peers, establishing and elaborating these activities often rely on repetitive sequences and routines (Garvey, 1977; Iwamura, 1980). Nevertheless, at some primitive level the peers collaborate in joint activities on their own.

Thus it seems that it is not until the pre-school years that children can establish and sustain social interaction with a peer. Given the complex interpretive processes involved in the sharing of a joint activity, the finding that pre-verbal toddlers are unable to establish joint activities with their peers is not surprising. Yet children of the same age (as well as those even younger) have been characterized as participating in essentially reciprocal interactions with their caregivers (cf. Brazelton, Koslowski & Main, 1974; Ryan, 1974; Stern, 1974; Sutton-Smith, 1980). Research concerning caregiver-child interactions suggests that *both* partners are actively engaged in a system of mutual regulation, working together towards more and more sharing of their individual worlds.

A partial explanation for why toddlers are said to be able to construct joint activities with more experienced adults, while unable to construct such activities with age-mates draws upon the Vygotskian notion of zone of proximal development, and the transition from inter- to intrapsychological functioning. Though both caregiver and child contribute to the construction of joint activities, they play different roles in this process. Caregivers can be thought of here as giving the child an "entry point". More experienced, knowledgable, and flexible about the specific demands of various communicative situations, caregivers assume much of the responsibility for organizing and sustaining shared activities (cf. Kaye, 1980). Elaborating on Vygotsky's notion of the zone of proximal development, this sort of special assistance on the part of the adult has been referred to as *strategic assistance* by Wertsch (1979, 1980) and as *scaffolding* by Wood, Bruner & Ross (1976). These terms refer to the specific structuring that adults or more experienced peers often provide as they attempt to interact with young children. The caregivers act as a finely tuned support system that first takes on much of the work so that a shared perspective can be achieved (cf. Camaoini, this volume).

We would like to stress the point that an evaluation of the child's abilities to construct joint communicative activities with others must take into account who the child is interacting with. The peer-interaction literature indicates that until the pre-school years, children have great difficulty in constructing activities with age-mates. In contrast, children before the pre-school years can be actively involved in establishing shared activities with caregivers. This seeming regress in interactive skills can easily be accounted for by considering the distinction Vygotsky draws between interpsychological and intrapsychological levels of functioning. When the toddlers interact with their caregivers, they construct joint activities at the interpsychological level. At this point they require the guidance of more capable interactive partners who use particular communicative strategies. It is only at some later point in development that the children can regulate the construction of joint activities without the guidance or scaffolding of more experienced others. Fluid constructions of joint activities without the assistance of some sort of scaffold must await a time when the child can also function on the intrapsychological plane.

3. The Transition from Caregiver-Child to Peer Interaction

In the previous section, we have suggested that the child's initial success at organizing joint activities with others is very much dependent on what Vygotsky referred to as the interpsychological functioning. At this point, we will return to a consideration of the actual transition from being able to interact only under the special guidance of more experienced others to being able to organize activities with age-mates. We will focus on the gap that exists between studies of toddler peers and those of pre-schoolers, in an attempt to shed light on the transition from caregiver-child to peer interaction.[2]

Our discussion centers around two ways young children achieve mutual agreement when interacting with one another. We begin with a discussion of the role of caregivers in peer interaction. We then discuss what we have called *shared understanding* and its contributions to the establishment of joint activities among peers. We also highlight some of the ways that these two factors interact.

The data we draw on are from a year-long, longitudinal study of two 2 year old girls' interactive development. The children came from similar family backgrounds: their parents were white middle class, college educated residents of a university community in Northern California; their fathers were employed fulltime, while their mothers held part-time jobs and took on the role of primary caregiver.[3]

Six months prior to our study the children and their mothers became acquainted at a local recreation center, and started meeting one afternoon a week. We observed their play sessions once a month. We video-taped whatever activities took place from the time the visiting mother-child dyad arrived until they left (we taped in alternating homes). These play sessions lasted an average of 2 hours. Our video-tapes begin at the point where the peers first started talking to one another. Our own role in the play group was that of participant observer.

3.1. Caregivers: A Support System for Peer Play

As adults, we frequently take for granted the ability to construct activities jointly with another person. Arriving at a mutual focus by soliciting a partner's attention or by joining into an ongoing activity, seems rather straightforward. But to many young children, especially those who have interacted primarily with attentive caregivers who shape almost any response on the part of the child into a common frame, the actual process of *how* to negotiate joint activities is a major obstacle.

The caregivers in our study are instrumental in the successful negotiation of the peers' joint activities and the organization of peer play. The mothers are not directly involved in the actual play of the children. Instead they encourage their children to *play with* or *next to* each other. They closely monitor their children's activities. The mothers assist their children by suggesting ways that the children could use their communicative resources for the purpose of negotiating shared activities.

Initiation. One of the primary kinds of strategic assistance the mothers give to the children concerns the *initiation* of joint peer play. The mothers continually point out to the children various ways in which a child could attempt to work out a common activity. Three major types of suggestions are made by the mothers, namely that:

(1) Child 1 SHOW Child 2 her activity
    "Show Jackie your new book"
(2) Child 1 OFFER that Child 2 could participate
    "Tell Jackie she can play too"
(3) Child 1 INSTRUCT Child 2 in how to participate
    "Tell Jackie how that works"

In all of the above suggestions, the mothers make more or less explicit the ways *Child 1* might invite her friend to play. Especially in the earliest sessions, the children display little awareness that one must solicit a co-participant's attention or participation for joint activities to take place.

Joining in. A second way in which the mothers contribute to the negotiation of peer interaction is to suggest to *Child 2* ways in which she could *join in* the activity that Child 1 is carrying out. Mothers accomplish this by making three kinds of suggestions:

(1) Child 2 should WATCH what Child 1 is doing
    "Oh look at what Susie's making!"
(2) Child 2 should HELP Child 1
    "Why don't you help Jackie"
(3) Child 2 should ASK Child 1 how to participate
    "Ask Susie, she can show you how to play"

As was the case with initiations, the children rarely attempt to join in each other's activity without the mother's prompting.

By facilitating the children's negotiation of a mutual focus, the caregivers are scaffolding particular sorts of activities. Interestingly, the mothers never suggest that their children negotiate or plan together what the children *could* play. We never found instances of mothers instructing their children to ask the other child what they could do next. Rather, the mothers attempt to frame a joint activity around an activity that has *already* been undertaken by one of the children. It seems that negotiating a joint activity from the vantage point of one that has already been started by one child is a less complicated endeavour. It remains an empirical question whether at a later point mothers scaffold the planning of activities in which neither peer is involved.

Maintenance. Up until this point, our discussion has focused on some ways in which the mothers have contributed to the *initial organization* of a joint activity between the children. But once the children are successful at finding a mutual focus, the mothers still play a significant role in making sure that such focus is *maintained*. It is not the case that the children merely need assistance in initiating joint activity. The children also require support to help insure that previously established joint focus is maintained. The mothers help achieve this by suggesting how to increase or preserve mutual focus between the peers. Thus, though often the mothers succeed in getting both children to focus on the same activity, the peers still seem unaware that they could work together towards achieving some interpersonally agreed upon goal within the context of that activity. For example, the mothers might succeed in getting their children to both play with clay, but the children still do not attempt to plan a common activity together around the clay. The children might observe what the other is doing, and even imitate or copy some aspect of the peer's behavior, but at best, such activities could be defined as joint only in that both children are "doing the same thing".

The mothers attempt to preserve or maintain the children's joint focus by encouraging them to check in on each other. They encourage the children to:

(1) RECOGNIZE the activity AS a MUTUAL one.
   "Show Susie what you just made"
(2) ASK one another for help.
   "Ask Jackie how that puzzle piece goes"
(3) SHARE resources.
   "You share with Susie she wants to help"
(4) ACKNOWLEDGE instances of sharing and help.
   "Say thank you."
(5) APOLOGIZE for transgression
   "Look what you did — you got her all wet.
   You better tell her that you are sorry!"

In summary, the mothers exert much effort to make the children recognize each others' point of view. The peers often lack awareness that they could use their existing communicative resources in order to establish and sustain a shared activity. The mother-child dyad functions as a unit. Each mother tends to team up with her own child. The kind of strategic assistance given by the mothers is illustrated in the following sequence:

Example 1:
    Session I, C 1 = 2;6; C 2 = 2;3
    C 1 is by tub of water playing with
    a toy goose. C 2 is sitting on M 2's lap.
1 M 1: Maybe the goose should go on the swing.
2 C 1: I'll give him a swinger-binger (taking goose to the swing area).
3 M 2: Wanna help C 1 give him a swing?
       (to C 2)
4 C 2: (approaches swing and helps C 1 push)
5 C 1: I need to do that! (glances at M 1)
6 M 1: You share with C 2, she wants to help.
7 C 1: She can help.
8 C 2: (removes goose from swing, takes it to a tub of water and runs to M 2)
9 C 1: She's getting him out. She's throwing him out.
10 C 2: I threw him back in.
11 M 2: You want to put a boat on the swing?
       (to C 2)

In the first part of this example (in particular in lines (1) and (3)), the mothers attempt to get their children to recognize a mutual focus. By line (4) both children are at the swing together. Despite the children's mutual focus, they encounter problems in elaborating this frame: In line (5) C 1 wants to be the 'pusher' of the swing; her mother reminds her to share her toys and expresses C 2's intentions. Though things seem patched up by line (7), difficulties arise in lines (8 − 10). We see in line (11) that the elaboration of this play frame is dependent upon a suggestion from one of the mothers.

The extent to which the mothers act as a support system in the negotiation of joint activities is even more apparent in situations where one peer knew about how to carry out an activity, but the other peer did not. With respect to such situations, we raised the question: to the degree that each partner must assume a particular role in an activity because of the relative familiarity of the participants with that activity, do the mothers indicate this, and if so how? In fact, the mothers capitalize on such activities as opportunities to draw attention to role demands. The mothers explained to the 'Expert' that the 'Novice' could be expected to require information and assistance from her, and they made explicit for the children why the 'Expert' should be appealed to: only she knew how, only she could explain the task at hand. Interestingly, at these junctures, such secondary aspects of negotiating joint frames, such as reminding the children to be polite, were backgrounded and instead mothers focused on role demands (cf. Strage, Bamberg and Budwig, 1981).

So, why do the caregivers put so much effort into helping their children organize joint activities. We suggest that, for this culture anyway, caregivers feel it is important that children at this age begin to interact with age-mates. They may be preparing their children for school situations, where many of their interactions will involve peer play. This is just one way caregivers' self-appointed role of socializing agents of communication skills manifests itself. In informal discussions after the completion of this study the mothers indicated to us that the purpose of arranging informal gatherings such as this play group was to provide the children with the opportunity to play together before entering more formally organized pre-school situations. Within such a setting the caregivers can provide a framework which suggests to the children potential ways to turn solitary play into joint activities, often by getting the children to make use of their burgeoning linguistic resources.

In this section we have emphasized that the mothers attempt to assist their children to participate in cooperative activities. We have also claimed, more specifically, that the mothers provide an important role in language socialization. The mothers illustrate how language can be used to foster joint activity. Our results are consistent with other studies that find that caregivers' input plays an important part in language socialization. As was mentioned above, caregivers act as a sort of support system for a variety of aspects of language acquisition. Our conclusions are more far-reaching than previous studies, since we suggest that caregivers act as a support system in activities larger than those involving dyads. Furthermore, we suggest that mothers' input assists in the acquisition of the more open-ended discourse demands of joint peer activities: when to ask, when to tell, and how to converse about what one is doing.

3.2. Shared Understanding

Thus far we have discussed the role of the caregivers in helping young peers negotiate joint activities. In highlighting the role of the caregivers, one might conclude that the transition to peer play merely involves the peers acquiring particular discourse skills, skills that are acquired with the help of a support system. Simply focusing on the mothers' scaffolding obscures another related and very important factor that contributes to the development of peer interaction — a factor we refer to as *shared understanding*.

In order to coordinate joint frames, regardless of whether they center around play or other forms of communication, interactants need some degree of *shared understanding*. Our notion of shared understanding implies the individual's competence to fit their own experiences into a scenic understanding and thereby construct meaningful wholes, wholes that are not only meaningful to the individual, but also to other members of a community or culture. The meaning of particular scenes and/or experiences must be shared intersubjectively in order to be interpreted as meaningful (cf. Bamberg, 1980).

It often is the case within other models of communication that the complex process of shared understanding is a given: researchers working within the information processing paradigm for instance, often take for granted that members of a particular culture share a knowledge base which they can draw on in order to communicate with each other. We do not find this rather static view of a pre-existing knowledge store appropriate. Instead it is our aim to show how individuals, and in particular young children, gradually *develop* such a common knowledge base through processes of understanding. We start from the assumption that children have differing experiences, and that children must learn to take into account the co-participant's individual experiences, and to relate these to their own perspective. By learning to communicate *across* their differences, children build up shared understanding.

At this point it seems necessary to consider the notion of shared understanding in terms of the child's first interactions with others. To what extent must the child take into account a co-participant's point of view when interacting with adults — and most frequently a familiar caregiver? The literature on children's interactions with caregivers in Western culture suggests that caregivers tend to center interactive activities around their children (cf. Ochs & Schieffelin,

1984). When interacting with caregivers (noted for going to great lengths to interpret their children's utterances and behavior), children often seem able to establish joint interactions without considering their partner's background experiences and perspective. Children can successfully construct joint frames with adults, not only because of the adult's extensive efforts but also because the caregiver has shared many of the child's previous experiences. If, however, one considers the nature of interactions between young children it becomes clear why the evolving process of *shared understanding* is so important. Peers must come to recognize that their partner may *not* always share their perspective and furthermore, soon after they begin interacting with an age-mate, the children discover that peers are not as attentive and responsive as are their caregivers. A central issue, then, when considering the transition from caregiver-child to peer interaction concerns the establishment of shared understanding.

In this section we will focus on the question of how it is that two peers arrive at some level of shared understanding. How do the playmates construct ways to express their views of a situation such that they are meaningful to one another? More generally, how is it that the children learn to coordinate activities across differences in perspective and experience? In what follows, we will suggest some ways that the mothers contribute to the construction of shared understanding between the peers and then, in the remaining pages of this section, we will document the children's growing sensitivity to the process of establishing shared understanding.

In the previous section of this paper we stressed the role of the mothers in fostering joint focus between the peers. Indeed the mothers' role could be interpreted as one of helping the children arrive at shared understanding. Clearly, the mothers help with the mechanics of negotiating joint frames. In mediating the peers' interactions the mothers draw attention to experiences that both peers have in common, such as activities that both children were familiar with. In addition, the mothers call attention to differences in the children's perspectives and at times remind the children to consider the point of view of their peer.[4] While there is little doubt that the mothers contribute to the coordination of the peers' activities, as well as to the development of shared understanding between the peers, the children's achievement of shared understanding cannot be viewed as the product of the mothers' input, exclusively. This view would underestimate the children's active role in the establishment of shared understanding.

We now turn to the ways the children *themselves* construct play activities through the use of their growing sense of shared understanding. This becomes clearer if we illustrate how the children in the earliest video sessions make use of the restricted means they have available for coordinating play interactions together.

In the first video sessions joint peer play involves, almost exclusively, some form of repetition. The peers rely heavily on sound play, such as repeating and varying the contours of each other's previous utterance, or taking turns performing a similar action, such as throwing small wooden blocks one at a time into a tub of water. What is most characteristic of the earliest joint activities established between the peers is the extent to which the peers rely on doing the same thing to glue their interactions together. In one such play sequence the children took turns jumping across the couch, rhythmically repeating the sounds *Ja, ja, ja*. The peers continued this activity with roars of laughter for more than ten minutes, until they were too dizzy to continue. The following excerpt from this interactive sequence is typical of the sorts of early activities the peers constructed on their own.

Example 2:
  Session III, C 1 = 2,8; C 2 = 2,
  C 1 & C 2 have been jumping across
  the couch saying the following:
1   C 2: Ja, ja, ja (laughter)
2   C 1: Ja, ja, ja (laughter)
3   C 1: Ja, ja, ja (laughter) (tumbles over)
        Mommy I keep falling down — backwards
        Mommy I keep falling down — backwards
4   C 2: Ja, ja, ja, ja, ja (laughter)
5   C 1: Ja, ja, ja, ja, ja (falls over)
6   C 2: Ja, ja, (slight pause) ja, ja, ja

While at first glance such an interchange seems to involve very little in the way of shared understanding, the peers have successfully organized, on their own, a mutual frame, centering around the limited means they each bring to the interaction. Not only do the peers collaborate in deciding on a mutual focus, but also they agree on ways to elaborate this frame. In the first utterance of Example 2 (line 1), C 2 has offered her peer one of many possible perspectives that can be taken on this setting. By joining in and repeating C 2's utterance (line 2), C 1 is not only acknowledging her acceptance of C 2's initiation, but in copying C 2's actions, C 1 suggests that she views her peer's utterance (line 1) as an initiation bid — a bid that could be both understood and responded to. Three elements, the opening initiation, the response, and the satisfaction found in the experience, foster a sense of cooperation between the peers, regardless of the relative simplicity of the play frames. This rather simple play sequence takes on new light when it is interpreted as an early form of cooperation between the peers. The coordination of such frames seems to be an experience the peers find mutually satisfying and enjoyable. Within the context of these early play interactions the peers are developing a sense of intimacy which enhances their shared understanding of one another. This sense of intimacy stems not only from the enjoyment of the play, but also from the enjoyment of successfully working out a joint play activity with an agemate.

In the short span of this study, the peers developed a greater sense of shared understanding. This was reflected on one level by their increasing ability to organize joint activities on their own, and on another, by the fact that the peers came to base their interactions on an ever-expanding background of shared experience. The peers' joint interactions no longer consist of merely doing or saying the same thing — by the mid-point of the twelve month study the peers were able to construct some joint frames around themes other than repetition and variation sequences. The children displayed a growing awareness of the need to solicit their partner's attention and unlike many of their previous (and unsuccessful) initiation bids, the children attempted to construct frames around themes and activities in ways that allow their peer a chance to participate. The children were consequently more likely and willing to join into an activity initiated by their peer. The following example captures the more elaborate nature that the peers' negotiations have taken on. In this example C 1 has been reading a storybook with one of the researchers. C 1 notices that C 2 is playing on the floor nearby and approaches her peer. This example is an excerpt from the interaction that ensued:

Example 3:
        Session VII, C 1 = 2;12: C 2 = 2;9

> C 1 has approached C 2 who is
> on the floor examining a stamp
> pad and stampers. C 1 requests
> water & paper from M 1. C 1
> returns with the supplies.

1 C 1: Mesty-mesty bing bing (singing).
         Look C 2.
2 C 2: A-ABCDEFG, HI (singing)
3 C 1: (joins in) HIJKLOmenOG, Jill, R (stamping)
         Make a 'C'! How about this? You do
         this one. Look. Put it in here.
         You don't put 'em both in there.
4 C 2: (inaudible)
5 C 1: And you put the thing in there.
         Where's the lid? (slight pause)
         Where's the lid Mommy? Where's the lid?
6 C 2: Right there (softly).
7 C 1: Mommy, where's the lid?
8 C 2: Here (hands C 1 the lid to the stamp pad).
9 C 1: Thank you. Thank you for giving me the lid.

In the above example the two peers have constructed an activity centering around a stamp pad and stampers that belong to C 1. While C 2 is examining these objects, C 1 recognizes that her peer has neither the water nor the paper necessary for making the stamps function. C 1 requests these supplies from her mother and returns from the kitchen with paper, singing a song that is seemingly created on the spot. Her peer, not familiar with this particular song, joins the singing activity by chanting a version of the 'ABCs'. C 1, familiar with this song, acknowledges the appeal to shared background by switching from her song to that of her peer. In line (3) C 1 begins explaining the mechanics of "stamping". While in earlier sessions repetition was the stuff of the peers' interaction, now the peers converse back and forth as they take turns using the stamp pad and stamps. C 1's explanation of how to use the stamps indicates her growing awareness that her peer may not have the same background knowledge of how to use the toys as she herself does. This is exactly the sort of information that we have suggested that the mothers had often needed to provide a few months earlier. Furthermore, C 1's explanation suggests her ability to communicate *across* such experiential differences, as does her attempt to solicit her peer's attention in lines (1) and (3). In line (6), C 2 also displays the extent to which she is monitoring her friend's talk. When C 1 asks her mother a question, C 2 attempts to provide the answer and in line (8) she actually gives C 1 the object she has misplaced. The children not only are able to establish joint dialogues and maintain them across several turns, but they acknowledge their appreciation of their peer's responsiveness (cf. for example line (9)). Throughout this example one senses the cooperative spirit underlying the peers' play. Because of a growing base of shared understanding, the peers are able now to construct joint activities through the use of their budding linguistic resources.

We contend that as a result of the gradual development of shared understanding and the children's growing ability to rely on verbal resources, the peers' interactions in the later sessions more closely approximate the sophisticated interactions of pre-school peers described by other researchers (cf. above). We do not want to suggest, however, that by the end of our last video session, the peers' negotiations were unproblematic. As the next example illustrates, despite a growing amount of shared understanding, the construction of joint activities was not always smooth. This was particularly true in instances of fantasy play, where the children were more likely to have different perspectives on the activity in which they both were engaged. Such instances were common in the doll play episodes which occurred in the later sessions, as well as in the children's play with clay as displayed in the following example:

Example 4:

        Session VII, C 1 = 2;12; C 2 = 2;9
        C 1 & C 2 are playing with clay.
        C 1 is explaining that she has
        a 'boulder' (a marble) stuck in
        her clay. M 1 & M 2 talk together
        on the couch nearby.

1   C 2:   (responding to C 1) A boulder?
2   C 1:   (doesn't seem to hear C 2) Look.
           (pause) Look (holds up clay).
           (2 second pause) Look (6 second
           pause). Look, Look C 2, look (holds
           clay closer to C 2) look, look.
3   C 2:   I'm making a pancake!
4   C 1:   Look, (puts clay even closer) look!
           (marble falls out of clay)
5   C 2:   That's silly (refers to marble)

      Uh-oh, fell off.
6   C1: N-no this is not — it didn't fall
      off — didn't fell off — it just —
      look at it. Look at. This is not —
      Look at. This is not — don't say it
      fell off, it just bouldered!

In this example the peers have difficulty arriving at a shared perspective on how to view the clay they are manipulating. C 1 explains that the marble stuck in her clay is to be viewed as a boulder at the start of this episode. C 2, not understanding, questions her peer, but her utterance (line 1) is spoken in a rather soft tone and goes unanswered by C 1. Instead, C 1 attempts to solicit her peer's attention with no success (line 2). When C 2 does respond in line (3), C 1 seems dissatisfied, and less interested in what her friend has constructed and more involved in sharing her particular view of her own wad of clay. It is not until line (5) that C 2 does acknowledge C 1's clay, but still no mutual perspective on how to view the clay is reached. Despite the growing foundation of shared understanding that has developed over time, the peers still have difficulty negotiating shared activities. In Example 4 the peers finally opt to work independently on their own clay constructions rather than attempting to further negotiate a joint frame. Nevertheless, even this episode reveals the extensive efforts that the peers invest in their attempts to construct shared frames.

In this section we have suggested that the notion of shared understanding, the child's ability to construct singular experiences into meaningful wholes which are meaningful to others, is a necessary factor contributing to the successful negotiation of peer play. It has been our contention that interaction itself contributes to the attainment of a greater sense of shared understanding between young peers, not only in terms of an increased amount of shared experience, but also in terms of a sense of intimacy that allows the peers to communicate despite their different perspectives. The fact that peers have quite distinct perspectives on particular situations makes the construction of joint frames all the more challenging for them. Interestingly, while the peers could have opted to play alone or only with their caregivers, they spent much of their time attempting to engage each other in joint play. Their increasing success seems to depend not only on their mother's strategic assistance, but also on the *process of interaction*, itself, through which they develop a greater sense of shared understanding.[5]

3.3. The Relationship Between Caregivers' Scaffolding and the Development of Shared Understanding

Thus far we have described two factors contributing to the development of peer interaction. We have stressed the role of the caregivers, who through a scaffolding process, act as a support system which facilitates joint focus between the peers. In addition, we have considered ways in which the peers themselves make use of their growing sense of shared understanding in establishing joint activities. We have not intended to minimize the inter-relationship between the scaffolding process and the peers' development of shared understanding. In this section we will discuss the inter-dependence of these two factors.

The interaction between scaffolding and the development of shared understanding can be found both *microdevelopmentally* within particular interactions, and *macrodevelopmentally*, across the various play sessions. In fact, in several instances the peers rely on shared understanding as well as on their mothers' scaffolding in their attempts to coordinate play. Consider the following example taken from the fifth video session:

Example 5:
> Session V, C 1 = 2;10; C 2 = 2;7
> C 1 & C 2 are working on a craft task
> that C 1 has brought to C 2's home.
> After M 1 helps explain the task
> of decorating 'little people' with
> markers and stickers she joins M 2
> on the couch.

1   C 1:   (referring to stickers) I got a lot.
            Stick 'em on the table.
2   C 2:   (reaches for stickers in C 1's hand)
3   M 1:   C 2 needs one (8 sec. pause, C 1 lets go)
4   C 1:   She has one (looking at M 1).
5   C 1:   I'm sticking 'em on the table and then
            I'm gonna put 'em on the man.
6   C 2:   I'm gonna put some buttons on 'em (tries
            to get roll of stickers from C 1).
7   C 1:   I'll give you one. Here.

In this example, C 1 and C 2 have jointly coordinated a frame around decorating small containers with colored stickers and marking pens. C 1's mother provides strategic assistance throughout this play frame of the sort offered in line (3). Note how the scaffold quickly recedes: M 1 returns to her conversation with M 2 after she has patched up the situation. In line (6) a similar incident arises: again, C 2 wants to use the roll of stickers that C 1 is holding. This time the peers work out the problem for themselves. It is not that the mothers only scaffold the earlier play sessions, that is throughout the first months, and later leave the children with sole responsibility for the negotiations. The mothers continue to be quite sensitive to the needs of their children, and lend assistance within particular frames when necessary, allowing the children to rely on their growing sense of shared understanding whenever possible. Thus, the mothers and the children work together making interaction possible.

There is also an interrelationship between the scaffolding process and the peers' reliance on shared understanding at the *macrodevelopmental* level. Early in this study the mothers intervene more frequently than in the later sessions. In the first sessions the peers know very little about the mechanics of negotiating frames and in addition, the children do not display much awareness that their peer might have a different perspective. Consequently, the mothers assist when necessary to assure that a mutual focus is established. As the peers come to share knowledge about ways to negotiate joint play frames and as their relationship grows and the peers develop an increasing sense of shared understanding, the children rely less on the strategic help provided by their mothers. Over the time span of this study, the peers themselves gradually took on more responsibility for negotiating joint activities.[6]

In summary, we believe that neither the scaffolding process nor the children's reliance on shared understanding alone leads to successfully coordinated peer interaction. We have suggested that it is the *finely coordinated interaction* between these two factors that is critical to how young peers come to play together.

4. Concluding Comments

One question has been central to this paper: how do children begin to construct joint activities with their peers? Previous research has documented that toddlers can successfully construct activities with more competent collaborators, such as older siblings and caregivers, though it has been suggested that establishing extended activities with a peer is rarely accomplished before the age of three. The findings from our own longitudinal study indicate that the development of the ability to construct joint frames with an age-mate spans an extended period of time. The peers did not pass quickly from a phase of relatively little joint interchange to a phase of more frequent mutual involvement. And furthermore, the actual *way* in which the joint activities are constructed is reorganized over time.

In focusing on the transition from caregiver-child to peer interaction, we have said that the mothers in our study offered strategic assistance both at the macrodevelopmental and microdevelopmental level of analysis. As was the case in our discussion of dyadic caregiver-child interaction, we suggest that the Vygotskian notion of the zone of proximal development offers a partial explanation for the transition to successful peer interaction. We have illustrated some of the ways mothers offer their children necessary guidance, at the same time challenging the child to take over more and more of the responsibility for constructing a joint focus with a peer. Clearly, before being able to construct joint activities on their own, the young peers relied on their mothers' help. Thus we claim that the mothers play a fundamental role not only in organizing dyadic interactions with their own child, but also in scaffolding the interactions with *another* child. Throughout our discussion of the caregivers' assistance, we have emphasized the special role of language. The mothers use language not only to direct the peers in how to construct joint activities, but also stress to the children the extent to which they can use their budding linguistic resources when constructing joint activity frames.

To a great extent, then, we have accounted for the successes and difficulties the children in our study had in constructing joint activities, and the role the mothers took on in terms of Vygotsky's notion of the zone of proximal development. We have, however, also claimed that the transition to peer interaction cannot be accounted for completely by this construct. Learning to communicate across differences in perspectives does not develop out of interactions with more experienced collaborators alone. In the above, we have outlined some ways that actual interactions with an unexperienced age-mate contributes to the development of the ability to establish and maintain a joint focus with others. The claim that peers play a role in creating a challenging zone of proximal development may at first glance seem to contradict the findings of McLane and Wertsch (1983), who compared the kind of strategic assistance adults and children provide in adult-child and child-child interactions. In their study, McLane and Wertsch conclude that the adults were more able to create a challenging zone of proximal development. We do not disagree that adults offer better strategic assistance than children. Our point is that scaffolding alone cannot account for the development of children's abilities to construct joint activities with an age-mate. Actual social interaction with an age-mate also provides an important forum that contributes to the creation of communicative strategies necessary for constructing shared activities with others.

It should go without saying that our findings may be limited to the population that we have studied. Clearly, the sorts of conclusions we have drawn from this study must be placed in a broader cultural perspective. We do suggest, however, that shared understanding is a necessary component of the successful negotiation of most all interactions taking place between peers. Furthermore, we would expect that in all societies, peer interaction is at first facilitated by the assistance of *some* support system. What the nature of this support system is and the specifics of its functioning may vary across cultures. In this culture, *caregivers* scaffold their children's activities, aiding the development of a sense of shared understanding between the peers. In other cultural groups, where children spend a great deal of time with older siblings, perhaps it is the older children who act as support systems. Our detailed analysis has in part isolated some culturally specific components that contribute to the development of peer interaction. But we believe that our study has raised questions concerning peer interaction that go beyond the population that we have studied. We leave it to researchers studying other cultures with different child-rearing practices to validate our claims about the role of support systems and of the process of establishing shared understanding in the development of peer interaction.

In this paper, the joint activities of children have been viewed as dynamically constructed by co-participants who make use of language to negotiate a mutual perspective on any given situation. We have outlined some developmental changes in the ways language is used so that such activities can be constructed. When children begin interacting with a peer the way in which the child must use language radically changes. Children must learn to use language in meaningful

ways despite differences in their communicative partner's background knowledge. It should be noted that the argument presented
here is not one in which the child is viewed as *moving out into* a
social world. Rather, at all times the child is viewed as an *active
participant* in a social world. What changes when interactions take
place with age-mates is the *nature* of that social world, a social
world that will continually be reshaped throughout development,
as a result of the child's specific interactions with a widening variety
of others.

Notes

1. Wertsch (1979) notes that much confusion has been generated by inaccu-
   rate translations of Vygotsky's writings. For example, the title of Vygotsky's monograph (Myshlenie i Rech) *Thought and Language* should have
   been translated as Thought and Speech. To avoid further confusion, we
   will continue to refer to the role of *language* though the reader should
   keep in mind that Vygotsky's interests were more with the dynamic and
   functional properties of language.
2. In focussing on this transition, we do not wish to imply that children
   first only interact with caregivers and at some later point interact with
   peers. Rather, our concern is with the transition from being able to
   construct a joint activity with a more experienced collaborator to being
   able to do so on one's own with a peer.
3. To help clarify the relationship between the two mother-child dyads, we
   will refrain from using names, and instead refer to the slightly older
   child and her mother as C 1 and M 1, and to the slightly younger child
   and her mother as C 2 and M 2. While somewhat impersonal, we hope
   this will contribute to the flow of this chapter.
4. Hoffman (in press) makes reference to a similar scaffolding process
   which assists children in learning to take into account a peer's well-
   being. It is argued that parents express a playmate's feelings ("Don't
   yell at him. He was only trying to help.") and to this extent, the parents
   are said to contribute to the child's moral development.
5. While it may be the case that shared understanding in part grows out
   of interactions with a variety of age-mates, our discussion in this paper
   will be limited to consideration of interactions with one continual peer.
6. For a more detailed analysis of the interaction between the scaffolding
   process and the peer's reliance on shared understanding, see Budwig
   (1981).

References

Bamberg, Michael
   1980   "A fresh look at the relationship between pragmatic and se-
           mantic knowledge. Exemplified with data from the acquisition
           of first words", *Archives of Psychology*, 133, 23 – 43.
Becker, Jacqueline M.
   1977   "A learning analysis of the development of peer-oriented be-
           havior in nine-month-old infants", *Developmental Psychology*,
           13, 481 – 491.
Brazleton, T. Berry, Koslowski, Barbara and Main, Mary
   1974   "The origins of reciprocity: The early mother-infant interac-
           tion", *The effect of the infant on its caregiver*, edited by Michael
           Lewis and Leonard A. Rosenblum (New York: John Wiley),
           49 – 76.
Bronson, Wanda C.
   1981   "Toddlers' behaviors with age-mates: Issues of interaction,
           cognition, and effect", *Monographs on Infancy*, Vol. 1, 127.
Brown, Ann L. and Ferrara, R. A.
   1985   "Diagnosing zones of proximal development. An alternative in
           standardized testing", *Culture, communication, and cognition:
           Vygotskian perspectives*, edited by James V. Wertsch (New -
           York: Cambridge University Press).
Budwig, Nancy A.
   1981   "Working it out together: The role of language in 2 year old
           peers' play", unpublished manuscript (Berkeley: University of
           California).
Burke, Kenneth
   1962   *A grammar of motives and a rhetoric of motives* (Cleveland:
           World).
Cook-Gumperz, Jenny
   1975   "The child as practical reasoner", *Socio-cultural dimensions of
           language use*, edited by Mary Sanchez and Ben G. Blount
           (New York: Academic Press), 137 – 161.
   1976   revised November 1977, *"The natural history of an activity"*,
           unpublished manuscript.
Cook-Gumperz, Jenny and Gumperz, John
   1976   *Context in children's speech*, Working Paper No. 46, Language
           Behavior Research Laboratory, University of California, Ber-
           keley.
Corsaro, Williams
   1979   "We're friends, right?", *Language in Society*, 8, 315 – 336.

Doyle, Anna B., Connolly, Jennifer and Rivest, L.
1980   "The effects of playmate familiarity on the social interaction of young children", *Child Development*, 51, 217−223.
Garvey, Catherine
1977   *Play* (Cambridge, Mass.: Harvard University Press).
Goffman, Erving
1974   *Frame analysis* (New York: Harper & Row).
Gumperz, John
1982   *Discourse Strategies* (Cambridge: Cambridge University Press).
Hoffman, Martin L.
in press "Affective and cognitive processes in moral internalisation", *Social cognition and social behavior*, edited by E. T. Higgins, D. Ruble, and W. Hartup.
Iwamura, Susan
1980   *The verbal games of preschool children* (London: Croom Helm Ltd.).
Kaye, Kenneth
1979   "Thickening thin data: The maternal role in developing communication and language", *Before speech: The beginning of interpersonal communication*, edited by Margaret Bullowa (Cambridge: Cambridge University Press), 191−206.
McLane, Joan B. and Wertsch, James
1983   *Child-child and adult-child interaction: A Vygotskian study of dyadic problem solving systems*, unpublished manuscript.
Mueller, Eduard and Brenner, Jeffrey
1977   "The origins of social skills and interaction among playgroup toddlers", *Child Development*, 48, 854−861.
Ochs, Elinor and Schieffelin, Bambi
1984   "Language acquisition and socialization: Three Developmental stories and their implications", *Culture Theory: Essays in Mind, Self and Emotion*, edited by Richard A. Shewder and Robert LeVine (Cambridge: Cambridge University Press).
Rogoff, Barbara and Gardner, W.
1984   "Adult guidance of cognitive development", *Everyday cognition: Its development in social context*, edited by Barbara Rogoff and Jean Lave (Cambridge, Mass.: Harvard University Press).
Rommetveit, Ragnar
1974   *On message structure: A framework for the study of language and communication* (New York: John Wiley & Sons).
Rubenstein, Judith L. and Howes, Carrollie
1976   "The effects of peers of toddler interaction with mothers and toys", *Child Development, 47*, 597−605.

Ryan, Joanna
1974 "Early language development: Towards a communicational analysis", *The integration of the child into a social world*, edited by Martin Richards (Cambridge: Cambridge University Press), 185–214.
Schwartzman, Helen B.
1976 "Children's play: A sideways glance at makebelieve", *The study of play: Problems and Prospects*, edited by D. F. Lancy and B. A. Tindall (New York: Leisure Press).
1978 *Transformations: The anthropology of children's Play* (New York: Plenum Press).
Strage, Amy, Bamberg, Michael, and Budwig, Nancy
1981 " 'It that any way to talk to your peer?': Mothers' input and the development of role-appropriate discourse among peers", *Papers and Reports on Child Language Development*, 20.
Stern, Daniel N.
1974 "Mother and infant at play: the dyadic interaction involving facial, vocal and gaze behaviors", *The effect of the infant on its caregiver*, edited by Michael Lewis and Leonard A. Rosenblum, (New York: John Wiley), 187–214.
Streeck, Jürgen
1980 "Speech acts in interaction: A critique of Searle", *Discourse processes*, 3, 133–154.
Sutton-Smith, Brian A.
1980 "A 'sportive' theory of play", *Play and culture*, edited by Helen B. Schwartzman (New York: Leisure Press).
Vygotsky, Lev S.
1978 *Mind in society* (Cambridge, Mass.: Harvard University Press).
1981 "The genesis of higher mental functions", *The concept of activity in Soviet psychology*, edited by James V. Wertsch (Armonk, N. Y.: M. E. Sharpe).
Wertsch, James V.
1979 "From social interaction to higher psychological processes: A clarification and application of Vygotsky's theory", *Human Development*, 22, 1–22.
1980 *Semiotic mechanism in joint cognitive activity*, Paper presented at joint US–USSR Conference on the theory of activity, Institute of Psychology, Academy of Sciences, Moscow, March, 1980.
in press "The zone of proximal development: Some conceptual issues", *Cognitive growth in children: The zone of proximal development*, edited by Barbara Rogoff and James V. Wertsch (San Francisco: Jossey-Bass).

Wertsch, James V., McNamee, Gillian D., McLane, Joan B. and Budwig, Nancy
    1980   "The adult-child dyad as a problem solving system", *Child Development*, 51, 1215—1221.
Wood, David, Bruner, Jerome and Ross, Gail
    1976   "The role of tutoring in problem solving", *Journal of Child Psychology and Psychiatry*, 17, 89—100.

The Social World of Kwara'ae Children: Acquisition of Language and Values

Karen Ann Watson-Gegeo and David W. Gegeo

When a Kwara'ae 2 or 3-year-old child performs a task well or accomplishes an interaction appropriately, its caregiver praises it with "You are almost *sari'i* (a maiden)/*'alako* (a young man) now." The utterance is accompanied by an exaggerated intonation contour, direct eye gaze, pronounced smile, and emphatic inclination and rise of the head. The marked character of this praise gives it the force of a generative metaphor (Schon 1979: 254): the child's accomplishment is singled out from the ongoing stream of behavior, and framed in terms of competence in the adult social world.

Sari'i/'alako praise exemplifies a strong theme in Kwara'ae children's socialization, the importance of becoming adult as soon as possible. In this chapter we show how a Kwara'ae child's world is shaped by a set of key values in adult culture, taught through important interactional routines and integrated into interpersonal relationships. Elsewhere we have looked at children's language acquisition (Watson-Gegeo and Gegeo, 1982). Here we are concerned with language as "intrinsically a 'social principle' for the child" (Cook-Gumperz 1975: 143), and socialization as "the acquisition of interactional competences" (Speier 1970: 189). Therefore we focus on how the young Kwara'ae child acquires the sense of everyday reality or "dense actuality" socially constructed and shared by Kwara'ae adults (Berger and Luckmann, 1967; Schütz, 1973; Cook-Gumperz, 1975).

We recognize that a child's sense of social structure differs from that of adults (Cicourel, 1970). In this paper, however, we are primarily concerned with the meaning of the world that Kwara'ae adults build around the child from birth to 5 years through language and interaction.[1] Our analysis is interpretive in nature (Taylor, 1979; Ricoeur, 1979), and attempts to integrate several perspectives: that of the Kwara'ae adult life-world (Husserl's *Lebenswelt*) together with its basis in tradition; Kwara'ae people's interpretations of their own behavior in childrearing, and the inferences they expect their children to make in interactions; observed instances of caregiver-child interactions; and our mutual and differing interpretations of individual events, as cultural insider and outsider often assigned caregiving duties ourselves when we were in the field.[2]

1. Some Features of Social Organization and Discourse

The Kwara'ae are a Melanesian people of Malaita in the Solomon Islands. Structurally, Kwara'ae society is both egalitarian and hierarchical. Under the national government, villages are led by an elected village committee and chief. In practice, decisions in small villages are still made as they were traditionally, by consensus among adult members. Particularly influential are the *gwaunga'i* (lit., "headness") men and women, who are heads of their families and of the social order. *Gwaunga'i* status, potentially open to everyone, is achieved by growing older, having at least one child marry, acquiring cultural skills, and exhibiting appropriate behavior. As a way of life or being which expresses Kwara'ae world view and values, *gwaunga'i*-hood is every adult's goal. It is achieved through a consensual process whereby, over a period of several years, one becomes increasingly recognized as *gwaunga'i*-like and finally *gwaunga'i*.

Within the patrilineal descent group and extended family, families are hierarchically ranked as "senior" or "junior" to each other. Within the extended and nuclear family, adults are senior in rank to children, and older siblings (and classificatory siblings) senior to younger. The oldest son will be the head of his sibling group through life, and one senior *gwaunga'i* male will become the head or *ara'i* of the descent group.[3] Often in childhood, however, the oldest daughter has a great deal of power in the household due to her supervisory role in family work. Because couples are socially judged by the skills and behavior of oldest daughters, most are kept out of Western schooling and reared to be completely traditional. Moreover, parents confine childrearing duties to themselves, their children, and unmarried brothers and sisters because they are concerned about the values their children learn. But their own reputations and possible future status as *gwaunga'i* are also at stake if they become the target of gossip for neglecting the care and teaching of their children (see Gegeo and Watson-Gegeo, 1983 a).

Kwara'ae social contexts and speech activities (Gumperz, 1982) are classified as either important (*'inoto'a, lalifu*) or unimportant (*kakabara, kwalabasa*); although unimportant contexts are clearly mundane, important ones are not necessarily seen as sacred. Unimportant contexts embrace everyday life, including polite and ordinary conversations among adults and most caregiver-child interactions. Such contexts and speech activities are associated with *ala'anga kwalabasa* (speech + "vine-like"), the level of discourse we call "low rhetoric". *Kwalabasa* suggests a root that goes down into the ground for a distance, and then suddenly splits into many lesser, wandering roots. Of speech, it implies ideas that go every which way. Important contexts and speech activities, including meetings, oratory at feasts, serious discussions of politics, religion, tradition, marriage, etc., poetry, and storytelling evoke *ala'anga lalifu* (speech + importantly rooted), or "high rhetoric". *Lalifu* is a tap root, the main root anchoring a plant. High rhetoric is characterized by a special vocabulary, a special set of pronouns, heavy use of underlying forms of words (most are metathesized in ordinary speech), very abstract phrasing, complex syntactical forms, special intonation contours, a set of graceful, somewhat stylized body gestures, and other discourse features. Competence in high rhetoric is an essential life skill for a Kwara'ae adult — one is unlikely to be called *gwaunga'i* without it. A child of 5 years who demonstrates a precocious ability in high rhetoric is praised, said to be *gwaunga'i*-like, and may be given special teaching.

In the working out of relationships in adult Kwara'ae society, there seems to be little tension between the egalitarian and hierarchical principles in the social order. We think the two principles are mediated by social organizational strategies, especially interactional strategies based on a set of key cultural values in *falafala* (tradition). We will first briefly define these values, then examine their role in interaction.

A *gwaunga'i* usually specializes in at least one area of *falafala* knowledge besides high rhetoric. In one sense, *falafala* is that body of lore, rules, 'case law', and life skills underlying Kwara'ae society and culture. In another, *falafala* constitutes the Kwara'ae world view, for it sets up "a meaningful relation between the values a people holds and the general order of existence within which it finds itself" (Geertz 1973: 172). *Falafala* is both arbiter (*"falafala* says ...") and standard (e. g., "it is congruent/incongruent with *falafala"*) in decision-making or disputes over rules, rights, and social obligations.

The eight key or "ultimate values" (Firth 1964: 174) that form the basis of *falafala*, the family, and the whole person, are regarded as equal in value, with all other values subsumed under them. Alphabetically, then: (1) *alafe'anga*, love, including obligations to kin as well as feelings of love; (2) *aroaro'anga*, peace, peaceful behavior; (3) *babato'o'anga*, emotional and behavioral stability and maturity, dependability, settling down in one place peacefully; (4) *enoeno'anga*, humility, delicacy, adaptability, gracefulness, tranquility ("Like a blade of grass bending in the wind, in times of difficulty one is to gracefully endure pain without resentment or anger, trusting that with inner strength, one will emerge at the end whole and well, and order will be restored" − Gegeo); (5) *fangale'a'anga*, giving, sharing, and receiving, as well as etiquette and manners (lit., eat + good); (6) *kwaigwale'e'anga*, welcoming, comforting, hospitality (lit., "bring to one's bosom to comfort"); (7) *kwaisare'e'anga*, feeding someone without expectation of return; and (8) *mamana'anga*, honesty and truthfulness, and power (both charisma and the power to make things happen, as in successfully inducing an ancestral spirit through prayer to bring aid).

2. Form and Style in Caregiver-Infant Interactions

Through a set of communicative routines (Boggs and Peters, 1982) introduced to infants beginning at 6 months, Kwara'ae caregivers shape interaction in the family, teach language, and transmit cultural attitudes and information. Through imperative and repeating routines children learn about rights, obligations, role, and cultural expectations according to gender and birth order; develop skills in work and other activities; and practice interactional skills. In the two following sections we will illustrate how children learn to present themselves through politeness routines, and how they learn key elements of Kwara'ae culture through counseling routines, including how to resolve family disputes, express and control emotions, and participate in cooperative family endeavors. Here we will discuss style in caregiver-infant interactions, and the more general issue of orienting the child to the adult world.

The key — that is, the tone, manner, and spirit (Hymes, 1974) — of caregiver-infant interactions reflects the cultural values of *enoeno'anga, babato'o'anga*, and *aroaro'anga*. The Kwara'ae down-play depression and anxiety; one's presentation of self, at least, is expected to be infused with a quiet happiness. Kwara'ae caregivers illustrate this theme through "happy talk" with their infants. They use light, gentle, affectionate tones, exaggerated rising pitch contours, cheerful facial expressions, singing, and other communicative strategies to stimulate infants, encourage smiles and laughter, and mitigate any discomfort they themselves or their charges may be experiencing. Infants are frequently urged to smile and told to be happy. We observed that only rarely are infants slapped or items roughly snatched from them. Instead, caregivers mildly scold their infants with *se!* (vocalized or unvocalized) or *abu!* (don't!, from *ābu*, tabu, forbidden, sacred). Or they redirect the child's attention with one of several distracting routines.

In fact, distracting routines that refocus the child's attention on something of interest (a bird, flower, airplane, passerby, missing parent or sibling) outside him/herself are widely used with young infants to stop them from fussing and crying. Distracting routines are among several socialization strategies used to get infants or young children to de-center, that is, to detach themselves from their own emotions and focus instead on social concerns. The Kwara'ae see de-centering and emotional control as important in two ways. First, the well-being of the social group takes precedence over the needs and feelings of the individual. Second, emotional control is seen as an essential characteristic of inner strength; the strength of the social group, in turn, depends on the inner strength of the individuals in it. Even the way caregivers hold and carry infants reflects a social theme: the child is always *faced* outward in the direction the caregiver is facing, towards the social group.

Among the earliest values taught through routines are *fanga-le'a'anga* (giving and sharing) and *kwaigwale'e'anga* (hospitality). If there are other children present, an infant of 6 months eating a fruit or a biscuit is told to give some of it to them. A very common routine is to hand an item to an infant, and tell it to give it to one of the adults present. Give/carry imperative utterances almost always indicate the recipient by kin term rather than by name.

From infancy, therefore, children learn who is to be given what, according to kin relationship. Young children also practice being hosts very early. For example, one afternoon as we arrived to visit a family, we saw only the 20-month-old male infant on the verandah, playing on the *tatafe* (bench). As soon as he saw us coming, he turned around on the bench to dangle his legs and straighten his back like an adult. Shifting to one side to make room for us, he dusted off the surface with his palm, inclined his head with a polite smile, and said, "Sit here, sit here".

Such early adult-like behavior is the result of a conscious attempt by caregivers to speed the child towards responsible behavior and adult norms of interaction as quickly as possible. To do this, adults include infants in social conversations from birth, speaking to them and for them. After the sixth month an infant's caregivers shift to a modified speech register with features of "baby-talk" found in many other societies, including simplifications, reduplication, altered vocabulary, repetition, expansion of infant utterances, question/answer sequences, and marked paralinguistic features. Caregivers explain this shift by saying that in order to rapidly bring a child up to adult interactive norms, they must start where the child is. From 10 months to 3 − 4 years of age, a young child's caregivers speak to it continuously, with interactions structured by dozens of routines and with caregiver register shifting towards adult speech norms as the child acquires greater competence.

Between 2½ and 3 years of age, Kwara'ae children undergo an important transition from infancy to responsible childhood. At this age caregiver talk shifts to the "language of socialization" (Gleason and Weintraub, 1978), children's speech and behavior are continually corrected by imperatives, and explanations are given for proper behavior. Girls at age 3 put on clothes, participate regularly in gardening and household work, and are given their first knife (a cut-down, sharpened bush knife) − all of which symbolize their entry into "womanhood." Three-year-old girls can already code-switch to "baby-talk" when caring for their younger siblings under adult supervision. They have been taught how to sit, stand, walk, and fold their skirts around their legs as adult women. Both boys and girls demonstrate competence in simple social conversations at this age. When their behavior is correct, they are praised as adult-like. When they fuss or cry, they are comforted but criticized with the scold *malangela* (childish or "pseudo-child").

On the other hand, proud or aggressive behavior in children is met with counseling (below) or ridicule. Humility is essential to the mediation between equality and hierarchy in Kwara'ae society; interestingly, "proud" in Kwara'ae is *alura'e*, lit. put + up/above. The culturally approved kind of humility is illustrated by the respected *gwaunga'i* widely recognized for his knowledge and leadership, and senior member in his family, who slips into a meeting quietly, sits at the back of the room, listens and watches, and rises to speak with quiet authority but no fanfare when the others have had their say. The *gwaunga'i* serve as cultural models, but teasing and gossip are the main strategies for ensuring humility in daily interactions. From infancy children are also teased in mild to sharp ways, and must learn to laugh rather than cry, willingly direct teasing at themselves, and tease back. Teases also carry important cultural knowledge which children must learn to infer, including information about the child's coming role as an adult. For example, once when a 3-year-old girl fussed and cried, her father's brother said in a stern but joking tone, "I'm sorry you arrived, but there's no pig to bake. What was it you and your husband fought over?" The child stopped crying at once. The tease implied that the girl was crying like a woman who had come home to her family to report a fight with her husband. The family's appropriate response would be to bake a pig, and take the woman and the pig back to her husband's village. This act implies that the woman has the protection of her family, who are willing to refund the brideprice and take her back with them if she is not properly treated. By saying that there was no pig, the father's brother was telling the child that the family did not approve of — would not support — her crying. Whether or not the girl correctedly inferred the message, she was embarrassed when the adults laughed (indicating all attention was focused on her behavior), and the juxtaposition of contexts effected by the metaphor roused her curiosity for an explanation (her face assumed the intense look typical with this child in direct teaching situations).

3. Politeness and Decorum: The Social Presentation of Self

As mentioned earlier, Kwara'ae social contexts are classified as either important or unimportant, and corresponding speech activities use high and low rhetoric, respectively. Now we want to illustrate these two kinds of contexts by focusing on politeness and on counseling.

"Happy talk" among caregivers and infants finds its parallel in adult polite social conversations (which are distinct from focused and casual conversations; see Watson-Gegeo and Gegeo 1982: 22 ff.). When adults meet on the road or in the village, or entertain guests/talk to hosts on social visits, they politely inquire after each other's affairs and engage in teasing and banter. People also call out from house to house, or as someone passes on the path, as a strictly social activity. Polite conversations are marked by wide pitch swings, strong stresses, and a lightly serious, friendly, but emotionally detached tone. These markers are associated with showing interest, concern, and politeness, and exchanging information on small matters. Because questions are used to indicate that one is showing an interest in even the most mundane affairs of other people — their well-being, problems, needs, and concerns — polite conversations are often structured by question/answer sequences, even when the inquirer already knows the answers. While prying and gossip are negatively sanctioned, concern for others is a high cultural value.

Caregiver-child "happy talk" interactions can be seen as an exaggerated form of polite conversational behavior. In fact, question sequences and teasing and banter among adults sometimes take the same exaggerated intonation contours and stress that caregivers use in "happy talk," and they are accompanied by smiles, laughter, gestures, and gross body shifts indicating "good humor." Interestingly, both politeness and caregiver speech contours are especially heard among female speakers, but also among adolescent boys and young unmarried men. Men's speech in such contexts is more reserved but also shifted towards the swings found in women's speech.

Polite conversations function as one strategy for mediating between equality and hierarchy in Kwara'ae society, for everyone regardless of status is expected to engage in these kinds of interactions. Teasing and banter play an important role in discouraging proud behavior; not only is a proud person the target of frequent direct and indirect ridicule, but those of high status often demonstrate their humility by teasing themselves. Politeness and decorum also seem a way to maintain *enoeno'anga* and *babato'o'anga* in adverse circumstances. Or, alternatively, one is expected to demonstrate endurance and acceptance of misfortune by carrying on politely and self-teasingly in the face of adversity, turning it into humor. People therefore often joke about their illnesses and disabilities, and even in a crisis inquire politely and in detail about others. Politeness and teasing are also ways to distance oneself from pain, the adult version of de-centering taught to very young infants, as we have seen.

Politeness strategies, including techniques of indirection, appropriate requests and questions of information, and socially acceptable forms of banter, are taught to infants and practiced with them in calling out and repeating routines. In adult society, calling out is used to locate someone, seek identity of an unseen person working nearby in the bush, and carry on a polite conversation across a distance. As one kind of repeating routine, calling out is first introduced to infants at 6 months of age to entertain or distract them, and then as the infant begins to speak, phrases and sentences are given to it to call out. The routine is elicited by the caregiver's imperative, *ako 'uana X* (call out + to him/her + X). Repeating is elicited by the caregiver saying *'uri* (thus, like this), and then modeling a sentence for the infant or young child, who then repeats whatever came after *'uri*, imitating the caregiver's intonation, phrasing, and stress. Special intonation contours are associated with calling out and repeating routines (see Watson-Gegeo and Gegeo, 1982), but by the time a child is 3 years old, he/she is expected to provide intonation, pitch, and stress appropriate to the context of situation. Caregivers recognize the role that these routines play in helping the child acquire language, e. g., through chunking (Peters, 1982). Repeating routines are often used like drills to teach labels, counting, the steps of and vocabulary associated with a task the child and caregiver are doing together, and to review knowledge already learned in another context.

The most frequent use of calling out and repeating, however, is as "scaffolding" (Bruner, 1978) in teaching children to converse with other children or adults, and to tease and respond to teasing. For example, the pre-verbal infant first encounters question/answer sequences as a caregiver strategy to entertain and stimulate infants. Infants are asked if they are hungry, full, thirsty, tired, sleepy, awake, hot or cold, well or sick; if they want to play, get up or down; where they slept last night or went with a caregiver; what they saw or are seeing; where their parents or siblings are and when they will return, and so on — that is, questions about their wellbeing, problems, needs and concerns parallel to questions asked of adults in polite encounters, but tailored to an infant's experiences. Adults answer these question on behalf of pre-verbal infants, often prefacing the response with *'uri*. Later as the infant begins to talk, *'uri*-prefaced statements are used to instruct it on appropriate ways to answer. Here is a typical example in which question/answer sequences are used both to entertain an infant and teach it responses: A mother was preparing nuts to be dried for a pudding while babysitting her 20-month-old infant, who was sick with malaria. In an exaggeratedly light and happy tone, the mother talked to the infant for more than half an hour, primarily through question/answer sequences. She repeatedly asked, "Are you sick? Very sick?" and since the infant did not respond, answered for her, "Yes, very sick." She asked the girl about her symptoms (was she hot? that is, feverish), where her brother had gone, whether she was hungry or thirsty, did she want to sleep, did she want to play, and so on. Often she gave no responses on behalf of the infant, but when she did she sometimes prefaced them with *'uri*, in an apparent attempt to get the infant to repeat. In this example as in others like it not involving illness, the manner in which caregivers inquire into an infant's concerns and needs is striking in its similarity to polite interactions among adults. The lightly serious tone with which topics like illness are presented seems to soothe a child and may help to distance it from its symptoms. Interestingly, 3-year-old children can be observed doing such question/answer sequences as "Are you sick? Very sick? Yes, very sick" with, say, sick pets.

Repeating is used to assist children in carrying on their side of conversations they or others may have initiated. In such cases the caregiver at first models the child's side of the conversation, line by line, with the child repeating. Once the child has a command of appropriate question and response forms, the caregiver may use an imperative to instruct the child on what comes next; e. g., "Ask about your cousin," and the child responds by asking his/her conversational partner, "Where is my cousin?" Repeating sequences are used to teach interaction in several varieties of *ala'anga kwalabasa*, from relatively formal greetings and interactions, to inquiries and joking in slang.

Infants are inducted early into simple teases and teasing rounds. A common teasing round involves body parts and appearance. Here

is a composite example based on several similar instances. While
cleaning up the kitchen after dinner, the father suddenly said to his
22-month-old son, "You flat buttocks", in a light, teasing tone. The
mother, laughing, told the boy, "*'Uri*, you long ribs", and the boy
repeated. She added, "You eat too much", and the boy repeated.
The father returned, "You *malangela*". The mother replied, "*'Uri*,
you tangled hair", and the boy repeated. A teasing round may go
on for two or three rapidly paced minutes, but then will be terminated by one of the interactants giving a non-teasing, direct reply
to a tease. Here the father replied, "My hair is tangled because I
couldn't find the comb after I showered. You children were playing
with it and lost it". His wife returned, "Oh, I put it on the shelf
where they couldn't reach it". A child is usually not given an *'uri*-
prefaced sentence to terminate a tease because teasing must be
directly terminated, and statements through a child are seen as
indirect. In order to keep the interaction with the child going,
however, the father told his son to go get the comb for him. If the
mother had wanted to continue the tease, she might have told the
son, "*'Uri*, you long ribs, go get it yourself. What are you doing
just sitting there chewing your betel?". This initiates a new round
of teasing, requiring a new direct termination.

Because statements coming through a child are seen as indirect
and humorous (apparently they are not seen as violating hierarchical
rank, either), adults often tease each other or another child through
an infant. As teasing through children begins with pre-verbal infants
who cannot repeat, *'uri*-prefaced teasing is a social fiction allowing
teases to be sharper than would be acceptable if said directly by
one adult to another. As a result, even with a verbal infant it is
not important whether the infant actually repeats. The following
example illustrates these points. At a social family gathering, a
respected and high-ranking *gwaunga'i* man joined some of his
younger relatives in smoking a cigarette; this was uncharacteristic
of his rank, since the ever-present pipe symbolized *gwaunga'i*-ship.
To entertain his 2-year-old grandson, the man began blowing
lungfuls of smoke all at once out through his nose, and making
comic gestures and facial expressions. The assembled adult relatives
were embarrassed by his behavior, as evidenced by their indirect
jokes. Had he been a lesser *gwaunga'i* his behavior would have
been ignored. Finally, his eldest daughter teased him through the
grandchild (her son), "*'Uri*, you continue with that and you'll

choke yourself".The boy did not repeat; there was restrained, self-conscious laughter from the adults. The *gwaunga'i* immediately stopped his comic behavior, took out his pipe and lit it, and resumed a dignified, *gwaunga'i*-like presentation of self. His daughter's underlying message was, "You're behaving childishly and we're all embarrassed. Smoke properly or don't smoke at all". If she had said either this or the tease directly to her father, she would have breached the pleasant conversational context and implied that she was angry.

The target of teases through a child can respond by teasing the initiator of the child back, or by taking the whole as a joke. In cases where a child actually repeats, the targeted adult has a moment to prepare a response before the tease is "socially heard" through the child.

By 5 years of age, children have learned to tease and tease back, as well as terminate teasing rounds. Repeating routines end by ages 4 – 5 years, after which children develop interactional skills by listening and practicing on their own, and by hearing caregivers correct them. Finally, remember that calling out and repeating routines are first introduced to distract crying infants, and later to entertain both caregiver and child while babysitting. It is therefore interesting that only *ala'anga kwalabasa* is taught through repeating routines, not *ala'anga lalifu; lalifu* cannot be associated with non-serious talk.

4. Counseling: Cultural Knowledge and Inference

Ala'anga lalifu is spoken in all *falafala* contexts, including discussions of tradition-governed subjects, dispute-settling, speech-making, planning, advising, and counseling. *Lalifu* talk is grave in tone, low pitched, melodic, rhythmical, and spoken in a quiet, relaxed voice. Its slow pace reflects the thoughtfulness of speakers and the fact that they do not need to compete for the floor. High rhetoric is also marked by parallel but abstract phrasing, meticulous attention to evidential and inferential detail and logical steps in argumentation, and formal introductions and closures at speech activity boundaries or for major turns. Diminuitive expressions show humility and contribute to the obliqueness of *lalifu* talk. Gestures accompanying speech are close to the body, and laughter at jokes is restrained. The mood of high rhetoric contexts is one of mutual respect, dignity, and honor. In fact, high rhetoric talk is often described in terms of the key values of *enoeno'anga, babato'o'anga*, and *aroaro'anga*. Another important value (one which some Kwara'ae regard as candidate for a ninth key cultural value) expressed in how an argument is presented is *fito'o'anga*, faith; that is, having confidence or faith in what one says.

One *lalifu* context is counseling, in which values are expressed, explored, elaborated, and reaffirmed, and behavior and issues measured against *falafala*. Adult family counseling sessions led by a *gwaunga'i* are held to resolve tensions among individuals or couples in the nuclear or extended family, or to deal with a member's behavior. Counseling sessions for children focus on their behavior and skills, and constitute lessons in cultural knowledge and inference.

Children may be counseled at any time about their behavior, but typically the parents do so after dinner in the evening. A session usually begins with a marked contextual shift; the parent switches to high rhetoric, and immediately the children fall silent and listen respectfully, their eyes focused in mid-space or on the floor. One or both parents may then speak about the children's actions that day, addressing both behavior and emotional issues within the cultural and moral context of *falafala*. If-then outcomes of misbehavior may be argued, especially if what the child did — e. g., taking fruit from someone's tree — can lead to public shame or having to pay compensation. Caregivers call counseling sessions *fa'amanata'anga*, teaching, or sometimes *fa'anaunau'anga*, making strong. *Fa'amanata* (lit., make + think) includes both therapeutic counseling and intellectual instruction; it implies shaping the mind. *Naunau* here is to speak fearlessly, an important *gwaunga'i* quality (see Gegeo and Watson-Gegeo, 1983 b).

Counseling is introduced to children at 18 months to 5 years of age, depending on the caregiver's assumptions about the child's ability to understand. The following two abbreviated accounts illustrate very early counseling routines.

Example (1)
A 2-year-old boy cried lustily when his parents put a plate of rice to be shared by him and his 10-year-old brother under the elder brother's control. The father took the infant into his lap as the mother arranged the plate on a chair between the two boys. Both parents softly and

seriously urged the infant to stop crying. When he was quiet, the father said in simplified high rhetoric and gentle counseling tones that they wanted the boy to *fangale'a* with his brother, who is older (*'a'ana* = adult, senior, grown-up) than himself. He pointed out that the boy's visiting cousins all *fanga kwaima* (eat in love) together, and he should do the same with his brother.

Discussion: At about age 2 years, distracting routines to stop infant crying are replaced by teasing (as we have seen) or by serious talk in either *kwalabasa*, or in *lalifu* if a counseling lesson is initiated. In this example the key value of *fangale'a'anga* — sharing — is explicitly taught, along with its corollary *fanga kwaima'anga*. The infant was also given a lesson in seniority: the 10-year-old was both older brother and the eldest boy of the sibling group.

Example (2)
During and after dinner, a father counseled his 3-year-old daughter as follows: That laziness is bad, that it brings in nothing, and you can be whipped for it. The girl asked, what about K? (a 9-year-old relative in the village). The father said, she's lazy and that's why her father whipped her the other day. There was a break. Then the father counseled the girl that if she cries and does silly things, S and G (her younger siblings) will imitate her; and imagine what you will all produce — darkness. After another break, the father counseled her on not playing "foolishly" and not copying other children when they swear; if she does, her mother's brother will whip her. Then her mother counseled the girl not to run after trucks or she would spank her. This topic was developed, with the girl asking questions and the father giving advice.

Discussion: Babato'o'anga is the primary focus of this lesson. At 3 years old, the girl was already beginning to assume caregiving duties for her younger twin siblings, and the father emphasized her responsibility as caregiver and model for them. She was also reminded that she should work with her mother, a point made frequently in different ways in this family's counseling sessions. "Foolish" play refers to boys and girls playing roughly together, which is forbidden by *falafala*; by age 3, girls should play with girls and not engage in rough or dangerous games. It is a common caregiver strategy to threaten a child with punishment by someone the child respects and fears; in this case, her mother's brother is a priest. *Lalifu* talk is filled with imagery, which is illustrated by the metaphorical "darkness" in this example.

Counseling contexts, then, are contexts for direct teaching of values and cultural knowledge. They are a way for parents and children to cross-check their mutual inferences about cultural expectations and meaning of behavior. While teaching in these sessions is direct, the language spoken is often oblique. Children are inducted into high rhetoric by early counseling in a simplified form of it. Both interpretive rules and communicative competence in *ala'anga lalifu* are learned by observation and practice. Caregivers do not directly teach *ala'anga lalifu* as they do *ala'anga kwalabasa*, through routines like calling out and repeating; but they will correct mistakes when children make them.

Conclusion

In this chapter we have explored the social world of Kwara'ae infants and young children, focusing on the use of language in socialization and enculturation, the transmission of values, and the relationship between the young child's experiences and the adult world he/she will enter.

Ochs and Schieffelin (1984) have suggested that societies can be contrasted according to two basic orientations towards child socialization: those that adapt the social situation to the child, and those that adapt the child to the situation. They argue that the first of these orientations, "adapt situation to child", is correlated with the child-caregiver interaction model typical of the white American middle class; this model has become the dominant paradigm in language acquisition theory. The second orientation, "adapt child to situation", and its corresponding child-caregiver interaction model is based on Ochs and Schieffelin's Western Samoan and Kaluli data, and studies of white and black working class Americans.

The Kwara'ae are an interesting test case for the model in that they correspond to lower or working class peoples elsewhere — they are subsistence horticulturists, usually non-literate or with a minimum of Western schooling, and economically very poor. Yet they share characteristics with both orientations and interactional models described by Ochs and Schieffelin.

More specifically, Kwara'ae caregivers use a simplified register and baby-talk lexicon, negotiate meaning with the child via expansion and paraphrase, cooperatively build propositions with the infant, respond to child-initiated verbal and non-verbal acts, and engage in frequent two-party conversations with infants — all characteristic of the "adapt situation to child" orientation. Yet they also model utterances for the child to repeat to a third party, direct the child to notice others, orient it to topics of situational concern, and engage in frequent multi-party conversations with infants — all characteristic of the "adapt child to situation" orientation (ibid.). Both sets of interactional strategies get equal billing in Kwara'ae caregiver-infant interactions.

Why is this the case? We think the answer lies in the Kwara'ae theory of socialization. The over-all Kwara'ae goal is to adapt the child to the situation; but, as we have seen, caregivers argue that the best and fastest way to accomplish this is by starting where the child is — by adapting some features of talk and situation to the child. Furthermore, the Kwara'ae behave as if they thought it inefficient to allow any potentially pedagogical situation to go by without making use of it. Thus, a child-initiated topic will be seized on as an opportunity for a lesson.

Classification systems like that suggested by Ochs and Schieffelin are useful exercises to help us understand how caregiver orientations relate to caregiver strategies. But care should be taken not to assume a direct or narrow correspondence between them. Ochs and Schieffelin's paper points out the need to examine the complex relationships among caregiver goals and values, and how they are strategically realized in different ways and at different levels in the ongoing situations that constitute the child's social world.

Notes

1. Thus "meaning" for us goes beyond linguistic meaning to experiential meaning — that is, meaning "for a subject, of something, in a field," or alternatively, the "meaning of a situation for an agent" (Taylor 1979: 34). In sociological terms, meaning refers to the "identification of social actions by their context in the broadest sense" (Firth 1964: 175). By "values" we mean "the referential norms by which meaning is judged, implicitly if not explicitly by the people concerned" (ibid.).
2. The data base for this analysis consists of: observational notes and audiotapes of adult interaction and discourse, and caregiver-child inter-

action, from six months in the field in 1978 and 1979; an intensive study of five families focusing on language socialization and childrearing over eight months in 1981, including observational notes, 80 hours of audiotaped interactions between caregivers and young children, and in-depth interviews with 10 families on child socialization; and Gegeo's knowledge as a member of Kwara'ae culture. NIMH and the Milton Fund partially supported our work in 1978, and the Spencer Foundation gave partial support from 1979 – 1982 through Harvard University seed grants. Our research was carried out in several Anglican villages of West Kwara'ae, and pertains especially to them.

3. Family/descent group rankings are traditional, dating back before the West Kwara'ae moved down to the coastal plain to live in Christian villages. Low-ranking families who acquire education or wealth today do gain respect because of it, but are still seen as junior to a poor but traditionally senior family. Illustrating the strength of seniority, a 19-year-old man once told us that he looks up to his identical twin brother and always follows his advice, "because he was born before me".

References

Berger, Peter L. and Thomas Luckmann
  1967   *The Social Construction of Reality* (Garden City, New York: Doubleday).
Boggs, Stephen T. and Ann Peters
  1982   "Interactional Routines as Cultural Influences Upon Language Development." To appear in *Language Acquisition and Socialization Across Cultures*, edited by Elinor Ochs and Bambi B. Schieffelin.
Bruner, Jerome S.
  1978   "The Role of Dialogue in Language Acquisition." *The Child's Conception of Language*, edited by A. Sinclair, R. J. Jarvella and W. J. M. Levelt (New York: Springer-Verlag).
Cicourel, Aaron V.
  1970   "The Acquisition of Social Structure", *Understanding Everyday Life*, edited by Jack D. Douglas (Chicago: Aldine), 136 – 168.
Cook-Gumperz, Jenny
  1975   "The Child as Practical Reasoner", *Sociocultural Dimensions of Language Use*, edited by Mary Sanches and Ben G. Blount (New York: Academic Press), 137 – 161.

Douglas, Jack D.
   1970   *Understanding Everyday Life: Toward the Reconstruction of Sociological Knowledge* (Chicago: Aldine).
Firth, Raymond
   1961   *Elements of Social Organization* (Boston: Beacon Press).
   1964   *Essays on Social Organization and Values* (London: University of London, Athlone).
Geertz, Clifford
   1973   "Ethos, World View, and the Analysis of Sacred Symbols." In Clifford Geertz, *The Interpretation of Cultures* (New York: Basic Books).
Gegeo, David W. and Karen Ann Watson-Gegeo
   1983 a   "Kwara'ae Mothers and Infants: Changing Family Practices in Health, Work, and Childrearing", Association of Social Anthropologist in Oceania Meeting, 9 — 13 March, New Harmony, Indiana.
   1983 b   "*Fa'amanata'anga*: Family Teaching and Counseling in West Kwara'ae", Conference on Talk and Social Inference: 'Straightening Out' Contexts in Pacific Cultures, 14 — 18 October, Pfitzer College.
Gumperz, John J.
   1982   *Discourse Strategies* (Cambridge: Cambridge University Press).
Hymes, Dell
   1974   *Foundations in Sociolinguistics: An Ethnographic Approach* (Philadelphia: University of Pennsylvania Press).
Ochs, Elinor and Bambi B. Schieffelin
   1984   "Language Acquisition and Socialization: Three Developmental Stories and Their Implications", *Culture Theory: Essays in Mind, Self, and Emotion*, edited by Richard A. Shweder and Robert LeVine (Cambridge: Cambridge University Press).
Peters, Ann
   1982   *The Units of Language Acquisition*, Cambridge Series of Monographs and Texts in Applied Psycholinguistics (Cambridge: Cambridge University Press).
Rabinow, P. and W. M. Sullivan (eds.)
   1979   *Interpretive Social Sciences: A Reader* (Berkeley: University of California Press).
Ricoeur, Paul
   1979   "The Model of the Text: Meaningful Action Considered as a Text", *Interpretive Social Sciences: A Reader*, edited by P. Rabinow and W. M. Sullivan (Berkeley: University of California Press).

Schon, David
1979   "Generative Metaphor: A Perspective on Problem-Solving in
        Social Policy", *Metaphor and Thought*, edited by Andrew Or-
        tony (Cambridge: Cambridge University Press).
Schütz, Alfred
1973   *Collected Papers I, The Problem of Social Reality*, edited by
        Maurice Natanson, 4th ed. (The Hague: Martinus Nijhoff).
Speier, Matthew
1970   "The Everyday World of the Child", *Understanding Everyday
        Life*, edited by Jack D. Douglas (Chicago: Aldine), 188 – 217.
Taylor, Charles
1979   "Interpretation and the Sciences of Man", *Interpretive Social
        Sciences: A Reader*, edited by P. Rabinow and W. M. Sullivan
        (Berkeley: University of California Press).
Watson-Gegeo, Karen Ann and David W. Gegeo
1982   "Calling Out and Repeating: Two Key Routines in Kwara'ae
        Children's Language Acquisition." To appear in abbreviated
        form in Elinor Ochs and Bambi B. Schieffelin (eds.), *Language
        Acquisition and Socialization Across Cultures*.

The Social Construction of the Sibling Relationship

Yvonne Schütze, Kurt Kreppner and Sibylle Paulsen

1. Introduction

It is remarkable that socialization research tends to analyze relationships between the child and its environment mainly by dealing with the absence of these relationships. Investigation of the mother-child dyad, for example, started by analyzing the effects of maternal deprivation. Research on the father-child relationship started about a decade ago with the analysis of father-absence. And now investigation of the sibling relationship is starting at a time when, at least in Western industrial societies, fewer and fewer sibling-relationships can be found. The reason for this, of course, is the general tendency to decrease the size of the so-called 'nuclear family', reducing the sibling group to two, three, or at the most, four children.

The influence of siblings on socialization, then, has rarely been considered in research so far. Until recently scientific interest in sibling relationships has been low — with the exception of a few pioneering works such as that by Dunn and Kendrick (Dunn and Kendrick, 1979, 1982 a, 1982 b; Kendrick and Dunn, 1980; Abramovitch et al., 1979; Pepler et al., 1981; Bank and Kahn, 1982). This assessment is not contradicted by the broad tradition of birth order research in which various human qualities are investigated to find out whether they are more likely to be found in older, middle or youngest children (Jones, 1933; Krout, 1939; Irish, 1964; Sutton-Smith and Rosenberg, 1970; Zajonc et al., 1979; Fröhlich, 1981). The genuine interest of this research lies in its contribution to the nature-nurture debate: "Since birth order was considered an environmental variable, systematic variance of diseases, character traits, specific abilities, etc. with birth order should at least prove a high degree of environmental determination" (Fröhlich 1981: 197). Although thousands of studies have been made, the results remain controversial and inconsistent. "No simple and unambigous correlations between birth order and psycho-social variables could be proved in the course of 121 years of birth order research" (Fröhlich 1981: 226). Birth order research in fact does not deal with sibling-relationships at all, in that is it ignores child-to-child interaction in the family system and simply examines the impact of birth order on individual development.

Neither is the tradition of research into siblings as competing for maternal affection pertinent to our interests here (Sewall, 1930; Levy, 1938; Legg et al., 1974). This research tends to presuppose that competition between siblings is the only determinant of sibling relationships. This seems to result from the general emphasis on the mother-child dyad that prevailed until a few years ago. Only if this dyad is understood as the only relevant relationship formed by the pre-school child does it appear plausible to treat sibling-relationships merely as a dependent variable of the mother-child relation.

Among the first to criticize this one-sided perspective on the sibling-relationship were Dunn and Kendrick (1982 a). The subtitle of their study, "Sibling, Love, Envy, and Understanding," indicates that they take into account the positive aspects of sibling-relationships as well. Our own study on "Early Childhood Socialization within the Family" was done before the work by Dunn and Kendrick was published, and it emerges that both projects developed similar kinds of questions. The questions on which we focused are:

1. How is the second child integrated into the family?
2. How is the sibling-relationship established?

In this paper I will deal only with the second question. Below is a brief description of the design of the project.

Sixteen families from different social backgrounds were observed for two years. Our observations began just after the birth of the second child. The older child was in no case more than 3 1/2 years old. In regular intervals — every 14 days for the first three months, then once a month — data on everyday situations in the family were collected by means of video recording. Data were complemented by three extended non-structured biographical interviews with the parents, at the beginning of the investigation, after nine months, and at the end of the field work. Furthermore, protocols were made after each visit with the family dealing mainly with the content of conversations with parents outside of video observation. We developed a fairly close relationship with the families, as is demonstrated by the fact that no family dropped out of the study. This seems quite remarkable in view of the experience of other longitudinal studies. When we returned to the families after one year for additional observation, we were welcomed; the families even indicated that they expected us to follow their development further.

2. Method

We proceeded without explicitly formulating hypotheses and without using standardized instruments. Even hardboiled advocates of quantitative methods would presumably accept such a procedure in this case, with available knowledge about the establishment of sibling relationships more or less limited to commonsense understanding, somewhat refined by socialization theory, and to scattered evidence from psychoanalytic literature consisting of histories of patients' childhood. Under these conditions a longitudinal study using the method of participant, non-standardized observation seemed appropriate. Nevertheless there are dangers involved in using a methodology of case studies without first formulating hypotheses. In the end, one may have interesting case histories and a huge amount of data but no generalizable characteristics which can be taken as rules governing the social actions observed.

When analyzing our cases we tried to avoid this danger by constantly making comparisons both within and between the families. Two goals were achieved by these studies: Specific cases were reconstructed over time, and typical problems that confront families when passing from a one-child family to a two-child family were elaborated. Comparisons between the cases enable us to go beyond the individual case and to identify general patterns of family interaction and problem solving strategies generated by the new two-child constellation.

3. Theoretical background

One goal of this project was to integrate theoretical approaches of socialization theory, systems theory, and human ethology. Such an integration seems appropriate in view of the specific limits of these approaches. Socialization theory focuses on the generation of the child's individual competencies through the mother-child relationship or on the specific aspects or factors such as social strata, or gender. Until now, socialization theory has not dealt explicitly with family dynamics, that is, with interactions between the various members of the family. And it definitly has not dealt with the social world of the child outside that of the parents.

Systems theory approaches do relate the formation of the child's personality to specific modes in which structural problems are solved within the family. They are not, however, concerned with the structural changes which follow from those biological und psycho-social developments in the child that transform the process of interaction within normal families. Systems theory of the family has derived its categories from the reconstruction of pathogenic family systems and has put much emphasis on balancing mechanisms for the sustaining of homeostasis and stability of the system. Until recent years the theory has conceived of transformations only as a means of passing from one state of homeostasis to another, without giving any importance to the process of transformation itself. It is only in human ethology that the effects of changes in the activity of the child are taken into consideration, i. e., the child's ability to actively interfere with the socializing interactions of the parents. Ethological approaches assume an inborn mechanism which generates interactions, such as those seen in the mother-child relationship. Until now research in the field has concentrated on the mother-child dyad.

We share the assumption of systems theory that the socialization process consists of solutions to structural problems which confront every family system. Furthermore, we assume that within a family system each member has a specific relationship to every other member. These assumptions constitute a general theoretical background to our question: First, what are the differences in the constellation of a family after the birth of its first child as compared to differences in the constellation after the birth of its second child? Second, what resources of the family system exist to fill in the missing relationship between the first and the second child?

In terms of systems theory, the answers to these questions would be as follows: The arrival of the first child induces a disequilibrium in the system which exists between the spouses. The exclusive affective relationship between the spouses is restricted because part of the capacity and time for interaction that thus far had been devoted exclusively to the partner are now absorbed by a third person. The child can either be a separating factor for the marriage or can newly integrate it. According to Georg Simmel the specific qualities of the marriage determine which effect the advent of the child will have upon the marriage.

> "Therefore, cold, intrinsically alienated spouses do not wish a child: it might unify them; and this unifying function would contrast more effectively, but less desirably, with the parents' overwhelming estrangement. Yet sometimes it is precisely the very passionate and intimate husband and wife who do not wish a child: it would separate them; the metaphysical oneness into which they want to fuse alone with one another would be taken out of their hands and would confront them as a distinct, third element, a physical unit, that mediates between them. But to those who seek immediate unity, mediation must appear as separation. Although a bridge connects two banks, it also makes the distance between them measurable; and where mediation is superfluous, it is worse than superfluous." (Simmel 1958: 128).

The child in a way represents the living outcome of the affective relationship of the couple and both parents feel a shared responsibility no matter how the tasks of education and care may be distributed between them in reality. The spouses get to know each other in a new way which may bring some conflicts: for both parents the child reactivates their relation to their families of origin. Spouses do not only consider each other as adults but also as representatives of maternal or paternal behavior continued or discontinued from their own childhood.

The constellation is quite different after the birth of the second child. The relationship with which the child interferes is no longer one of two adults of the opposite sex but instead, a triad. The exclusiveness of the relationship between the spouses was abolished by the arrival of the first child and has been replaced by a new exclusiveness, namely that of the triadic relationship between father-mother and their only child. This exclusiveness is again destroyed by the addition of a second child. It should be noted, however, that the second child should be a factor of reinforcement for the marriage since it will eventually lead to a differentiation of the family system into a parent-system and a children-system.

Though the arrival of the second child considerably increases the amount of work for the parents, it does not imply a major emotional change within the parent system. The emotional change in this case is demanded from the first child. He/she has to relinquish the position of being the only child and adapt to the position of being the elder child. Parents are faced with the complex situation of how to distribute attention and affection in a manner which is fair to the respective developmental levels of the children. A specific individuated relationship has to be continued with the first child and established for the first time with the second child. At the same time it must be conveyed to the elder child that he/she now must frequently stand back. The child also feels an ambiguity because, although the parents still intimate the beloved child, he/she must often be considerate and realize his/her signals are not and cannot be responded to as before. Between the parents, the distribution of domains and tasks needs to be renegotiated. Because of this increased burden on the couple and decreased possibilities to interact exclusively with one another, there is a danger for the marital subsystem to be absorbed into the parental system, a situation which would in the long run eliminate the basis for the marital relationship. At first glance, a distribution of tasks seems possible in which each parent primarily relates with one child either in permanent coalition or in a changing one. In the long run however, such a distribution would be dysfunctional for the total family system. It tends to suspend the marital system and to counteract the emergence of the sibling relationship. The only possibility of avoiding unilateral dyads that prevent differentiation of generational roles and to close the gap which exists in the system is to actively establish the sibling relationship. This establishment or social construction of the sibling relationship is achieved through an interesting mechanism. Parents behave counterfactually 'as if' a relationship between the first and the second child already existed. In other words, parents behave according to the theorem of W. J. Thomas: "If men define situations as real, they are real in their consequences." This is the same well known mechanism that operates in the interaction with an infant. Parents behave *as if* the child were already capable of language and social action. This counterfactual behavior of the parents does not imply that they believe the infant can understand what is said. By the same token, the parents behaving as if a sibling relationship already existed does not imply that they are blind to the difficulties of the first child.

It is possible to connect the theoretical construct of counterfactual behavior within the domain of family interaction to the broader perspective of social interaction theories, in particular Goffman's (1963) concept of phantom normalcy. This concept was developed as a paradigm to describe the interaction with stigmatized persons and was later extended to the analysis of everyday life. Goffman's construct implies that partners in interaction do realize the gap between normative expectations and reality but nevertheless act as if normative claims were fulfilled. The construct applies to the parent-child interaction as well. In this case the fiction of the sibling relationship must not go so far that it is taken literally by the parents or the older child.

The mechanism of the fictitious sibling relationship is a rule of socialization interaction which the parents follow but which they are not able to explicate by themselves. When this construct is explained to them, however, parents accept it as self-evident.

Our further hypothesis is that transition from the triad to the tetrad (that is, from the one-child family to the two-child family) is achieved when the fictitious sibling relationship becomes a reality. Analyzing our data we found this fictitious sibling relationship in some families but not in others. There is some counterevidence in those cases where there seems to be a need for the family system to prevent the establishment of an autonomous sibling relationship. Furthermore, one can assume that differences in the strategies parents use to establish the sibling relationship correlate with differences in the family structure and that these differences influence the course of the sibling relationship later on. Finally, we need to find indicators which identify the transition from the fictitious to a real sibling relationship.

Our preliminary results show that transition takes place in three phases during the first two years of the second child's life. The changes are characterized by advances in the individual development of the second child. In the first phase, the main problem is establishing contact between the children and introducing the elder child to its new position as the older one. Apparently the first phase represents a kind of "honeymoon" in the story of the sibling relationship. Never again is there so much positive behavior towards the younger child, and never again so little negative behavior. This idyll is probably due to two factors: First, the baby evokes attention and curiosity rather than feelings of rivalry. Second, mediating strategies of the parents primarily remain addressed to the older child, and his responses to the baby receive positive responses from the parents. Thus the positive behavior towards the baby mainly results from the parents' behavior. The second phase is characterized as the one in which real rivalry between the children arises. The change that induces conflict is the beginning of the independent movement of the second child around his/her 8th or 9th month. The second child is now able to actively interfere with the first child's sphere. In addition the parents are delighted with the second child's development and invest much more attention in him/her. At the same time they frequently warn the older child to have regard for the toddler and they no longer integrate the older child so closely into their interactions with the younger one. The three main activities of the first phase, feeding, bathing, and pampering, cease to take so much time. The typical scene is now the following: Mother and father are sitting on the floor playing with the second child, while the first child is somewhat left out and tries to get involved with their play.

The third phase begins when the younger child achieves active mastery of language between his/her 16th and 18th month. It can now talk to the elder sibling and thereby create new qualities of interaction.

The behavior of the parents changes strikingly. They seem no longer to consider it a major obligation to mediate between the children. Rather they leave it more and more to the children themselves to organize and manage their play and conflicts. The growing potential for conflicts between the children may be interpreted as an indication of a dynamic development of the sibling-relationship, which is relatively independent of the parental system.

4. How parents establish contact between the siblings

The following are three short scenes from our material which demonstrate different interaction strategies of parents to establish contact between the children. These three scenes are taken from the first video recording in each family.

Example 1
Family H.
Older Child: Christa, 2 years

Younger child: Thomas, 18 days
M to C: It's a baby rattle, isn't it? It's for Thomas, but you can also play with it. I guess.
After a while, while the mother is putting Christa's shoes on, Thomas begins to cry in the background.
M to C, who is still holding the rattle in her hand: You'll give this to Thomas afterwards, won't you?
Mother and Christa go to the kitchen where Christa gets her bottle. Then mother goes to Thomas and takes him out of the cradle.
M to T in a soft voice: Come there now, come.
Christa sitting some distance away on a bench, says: They're both coming.
Mother goes to Christa with the baby and shows her her little brother.
M: Good morning, look he's still asleep, good morning.
Christa holds the rattle out to Thomas.
M: He can't take it yet, no, can't take it yet at all. Shall we give him something to eat first, okay? Yes — I think so.
Mother sits down with Thomas on the parents' bed and starts nursing him. Christa sits on the floor at the other end of the bed.
M to C: Come over here a little — come on.
Christa climbs into the bed and comes close to mother and Thomas. She again holds the rattle out to the baby, murmuring something incomprehensible in a friendly tone.
M: Yes, that's for Thomas. But he's still a bit too little. He can't hold things yet. Give it to him. But he can't hold it yet, no my bunny.

Interpretation

When Christa plays with the rattle mother says *but it's a baby rattle* indicating that it is no longer a toy adequate for Christa's age level. With her next remark, she makes it clear that the rattle is a toy for the little brother and therefore Christa should not claim to possess it. After pointing this out she adds *but you may also play with it.* That is, although it is a baby rattle and belongs to Thomas, she may still play with it. Her final *I guess* may indicate that the mother considers her own behavior somewhat inconsistent, i. e. on the one hand pointing out property relations but on the other letting Christa play with the rattle, thus cancelling her own intention. It may be possible to paraphrase *I guess* as follows: At least property relations have been pointed out to Christa, and that is enough for the beginning. With her question as to whether Christa will give the rattle to the brother later, the mother prepares the handing over of the toy, although she knows that the brother will not be able to take nor hold the rattle. In this way the mother draws Christa's attention to the little brother.

As soon as the mother has taken Thomas out of the cradle she carries him to her daughter, integrating Christa into the interaction with the baby which now begins. The twofold *good morning* not only serves to welcome the baby but also to make it seem *as if* one child welcomed the other. She acts, so to speak, as different persons feigning a welcome ceremony between the children. Christa reacts by presenting the rattle to the baby, just as the mother had recommended a while ago. Here reality contradicts the fiction. Thomas cannot yet take the rattle. The mother has extended the fiction too far by asking Christa to give the rattle to the baby. Her proposal must necessarily fail. The mother manages the situation by introducing a new stimulus. She asks her daughter: *Shall we first give him something to eat*, pretending that it would also be Christa's decision to feed the brother and further pretending that they are now both taking care of him.

As with the proposal to give the rattle to the baby, the mother with this question also goes beyond what can be realized. What would happen if Christa answered *no*? The mother would, of course, feed the baby, leaving Christa with the feeling of being cheated. Christa, however, focuses not on the content level but on the metacommunicative aspects of the message of her mother; she is not being excluded when the baby is breastfed. When she is welcomed by her mother to sit nearby, she immediately tries again to give him the rattle. The mother confirms Christa's good intentions and again gives reasons why he cannot yet take the rattle. The following *give it to him* is contradictory to the reasons just given for his not yet being able to grasp. This is another example of the difficulty the mother has in assessing how far she can extend the fiction of a possible interaction between the children. One could also say that in mediating between the two children, the mother only takes into account the interaction capabilities of the first child and exaggerates the capabilities of the second child to such a degree that she repeatedly has to correct her own statements.

Example 2
Family K.
Older child: Anna 2½ years
Younger child: Sabine 14 days old

Sabine is lying on the floor, the mother is sitting some distance away on the sofa. The father and Anna are standing close to the baby. Anna is squeaking a toy cow at Sabine.

F: Exactly

M: She's listening now, hm?

F: She's listening now, see? See?

M: She's thinking: what's that, I've heard that noise before.

A: (turning to mother) She says 'what's that'.

M: She thinks 'what's that', she doesn't say it, but that's what she thinks perhaps. (laughing)

(Anna turns again to Sabine, continues squeaking)

A: Sabine peeping. (taking Sabine's hand)

Interpretation:

The father reinforces Anna's action, she is doing it "exactly" right. The mother interprets Sabine's perception: she is listening. She thus establishes a connection between the children. Sabine is listening to the noises Anna is producing. As far as Sabine's abilities are concerned it would not be justified to assume that she is really listening, i. e., intentionally hearing. The point is not, however, whether the mother indeed assumes that Sabine is listening. The point is rather that the mother acts as if intentional behavior on the part of Sabine were possible, thus making her a social partner for Anna. The father confirms his wife's assumption, emphasizing for Anna Sabine's ability to listen. The repeated *see* implies: "here you see it, I always knew what Sabine is already able to do". At the same time this encourages Anna to pay attention to Sabine's reactions.

The mother then goes one step further (from listening to thinking), thus extending Sabine's abilities. That Sabine is assumed to be thinking "What's that, I heard that noise before" implies that she had listened to Anna's squeaking before. This implies that Sabine has already reacted to Anna in the past, which in turn means that virtually from her first day on Sabine is considered a competent member of the family. At the same time the mother tries to make the baby attractive as a partner — for Anna — in that a child which is able to think and to remember may also be more attractive to interact with. Anna completely follows the proposal of her mother to consider Sabine as a child already capable of interaction. She even goes beyond her mother's remark and imputes to Anna the ability to speak.

The mother corrects this imputation, leading back to reality: *can't say it yet*. The mother anticipates the possibility of Anna's expectations being too high and brings them back to reality. By laughing, she indicates how much she is amused that Anna can be convinced of the fiction of Sabine's ability to react.

Anna feels reinforced and goes on squeaking: She is now herself stating Sabine's reactions: *Sabine peeping*. Anna now has the possibility of accepting the relatively passive baby as a virtual partner of interaction:

Example 3
Family D.
Older child: Julia, 2 years
Younger child: Oliver, 4 weeks old
Mother is sitting on the parent's bed and nursing Oliver.
M to Oliver: Not very hungry, hm, are you? (looking at him, long and attentively)
Julia is playing with toy blocks beside the bed. Then she climbs up and seizes her mother's legs saying: I come here.
M: Why don't you get your Oliver, too? Don't you want to get your Oliver, too?
Julia climbs from the bed immediately and runs out of the room. Mother is laughing quietly. After a short while Julia returns, saying:
J: My Oliver isn't there.
M: What, that's impossible, where could he have gone then?
J: (continuing her play with the toy blocks) Run away.
Now Mother and Julia talk about whether a teddybear can walk at all and to where he might have gone. After this dialogue Julia is playing quietly for a while, close to her mother. She only begins talking again when Mother talks to the baby.
M: Look, look, hello? Still tired?
J: (approaches the bed again) Perhaps he is in my car.
M: Who? Who is in your car?
J: Perhaps Oliver is in my car.
M: Hm, good, then have a look.

Interpretation:

It is Julia who starts interaction with the mother as she is busy with the baby. *I come here* indicates: "I am also here", "I want to be included". In this sequence it is not the mother who integrates the older child, but the child herself who demands participation in the mother-baby dyad. Mother reacts to Julia's announcement by proposing: *Why don't you get your Oliver, too*. Julia's Oliver is a teddybear, whose name used to be *Pooh Bear*, but after the birth of the little brother he has been renamed *Oliver* and has been cared for like a baby by Julia, in imitation of her mother's behavior.

By advising Julia to get her own Oliver, the mother declines to interact with Julia as mother and child. At the same time, she is constructing a constellation in which the daughter can identify with the mother as they do something together ("We mothers are breastfeeding our babies"). The relationship to the brother is not constructed through pointing Julia directly to her "dear little brother" but rather through the symbolic Oliver-teddy interaction. Julia is to anticipate the sister-brother relationship by playing with her teddybear. She accepts her mother's advice and leaves to look for her Oliver. The search does not last long, however, and she returns announcing that her Oliver is not there. Julia leaves the level of common activity proposed by her mother, and now acts again as a child, implicitly expecting and demanding that her mother help her look for the things lost. Normally the mother would comply with this expectation. In this case, however, her asking back indicates that she is not prepared to start searching now. At the same time she introduces the following dialogue, implying that Oliver-Teddy is a living being. She does not ask "Where could he be?" but instead *Where could he have gone?*

Julia understands the meaning of the question correctly and accepts the proposed game, answering, *run away*. During the following conversation about where the teddy could have gone, the mother does not pay any attention to the baby. When Julia starts again to play with her blocks, the mother uses this opportunity to turn to Oliver again. Putting him to her other breast she tenderly addresses him: *Look, look, hello, still tired?*

This interaction of mother and Oliver induces Julia to enter the scene again. The teddy, *her* Oliver, comes to her mind again. Besides wanting to be assured that her mother will react to her, it is also possible that she wants to interrupt her mother's dialogue with Oliver. Whether or not it was really her intention, she does, in fact, interrupt the dialogue by asking a question and hence demanding an answer. Her comment *Perhaps he is in my car* implies that the mother of course knows who is meant by *he*. Julia continues the interrupted dialogue at the point of 'looking after teddy'. The mother, in turn, by her question *Who is in your car?* indicates either that the conversation she has just had with Julia was not very important to her, that she had already forgotten it (which is not very likely), or that she is now so much involved in the interaction with Oliver that she did not pay attention to Julia's remark. Her own asking back only is a minimally required response to Julia. Julia patiently explains to her mother whom she is talking about: *Perhaps Oliver is in my car.*

In each of the scenes presented here, the parents achieve their goal of enhancing the relationship between the children, either by trying to make the elder child understand what the younger is supposed to feel and think (examples one and two) or by showing her how to deal with a baby (example three).

Dunn and Kendrick made similar observations, namely that some "mothers who encouraged their first children to take joint responsibility and who discussed the baby as a person, were more likely to have children whom they reported to be particularly inter-ested in and affectionate toward the baby" (Dunn and Kendrick 1982: 73). We have been unable to find such a correlation. This is probably due to two reasons. The first reason is that parental strategies for bringing about contact between the children depend on the age difference. We have in our sample four pairings with a rather low age difference (eleven to sixteen months). In these cases parents do not try to explain the subjective constitution of the baby to the elder child, who cannot yet speak him/herself. They confine themselves to coordinating the clumpsy approaches of the child to the baby and to stimulating acts such as touching, caressing, etc.

The second reason is that the communicative strategies of the mothers, although they converge in informing the elder child about the baby as a person, also differ in important aspects. This may be relevant for the kind of attitude the child develops toward the baby.

In the first case, the mother predominantly focuses on the older child. In trying to make the baby attractive for the older child, she constantly takes the fiction of a relationship too far, and then, faced with actual or potential failure, she must withdraw her own demands and statements.

In contrast, in the second case, the parents account for the level of interaction of both children. Here, too, a capacity for interaction is feigned for the second child. The fiction does not however go so far that it will necessarily be wrecked by reality as in the first case. In this case a good balance exists between the anticipation of future development and an awareness of what is presently possible. In the third case, the fiction operates on a different level. Interaction is limited to two dyads, each consisting of the mother and one child. The mother addresses both children on their respective level of development. She does not directly try to establish a relationship between the siblings. Instead this relationship is initiated indirectly through a symbolic game. By dealing through a game with the fictitious teddy-brother, the daughter learns to deal with the real brother. At the same time her identification with the mother is reinforced.

In the interpretation of these scenes, one can see different strategies developed by parents to deal with *one* of the structural problems implied by the arrival of the second child: the problem of initiating contact between the children. Further progress in the development of the second child, for instance the ability to move independently or the acquisition of language, poses new tasks for the parents for which strategies have to be found. The analyses will have to show whether the different strategies of interaction are basically reproduced in later phases or whether these are beginning strategies which are later transformed through the course of time, perhaps due to the activities of the children themselves.

5. Conclusion

Methodologically, we wanted to demonstrate how hypotheses can be generated by going back and forth from the interpretation of data to theoretical preassumptions. We call this procedure "iterative heuristics". Hypotheses generated by this procedure (in this case the hypothesis that parents establish a relationship between the siblings by pretending it exists) may be tested in other everyday situations which are comparable to the one which led to the generation of the hypothesis. In doing this, the procedure can be compared to a series of natural experiments. In this respect we analyzed everyday interactions in the family in order to identify those strategies of communication which construct a relationship between the siblings and those which delay or prevent these relationships from forming.

References

Abramovitch, Rona, Corter, Carl and Sander, B.
   1979   "Sibling interaction in the home." *Child Development 50*, 997–1003.
Bank, Stephen P. and Kahn, Michael D.
   1982   *The Sibling Bond* (New York: Basic Books).
Dunn, Judy and Kendrick, Carol
   1979   "Interaction between young siblings in the context of family relationships." in Michael Lewis and Leonard A. Rosenblum (Eds.), *The child and its family*, (New York: Academic Press).
   1982 a   *Siblings: Love, Envy, and Understanding*. (Cambridge: Grant McIntyre).
   1982 b   "Siblings and their mothers: Developing relationships within the family". In Michael E. Lamb & Brian Sutton-Smith (Eds.), *Sibling relationships: Their nature and significance across life-span*, (Hillsdale: Lawrence Erlbaum), 39–60.
Ernst, Cécile and Angst, Jules
   1983   *Birth Order: Its Influence on Personality*. (New York: Springer).
Fröhlich, Gerhard
   1981   *Kumulativer Erkenntniszuwachs. Inkonsistenz empirischer Befunde und Barrieren der Wissenschaftlichen Kommunikation in der Geschwisterforschung*. Dissertation. (Wien)
Goffman, Erving
   1963   *Stigma. On the management of spoiled identity* (Englewood Cliffs: Prentice Hall).
Irish, Donald P.
   1964   "Sibling interaction: A neglected aspect in family life research." *Social Forces. 42*, 179–288.
Kendrick, Carol and Dunn, Judy
   1980   "Caring for a second baby: Effects on interaction between mother and firstborn." *Human Development, 16*, 303–311.
Krout, M. H.
   1939   "Typical behavior patterns in twenty-six ordinal positions." *Journal of Genetic Psychology, 5*, 3–30.
Lamb, Michael E. and Sutton-Smith, Brian
   1982   *Sibling Relationships* (Hillsdale: Lawrence Erlbaum).
Legg, Cecily, Sherick, Ivan and Wadland, William
   1974   "Reaction of preschool children to the birth of a sibling". *Child Psychiatry and Human Development. 5*, 3–39.
Pepler, Debra J., Abramovitch, Rona and Corter, Carl
   1981   "Sibling interaction in the home: A longitudinal study," *Child Development, 52*, 1344–1347.

Sewall, M.
    1930   "Two studies in sibling rivalry." *Smith College Studies in Social Work. 1*, 6–22.

Sutton-Smith, Brian and Rosenberg, Benjamin G.
    1970   *The Sibling* (New York)

Wolff, Kurt H. (Ed.)
    1956   *Essays on Sociology, Philosophy and Aesthetics by Georg Simmel* (Ohio: Columbus State University Press)

Zajonc, R. B., Markus, H and Markus, G. B.
    1979   "The birth order puzzle." *Journal of Personality and Social Psychology. 37*, 1325–1341.

Rules in Action: Orderly Features of Actions that Formulate Rules

Anthony J. Wootton

Those in charge of children are more than caretakers. As well as supervizing upkeep they claim a responsibility for turning children into acceptable moral beings. In English society that means such things as encouraging them to express gratitude, to speak the truth, to be polite; discouraging them from biting, fighting and the like. In other words children are exposed to a variety of prescriptive and proscriptive requirements which are designed to influence the course of their moral development. Empirical investigation of these issues sociologically has focussed on revealing intra and inter cultural differences in these respects, usually through the procedure of interviewing parents about their childrearing practices. Their examination *in vivo* has only occurred in more recent years, and has been largely spearheaded by psychologists and anthropologists, especially those interested in children's acquisition of linguistic routines (eg. Gleason and Weintraub, 1976; Greif and Gleason, 1980; Wilhite, 1983).

In section 1 of this article I present a number of limitations to the strategy of placing an explication of these prescriptions in the forefront of sociological analysis. These arguments derive from ethnomethodological work addressing the analysis of rules/norms in sociology more generally (Garfinkel, 1967; Cicourel, 1972; Wieder, 1974). They have the merit of suggesting alternative ways of analysing social requirements, and in section 2 I hope to illustrate what one such alternative analysis might look like, and what forms of systematicity it can reveal. In the light of this I go on to offer some brief remarks about the investigation of children's moral development in section 3.

1. Preliminary Considerations to the Analysis of Rules

1.1. The first problem with placing the explication of rules in the forefront of sociological analysis is that of deriving the rules from the occasions on which they appear to be used. This point can be introduced through an example (extract 1) in which the politeness of a request is at issue, a routine phenomenon which can occur in the homes of many, if not most, young children.

(1) Jo/Ch (3; 10)*
       Ch: ↑ Put on the li::ght
              (.9)
       M: Pa:rdon
              (.)
       Ch: Put on the light please
              (.)
       M: (Thats) better

The first point to stress about extract (1) is that the mother, in saying *(Thats) better* treats the child's initial turn, *Put on the light*, as deficient, as not meeting some standard. Parents do have available to them, then, forms of turn design which imply that there are standards. But from the fact that parents can act as if there are such standards/rules it does not follow that these standards/rules can be identified by an analyst, nor is it necessarily the case that parents have 'in mind' some describable standard when dealing in this way with their children's requests. These problems can be illustrated by an analysis I have carried out of all the requests occurring in the homes of four 4 year old children.[1] If we examine those cases in which parents are confronted with the absence of *please* from their children's requests a number of points emerge. Firstly, children rarely use *please* in the design of their requests — in under five per cent of all their requests — so parents are frequently confronted by its absence. Secondly, parents act so as to notice the absence of *please* (in cases like extract 1) very rarely — in a total of 517 requests (including imperative and declarative/I *want*/ requests) parents only acted in this way on eight occasions. On these grounds it would be difficult to claim that parents or children

---

* See the end of the article for transcript conventions.

are operating with a rule which requires *please* to be routinely introduced into the design of all children's requests. A more sensible tack might be to investigate the distinctive features of those requests in which children did incorporate *please* (spontaneously), and of those instances where parents in some way draw attention to their absence. One might then be in a position to say that under X conditions either parents or children employed *please* in their requests, and in so doing followed a describable rule. But neither other analysts nor ourselves have been able to locate what these conditions might be; on the face of it there is no obvious systematic difference between those few occasions where children use *please*, for example, compared with those where they do not.

Two points emerge from this discussion. Firstly, that parents (and children for that matter) have available to them ways of acting/ talking which treat the behavior of others as deficient, as not meeting some standard.[2] But, secondly, even in these cases, which are relatively clearcut, there are formidable difficulties in locating and claiming the rule like prescriptions which may underlie the set being considered. And similar issues are likely to arise in all domains of children's conduct where rules may be thought to exist.[3]

1.2. A second issue concerns how an analyst is to locate the rules that are to be studied. To propose a study of prescriptive rules in childhood is to imply a distinction between domains of conduct where such rules may be operative as compared with those where they are not. This 'flights and perchings'[4] model of social structure seems inappropriate however in that there appears to be no analytic basis on which to exclude *any* sphere of children's conduct as being potentially rule governed. There can be a right and wrong way of requesting, interrupting, eating, sitting, standing and playing. The list is *essentially* undefinite. There is no way, for example, of anticipating all those forms of behaviour which parents may, in certain circumstances, treat as deficient according to some standard. Even where rules *are* explicitly formulated by parents, far from articulating those general social rules anticipated by theorists such as Bernstein[5] they can address highly particular matters. For example, in extract (2) the mother's stress on Angela being careful where her feet are seems closely linked to her analysis of what has caused the specific just-prior accident in which Angela has fallen off the chair:

(2)   To/Angela (3; 10)
      M: (An') when you ↑ stand up on things Angela you must be
           (.)
      M: *Very* careful where your *feet* a:re

There seems then to be an essential indefiniteness not just about the character of rules, but where the analyst is to locate them and the forms of conduct to which they can be made relevant.

1.3. In the light of such considerations ethnomethodologists propose alternative ways of investigating the part that rules play in human conduct. They argue generally that instead of investigating human behavior with a view to extracting from it the nature of local social requirements, we can investigate how behaviour is organized so as to exhibit its accountability. Garfinkel writes:

> The policy is recommended that any social setting be viewed as self-organizing with respect to the intelligible character of its own appearances as either representations of or as evidences-of-a-social order. Any setting organizes its activities to make its properties as an organized environment of practical activities detectable, countable, recordable, reportable, tell-a-story-aboutable, analysable — in short, *accountable*. (1967: 33)

For him the sense that can be attached to any human behaviour, its accountability, arises from the way that conduct is organized, the details of its design.[6] So if we are interested in rules we can examine the *ways* in which people exhibit, in the design of their actions, recognitions and displays of rules. I use the term *ways* because it is evident that there are a large variety of action designs through which people can exhibit such displays.[7] For example, the procedures employed by the parent in extracts (1) and (2) both locate some failure on the part of the child, but their designs as forms of action are very different. A suggestive general account of such designs is given by Goffman (1971, Ch. 4), who describes techniques whereby people orient to offences they might give to others (e. g. through requests, apologies and the provision of reasons for action) as well as techniques used to redeem the self from potential defamation. More systematic empirical enquiry into the social organization of offences, blame, complaints and the like is to be found in the work of various conversation analysts (e. g. Sacks, 1969, 1971; Pomerantz, 1978; Atkinson and Drew, 1979, Ch. 4 — 5).

The logic of this approach suggests a shift away from treating rules as the topic of enquiry to treating rules as a resource that people can and do make use of in making action accountable. Given that there are a variety of ways that rules can be made use of, a variety of techniques through which people can exhibit some orientation to social requirements, these ways each require careful description with a view to identifying the kinds of action thereby being revealed. In this article an unusual way of exhibiting orientation to a rule will be investigated, cases like extract (2) where rules are explicitly invoked. These are unusual in that they occur very infrequently in the parent-child transcripts which constitute my main data resource.[8]

2. An Analysis of Rule Statements

2.1. In fact my data search yielded rule statements which seemed to have *two* distinctive forms of linguistic organization. Cases like extract (2) have a (conditional clause + main clause) structure, and in the main clause a course of action is recommended which is appropriate in the circumstances described in the conditional clause. These will be called *type B* rule statements, and two further examples are given below in extracts (3) and (4). In the context of parent-child talk these statements were only made by parents:

(3) Fo/Dh (4; 0)
    M: Well: when ↑ *you:* go on a swing ↓ you've gotta watch that its not anywhere near Richard before you start moving

(4) Ga/Ch (3; 10)
    M: If you do a job you've got to finish it properly by tidying up an' (.) seeing that things are (.) left neat and tidy

In what will be called *type A* rule statements the rule is simply announced. These were used by both parents, as in extract (5), and children, extract (6):

(5) Mu/Nicky (2; 0)
    M: ↑ Ni:↓cky ↑ (Y'know) you must only draw on paper
         (.5)
    M: *Only* on paper *not* on the doo:rwa:y

(6) Ma/Av (3; 10) Martin (about same age)
    Av: Yer no'allowed for *your* voice Martin

These two types of statement have interesting similarities and differences that will be discussed. One similarity is that they both occur in the environment of what can be called *untoward events*.

2.2. In some cases the prior occurrence of an untoward event is self-evident to all concerned. Prior to extract (2) Angela has been crying as a result of falling off a chair; prior to (3) recipient's younger brother has been hit on the head by recipient's swing. In other cases participants identify the untoward event in their immediately prior talk. For example:

```
(7)   Mu/Nicky (2;0)
  → M:   Did you do tha:t
              (.5)
  → Ch:  °Ye::(s)
              (.9)
  → M:   ↓ °A(hh)::::w °°dea:::r
              ⋮
    M:   ↑ Ni:↓cky ↑ (Y'know) you must only draw on paper
              (.5)
         Only on paper not on the doo:rway
```

But in further cases it is the rule statement itself which does the work of giving a prior event its untoward quality. In (8) Martin's prior *Hello* could clearly be identified as a greeting; it is Av's next utterance which makes it potentially inappropriate. And in (9), S's *We're not allowed to spit* performs a similar role in relation to the prior turn:

```
(8)   Ma/Av (3;10) Martin (about same age) ((Ma speaks close to the
      microphone on Av's back))
      Ma: Hello
      Av: Yer no'allowed for your voice Martin

(9)   9
      L:   Pew did you have a fright (('Pew' is a gunfiring sound))
      S:   No
      L:   Pew pew pew
      S:   We're not allowed to spit
```

Even in those cases where the prior untoward event is self-evident it is important to note that the rule statement contains a formulation of what actually happened. It embodies *a* version of what took place. For example, when a child falls off a chair the effective cause could be located in some property of the chair (e. g. wobblyness), some feature of the surroundings (e. g. she was pushed) or in a variety of failings on the part of the child (e. g. the chair was not placed close enough to that being reached). To say *(An')* *when you stand up on things Angela you must be (.) very careful where your feet are* is to propose a particular version of what happened, to constitute a version of the context to which that utterance is relevant.

2.3. A further feature that both types of rule statement share is that they locate recipient as *at fault* in some way. This is part of their business as interactional objects. In type A the turn is constructed so that an action which has occurred can be recognized as in breach of the rule now being stated. This is done by invoking a wider prescription of proscription which recognizably covers a prior action of recipient(s). In (8) the proscription is wider in that it could cover other vocal contributions than *Hello*; in (9) the proscription *We're not allowed to spit* is constructed as a general requirement binding not only on L but also, at least, on A; in (7) the prescription locates the place where drawing should be done in contrast with an indefinite set of other places where it should not be done; and in (10) the prescription requires the boys to stay the other side of the line not just when the ball comes towards them, but at *all times*:

(10) ((Stated by a man over a loud speaker to spectators at a cricket match. Some small boys had just picked up the ball after it had been hit towards the edge of the field by a batsman, but before it had crossed the formal line which would have merited the award of four runs to the batsman.))
   A: It is most important boys that you stay the other side of the fence at all times

Indeed it is the wider way in which the prescription/proscription is constructed which contributes to the rule-like quality of these statements, which makes them different from statements like 'You mustn't do that' or 'You shouldn't have done that'. In type As what has happened is overtly treated as just an instance of a wider set of non-allowable actions.

In type B fault is constructed differently. These turns index what has occurred by giving an action description which *indirectly* describes what *recipient* was doing. In (11) with *when you go on a swing* (not, for example, 'when children are swinging' or 'when Richard's near the swing' or 'when you went on that swing'); in

(12) with *(An') when you stand up on things*; in (13) with *If you do a job*. These descriptions index the state of affairs which obtained at the time of the untoward event, and permit the rule to be heard as concerning those affairs, but they are not constructed as actual descriptions of those affairs. In these reconstructed contexts courses of action are recommended. In (11) ... *you've gotta watch that its not anywhere near Richard before you start moving*; in (12) ... *you must be (.) very careful where your feet are*; in (13) ... *you've got to finish it properly by tidying up* etc.

(11) Fo/Ch (4; 0)
    M: Well: When ↑ *you:* go'on'a swing ↓ you've gotta watch that its
        not anywhere near Richard before you start moving

(12) To/Angela (3; 10)
    M: (An') when you ↑ stand up on things Angela you must be
        (.)
    M: *very* careful where your *feet* a:re

(13) Ga/Andrew (3; 10)
    M: Andrew pick up these pieces of paper
          :
    Ch: (Will) s:omebody please he:lp me
        ⌐(.)
    M: °No:w
        (5.3)
    Ch: (   )
        (.)
    M: What would happen if everytime mummy did something
        (.7)
    M: She didn't want to tidy up an' she 'ad to shout ↑ 'Will somebody
        please come and help me'
        (1.8)
    M: Mm::
        (1.2)
→ M: If you do a job you've go to finish it properly by tidying up an'
→   (.) seeing that things are (.) left neat and tidy

These courses of action are recognizable ways through which the untoward event which has taken place (in 11 and 12), and which may still be taking place (in 13), can be avoided. They are precautions for avoiding those undesirable outcomes. In the case of (11) and (12) these turns treat what has occurred as avoidable if recipient had acted otherwise. By implication recipient is held responsible, and at fault, in that s/he did not take the requisite precautions. In (13) the course of action being recommended stands as a description either of that which the child has not done, or is not doing. Through not meeting this requirement the child's past or present behaviour is treated as at fault.

Both type A and type B rule statements, then, propose their recipients to be at fault. And their recipients can exhibit recognitions of this by then formulating a defence of that which is treated as faulty. In (14) L, in disclaiming that he is spitting *at* S, proposes that her application of the rule to his prior action is inappropriate. In (15) the child invokes circumstances which prevented her from taking the precautions that the mother, *by implication*, has stated that she should have taken:

(14) S: We're not allowed to spit
→ L: pew pew I'm not spitting on S (   ) pew pew
   S: Here we go round the table ((this is sung))

(15) Fo/Ch (4; 0)
   M: Well: When ↑ *you:* go on a swing you've gotta watch that its not anywhere near Richard before you start moving
→ Ch: ·hh Ah'bt' I wanted te'go
        (.)
→ Ch: Quick
   M: It doesn't matter he's been crying ever since an' I cant get my hai:r done

2.4. Although defences *can* be constructed to these rule statements it also seems to be the case that they are not required in this position. Where they are absent, for example, they are never then solicited by the rule stater. And even where defences are provided, as in (14) and (15), the rule stater does not then enter into negotiations about what took place. In (14) S switches topic and begins singing; in (15) the mother brushes the child's defence aside and focusses on the misfortunes for *her* that have followed on the untoward event.[10] The official business of these rule statements is not to initiate forensic enquiry into what took place. Quite the reverse. These statements are overtly designed as instruction like informings. In this way they treat recipients as here and now inadequately aware of the precepts they articulate. In doing this

they indirectly proffer an explanation of recipient's role in the
occurrence of the untoward event itself. Recipients' action or inac-
tion arose out of inadequate awareness of the precept now being
articulated. But the official business of these turns is with the present
and the future, with making recipient now aware of the requirement,
and ensuring that the untoward event does not recur.

What is important, and consistent with this account of these
turns, is what does *not* take place after them as much as what does.
Parents can attend to the occurrence of untoward events in a whole
variety of ways. They can enquire into what took place, re-describe
its gravity, make overt moral evaluation of the offender and so on
(see, for example, extract 22). Such matters are not generally pursued subsequent to these rule statements; the latter, in effect, have
the capacity to treat what has occurred as over and done with.
Where matters are pursued they are specifically touched off by the
way in which recipient treats the rule statement. In (16), for example,
the mother is clearly unhappy with Nicky's demeanour after she
has spoken to him, and this leads to further re-statements of the
rule. In (17) Martin says *Hello* again in response to Av's first rule
statement, thus presenting Av with a further similar action with
which to deal, and which will be discussed more fully later:

(16) Mu/Nicky (2; 0)
    M: ↑ Ni:↓cky ↑ (Y'know) you must only draw on paper
         (.5)
    M: *Only* on paper *not* on the doo:rwa:y
         (.5)
    M: ↑ Ni:↓cky(h)::
         (.)
    N: Yea(hh)::
    M: ↑ Thats not funny
    N: ·hhh °Yeah
         ⋮
    M: ↑ But you mustn't
         (.)
    M: Drawing must *only* go on paper

(17) Ma/Av (3; 10) Martin (about same age)
    Ma: Hello
    Av: Yer *no*'allowed for *your* voice Martin
    Ma: └Hello:
    Av: Yer ↑ *no*'allowed for *your* voice only *my*: voice

These rule statements therefore formulate a particular version of the prior event, locate recipient as at fault and locate that fault as arising out of inadequate awareness of the precept being articulated. But they do this indirectly, and through being constructed as instructions/informings they represent a move away from the particulars of the prior untoward incident, and permit the whole matter to be dropped, there and then. The only action they require from their recipients is some evidence of them 'taking in' that which they have just been told;[11] then the discussion can perfectly well terminate. In (18) the topic is dropped after the mother solicits some minimal confirmation of what she has said (*Mustn't ye*), and the production of the endearment term *tattie*, through which some sympathy (at last!) is expressed to the victim; in (19) the teacher simply continues with her original topic after a brief pause subsequent to the rule statement — *(.5) but the snow's all gone now ....*:

(18) To/Ch (3; 10)
    M: Now are ye allright
    Ch: No:::(hh)= ((voice still quavering))
    M: =(An') when you ↑ stand up on things Angela you must be
                          (.)
    M.   *Very* careful where your *feet* a:re=
    Younger Ch: =(   )=
    M: = Mustnt ye:
                          (1.7)
    M: Tattie

(19) [12] (T = teacher; children aged about 6)
    T: Thats right yes good boy there was too much snow on the ground and a:ll the schools were closed because the children (couldnt go)
    Several children: (   )
    T: Em: (.) *please* if you want to say something remember to put your hand up (.5) but the snows's all gone now hasn't it Mia (.) what's happened to it

And it is this potential to terminate the speaker's concern with what has occurred, as well as to initiate it, which technically fits this type of turn to the business of doing something entirely self-contained like the loud speaker announcement that occured in extract (10).

2.5. The argument about these turns so far has glossed over an important aspect which will now be mentioned and illustrated, but which the discussion here will not do full justice to. This concerns their sequential placement. Rule statements can be placed in a variety of positions in those sequences where an untoward event is discussed. And *where* they are positioned contributes significantly to how they can be treated by recipients. This does not undercut the main line of argument above, but it does complicate it in important ways, and these complications will be illustrated in a discussion of two sequences which both contain what I've called type A rule statements, and which are reproduced in full below:

(20) Ma/Av (3;10) Martin (about same age) ((Ma speaks close to the microphone on Av's back))

```
Ma: Hello
Av: Yer no'allowed for your voice Mar⌈tin
Ma:                                    ⌊Hello:
Av: Yer ↑ no'allowed for your voice only my: voice
         (1.0)
?:    (        ) ((obscured by other children's talk))
```

(21) Mu/Nicky (2;0) David (4;2)

```
 1   M:   Who di'tha:t
 2          (.)
 3   D:   °Nicky
 4          (1.4)
 5   M:   ↑ Nicky:
 6          (.8)
 7   M:   ↑ Did you do tha:t
 8          (1.5)
 9   M:   Did you do tha:t
10          (.5)
11   N:   °Ye::(s)
12          (.9)
13   M:   ↓ °A(hh)::::w °°dea:::r
14          (.)
15   N:   Ye:s
16          (.)
17   M:   ↑ Ni:↓cky(hh): =
18   N:   =(        ) =
19   D:   ↑ (No:) Nicky did i' right up t'there =
20   N:   (                        there)
21   M:   ↑ Ni:↓cky(hh)::
```

```
22              (.)
23    M:    ↑ Ni:↓cky ↑ (Y'know) you must only draw on paper
24              (.5)
25    M:    Only on paper not on the doo:rwa:y
26              (.5)
27    M:    ↑ Ni:↓cky(h)::
28              (.)
29    N:    Yea(hh)::
30    M:    ↑ Thats not funny
```

By differential positioning of rule statements I am referring to the
fact that in (20), for example, Avril's initial *Yer no'allowed for your
voice Martin* is placed immediately subsequent to that which is
treated as the untoward event, Martin's *Hello*. Whereas in (21) M's
Nicky (Y'know) you must only draw on paper occurs subsequent to
other discussion of the untoward event.

In (20) Avril's initial turn is a selection from a set of alternative
action designs which might be usable in dealing with an untoward
event. She might have said such things as — 'You shouldn't have
done that', 'If you do that again I'll ...', 'Stop it' and so on. The
identification of members of the set is really a matter for extensive
empirical enquiry as to which turn constructions Avril, and other
children of her age, can and do employ in such a position. As yet
that has not been undertaken.[13] On the face of it, though, one can
say, on the basis of analysis done in sections (1 – 4) above, that in
choosing to employ a rule statement she is choosing to treat what
has occurred as of less significance than she might have. She avoids
making direct reference to what has occurred and indirectly proffers
an account for Martin's action which treats him as unaware, when
he committed the offence, of that which he is now being informed
of. And the reduced significance being attached to what has happened may constitute an environment where less risk is involved in
the production of a challenge, which the *Hello* in Martin's second
turn will be construed as. The response to this second turn by Av
is most interesting. Although Martin's second *Hello* could be treated
as a challenge, Avril instead chooses to treat Martin as having
inadequately monitored her first statement. She repeats her first
statement, though includes an additional clarifying phrase (*only my
voice*) which also treats her own prior turn as potentially in need
of repair, and thus Martin's action (*Hello*) as possibly arising out
of its inexplicitness. The crucial point here though is that in her

second turn Avril can be identified by Martin as transparently choosing to deal with his second *Hello* in one way rather than another. That his second *Hello* is a deliberate challenge to Avril's first turn is a reading available to both of them; and Martin has a basis, of course, for knowing that it is available to Avril. What is available to Martin then is that Avril, in treating his second *Hello* as arising from an inadequate grasp of her first statement, is choosing not to treat his second *Hello* as a challenge. In this sense there are important differences between Avril's first and second rule statements; most notably the sequential position of the second makes it a *transparent* choice between *certain* alternatives in a way that was not true of the first.[14]

In extract (21) the rule statement at lines 23–25 occurs only after prior discussion of the matter between Nicky, his mother and his elder brother David. At lines 7–11 an admission of responsibility is obtained from Nicky; the gravity of what has happened is exhibited (line 13); there may then be some attempt by Nicky to shift or mitigate the offence judging by David's turn at line 19. Subsequent to that the rule statement is produced by the mother. Although systematic analysis of such sequences has not been completed, inspection of other materials suggests that such prior handling of what has happened by a parent can project that the child is at least to be morally censured for what has occurred. In extract (22), for example, similar initial treatment of an offence (i. e., drawing attention to what has been done, heightening its gravity) leads to overt moral evaluation by the parent — *Oh ye bad boy:*.

(22) Ma/Av (3; 10) Al (1; 6)

```
    M:   ↑ Oh ↑ A::la:::n look at yer (.) ca::t sui:t
              (.)
    M:   ·hhhhhh ↓ Oh::::: (hh)A::la:n
              (4.5)
    M:   °°Look what he's done Avri,l
    M:                          └°°Ah::
              (.6)
    Av:  °∮No:=
    M:   =°∮Oh ∮∮(hh)A:la:n tha:ts one of your ↑ne::w ones
              (1.0)
    M:   Oh ye ba::d bo:y how did ye do *tha::t*
              (1.0)
    Al:  Nw ba:: ((vowels transcribed phonetically))
    M:   You *a:re ba::d*
```

The preliminary sequence in extract (21) may not just project such a possibility. It could be argued that certain parental turns either permit or look for some vocal or non-verbal display of penitence on Nicky's part. Such a display would seem, for example, to be a fitted response to the address terms at lines 17 and 21. If all this is true then the parent's use of the rule statement at lines 23 — 25 marks a shift towards a more lenient position on the part of M from that which was projected in the earlier part of the sequence. Although Nicky is still being treated as at fault, in treating him as inadequately aware of the rule the parent is not treating Nicky as wilfully committing an act for which he should have known better. It is a shift that can be received with a sense of relief by the child rather than one of foreboding: it is only *after* the rule statement that from our audio material we have any suggestion of the child acting in a manner construable as not taking the matter seriously — i. e. in M's turn *That's not funny* at line 30. Again then the character of the rule statement needs considering in the light of those other forms of action which could have been positioned there in the sequence: in an important sense what that action *does* hinges on which set of actions it is a selection from, and that set is an analysable product of the sequence as it has developed up to that point.

3. Rules and Moral Development

So far in this chapter I have advanced various reasons as to why there may be analytic advantages in choosing to investigate the manner in which people invoke rules rather than attempt some explication of the content of rules. To demonstrate this form of analysis I chose to examine a manner of invoking rules which occurs infrequently, namely cases in which rules are explicitly stated. The analysis has suggested that such statements, although occurring in a variety of different contexts, organize the flow of events in interaction in similar ways. If we take due consideration of their sequential positioning it seems likely that powerful pragmatic generalizations will be possible concerning this technique of invoking rules, and that detailed investigation of other techniques of orienting to rules is also likely to demonstrate that they embody distinctive interactional practices.

Finally I shall make some brief remarks on how the approach and analysis that has been reported bears on the general issue of children's moral development. The major research tradition represented in the writings of Kohlberg (1976), Damon (1977), Turiel (1983) and others has investigated social rules by raising questions about children's *knowledge* of those rules. Their aim has been to discover developmental changes in the character of this knowledge by showing, for example, how children at different ages have different conceptions of the purpose of rules, their scope and how they originate. In particular they have been concerned with whether developmental changes in such respects are uniform across all types of rule or whether children from an early age make distinctions between, say, conventional rules (e. g., table manners) and moral rules (e. g., stealing). The investigative techniques have primarily, though not exclusively (Much and Schweder, 1978), involved questioning children — asking them, for example, to talk about the rights and wrongs of particular hypothetical instances. In their actual dealings with other people, however, children are not just in the business of acquiring and displaying knowledge of rules, they are participants continually involved in the production and comprehension of illocutionary acts. And children have an emerging repertoire of such actions for dealing with occasions where misdeeds have arisen or may arise. One such action, for example, that children aged four can employ (see extract 20) is what I have called a type A rule statement, but there are obviously many others — warnings, prohibitions, requests, reportings and so on. In turn, one can ask developmental questions about the organization of these actions in relation to misdeeds; about the order of emergence of items in the repertoire, about the way that different items co-occur as strategies within particular sequences and about the different types of relationship thereby being revealed. And, of course, one can explore whether and when children employ these action designs in the way that adults do. To investigate such matters we need to employ research techniques which can do justice to the complexity of ongoing interaction processes, but which at the same time offer findings which are both rigorous and revealing with regard to competences that children share. Although this article has not been primarily concerned with children's practices I hope to have illustrated how the type of conversation analysis that has derived from ethnomethodology suggests such a domain of enquiry, and offers promising techniques with which to explore that domain. Such research into children's moral practices is potentially a distinct field of study, though it would also seem likely to play an important part in any ontogenetic account of the emergence of children's knowledge about rules. But, for the reasons I outlined in section 1 of this article, careful analysis of children's practices may also be more rewarding given the difficulties, especially in the early years of children's lives, attached to locating in any de-contextualized way the rules that parents and children are supposed to have knowledge of.

Notes

Versions of this paper have been given to the British Sociological Association Language Study Group at the University of Lancaster, England, in June 1982; and to the Department of Sociology at the University of Lodz, Poland, in October 1983. I am grateful to Peter French and Roger Peskett for their useful comments on an earlier draft. The research was originally funded by the Foundation for Child Development.

1. These transcripts are based on audio recordings made in children's homes with the aid of a radio microphone system in Aberdeen, Scotland, during late 1969 — early 1970. Twenty first born four year olds were recorded, half of the children being selected from working class homes (with semi-skilled fathers) and half from middle class homes (with professional and managerial fathers). Approximately 10 hours of recording were made in each child's home.
2. Collett (1977, especially p. 20) makes very similar points in his useful discussion of rules.
3. Take, for example, children's giving of thanks of being given a gift, recently studied by Grief and Gleason (1980). There is an important conventional connection between gift giving and appreciation. But it seems wrong headed to ask the question 'What is the nature of the prescriptive rule being operated here?' Grief and Gleason found that on being given a gift by an experimenter children infrequently said *thank you* spontaneously, and that where they did not roughly half of their parents prompted them to say this. Would we then want to say that those parents who prompted their children were operating with a different interpretation of this rule, and, if so, how could we explicate in a general (i. e. not specific to this event) and rigorous way the nature of these differential interpetations?

4. A phrase used in this way by Garfinkel, though quite where I am not sure.
5. Bernstein (e. g. 1971, Ch. 8) predicted that in working class homes what he calls 'positional' statements would be more frequently articulated. In these statements, for example, children's actions would be treated as inappropriate by parents invoking "norms which inhere in a particular or universal status" (157), e. g. 'little boys don't do that'. For related empirical enquiry see Cook-Gumperz (1973) and Turner (1973). Note how in every instance of overt rule formulations cited later in the article there is never reference to a universal category of people. The only possible exception is extract (10), though here I take *boys* crucially not to refer to all boys in the crowd, let alone boys even more generally, but to those boys who have just committed the offence, and others (not necessarily boys) who may consider doing likewise.
6. For a clear secondary account of Garfinkel's work which also addresses various criticisms, and comments on some of the differences between his approach and that of Cicourel, see O'Keefe (1979): the most authoritative secondary account of Garfinkel's work is now Heritage (1984).
7. In general terms Garfinkel identifies rules as being used by members of a society to justify and legitimate prior courses of action. Other non-ethnomethodological writers have argued in similar vein. Oakeshott, for example, writes that "The abstract character of a moral practice identified as a system of rules and their like is revealed in that idiom of *ex post facto* persuasive discourse which is designed to relate actions performed to a moral practice; namely, the engagement to 'justify' a performance" (1975: 68).
8. Except where indicated the extracts are derived from the data base outlined in note 1 above. I should emphasize that all the data with which I am dealing is audio only. At several points the limitations of this will become clear. I have examined about three quarters of this material with a view to locating rule statements, which is approximately 150 hours of recordings. Only two clear cases have been omitted, not because they undercut the line of argument, but because their inclusion would make the discussion unwieldy. Those cases in the text therefore constitute the large majority of such instances in my transcripts. The relative absence of these types of statement from recordings in other settings where one would expect them to occur is also striking (e. g., courts, institutions for juvenile offenders, psychiatric hospitals).
9. I would like to thank Jenny Cook-Gumperz for permission to use this extract. I rely on her transcription here.
10. This is especially striking in (15) as in her defence the child provides the mother with material which could be used, for example, as a basis for treating the child as at least reckless. At worst the child may be

implying that she placed her own concern to go quick before her concern with her brother's safety. As a 'defence' therefore it is weak as it could be construed as bringing into question the more charitable version of what happened implied in the mother's prior rule statement. I'd expect that in some such sequence such a defence *could* lead the rule stater to revize the approach they are taking to the incident, i. e., not to take it so lightly. In itself that would not undercut the argument so long as such a move by the rule stater was constructed as a *revision* of the position projected by their rule statement. Currently I do not have such a case though.

11. For this reason the examination of the social organization of·demeanour and face-work in this sequential position would be most interesting. How children act so as to appear to be taking such a matter in has not been explored to my knowledge. Intuitively one suspects that older children could convey 'insolence' in this position by distancing themselves from the sequentially fitted behaviour.

12. I would like to thank Peter and Jane French for both, independently, drawing this example to my attention: I rely on their transcription.

13. Much work in conversation analysis has concerned the systematic choices that members of a society make between alternative action designs in particular sequential positions. See especially Schegloff, Jefferson and Sacks (1977), Pomerantz (1978, 1984), Wootton (1981). For more general overviews of such work, particularly that concerning 'preferences', see Levinson (1983, Ch. 6) and Heritage (forthcoming).

14. For a useful discussion of repeated offences which bears on this extract see Goffman, 1971, 201 − 2. Perhaps I should also mention, in case readers think otherwise, that no formal instructions were given by the researcher that other children were not to speak during the recordings!

Transcript Conventions

Underlining	— emphasis on that word
( )	— unsure transcription or words not transcribed
o/oo	— works spoken softly/very softly
⌐⌐	— pitch contours
↑ ↓	— at turn beginning marks an utterance at noticeably higher or lower pitch than is normal for that speaker: elsewhere marks sharp upward or downward pitch jumps
:::	— extension of the prior sound
(.)	— pause of under half a second

	— marks points of overlap in speech or speakers beginning their utterances simultaneously
(hh)	— audible outbreath
·hh	— audible inbreath
=	— no gap between speakers' turns
:	— part of that sequence omitted
(( ))	— further comments of the transcriber

These conventions were originally devized by Dr. Gail Jefferson.

Prior to each extract cited is an identification of the home in which it took place and the chronological age of children concerned. In extract (1), for example, Jo identifies a specific household, and the child's (Ch) chronological age is 3 years 10 months.

Bibliography

Atkinson, J. Max and Drew, Paul
    1979   *Order in court* (London: Macmillan).
Bernstein, Basil
    1971   *Class, codes and control* (London: Routledge).
Cicourel, Aaron V.
    1972   "Basic and normative rules in the negotiation of status and role", *Studies in social interaction*, edited by David Sudnow (New York: Free Press), 229–258.
Collett, Peter
    1977   "The rules of conduct", *Social rules and social behavior*, edited by Peter Collett (Oxford: Blackwell), 1–27.
Cook-Gumperz, Jenny
    1973   *Social control and socialization* (London: Routledge).
Damon, William
    1977   *The social world of the child* (San Francisco: Jossey-Bass).
Garfinkel, Harold
    1967   *Studies in ethnomethodology* (Englewood Cliffs: Prentice Hall).
Gleason, Jean Berko and Weintraub, Sandra
    1976   "The acquisition of routines in child language", *Language in Society* 5: 129–166.
Goffman, Erving
    1971   *Relations in public* (London: Penguin Books).

Greif, Esther Blank and Gleason, Jean Berko
  1980   "Hi, thanks and goodby: more routine information", *Language in Society* 9: 159—166.
Heritage, John
  1984   *Garfinkel and ethnomethodology* (Cambridge: Polity Press).
Heritage, John
  forthcoming "Recent developments in conversation analysis", *Sociolinguistics Newsletter*.
Kohlberg, Lawrence
  1976   "Moral stages and moralization", *Moral development and behaviour*, edited by Thomas Lickona (New York: Holt).
Levinson, Stephen C.
  1983   *Pragmatics* (Cambridge: Cambridge University Press).
Much, N. and Schweder, R. A.
  1978   "Speaking of rules: the analysis of culture in breach", *New directions for child development*, edited by William Damon (San Francisco: Jossey-Bass).
Oakeshott, Michael
  1975   *On human conduct* (Oxford: Oxford University Press).
O'Keefe, D. J.
  1979   "Ethnomethodology", *Journal for the Theory of Social Behaviour* 9: 187—219.
Pomerantz, Anita M.
  1975   *Second assessments: a study of some features of agreements/disagreements* Ph. D. dissertation (University of California, Irvine).
  1978   "Attributions of responsibility: blamings", *Sociology* 12: 115—121.
  1984   "Agreeing and disagreeing with assessments", *Structures of social action*, edited by J. Maxwell Atkinson and John C. Heritage (Cambridge: Cambridge University Press).
Sacks, Harvey
  1969—71 Unpublished lectures (transcribed and indexed by Gail Jefferson) University of California, Irvine.
Schegloff, Emanuel A., Jefferson, Gail and Sacks, Harvey
  1977   "The preference for self-correction in the organization of repair in conversation", *Language* 53: 361—82.
Turiel, Elliot
  1983   *The development of social knowledge* (Cambridge: Cambridge University Press).
Turner, G. J.
  1973   "Social class and children's language of control at age five and seven" *Class, codes and control*, Vol. 2, edited by Basil Bernstein (London: Routledge) 135—201.

Wieder, D. Lawrence
   1974   *Language and social reality: the use of telling the convict code*
            (The Hague: Mouton).
Wilhite, Margaret
   1983   "Children's acquisition of language routines: the end of meal
            routine in Cakchiquel", *Language in Society* 12: 47−64.
Wootton, Anthony J.
   1981   "The management of grantings and rejections by parents in
            request sequences", *Semiotica* 37: 59−89.

Nursery School and the Early Grades

The chapters in this section focus on children's social worlds, language and social cognition during the period from nursery school to the first grades in school. Although the chapters cover a diverse set of topics (which include the social representations, communicative skills and peer routines of nursery school children; the peer culture of deaf children; and fictitious play), they all share a common interest in discovering and documenting stable features of young children's perception of and strategies for participating in their social worlds.

In chapter 8 Shields and Duveen examine nursery school children's cognitive representations of common characteristics of persons and their typical roles and activities in the social world. Whereas previous research in this area primarily focused on children's understanding of *individual differences*, the aim of this research is to explore children's fundamental sociological conceptions regarding *general* features of the interpersonal world. Shields and Duveen stress that the understanding of similarities in the intersubjective field is a more fundamental achievement than that of individual differences, and that children from an early age have a clear grasp of the fact that the world is conceptually shared by all humans. The results of the study indicate that nursery school children have fairly realistic conceptions of persons and believe that all humans are endowed with basic capacities. The authors argue further that the wide-spread belief in children's animistic thinking is a mistaken interpretation of the frequent use of metaphor in children's speech, a phenomenon which according to Shields and Duveen is better explained as a cognitive strategy for assimilating new information to old conceptual categories.

Auwärter's paper (Chapter 9) supplements Shields and Duveen's findings. While Shields and Duveen show that children's fantasies are parasitic upon realistic conceptions of the social world, Auwärter investigates various linguistic means with which children (of 3 to 10 years) constitute fictitious play reality. Auwärter distinguishes nine "levels of reality" in his data, each of which is defined by the parameters "speaker identity" (everyday vs. role-play identity) and "reality claims of utterances" (about ordinary vs. fictitious reality). On the basis of a linguistic analysis of different markers used by children to situate their play-related utterances at the various levels, Auwärter argues that there is, over the years, an increase in utterances made *from within* the play-identity and a complementary decrease in "serious" frame-related comments. In addition, Auwärter finds that around the age of 5 − 6 years, children appear to enjoy the linguistic construction of play-frames more than their actual enactment.

Corsaro's article (Chapter 10) is an interesting sequel to the chapters of Shields and Duveen and Auwärter because it investigates the relationship between children's social representations and their developing interactive and communicative abilities by examining the structure and function of several basic routines in the peer culture of nursery school children in the U.S. and Italy. According to Corsaro an activity can be classified as a routine if it is communal, predictable and adaptable. Corsaro identifies and discusses several such routines which appeared consistently in peer interaction in the nursery schools he studied. In his discussion Corsaro demonstrates how these routines can be seen as a part of peer culture since they perform a range of social functions, all of which are generally related to the children's attempts to break down adult authority and their sharing of a sense of control over their everyday lifes. More generally Corsaro relates his findings to Moscovici's (1981) conception of social representations and his ideas regarding the basic processes of familiarization in everyday life. According to Corsaro, children, through their production of and participation in peer routines, are attempting to make the unfamiliar familiar. They are attempting to transform confusions and ambiguities from the adult world into the familiar and shared routines of peer culture. In this process, argues Corsaro, the children's peer world is always changed somewhat; it always becomes a bit different in that some social development has occurred.

In chapter 11 Coenen presents a phenomenological analysis of the peer world of deaf children. He begins with the question: how do, in deaf children's interaction, the many possible aspects of corporeal movement and sense perception intersect and hook into one another, so that meaningful structures come into being, get changed, fall to pieces, etc.? In addressing this question Coenen describes three types of incorporation: (1) how he was incorporated as a stranger into the children's worlds; (2) how children new to the school setting were incorporated into the group; and (3) how the children incorporated given tasks and imposed regulations of the school into their own peer world. Coenen's work is one of the very few naturalistic studies of peer interaction among deaf children, but it also adds to childhood socialization theory. The deaf children in Coenen's research, like hearing children in the papers by Auwärter and Corsaro, develop communicative skills and social knowledge through their practical actions in everyday events making up peer culture. Coenen argues that communication should not be viewed primarily in the verbal channel, but should be seen as activity of the body. And this activity should be taken in a broad sense: on the one hand it consists of a very wide range of expressive and perceptive aspects and forms, on the other hand it is not confined within the boundaries of the individual subject but rather is experienced as a common field in which a plurality of subjects is involved. The importance of communal sharing of experiences seems to be a central element of peer culture among preschool children (see Corsaro, this volume; 1985).

References

Corsaro, W.
   1985   *Friendship and Peer Culture in the Early Years.* (Noorwood, N. J.: Ablex).
Moscovici, S.
   1981   "On Social Representations." *Social Cognition,* edited by J. Forgas (London: Academic Press), 181 – 209.

The Young Child's Image of the Person and the Social World: Some Aspects of the Child's Representation of Persons

Maureen M. Shields and Gerard M. Duveen

This paper is a report of the first phase of an investigation into some of the child's representation of persons and their roles and activities in the social world. It arose from an interest in the pragmatics of human communication which are concerned with the presupposed inter-subjective material that makes communication possible. Because pragmatics deal with what everyone knows about and takes for granted, its material is apt to appear obvious and banal and, so, to have been neglected by developmental psychologists and psycholinguists in favour of the study of individual differences. Yet, the common and banal ... like the universal fact that unsupported bodies fall to the ground ... can often be worthy of study, and science appears to progress by revealing the strangeness of the obvious. It is precisely this common knowledge in individual minds that allows them to communicate by means of language, for without this common knowledge, linguistic reference and the co-ordination of human activities through talk would be impossible.

The acquisition of this common knowledge is an astonishing human achievement through which the child becomes a communicating member of human society and absorbs the taken-for-granted element of his culture and sub-culture. The amusing anecdotes which abound in the literature of how children get things wrong — any parent will have a store of these, — should not blind us to the fact that such errors are peripheral to an accumulating world image which is constantly being tested against the realities of experience and the exchange of communication. The work described here was aimed at exploring a small part of the 'taken-for-granted' knowledge of the young child about his fellow humans and some of their social roles. The investigation* was planned in two phases: the first, which

* This investigation was supported by a grant from the S.S.R.C. (U.K.).

is reported here, concentrates on aspects of the child's knowledge of human characteristics in general, i. e. some of the features which the child expects any human person to have. The second phase was aimed at eliciting some aspects of differentiating characteristics, roles, relations and transactions within the social world and their intersection with concepts of age, gender and skill. Some of the work on the second phase is reported in Shields and Duveen (1984 and forthcoming) and Duveen and Shields (1985 a).

1. Background

1.1. The importance of representation

Research on children's thinking has largely concentrated on their ability to tackle problems, usually of a mathematical or logical kind, but there is relatively little on their image of reality, especially their social reality which is built up from their experience and observation as members of a human community. Miller, Galanter and Pribram (1960), in a seminal work, pointed out the importance of the image of the world which underpins planning and action. Recent research on artificial intelligence (Schank and Abelson, 1977) has indicated that the elaborate logical processes of computers cannot operate everyday problems without the equivalent of such an image in the form of a scenario or script. This investigation is concerned with the kind of representation or image of a person which children may have, and the way this knowledge changes as they develop. It is focussed on the *content* of such representations, that is on the 'know that' aspect of representation, or declarative knowledge as it is sometimes called because of its alleged greater availability to propositional expression. Children, like adults, rapidly learn to cope practically with the situations in the material and social world in which they are immersed, but procedural 'know how' is more complex than 'know that' because it involves serial inference and serial planning and co-ordination of action. Such serial inference and planning is made easier by information reduction mechanisms, which yield handy stripped down categories which can be used to sort the familiar and isolate the unfamiliar for attention thus fitting our plans and activities appropriately to the personal and impersonal environment. These handy schemes and categories form the basis of our image or representation about the world and both arise from and facilitate our 'know how'. Jean Mandler has recently written an exhaustive review of the whole topic of representation. It is sobering to realise that while taxonomic categorisation and the representation of space all receive exhaustive coverage, the representation of people is absent except in the form of characters in a story (Mandler, 1983).

1.2. The development of representation

Most of the now very numerous studies of infant social development show how very early babies manifest some of the procedural skills of interpersonal reaction which appear to depend on the accumulating observation and tested prediction of the behaviour of others (Schaffer, 1977; Bullowa, 1979; Hubley and Trevarthen, 1980). The kind of representation constructed by the infant from this intimate and extensive experience, however, remains a matter of speculation.

Young babies appear to develop canonical expectations about the appearance and orientation of human faces (Fagan and Shepherd, 1979). Five or six-month old babies can distinguish male, female, child and adult faces (Fagan and Singer, 1979). Infants as young as four months have been found to differentiate between joy, anger and neutrality in facial displays (La Barbera et al., 1976). Later, at the toddler stage, there are studies which explore the child's representation of such common human characteristics as age and sex (Brooks and Lewis, 1979; Brooks-Gunn and Lewis, 1978; Lewis and Feiring, 1979). Studies of the mental and internal states of others usually begin at a later age, often six years, which marks the age when psychological subjects enter the school trap in the U.S.A. and become more available for investigation. Children's ideas on thinking have been studied by Miller and her colleagues (Miller et al., 1979) and by Johnson and Wellman (1982). There are also studies on memory (Kreutzer et al., 1975; Spee and Flavell, 1979), attention (Miller and Bigi, 1979). Camras (1980), Borke (1971) and Odom and Lemond (1972) have looked at children's identification of emotion from facial displays. Empathy and affect have inspired numerous studies in the Piagetian tradition, and now also have a considerable experimental background (Mussen and Eisenberg-Berg, 1977; Strayer, 1980).

There is, therefore, evidence that children have representation about various aspects of the human person, but there has so far been little attempt to map out this conceptual field as such. Is there any reason to suppose that children have a generalised representation of a human being which can be extracted from their considerable episodic and procedural knowledge? It seems probable that such a prominent, value-soaked phenomenon of the child's experience should rapidly produce an image which brings together the many recurring features of human beings manifested in encounters.

Nelson (1981) has suggested from her study of children's grasp of event scripts that the syntagmatic relations between events, between objects and between persons and objects and events in these scripts could give rise to paradigmatic relations as their occurrence in different episodes was noted.

In this way the child's original representations are based on procedural learning organised around enactive and interactive episodes, and this procedural knowledge gradually develops a system of mobile schemata which can be combined with other schemata arising from different episodes. If this is a likely description, then human beings must be the foremost candidates for early schematic representation because of their ubiquity in the child's experience of events. Moreover, the schemata concerning human beings are likely to become mobile, and therefore abstract at an early stage. In a somewhat similar vein Sinha suggests that knowledge about objects is modified by growing knowledge of relations between objects, and that this gradually prises them away from their embeddedness in canonical procedures (Sinha, 1982). If this is true about children's knowledge of cups and containers, which form the content of this research it must, a fortiori, be true of their representations of human persons who enter into many more relations with each other and with things.

Emerging categorical knowledge of the common features of persons will, in so far as it is generalised, accompany and structure the child's perception of persons as a tacit taken for granted substratum for the very varying roles and activities which she will observe them engaging in. This knowledge of common characteristics allows the child to attend to what is new or different in human behaviour. The framework of categorisation then becomes tacit, and drops below the level of immediate conscious attention unless it is challenged by some strikingly anomalous information.

However, it may be that categorical knowledge, or the kind of categorical knowledge usually investigated in studies of taxonomies of classification may be a less important and more task contingent form of representation than we have supposed. If the primary framework of human knowledge is of persons and the social world, then one element that must be present in it is the sequence of actions in time. As time is one way and open ended, there must be a strong element of contingency or potential in any categorisation of human beings. The kind of disembedded knowledge that goes with taxonomic classifications might be more useful in handling static elements of the environment, backgrounds, non-agents and manipulanda. When it comes to understanding human action and interaction, the time sequence of successive events demands an inferential chain, and episodic representation and event schemata might be more effective.

The work on the understanding of stories which is a new and burgeoning field of research shows that young children like adults use schematic models in their understanding of stories, and are able to bring these internal episodic representations to bear on sequentially organised material (Kintsch, 1977; Kintsch and Green 1978; Mandler and Deforest, 1979; Rumelhart, 1975, 1980).

If we look at representation through and by means of language there are certain features such as naming which seem to imply a sorting and labelling activity, and others such as predication which imply knowledge of events and processes. However, events and processes can be nominalised, and nominals can metamorphose into predicates so it would seem that human thinking can swing between a time tagged event representation and a static categorical representation as need demands.

The representation of persons would need storage of a 'manifestation', as Bobrow and Winograd (1977) call a group of descriptions belonging to an individual or a set of individuals. As human individuals as opposed to logical individuals live and act in time, at least part of these descriptions must consist of potentials and roles which link them to the episodes and events which form part of the stored representation of human social life.

2. Language and Representation

The exchange of meaning through language which is the backbone of social life is based upon the creation of a basic model of another person who resembles the message sender and shares a world with him or her.

It is a logical inference from the nature of the human communication that the child who is acquiring communication skills must be able to represent to herself what others can perceive, attend to or remember, for without this both the referring and predicating operations of communication would be impossible. It is also logically necessary that the child should be able to develop at least a rudimentary idea about other people's states, action potential and intentions, for without these, the child could not sustain reciprocal action with another person, or hope to modify their behaviour by means of language or adjust to reciprocal demands.

Developing this line of logical inference from interactional communication, M. Shields (1978) set out twelve constants which might be the skeletal basis of the child's construction of a person. These were: (1) identity over time, (2) self-motivation, (3) interpersonal recognition, (4) similarity of perception, (5) similarity of conceptual constructs, (6) intentionality, (7) similarity of emotional potential, (8) communicative abilities, (9) same and different action potentials, (10) predictability within context, (11) memory, (12) rule-observing behaviour.

This is, of course, a very abstract list of headings, and to operationalise such abstractions at the level of comprehension and experience of a three or four year old child is extremely difficult. Yet in their everyday interactions, children appear to assume continuous identity of parents, siblings, peers and familiar adults, give and expect interpersonal recognition, seem to assume that the world is perceptually shared, and that concepts of common objects are similar. Children apparently believe that persons will remember previous events and transactions, that they will initiate behaviour, and act in reciprocity in a way that can often be predicted from the context. Children are people watchers and close observers of the done thing which they assimilate and adapt to their own schemes of behaviour. They appear to absorb models of behaviour as procedural episodes and recreate them with variations rather than imitating them mechanically. Unfortunately the immense feat of learning which underlies the development of basic representation concerning human persons tends to be taken for granted, or recognised at the margin, i. e. where it is uncertain or ineffective, and our conceptions of children's minds are correspondingly impoverished.

3. Plan of Investigation

This investigation was designed to discover if some of the inferred elements of the child's representation of persons set out above also formed part of the declarative knowledge of young children, i. e. that part of their thinking which was available for inspection and capable of being verbalised.

Areas 1, 2, 4, 7, 8 and 11 were selected, and two more areas, that of the distinction between animate and inanimate objects and gender constancy were added. The areas were mapped onto a segmented questionnaire and were presented in the form of a play interview based on simple tasks in manipulating and making judgements about pictorial material. The pilotage took place in a large nursery centre and both investigators participated as auxiliaries in the children's rooms, read to and played with the children both indoors and out and talked to the children as individuals and in groups. The original plan of a paired interview of the target child and a chosen friend was abandoned, for although the children were more relaxed, the play and fantasy element in the children's behaviour also became more prominent and it was too difficult to maintain reality orientation for the necessary time, or rather the interviews would have had to be extremely prolonged to obtain the information sought. A didactic interview was therefore planned round four contextualising tasks.

Although the interview was based on a set of questions, topics introduced by the child were also developed so that the assymetry of the interview situation could be mitigated and a more normal interpersonal conversational flow maintained. The interview could easily be broken up into sections to allow for the powerful interest the younger children had in returning to their group, though the majority of the children interviewed were sufficiently interested in the investigator and the material to give up some of their time and even come back for more.

The Subjects

Subjects were children in the second half of their third, fourth and fifth year who were pupils in the nursery and reception classes of four London Schools. The sample was both teacher and selfselected and consisted only of children able and willing to participate. The age and sex distribution is given in Table 1:

Table 1 Age and Sex Distribution of Sample (Mean age in parentheses)

Age	Boys	Girls	Total
1. 3 years 6 months to 4 years	14	13	27
Mean Age (months)	(45)	(45)	(45)
2. 4 years 6 months to 5 years	14	17	31
Mean Age (months)	(56)	(55)	(55)
3. 5 years 6 months to 6 years	15	18	33
Mean Age (months)	(68)	(68)	(68)
Total	43	48	91

The topics covered in the interview are presented here in the following order but this does not represent the order in which they were presented to the children. (1) The distinction between persons and other animate and inanimate objects, (2) the sequence of human development, (3) the child's continuity of identity through development, (4) gender constancy, (5) sensory abilities, (6) basic skills, (7) emotions. The areas of autonomy and memory were also explored but will not be dealt with here.

4. The distinction between persons and animate and inanimate objects

In his early work Piaget (1929, 1930) argued that one characteristic of the young child's mode of thought, of his representation of the world, was a tendency towards animistic thinking. Piaget defined animistic beliefs as a "tendency to endow inanimate things with life and consciousness" (Piaget 1929: 132).

For many years following the publication of Piaget's work the debate which ensued concerned the question of whether or not such a tendency towards animism was actually present in the young child's thinking. More recently Gelman and Spelke (1981) have returned to this theme but set it in a new theoretical context. For them the issue concerns the development of cognition about animate and inanimate objects in so far as this related to a more general distinction between social and physical cognition. They are critical of Piaget's work on the grounds that his questioning concerned objects which were remote from the child's practical experience (the sun or the moon), that his questions were frequently anomalous in the sense of presenting difficulties even for adults to resolve satisfactorily (e. g. "does the sun know where it is moving?") and that his method required a degree of reflective thought which was difficult for young children.

The present study aimed to examine whether or not young children, given a straightforward task, do indeed believe that the world is comprised of objects which sense, feel, think or talk whether or not an adult would distinguish some objects as animate and others as inanimate.

Method

The experimenter showed the child a picture of a farmyard and asked the child to name the objects depicted. Particular attention was paid to four objects, the farmer, a cow, a tractor and a tree. The experimenter then showed the child smaller pictures of these four things and asked the child to identify which of these four could do certain things. The questions were as follows:

1. Which of these eats?
2. Which of them goes to sleep at night?
3. Which of them can move by itself?
4. Which of these can smell flowers?
5. Which of them can talk?
6. Which of them can feel angry, can feel sad or can feel happy?
7. Which of them can decide for themselves what they want to do next?

The child was asked to make a response to these questions for each of the four objects.

Results

The responses to these questions are shown in Table 2. The questions concerning eating, sleeping and smelling have been combined into a single category of biological functions; those concerning feeling angry and happy have been combined into a category of emotions.

The results are shown as percentages of positive responses to each question or group of questions in respect of each of the four things. Although the age groups have been separated the sexes have been combined:

From this table it is apparent that for each type of question the four objects are divided into two groups of two, the Man and the Cow attracting a great many positive responses while the Tree and the Tractor attract very few. This pattern was firmly established at each age level. It would seem therefore that this sample of young children did not show any very high degree of animistic beliefs in the sense of attributing animal functions to inappropriate objects. Even the youngest age group knew that a Tractor moved only through human agency. Indeed some of the youngest age group evidenced a great surprise at being asked to respond to such apparently obvious questions. Of the four objects it was the Cow which attracted the most varied responses as to whether or not it was capable of performing any of the functions. A large number of the children who said that the Cow could talk maintained that it talked with other cows, or with the farmer; there seemed to be a sense that communication was possible with the cow, and that this could be adequately denoted by the word 'talk'. In this sense the talking cow seemed to be an example of the child's linguistic problem in articulating a specific idea rather than an indication of any animistic belief.

Overall, therefore the results of this study are in agreement with the position of Gelman and Spelke (1981). Faced with the task of making a straightforward judgement these young children showed very little trace of animistic thinking, indeed their sense of the practical realities of which objects could perform which functions appeared to be as sophisticated as any adult's.

When however the children were asked to give reasons why the tree or the tractor could not do something, that is when they were asked to reflect on their knowledge of these objects, a number of them did in fact respond with animistic explanations. The tractor for instance didn't go to sleep "because it stays up", or the tree could "decide to make the wind blow". It may well be, therefore, that in speaking about the question of agency or in giving reasoned explanations for what appears to be common sense knowledge that the children had recourse to animistic thinking.

Table 2 The distinction between persons and other objects

| Questions | Age Groups | | | | | | | | | | | |
| | 3½ years | | | | 4½ years | | | | 5½ years | | | |
	Man	Cow	Tree	Tractor	Man	Cow	Tree	Tractor	Man	Cow	Tree	Tractor
1. Biological Functions	91	84	7	5	97	87	1	1	100	96	6	3
2. Moves by Itself	89	96	7	7	97	70	6	16	100	100	0	3
3. Talks	96	63	4	0	97	37	3	3	100	42	0	0
4. Emotions	96	51	4	4	96	43	3	1	98	70	1	0
5. Can Decide for Self	96	78	0	0	100	45	10	0	100	66	6	3

It may also be that the language available to them for answering such questions has a strong bias towards agency because of its foundation in human interaction, and that the interviewer by asking the question why a tractor or tree can't do something automatically switches in a discourse matching procedure and elicits animistic answers to what are in the child's view, given its naïveté about scientific causation, animistic questions.

5. The sequence of human development

The aim of this section of the investigation was to discover if young children had any conception of the fact that all human beings start as babies and grow into adults, that they are looked after by mothers when immature, and that the process of growth is irreversible. It was not intended to go deeply into the exchange of generations, or to discover children's view of biological parenthood, a subject which is heavily affected by cultural transmission (Goldman and Goldman, 1982). Children also have a very limited concept of kinship (Haviland and Clark, 1974; Duveen, 1974) and it was not proposed to enter into this area either.

Method

The interview was contextualised by the child being asked to sort into chronological order four or five photographs of a child growing up from babyhood. The great majority of the children were able to do this successfully. There was no difficulty in anchoring the beginning and end of the series though a minority of children hesitated about one or other of the middle group. The following questions were asked:

1. Were you a baby once?
2. Was the experimenter a baby once?
3. Were their teachers and head teachers once babies?
4. Was their mother once a baby?
5. Did their mother have a mother?
6. Was their father once a baby?
7. Did their father have a mother?
8. Was everyone a baby once?
9. Would they like to be a baby again?
10. Was it possible to become a baby again?

Results

Combining the answers to 2 and 3, 4 and 6 and 5 and 7 the results were expressed as percentage of affirmative answers (Table 3).

Table 3

	Children aged 3½ %	Children aged 4½ %	Children aged 5½ %
1. Child was baby once	92	96	100
2. Unrelated adults were babies	74	92	93
3. Parents were babies	62	92	95
4. Parents had parents	61	91	96
5. Everyone was a baby	70	90	100
6. Child would like to be baby again	22	58	39
7. Possible to be baby again	15	10	7

There were one or two children among the four or five year olds who were not sure about or denied either that one of their parents was a baby, or that their teacher or head teacher had been a baby, but on the whole the response conventionality was over 90%. The interesting deviants were the three year olds who were struggling to co-ordinate two different frames of representation. For young children babyhood is a socially inferior position carrying lower role status, and this is confirmed by frequent admonitions about being babyish or behavioural exhortations with the argument "you're a big boy/girl now". It is clearly difficult to combine the biological status of babyhood with the authority status of teacherhood and parenthood, and as the latter carried a heavier evaluative tag, it won out.

There was, however, a high consensus that return to babyhood was impossible ... without the help of magic:

L.5.7   Once I'm grown up, I'm grown up.

J.5.7   No, because you have to grow ... and then when you're really old, you often die.

D.4.8   No ... only by magic ... if I was a witch and I had a stick I could change.

Two of the most interesting interviews were with five year olds who initially maintained that neither their head teachers nor their parents had been babies, but on being asked whether everyone was once a baby, they then affirmed this and went back over their previous answers and revised them. This appears to have been an instance where the child realised the contradiction between what they had asserted previously, and the logic of the general proposition. Most of the four and five year olds attempted to cut this section short after question 2 by asserting that everyone was once a baby.

> S.4.7   Well a long, long, long, long, long time ago ... giants must have been babies once

These results seem to indicate that four and five year olds have an elementary life span perspective, but that for the three year olds and one or two four year olds there was inter-concept interference between biological development and social role.

6. The ability of the child to envisage personal continuity from babyhood

In the second part of this section of the interview, there were a group of questions aimed at eliciting whether the child had some idea of continuity between his or her present self and babyhood. The questions were:

1. Are your eyes the same eyes as when you were a baby? (repeat for ears, hand and mouth)
2. Could you talk when you were a baby? or did you have to learn?
3. What things can you do now that you couldn't do then?
4. Are you the same (child's name) as when you were a baby?
5. What is different about you now?

The questions were difficult to formulate because personal identity and historical identity are both extremely difficult concepts even for adults to handle. Because of the one way flow of time our past selves have ceased to exist except in so far as they are rolled up in our present selves as biography. This biography would be tenuous indeed if it depended solely on intra-mental recollection, but the developing or historical self is buttressed by the possibility of inter-subjective exchange of recollections, and one of the important roles of the family is to create and maintain a common biography.

Friends, acquaintances and even enemies help to keep our past selves alive for us. Diaries, photographs and other external evidences also play a role. How does a young child maintain autobiographical touch with his previous self? For this idea of personal historical continuity will be bound up with the concept of human lifespan, being born, growing up, adulthood and aging which is a substratum of our knowledge of persons and our relations to them.

Children have a recognition memory from very early in their lives and this allows them to make a start on ordering their experiences. Recall memory, however, is dependent upon the development of cognitively based expectations and the ability to make inferences which develops over time. The pilotage of the interview showed that children are very poor at recalling *extempore* any incident from their past unless it had been consolidated by family discourse into part of a family biography. The little girl who replied readily to the question whether she remembered anything that happened when she was a baby: *Yes, I had measles, mumps and chickenpox* was calling on such a constructed biography in which her specific memory of going to hospital had become embedded.

This difficulty with recall is also likely to have been a factor in the low ability to assign reasons for feeling cross, happy or sad which the younger children found when answering questions on Emotions, though there may also have been an element of repression in addition.

Another hazard was, of course, the formulation of questions which inevitably had to use the terms 'same' and 'different' with their ambiguity of reference. Sameness can refer to having the same identity, or having the same qualities, different can mean having a different identity, or maintaining identity but having qualitative differences. If the child was asked whether their eyes were the same and replied:

Cla:3.8   No ...I had ... I had ... black all the way round, I had black
          pupils ... black outside, and black everywhere in my eyes

did this constitute a reply which maintained identity by the use of 'I' and the past tense but noted qualitative difference? Strictly speaking discourse-wise, the use of the phrase *when 'you' were a baby* and the employment of 'I' by the child in return is an implicit assertion of identity.

However, as well as the tacit claim to identity underlying the use of 'I', most children asserted identity explicitly as well (Table 4).

Table 4

	Children aged 3½ %	Children aged 4½ %	Children aged 5½ %
1. Features the same	93	100	93
2. Size the main difference	52	58	27
3. Had to learn to talk	78	94	93
4. Greater skills and opportunities	51	50	52

As the questions referred to physical features it is hardly surprising that size was the first, and often the only mentioned variable, but it is likely that increase in size is also the main index of growth for most children. Only the five year olds, all of whom were in their first year of school, began to mention skills or opportunities in greater numbers as the first differentiating variable instead of size.

What are the achievements of growing up? At three, the children had to rack their minds, the question was a difficult one ... for what significant achievement could be chosen out of the diffuse sense of 'being grown up'? Small things were mentioned, mostly recent achievements such as not having to have help on a climbing frame, catching balls, drawing and painting ... or being able to play with knives. The four year olds had more reflective power and more means of comparison in the behaviour of toddling younger siblings:

    Abi: 4.11 ... when I was little I learned not to do pees in my pants
               and guess what ... when I was ... guess when I stopped
               doing pees in my pants.
    MMS: How old were you?
    Abi: When I was three!

The responses of the five year olds add little to those of the four year olds. Reading and writing began to enter the list of achievements and more sophisticated forms of drawing like drawing people. Accomplishments like riding a two wheeler and playing the piano appear and the opportunity to go out to play and to visit one's friends and neighbours by oneself were also mentioned. Girls have become more conscious of changes in appearance, and four or five mention differences in hair. The main response difference however, lies in the fact that being bigger forms a lower proportion of the initial responses of five year olds, and other differences begin to be more prominent.

To sum up this section, children affirm their continuity with their younger selves, but are not able to contrast themselves with earlier developmental stages except in respect of being bigger or growing up. This is an area which it might be worth exploring in depth with a more elaborate technique in order to probe for the parameters of children's concepts of developmental transformations.

7. Gender Constancy

In presenting his cognitive-developmental analysis of children's sex-role concepts Kohlberg (1966) argues that an understanding of the constancy of gender appears in young children around the age of 5 — 6 years. Prior to this age he notes that the child may be able to provide the correct label for his or her own gender by the age of three and over the succeeding two years comes to be able to label others. For Kohlberg the importance of gender identity is that it provides a "stable organizer of the child's psychosexual attitudes" (Kohlberg 1966: 95). This is only possible, however, when the child is categorically certain of the unchangeability of his or her gender identity. Whilst self-labelling and the labelling of others may be a necessary step in this direction it is not a sufficient criteria for the constancy of gender identity.

To test this, Kohlberg and later investigators (Marcus and Overton, 1978; Gouze, 1980) used photographs of children which could be transformed by conventional opposite sex overlays. If the child said that such overlays could affect a gender transformation, they were assigned to the group uncertain of gender. It is on the basis of responses to this task that Kohlberg argues that children younger than 5 — 6 years are not certain of the constancy of gender identity. It was only at this age that children refused to accept that the photographed girl could be a boy; at younger ages (4 years) most children said that she could be a boy if she wanted to or if she dressed appropriately.

Method

In part of the interview dealing with knowledge of sensory processes the child had been introduced to a figure drawing and asked to identify it as male or female. The figure had then been dressed appropriately, a dress for a girl and a jumper and jeans for a boy. At the conclusion of the questions on sensory processes and emotions the Experimenter drew the child's attention back to the figure and swapped its clothes for those of the opposite gender. The child was then asked the following questions:

1. Now I've changed this boy/girl's clothes does that turn him/her into a little girl/boy?
2. If you changed your clothes could you be a girl/boy?
3. When you grow up will you be a man or a woman?

If the child answered (2) by saying that he or she could become a member of the opposite sex, they were asked whether they really could or whether they could only play the opposite gender role as 'pretend'.

Results

The responses to these three questions are shown in Table 5, the responses for both sexes are combined since no appreciable differences between were found.

Table 5 Gender Constancy

	Age Groups		
	3½ years N 27	4½ years 31	5½ years 33
1. % responses that the sex of the figure could change	78	81	81
2. % responses that sex of self could not change	96	97	97
3. % responses that sex would remain unchanged when grown up	85	90	100

These results are clear and unambiguous, even the youngest children in the sample appear to have a stable concept of gender identity. Very few children (in point of fact only one child in each age group) thought that their own gender identity could be changed by a change of clothes, even though about 80% of children at every age thought that the gender of the figure could be changed by changing its clothes. Of those children who thought that the sex of the figure could not be changed some claimed to be able to identify some physical feature of the drawing which identified it as male or female (its eyes or its hair) whilst others who had originally identified the figure as a girl maintained that girls too could wear trousers. In respect of themselves many children thought that they could pretend to be the opposite sex, but their own gender identity appeared to them as an immutable given, a fact of life!

For the third question there was again an overwhelming majority of children at every age who maintained that their gender would not change as they grew up. The few children at the younger age levels who did not fall into this category claimed not to know what they would be when they grew up, they did not claim that they could grow up to be of the opposite gender.

These findings are then, in direct contradiction to Kohlberg's claim that an understanding of the constancy of gender identity only appears around the age of 5 – 6 years. Gouze (1980) also found that self gender was constant earlier than the gender of others, but she too used the figure and overlay techniques employed by Kohlberg.

In the present study even the youngest age group of 3½ year olds showed a clear understanding that gender identity is a stable and unchangeable characteristic. This investigation also strongly suggests that Kohlberg's results are an artifact of his method. He questioned children about a hypothetical transformation of a photographic representation of a girl. Yet as the responses to the figure drawing in this study showed these young children are aware of the difference between representation and reality. The gender identity of a drawing could be changed at will although their own gender identity remained constant. This difference was clearly articulated by many of the children interviewed; one girl in the middle age group for example simply said that although the drawing could change sex she herself could not "because I'm real". Even at these young ages, therefore, it appears that children are sophisticated manipulators of representation; it is only when the gender identity of real persons, themselves, is put in question that their sense of its constancy becomes apparent.

8. Sensory abilities

The fifth area to be probed in the interview was that of sensory abilities and equipment. It is clear from the development of language that there is a tacit assumption that the interlocutors share an experiential world, otherwise the operation of reference could not get off the ground. There is also an assumption that people can hear, or there would be no signal value in vocalisation. It was decided to concentrate on the two main distance receptors sight and hearing, with smell thrown in to see if the ambiguous transitivity of the word 'smell' combined with a less ubiquitous use of the sense of smell made any difference.

Our assumption that other people have the same sensory abilities as ourselves is so taken for granted that it is difficult to imagine being without this kind of representation. Yet it must also be a feat of learning, and a feat of a very special kind in which interactional intersubjectivity must play a vital role. Inferences about the sensations of others require a combined vision from an inner looking and an outward looking perception which can bring together within-person sensations and between-person activities to achieve that ego-projection and alter-introjection which allows us to equate our experiences with those of others. The fact that the concept of egocentricity has concentrated on the periphery of this achievement where too much commonality of perception and experience is assumed, should not blind us to the fact that this is a major feat of learning, and absolutely essential for almost all important cognitive achievements.

Method

The method adopted was to use a large, tinted, line drawing of a person of ambiguous age and sex, which had eyes, nose and ears missing, together with an identikit set of detachable features. The children were then asked what was wrong with the figure, and whether they could put it right, and as they attached the features to the face they were asked what each feature was for, whether it was needed for the function named and whether everybody could exercise that function. They were also asked what other uses there were for a nose to see if they were aware of alternative functions. The results are set out in Table 6.

Table 6 Sensory abilities

	Children aged 3½ %	Children aged 4½ %	Children aged 5½ %
1. Eyes are for seeing	96	100	100
2. Everybody can see	96	100	100
3. Exceptions mentioned	–	19	36
4. Ears are for hearing	89	97	98
5. Everybody can hear	89	94	94
6. Exceptions mentioned	–	16	27
7. A nose is for smelling	70	97	94
8. Other uses for nose	33	39	97

Sight is the most clearly represented of the sensory abilities, but hearing runs it fairly close. Smell is not a clear concept of the younger children who were not helped in their answers by the fact that many of them had runny noses. The younger children also showed response rigidity over alternative uses for the nose, as they did in the next section over alternative uses for the mouth. Having initially said that a nose was for blowing, or that ears were for cleaning, it might take several more exchanges before they produced an alternative use. Basically this may be evidence that procedurally organised knowledge which would place ears and nose in the context of frequent ministrations from caretakers, was taking precedence over conceptually organised knowledge, though the fact that they could in the end produce an answer in terms of function showed that the two systems of organising knowledge were running in parallel. There may also be a discourse effect in that the children, not being sure what their interlocutor had in mind, produced a perfectly good conversational response turn with interesting possibilities for development, and did not see any particular reason for altering it. The didactic question with a 'correct' response is only beginning to play a part in the lives of these preschoolers.

The four and five year olds, on the other hand, were more flexible and some of them showed awareness that there were blind and deaf people as exceptions to the universality of vision and hearing. The five and a half year old children were much more conscious of breathing as an alternative function for noses and the proud possessor of a rabbit added twitching.

9. Basic skills

Bipedal gait and the ability to talk are skills which, in combination, distinguish man from all other animals. Learning to walk and talk is also a distinguisher between babies and toddlers, and pretty familiar to young children who are nearly always acquainted with a range of such achievements in siblings or children of the families of friends. Do they also form part of the basic representation of a person? The questions in this section followed on the ones in the previous section, using the same figure and asking what its mouth was used for, and what it might do with its legs, whether everybody could walk and talk and whether it was possible to forget these skills. The results are set out in Table 7:

Table 7 Basic Skills

	Children aged 3½ %	Children aged 4½ %	Children aged 5½ %
1. The mouth is for talking	100	100	100
2. Other uses for mouth	33	77	88
3. Everyone can talk	100	97	100
4. Not possible to forget how to talk	88	97	100
5. Legs are for walking	100	97	100
6. Other uses for legs	44	32	48
7. Everyone can walk	85	94	100
8. Exceptions mentioned	–	6	15
9. Not possible to forget how to walk	74	87	94

There seems no doubt about walking and talking being part of the representative schema of a human being. Also that the older children did not think that these basic skills could be forgotten once learned. Again the problem of response rigidity was encountered with the younger children. If, for instance to the question about what mouths were used for the child answered 'eating', then this topic had to run into several exchanges about food before a second probe elicited 'talk'. Eating was not a topic which the young conversationalist would surrender lightly.

10. Emotions

For a long time the notion of early childhood egocentricity led to a masking of the child's understanding of other people's feelings. The young child's difficulties in role-taking tasks were adduced as evidence that he or she could not represent to themselves the internal states of another. A new interest in the subject has arisen from two strands of research, one connected with moral development which has looked at empathy as a necessary component in altruism (Hoffman, 1975, 1977, 1981; Feshbach, 1977; Bryant, 1982). A second line of study has been the identification and response to human emotion as shown in facial expression. Infants as young as four months have been noted as distinguishing between joy, anger and neutrality in facial displays (La Barbera et al., 1976). The focus of the present enquiry was slightly different. What it aimed at was some elucidation as to whether children made a general attribution of emotional potential to human beings or how far this was still embedded in specific interactional episodes.

Method

The same figure was used for this as for the questions on gender constancy and sensory abilities combined with three heads designed to overlay its existing head. Each head was designed to portray an emotion in a slightly exaggerated cartoon-like manner, either anger, happiness or sadness. The face portraying sadness had visible tears as well as the standard droop of mouth and eyebrows, and inclination of the head. There was a difference in procedure between two groups of children, 39 were asked to select a head named by the investigator as happy, sad or angry and put it on the figure (comprehension condition), and the other 52 were asked to name the expressions themselves before putting them on the model (production condition). Only two children did not succeed in choosing the labelled face under the comprehension condition, but under the production condition 38% of the three year olds, 37% of the four year olds and 32% of the five year olds labelled the cross face as sad. Similarly 83% of the threes, 81% of the fours and 38% of the fives labelled the sad face as 'crying' picking out the tears as the most significant index of emotion and using a term relating to the outward manifestation rather than the inner state. The happy face presented no problems. After the child had identified the emotions, she or he was asked whether they ever felt cross, whether their mother was ever cross, whether their teacher was ever cross, and to give suggested reasons in each case. They were then asked whether they thought everybody sometimes was cross. The same procedure was employed for happiness and sadness.

The responses are given in Table 8 in percentages counting 'crying' with sad as a correct identification of the sad face:

Table 8

	Cross			Happy			Sad		
	3½ %	4½ %	5½ %	3½ %	4½ %	5½ %	3½ %	4½ %	5½ %
1. Child identifies expression	51	54	84	100	100	100	100	90	100
2. Child feels emotion	48	90	78	100	96	96	40	61	75
3. Reason given	44	87	72	66	61	54	33	54	51
4. Mother feels emotion sometimes	74	90	100	92	93	100	22	38	69
5. Reason given	62	77	84	25	61	69	22	35	51
6. Teacher sometimes feels emotion	66	83	96	66	83	66	22	32	51
7. Reason given	48	67	84	62	54	24	11	29	39
8. Everyone sometimes feels emotion	62	96	90	74	96	100	66	83	96

These figures present problems. Some of these are no doubt due to defects in the methodology and clearly more work is needed to look closely at the child's representation of emotions. If taken at their face value the different proportions of the children prepared to answer as between the emotions are interesting. Happiness was the most certainly identified of the facial expressions and the state most frequently claimed for both child and mother, and to a lesser degree the teacher. Sadness was the least clearly attributable emotion and this may be because the younger children who were more structured by the crying expression were unlikely to have seen an adult shed tears. Furthermore, it was clear from the reasons for sadness that the younger children gave that these did not differ in any substantial way from the reasons given for feeling cross. The reasons for being happy were also very largely the converse or negative of the reasons given for feeling cross. Mothers and teachers got cross when the children were noisy, naughty, aggressive, and caused damage, mothers and teachers were happy when the children were not noisy, were good and didn't fight. The majority of reasons given were based on a presupposed rule governed interactional situation where the children's roles were specified in certain ways both to each other and towards the adults. If either party stepped out of the expected role behaviour, the breach caused temper or tears. Otherwise everybody was mostly usually or always happy. The children appeared to be operating with a two factor model of emotion steady state (happy) when interpersonal behaviour went as expected and upset state (cross or sad) when there was some breach of expected role. In the case of the older children, however, there was more personalisation and sophistication in some of the reasons given for happiness and sadness:

Lia: 5.6   My mummy cries sometimes ... my dad ran away and my baby was really dying
Zab: 5.11   My mum feels sad sometimes when her dad ... her dad died
Kri: 5.9   Last year I saw a lady who was sad because her boy friend left her
Sar: 5.10   (of her mother) She gets extremely happy when she goes to our other nanny's

The 'upset' state which seems to dominate the thinking of the younger children is giving way to a differentiated presentation where empathic understanding is beginning to acquire depth. This area was further investigated by Shields an Ireson (1985) and a lack of differentiation between negative emotions such as anger and sadness continued to be a feature of the thinking of four-year olds.

11. Discussion

This investigation covered a wide area, too wide to be explored in depth. It was, however, planned as a mapping exercise in the hope and expectation that a sketch plan of this fascinating field would encourage more profound investigation. What we hope we have clearly demonstrated is that young children under six have a sub-stantial understanding of some of the generalisable characteristics of human beings. They differentiate them from inanimate objects and plants, though they acknowledge some shared characteristics with animals. They know that people start as babies and then grow up, though the younger children cannot co-ordinate this concept with others concerning adult status and role. They know that the process of growth is irreversible. They are sure of their own gender and its constancy ... only magic could make one switch sex. They maintain biographical identity with their past selves. They endow all human beings with sight and hearing and the ability to walk and talk, and they do not think that the latter skills can be forgotten, though the older children are aware of injury and handicap. They also endow people with a capacity for emotion, but the difference between the younger children and the older children in the degree of differentiation of emotions is quite pronounced.

There were the odd few exceptions to this generally adult-like grasp of the human state, but the high scoring of the majority of children indicates that their scheme of a person is already very firmly established and is available through talk. This image must have been formed during the sensori-motor phase of development as the child begins to form general expectancies about his human social partners, and probably has its roots well back in the first year of life.

Those areas in which there seemed to be particularly high agreement between the scores of the older and the younger children were the distinction between persons, and plants and tractors, the irreversibility of growth, the constancy of gender. The universality of sight, hearing, walking and talking appear already to be so taken for granted that the children considered our questions odd. In the areas where there were differences between three and four year olds, and to a much lesser extent four and five year olds, the children revealed some of the difficulty in logical co-ordination which is involved in superimposing two discrete frames of reference as in the case of the tendency of a minority of the three year olds to deny that teachers or parents had once been babies. The different valence of the concepts of parenthood, teacherhood and babyhood was an additional complicating factor in the class inclusion task: all people were babies, some people are teachers/parents. The shift in time from now to the past would not make this any easier. Indeed, in view of the difficulty of the intellectual task, it is surprising that the majority of the children who were in Piaget's pre-operational stage coped as well as they did.

The difference between the older and the younger children in their apparent grasp of emotions is of a different kind. It was clear from the responses of all ages that the children were faced with a problem in co-ordinating situation bound knowledge of individuals and general knowledge that people had the potential to feel emotion given the appropriate situation. This would require a degree of generalisation across a number of recalled situations, which the younger children were not able to perform.

This phase of the investigation was concerned with the skeleton of the child's representation of persons and dealt with some of the taken for granted characteristics which would hold across human encounters. There is much more to people as embodied in the real world where they play many social roles, and interact in numerous ecological settings. The task of the next phase is to see how far the three to five year old child has grasped some of the more specifically social activities of persons in the settings which they have under observation.

References

Bobrow, Daniel G. and Terry Winograd
    1977   "An Overview of KRL, a Knowledge Representation Language", *Cognitive Science*, 11: 3–46.
Borke, Helen
    1971   "Interpersonal perception of young children: egocentrism or empathy", *Developmental Psychology*, 5: 263–269.
Brooks-Gunn, Jeanne and Michael Lewis
    1976   "Infants' responses to strangers: midget, adult and child", *Child Development*, 47: 323–332.
    1978   "Early social knowledge: the development of knowledge about others", Harry McGurk (Ed.). *Issues in Childhood Social Development* (London: Methuen).
Bryant, Brenda K.
    1982   "An index of empathy for children and adolescents", *Child Development*, 53.2
Bullowa, Margaret (ed.)
    1979   *Before Speech: The Beginning of Interpersonal Communication* (Cambridge: Cambridge University Press).

Camras, Linda A.
   1980   "Children's understanding of facial expression used during conflict encounters", *Child Development*, 51: 879—885.
Duveen, Gerard M.
   1974   *The Child's Conception of Kinship: An Exploratory Study*, unpublished masters thesis (University of Strathclyde).
Duveen, Gerard M. and Maureen M. Shields
   1985 a   *Children's Ideas About Work, Wages and Social Rank*, paper presented at the International Society for the Study of Behavioural Development Tours Conference, June 1985.
   1985 b   *An Artifact in Developmental Research on Gender Knowledge.* A reconsideration of the distinction between gender knowledge and gender constancy. Department of Child Development, University of London Institute of Education, to appear.
Fagan, Joseph F. and Patricia A. Shepherd
   1979   "Infants' perception of face orientation", *Infant Behaviour and Development*, 2: 227—234.
Fagan, Joseph F. and Lynn T. Singer
   1979   "The role of simple feature differences in infants' recognition of faces", *Infant Behaviour and Development* 2: 39—45.
Feshbach, Norma D.
   1977   "Studies in empathic behaviour of children", Brenda H. Maher (Ed.). *Progress in Experimental Personality Research* (New-York: Academic Press).
Gelman, Rochel and Elizabeth Spelke
   1981   "The development of thoughts about animate and inanimate objects: implications for research on social cognition", John H. Flavell and Lee Ross (Eds.). *Social Cognitive Development. Frontiers and Possible Futures.* (Cambridge: Cambridge University Press).
Goldman, Ronald J. and Juliette Goldman
   1982   "How children perceive the origins of babies and the role of mothers and fathers in procreation: a crossnational study", *Child Development*, 53: 491—504.
Gouze, Karen R.
   1980   "Constancy of gender identity for self and other for children between the ages of three and seven", *Child Development*, 51: 275—278.
Haviland, Susan E. and Eve V. Clark
   1974   "This man's father is my father's son: a study of the acquisition of English kin terms", *Journal of Child Language*, 1: 25—48.
Hoffman, Michael L.
   1975   "Developmental synthesis of affect and cognition and its impli-

cations for altruistic motivation", *Developmental Psychology*, 11: 602 – 622.

1977 "Empathy, its development and pro-social implications", Charles B. Keasy (Ed.). *Nebraska Symposium on Motivation*, Vol. 25, (University of Nebraska Press).

1981 "Perspectives on the difference between understanding people and understanding things", John Flavell and Lee Ross (Eds.). *Social Cognitive Development: Frontiers and Possible Futures*, (Cambridge: Cambridge University Press).

Hubley, Penelope and Colwyn Trevarthen
1979 "Sharing in task in infancy", Ina Uzgiris (Ed.). *Social Interaction and Communication During Infancy: New Directions for Child Development*, 4, (San Francisco: Jossey Bass), 57 – 80.

Johnson, Carol N. and Henry M. Wellman
1982 "Children's developing conceptions of the mind and brain", *Child Development*, 53: 222 – 234.

Kintsch, Walter
1977 "On comprehending stories", Marcel A. Just and Patricia Carpenter (Eds.). *Cognitive Processes in Comprehension*, (Hillsdale, N. J.: Erlbaum).

Kintsch, Walter and Edith Green
1978 "The role of culture specific schemata in the comprehension and recall of stories", *Discourse Processes* 1: 1 – 13.

Kohlberg, Lawrence
1966 "A cognitive-developmental analysis of children's sex-role concepts and attitudes", Eleanor Maccoby (Ed.). *The Concept of Sex Differences*, (Stanford: Stanford University Press).

Kreutzer, Mary Ann, Sister Catherine Leonard and John Flavell
1975 "An interview study of children's knowledge about memory", *Monographs of the Society for Research in Child Development*, 40.1 (Serial 159).

La Barbera, Valerie, Caroll E. Izard, Peter Veitze and Sam Parisi
1976 "Four and six-month old infants' visual responses to joy, anger and neutral expression", *Child Development*, 47: 535 – 538.

Lewis, Michael and Candice Feiring
1979 "The child's social network: social objects, social functions and their relationships", Michael Lewis and Leonard Rosenblum (Eds.). *The Child and its Family: the Genesis of Behaviour*, (New York: Plenum).

Mandler, Jean
1983 "Representation", John H. Flavell and Paul Mussen (Eds.) *Cognitive Development*. Vol 3 of Paul Mussen (Ed.) *Handbook of Child Psychology*. (New York: Wiley)

Mandler, Jean and Marsha Deforest
1979   "Is there more than one way to recall a story?" *Child Development*, 50: 886—889.

Marcus, Dale E. and Willis F. Overton
1978   "The development of cognitive and gender constancy and sex role preferences", *Child Development*, 49: 434—444.

Miller, George A., Eugene Galanter and Karl H. Pribram
1960   *Plans and Structure of Behaviour* (New York: Holt).

Miller, Patricia H. and Linda Bibi
1979   "The development of children's understanding of attention", *Merill Palmer Quarterly*, 24.4

Miller, Patricia H., Frank S. Kessel and John H. Flavell
1970   "Thinking about people thinking about people thinking about ... a study of social cognitive development", *Child Development* 41: 613—624.

Mussen, Paul and Nancy Eisenberg-Berg
1977   *Roots of Caring, Sharing and Helping* (San Francisco: Freeman).

Nelson, Katherine
1981   "Social cognition in a script framework", John H. Flavell and Lee Ross (Eds.). *Social Cognitive Development: Frontiers and Possible Futures* (Cambridge: Cambridge University Press).

Odom, Richard G. and Carolyn M. Lemond
1972   "Developmental differences in perception and production of facial expression", *Child Development* 43: 359—369.

Piaget, Jean
1929   *The Child's Conception of the World* (London: Routledge and Kegan Paul).
1930   *The Child's Conception of Physical Causality*, (London: Routledge and Kegan Paul).

Rumelhart, David E.
1975   "Notes on a schema for stories", Daniel Bobrow and Allan Collins (Eds.). *Representation and Understanding: Studies in Cognitive Science*, (New York: Academic Press).
1980   "Schemata: the building blocks of cognition", Rand Spiro, Bertran Bruce and William Brewer (Eds.). *Theoretical Issues in Reading Comprehension*, (Hillsdale, N.J.: Erlbaum).

Schaffer, Rudolph
1977   "Early interactive development", H. R. Schaffer (Ed.). *Studies in Mother-Infant Interaction* (London: Academic Press).

Schank, Roger and Robert Abelson
1977   *Scripts, Plans, Goals and Understanding* (Hillsdale, N.J.: Erlbaum).

Shields, Maureen M.
  1978   "The child as psychologist: construing the social world", An-
          drew Lock (Ed.). *Action, Gesture, Symbol: The Emergence of
          Language* (London: Academic Press).
Shields, Maureen M. and Gerard M. Duveen
  1984   "Cultural knowledge and belief systems of very young chil-
          dren", paper given at European Seminar on the Role of Behav-
          iour in Evolution and Development, sponsored by the Econ-
          omic and Social Research Council, Avery Hill, March 1984.
  forthcoming "Dialectics, dialogue and the social transmission of
          knowledge", John H. Danks, Ida Kurcz and Grace W. Shugar
          (Eds.). *Knowledge and Language* (Amsterdam: North Holland).
Shields, Maureen M. and Judith M. Ireson
  1985   *Report on the Development of the Child's Representation of
          Emotion.* Economic and Social Research Council. Grant No.
          COO 232 109.
Sinha, Christopher
  1982   "Representational development and the structure of action",
          George Butterworth and Paul Light (Eds.). *Social Cognition
          Studies of the Development of Understanding* (Brighton: Har-
          vester Press).
Spee, James R. and John H. Flavell
  1979   "Young children's knowledge of the relative difficulty of recog-
          nition and recall memory tasks", *Developmental Psychology,
          15*, 2: 214−217.
Strayer, Janet
  1980   "A naturalistic study of empathic behaviours and their relation
          to affective state and perspective taking in pre-school chil-
          dren", *Child Development* 51: 815−822.

Development of Communicative Skills: The Construction of Fictional Reality in Children's Play

Manfred Auwärter

1. Introduction

I shall try to show some differences in the means by which children of different ages and developmental stages generate the social and communicative situation 'play' or 'fictionality'. The material to be analyzed will be transcripts of the hand-puppet play of children in the age range of 3 to 10 years.

To create fictionality, the children must mark some of their utterances as 'deviant', as playful or pretended, as not claiming validity in normal, everyday reality (cf. Bateson, 1955). They must bracket the ongoing activities and key the parts within the brackets as fictional ones (cf. Goffman 1974: 41 ff.). This keying, or transformation of serious, real actions into something fictional or playful, can be done in two ways: Either by marking the utterances themselves, or by creating contexts which transform utterances which look normal or mundane by any criteria, into fictional ones.

In general, the context of utterances not only influences the meaning speakers and listeners attribute to them, but also whether they consider these utterances to be pertinent, necessary, or adequate (cf. Hymes, 1972; Erickson and Shultz, 1981; Fillmore, 1972). In this connection we must not forget that the context of an utterance cannot be conceived of only in objective terms, e. g. in terms of such features as the material situation, as the linguistic context in the sense of preceding and subsequent utterances, or as the social characteristics of the addressees or other listeners (like age, sex, or social class). Such 'objective' contextual features (1) have their communicative effect only via the interpretation given to them — and the interpretations of speaker and listener may differ — and they include (2) the shared or presumedly shared background knowledge and background expectations of the participants in a social encounter. These potentially differing contextual interpretations by the participants in an encounter (e. g. the hand-puppet play) must be coordinated so that the communicative or interactive moves of the participants become mutually understandable, and so that a story line can be built up which satisfies the participants' expectations concerning logical or normative consistency. This means that the participants of the encounter must cooperate in deciding which aspects of the objective, material context, of the verbal context, of the background knowledge and expectations, of the social norms and value orientations are relevant or valid in a given communicative move. This has to be done explicitly when different interpretations, i. e. misunderstandings, arise.

The consensual construction of a fictional level, a play context achieved by using various communicative means and by activating specific social background knowledge etc., is analyzed as an example of the process of constructing contexts for utterances in general: An example which potentially shows some of the underlying mechanisms and some of the ongoing processes more clearly than the normal, everyday processes of generating common social frames for communication processes. The study of processes of contextualiation carried out in a developmental, sociological and psychological perspective seems the appropriate method to bring forth possibly differing modes of generating contexts for utterances, as well as to analyze whether these differing modes are viable alternatives for a particular communicative situation or whether they are to be arranged in a developmental hierarchy.

The question of how contexts for possible utterances are generated has lately been studied from two points of view. On the one hand there are analyses about how social knowledge is organized so that it is mutually shared or can be presumed to be shared (cf. Schank and Abelson, 1977; Berger and Roloff, 1980); on the other hand there have been studies about how the 'negotiation process' or the 'construction process' of generating common context takes place (cf. Sacks, 1978; Schenkein, 1978; Cronen, Pearce and Harris, 1979).

This question is becoming more and more important, for although the social foundations of all communication processes have become manifest (cf. Lakoff, 1972; Sanches and Blount, 1975; Bates, 1976; or Ochs and Schieffelin, 1979), the pertinent studies regarding the social-cognitive development of children on the one hand and regarding the microprocesses of social interaction on the other have largely been neglected by both sociology and psychology.

To analyze how children generate fictional reality in their socio-dramatic hand-puppet play, and how they consensually maintain the boundaries between play and reality, I shall (1) develop a conceptual schema for categorizing the children's utterances during their sociodramatic play, using the speaker's role identity and the validity claimed for a specific utterance as parameters. I shall (2) attempt to exemplify the communicative or linguistic means the children use to differentiate between the categories defined according to this schema, and I shall (3) look, using a rather small sample of protocols, for developmental changes in the children's mode of constructing and maintaining fictional reality, i. e. whether or not there are developmental trends in the distribution of the children's utterances across the categories defined according to the schema presented.

2. Observational Setting

Groups of 3 to 5 children in a German kindergarten were invited to play with some hand-puppets, a doll house, and some props in a separate room of the kindergarten. They were to play freely with these puppets (i. e. without prescribed story lines or other thematic instructions) and they were only to play for themselves, not for spectators. Sometimes, and especially at the beginnings of the play periods, an adult observer was present, but he tried to withdraw as soon as the play started.

The doll house consisted of a foldout cardboard, pasted over with foils, with a door, windows, a table, and a bed. Two detachable covers of the house were to be used to create additional rooms. The hand-puppets did not represent fairy tale or similar figures, but everyday persons, like father, mother, grandmother, grandfather, boys, girls, a policeman, a nurse, a cook, and a teacher.

The props which were put into the doll house and which seemed to have inspired some of the 'scripts' of the play consisted of a shopping basket, a kettle, a small metal bell, two wooden figures of a dog and a fox, a small finger-puppet, a toy-tractor, a set of play cards, and a thermometer.

Almost all of the children agreed to play with the hand puppets, the doll house, and the props for some time; they were promised small gifts (balloons, toy cars, plastic figures, etc.) for their effort. The play situation was recorded on a tape recorder via four microphones hanging from the ceiling in different parts of the room, and sometimes additionally with a videocamera. As indicated, the room was a separate room without too much interference from other play groups in the kindergarten.

In this play situation the scripts or action plots were the children's own choice and creation. The children made their puppets talk and act without agreeing beforehand on the story lines, so that spontaneity is one of the essential elements. In the play situation recorded, as a rule, the topics staged were not taken from the fairy tale world in the narrower sense of the term but consisted of everyday scenes such as 'shopping', 'cooking', 'celebrating a birthday', 'hunting', or 'getting married'. The sequences so staged were essentially fictional in that while performing them the children's speech actions were no longer related (or no longer exclusively related) to the everyday reality of the kindergarten.

In other words, when some children are playing 'having supper' they do not only act in their everyday roles as members of the kindergarten, but for some of the time they bring their hand puppets into action, they speak as these puppets, explain and make comments on the staged action, and make proposals or requests concerning the play situation to the other participants.

3. Methods of Analysis

In the following, an analytic instrument is developed which allows us to categorize the children's utterances when they are building up or preparing their hand-puppet play and when they are really acting with their hand-puppets. These utterances are analyzed in terms of two parameters which are probably constitutive for any kind of role play. The utterances were first categorized according to the scope of validity they implicitly claim, i.e. whether the speaker in using them is referring to the everyday reality of the kindergarten or to the enacted fictional play reality. In the first case, a chair is a chair, in the second case a chair may be a mountain or a swimming pool. In the first case the children are playing on the second floor of their kindergarten, in the second case they may be riding through a desert. Second, the utterances were categorized according to the identity the speaker projects by uttering them, i.e. whether he is displaying his everyday identity as a child or a fictional role identity. In the former case, Nadja is talking to Linne as Nadja, in the latter case, she is speaking as 'grandmother' to 'mother'.

These two distinctions are by no means identical, for, as the data show, the participants may make utterances in a fictional role identity, e.g. as the 'grandmother', which pertain to the normal reality of the kindergarten, and they may make utterances in a normal everyday speaker identity which claim validity only in relation to some fictional reality. But what is more important is that there are a number of positions which range between these extremes.

These are utterances which hold intermediate positions between the extreme points in the dimension of the projected speaker identity and in the dimension of the scope of validity claimed for an utterance. On the one hand these are utterances which refer neither to the normal reality of the kindergarten nor to the fictional play reality, but which are made to prepare the stage for fiction to occur without being themselves completely fictional (in Table 1, these are utterances on the levels 2a, 2b and 2c). On the other hand, these are utterances which do not project the speaker in his usual everyday identity nor in a fictional role identity, but which are neutral with regard to speaker identity. In using these utterances the speaker does not commit himself as a performer — either as a member of the kindergarten or as a character in the play — but he assumes the role of an impartial observer who talks about what is going on in an impersonal manner. We can describe these positions as third-person speaker identity. At any rate, with respect to their form, these utterances do not preclude such a classification (in Table 1, these are utterances on the levels 1b, 2b, and 3b).

Table 1 Levels of reality in children's hand-puppet play.

Speaker Identity	Scope of Validity		
	Everyday Reality	Transition from Reality to Fiction	Fiction, Staged Reality
Everyday Personal Identity	1a	2a	3a
Neutral Observer Identity	1b	2b	3b
Role Identity, Character	1c	2c	3c

Altogether, if we apply these two parameters and take into account not only the extreme positions but also the intermediate ones just described, we can distinguish nine 'levels of reality'. These nine levels of reality will be explained and exemplified by short sequences of the transcripts obtained. A list of the communicative means used to distinguish between these levels can be found at the end of this chapter.

3.1. The 'Canonical Forms': Everyday Reality and Completely Staged Fiction

Utterances located on *level 1 a* concern the everyday reality (of the kindergarten) and show the speaker in his everyday personal identity. These utterances either do not refer to the fictional level at all or they do it in a way that does not imply any kind of commitment to the 'play'. For the staged play with hand puppets they can have the function of a supporting frame.

Examples for utterances on this level can be seen in the following sequence. Daniela, Barbara, and Kathi leave the play group, Linne and Nadja are left alone with the doll house and the hand puppets:

Sequence 1: Now we can play by ourselves!

Da:	Mhm. Barbara, do you wonna play some more?	1 a
	I wonna ride the tricycle, and you?	1 a
	((Pause, Ba and Da run away))	
Li 1:	Go away! ((low))	1 a
Ba:	Come on! ((to Kt, in the background))	1 a
Li 1:	Now we can-	(1 a)
Da:	Come, Kathi, come! ((whispering))	1 a
Ka:	No, you- ((walks away))	1 a
Li 1:	Now we can play by ourselves, right? ((whispers))	1 a
Na:	Gee, that's great! Now we can play by ourselves!	1 b, 1a
	((whispers with exaggerated accentuation))	

(For the age of the children, cf. Tables 3, 4 or 5; for the transcript conventions, cf. the Appendix.)

Of course, the doll house and the puppets are the indirect topic of the conversation, but the children are neither acting on a fictional level nor are they building it up or preparing it, e. g. by defining the objects or naming the puppets. Instead they organize the subsequent course of activities in the kindergarten. They address each other by their real names and speak in their usual tone of voice — even when they are whispering.

In clear contrast to this level is *level 3 c*, the level of the completely staged fiction. Here the speaker is fully identified with the part or character he assumes while engaged in the play; the utterances refer to the objects, actors, and topics of the staged play and as such they are subject to the particular norms of the enacted situation and the enacted plot or story line.

In the following sequence it is not Linne and Nadja who meet, but 'mother' and 'grandmother'. Only this explains why they greet each other. And it's not Linne and Nadja who quarrel about who is taking too much space in the doll house but it's grandmother and mother quarreling about getting more space for themselves in the 'swimming pool':

Sequence 2: Don't make yourself so big!

Li 1:	Hallo! ((with changed voice; meet in the 'swimming pool'))	3 c
Na:	Hallo! ((with changed voice)) Tschsch.	3 c, 3 b
Li 1:	Don't make yourself so *big*! ((very loud; the 'swimming pool' is barely as wide as two hand puppets))	3 c
Na:	I can't make myself so bi-*bigger*. ((the last word with a drawl, laughing)) ((swimming noises from both))	3 c
Na:	I'm gonna swim⌈over there.	2 c
Li 1:	⌊Now I'll get out and dry you off.	3 c
	I'm gonna lie down here. ((low))	2 c
Na:	Me too, ((very low))	2 c
Li a:	Ah, how nice! Ahh, ahh, Mmmmmm! ((utters sounds of pleasure))	3 c
Na:	Hello, mother! ((with changed voice))	3 c
Li 1:	Hello!⌈Today, I'm gonna make the coffee right now. Father, you=	3 c
Na:	⌊Can- ((low with high pitched voice))	(3 c)
Li 1:	= lie down⌈for a bit longer ((sounds busy))	3 c
Na:	⌊I don't want any coffee, I want tea! ((with changed voice))	3 c

The function of the objects and the meaning of references to time and space are symbolically transformed: 'tomorrow' means only 'later', etc. The roles are very often characterized by special intonation markers, e. g. when Linne in the second part of the sequence assumes an eager, taking-care-of-it-all voice which she feels fits the role of mother, or when Nadja represents grandmother by speaking in a rather high-pitched voice.

3.2. The 'Intermediate' Forms: Construction of Fiction

With most children, fictional reality as a shared context for the play utterances is not simply presupposed. The fictional world which will then function as a concrete context for the utterances is first built up and specified in its details. The children define the fictional situation — 'it's the father's birthday today' —, they decide upon the symbolic transformation of the props — 'this is gonna be the swimming pool' —, they define and assign the roles to be performed — 'I am the grandmother!' —, and they equip these roles with individual characteristics and sometimes even with a past history. In short, they introduce and explain the parameters which will (partially) determine the logic of the subsequent action, i. e. which legitimize subsequent action and make it predictable as well.

In addition, a plot is worked out, at least approximately, which enables the integration of the actions of the particular performers (cf. Garvey, 1979), and this plot must be accepted or consented to by the participants. The children must ascertain which elements of the plot must be agreed upon explicitly, and find out how far they can rely on presumably shared action plans, social scripts or schemes (cf. Schank and Abelson, 1977).

The generation of contexts for fictional play is not just a task which can be performed at the onset of a longer play period, but is rather an ongoing process, either because requirements of everyday life and of the play situation interfere or because the children seem to think it is necessary to re-define and re-assign the roles, to change the function of the props, or to elaborate the story line or the setting.

Fictional reality can be built up from at least three distinct speaker positions by using explicit communicative means (i. e. there are at least three levels on which a parameter for the play situation can be defined beforehand or brought in after the fictional play has begun (cf. Table 1)). By using utterances which can be located on *level 2 a*, a speaker contributes to the construction of fictional reality while still projecting his everyday personal identity. He expresses his own personal wishes for the fictional play activities, e. g. by declaring that he himself will play the character of the hunter, or by proposing that some object in the room should be transformed symbolically, e. g. the wastebasket into a washing machine.

In the following sequence, Nadja and Linne are choosing their puppets and thereby also their roles, but they have not yet adopted these roles for the play action and are still speaking as Nadja and Linne, in a normal, undisguised voice, while Michaela is already performing the role of 'mother':

Sequence 3: I'm gonna play the grandmother!

Mi:	Take a sip, baby, come on! ((which changed voice))	3 c
Na:	I'm gonna play the grandmother!	2 a
Mi:	You really⌈have to drink a lot. ((low, with changed voice))	3 c
Li 1:	⌊The hunter! ((laughs))	2 a
	I'm gonna wear this! ((the grandfather with a hunter's costume))	

On *level 2 b*, a speaker participates in the construction of fictional reality by defining parameters, making proposals with regard to the characters to be taken, etc., without presenting these proposals as his own personal wishes, and without having taken over a fictional role identity. It is because these utterances do not contain any formal references to the identity of the speaker (like personal pronouns) that they take the appearance of proposals for which the speaker should be able to give impersonal reasons or justifications. These more 'objective' reasons relate to social script knowledge regarding the normatively correct progress of social events; they are hints at a mutually-shared action plan, and indicate the practical requirements of the ongoing fictional play or other normative knowledge which is presumably shared.

The formal linguistic means by which the children generate this impression of impersonal proposals for the fictional play are very often the use of modal verbs and of the subjunctive mood (*mußt, müßtest, hättest, würdest, tätest, solltest*).

Examples for utterances on this level can be seen in the following sequence:

Sequence 4: You have to take the grandmother!

Ka 1:	Now grandma shouldn't be here any more, right? Should I take the other one? ((another hand puppet))	2 b, 2 b
Sl 2:	No, you have to take the grandmother!	2 b
Ka 1:	Now, a police is coming ((half singing, turning into laughter))	2 b

By using utterances on *level 2 c*, a speaker participates in the explicit construction of fictional reality while already enacting a fictional role, that is by claiming a fictional role identity at the same time. The speaker does not completely abandon the fictional play level while bringing in additional parameters, while changing the definitions of the situation or while giving explicit directives to the co-participants. She solves a problem of the staging of the fictional role, i. e. by claiming a fictional role identity, and she does so by transgressing, to some extent, the attributes of her fictional role. For neither a real grandmother nor a staged grandmother can suggest someone to be her granddaughter.

In using utterances on level 2 c, however, a participant in the fictional play makes his definitions of parameters, etc. explicit instead of merely presupposing them by making utterances on the level of pure fictional play (level 3 c). Examples for utterances which are to be located on level 2 c can be found in the following sequence:

Sequence 5: I have to drink all the soup.

Sl 2:	I have to, I have to drink all the soup, because I'm sick.	2 c
	Oh! Oh! Oh! Oh!	3 c
Ka 1:	I'm pouring some.	2 c
Sl 2:	Now I have to sit down here. Otherwise I won't be with my mother.	2 c

In these examples, the children maintain their fictional role identity — as a sick child and as a mother — but they comment on their actions in a manner which children who are 'actually' acting (rather than playing to act) would not be able to do.

3.3. The 'Neutral' Forms: Comments of the Observer

It is possible, as we have seen, to distinguish — in terms of the projected speaker identity — three levels on which the context for fictional utterances is built up explicitly (2 a, 2 b, and 2 c). In a similar way it is possible to distinguish three different categories of utterances on the plane of an 'impartial' observer, i. e. 'impartial' utterances whose range of validity is the everyday real world (1 b), the building-up of fictional reality (2 b, see above), or a fictional reality, the staged reality of the play (3 b).

Utterances on *level 1 b* relate to normal, everyday reality without containing any formal markers indicating the identity of the speaker. These utterances are communicative acts which either comment on the wider setting of the play encounter or which contain meta-comments concerning the fictional play itself. Because of their impersonal formulation they appear to be made from the position of an unconcerned or neutral observer who views the ongoing episode with some detachment.

In most cases, these communicative acts imply judgments of a technical, moral, or aesthetic kind. By implying these judgments, they relate, more or less explicitly, to normative issues or higher authorities and not to private, idiosyncratic views or wishes. An example of such 'higher authorities' is of course encyclopedic knowledge that is not challenged or that is presented as uncontestable. Examples can be found in the following sequence:

Sequence 6: I take the wolf!

Ka 1:	I take the wolf!	2 a
Ss 1:	I can't play at all. There are no nice ones in there. ((puppets))	1 b
Sl 2:	They sure are there.	1 b
Ss 1:	Listen, Karola! You can't do that, otherwise you won't win anything. If you make such a fuss!	1 b

Whereas utterances located on level 1 b represent impersonal comments on the everyday reality of the kindergarten, e. g. on the general action context of the encounter, utterances on *level 3 b* refer, in a commenting mode, to the fictional play reality itself. Normally, they also contain no formal markers of the speaker's identity. Because of the distance the speaker keeps from the fictional play in commenting on it, this level can best be characterized as 'narrative' fiction. The speaker gives a running commentary on the actions of the puppets or characters without his utterances being interpretable as enactments of any of the roles. This category also comprises those instances of onomatopoeia which represent specific actions symbolically. Although these onomatopoetic instances belong to the staged events in a narrower sense, they cannot be interpreted as enactings of a specific fictional role.

In the following sequence, both sub-categories of level 3 b utterances, narrative fiction, and onomatopoetic representation, are exemplified:

Sequence 7: The foxi is hiding.

Sl 2:	The fox is biting the kid. Happ!	3 b, 3 b

Ss 1:	Na-ana-ch ((sounds of eating))	3 b
Sl 2:	I throwed him into the room. ((throws the fox into the doll house))	(3 b)
Ka 1:	The foxi is hiding.	3 b

3.4. The 'Impossible' Forms: Interference of Reality and Fiction

An utterance can be located on *level 1 c* of Table 1, if somebody, while projecting his role identity, makes an utterance that claims validity in normal everyday reality. Two of the naturally rare examples can be seen in the following sequence:

Sequence 8: Can you put my finger in there?

((The children are playing 'having dinner'; Sl 2 is 'cooking', Ka 1 is already 'eating'))

Ss 1:	Can you put my finger in there? ((with high-pitched voice, as 'grandmother' to the adult observer; asks for help to put on the hand puppet))	1 c
Au:	You want to play this one? ((adult observer))	2 a
Ss 1:	Yeah, this one. ((normal voice))	2 a
	Can you put my finger in there? ((again as 'grandmother'))	1 c

An utterance can be located on *level 3 a*, when a speaker says something which shows him in his everyday personal identity but which raises no claims of being valid in everyday reality. One of the rare examples in our protocols is to be found in the following sequence:

Sequence 9: The fox bit me.

Ka 1:	I don't want to play any more ((very serious))	1 a
Ss 1:	Why?	1 a
Ka 1:	Because- because the fox bit me, that's why I don't want any more.	3 a
Sl 1:	For real?	1 a
Ss 1:	For real?	1 a
Ka 1:	Yes.	(3 a)

Karola really does not want to continue to play, and she puts forward an argument which could have meaning only in fictional reality − the fox is a wooden one, after all. (In some respects I think Sibel's and Susanne's questions "for real?", in German *in echt*?, should also get a 3 a-coding.)

4. Summary of Linguistic Markers Characterizing the Levels of Reality Described

I have now described nine possible levels of reality generated by utterances in the context of fictional play. This was done on the basis of a conceptual distinction between two parameters intrinsic to role playing in general, that is, the speaker identity projected by an utterance and the validity claims raised by it. These levels cannot only be distinguished conceptually, but also in terms of the linguistic markers which the speaker uses when realizing them and which the hearer must take into account when deciding upon the meaning of a specific communicative move. Some of these markers have been mentioned unsystematically in the description of the levels above. Table 2 gives a preliminary summary of the markers I have found thus far.

Because of the small number of examples found, levels 1 c and 3 a are omitted.

Normally, the specific level of an utterance is not determined by a single linguistic or communicative marker, but by a cluster of such markers. And additionally, a judgment about the level an utterance is located on, implies judgments about the reflexive relation that holds between a given utterance and the previously provided and the subsequently agreed upon context of this utterance (and this does not only apply for the scientist trying to categorize the utterances, but also for the other participants in the sociodramatic role play).

Having presented nine 'levels of reality' for categorizing the children's utterances during their sociodramatic role play, I will now try to analyze whether the distribution of the children's utterances across these categories can be interpreted in a developmental perspective.

5. Data Base and Coding Procedures

5.1. Subjects of the Study

The children whose utterances in the context of fictional play were to be analyzed should belong to a wide age range, but we also thought it was necessary that at least some of the children be

Table 2 Some linguistic markers of the levels of reality distinguished*.

Markers	Levels of Reality						
	1a	1b	2a	2b	2c	3b	3c
Prosodic Features							
non-habitual voice quality (pitch, volume, loudness, timbre)	−	−	−	−	+	−	+
typifying forms of speech (intonation patterns, rhythm, rate and accuracy of articulation)	−	−	−	−	+	−	+
Referential Markers							
self-referential pronouns	+	−	+	−	+	−	+
fictional terms for actors	−	−	−	−	+	+	+
pretend vocatives and address forms	−	−	−	−	−	−	+
symbolic transformations of objects	−	−	−	+	+	+	+
symbolic transformations of temporal and spatial relations	−	−	−	+	+	+	+
Stylistic Markers							
role-specific registers and routines (e. g. polite address forms)	−	−	−	−	−	−	+
event-specific formulas and routines (e. g. greetings in the course of play)	−	−	−	−	−	−	+
description of actions going on simultaneously	−	−	−	−	−	+	−
onomatopoetic representations of ongoing action	−	−	−	−	−	+	−
stage-like asides ('inner monologues')	−	−	−	−	−	+	−
Verb Forms in Main Clauses							
subjunctive mood	−	−	+	+	+	−	−
imperatives	+	−	+	−	−	−	+
modal directives and commissives	+	−	+	+	+	−	+
present tense obligatory	−	−	−	−	−	+	−

* These markers pertain to German role play situations; there might be other markers in English (cf. Garvey & Berndt, 1975).

represented more than once in the study because, in developmental studies, longitudinal data usually have more explanatory power than cross-sectional ones.

The subjects of the present study vary with respect to age between 3;1 and 10;0 years; all of them are girls and come from a middle to upper middle class social background. The sample is comprised of participants in the following four hand-puppet play sequences:
(a) One very long sequence in which a total of nine children actually participated but in which normally only about two to four children participated simultaneously — the joining in the play and leaving it being open. Additionally, an adult observer was present and participated in the play activities during half of the play sequence.
(b) Two sequences in which the same three children participated — once in the age range of 4−5, the second time exactly one year later. In both play sequences, adult observers were present only at the beginning and end of the sessions.
(c) One relatively long sequence in which three older children participated, this time without any adult observer.

Table 3 Subjects of the study; age in years and months; children participating more than once appear in the same column with different indexes.

Group 1	Te	Sl1	Kt	Ba	Na	Si	Mi	Li1	Da		
	3;1	3;1	3;8	4;3	4;3	4;10	5;7	5;9	6;2		
Group 2		Sl2						Ka1	Ss1		
		4;11						3;9	3;11		
Group 3		Sl3						Ka2	Ss2		
		5;11						4;9	4;11		
Group 4						Li2				Be	Sa
						8;6				7;8	10;0

Note: The children of the fourth group were visiting the kindergarten during their school holidays.

5.2. Coding Procedures

The protocols of these four sequences were coded in terms of the categories of Table 1, keeping to the following conditions:
    The units for the coding process were 'communicative acts'. These are loosely defined as coherent, separable 'messages'. Such a message may comprise several sentences, e. g. if someone makes a proposal and gives reasons for this proposal. Communicative acts may be interrupted by other participants' communicative acts and

continued afterwards. These instances are coded only once, i. e. as single communicative acts, if (1) the interruptions are not contingent (i. e., motivated by unrelated aspects of the ongoing interaction), if (2) they do not occur at possible completion points (cf. Sacks, Schegloff and Jefferson, 1974), and/or if (3) their continuation contains no elements of a reaction or response to the interruption itself.

A single turn of a participant in the play activities may comprise more than one communicative act, and on the other side, a single communicative act may be distributed over more than one turn of a participant in the communicative process. A communicative act is regarded as completed, at the latest, when new codings become necessary, e. g. when a 3 c-coding is followed by a 1 a-coding.

Incomplete, broken-off contributions which seem to have been rejected by the speaker herself, e. g. because she herself puts forward reformulations for these contributions, were not coded and are not included in the data. Examples for these coding procedures can be seen in the following two sequences:

Sequence 10: Oh my dear Lassie!

Sl 2:   You must do it like that, too. ((to Ss 1, in a normal voice;   2 b
         relatively low))
         Gee, I think, she can- somebody locked her up. ((normal   2 b
         voice))
         Lassie! Oh my dear Lassie! ((very exaggerated, theatrical   3 c
         'crying'))

The broken-off sentence "Gee, I think, she can-" is not coded because it seems to have been rejected by the speaker herself.

Sequence 11: Oh, Sweetie, But I have to-

Ss 1:   I want some more of that dessert- ((as 'child', with rising intona-
         tion))
Sl 2:   Oh, Sweetie, but I have to- ((as a mother in a state of stress; with
         tearful voice))
Ss 1:   with- with four cherries!

Both of Susanne's turns are regarded as a single communicative act.

In a number of cases, the categories of a communicative act could only be decided upon by referring to the coding of the preceding communicative acts which are contingent to the act to be coded. Such an approach to some extent reflects the fact that an utterance can have an effect on the subsequent verbal context, in this case, that it establishes a communicative level that remains operative as long as no indications to the contrary appear. An example can be seen in the following sequence:

Sequence 12: I must give him food.

Sl 2:	Go ahead and- Sweetie! Go ahead and pat the dog, he is so nice! ((changed voice, as 'mother'))	3 c
Ka 1:	Okay.	3 c
Sl 2:	I must give him food. Otherwise he would have starved. Doggie! Bessie! ((as 'mother'))	3 c, 2 c, 3 c

Karola's communicative move 'okay' gets a 3 c-coding, although it does not have 3 c-markers, because Karola participates in a fictional sequence which has been inaugurated by Sibel.

In some other cases a communicative act of a child cannot be classified unequivocally by referring to its formal markers, but it is disambiguated retroactively, by the subsequent utterances of the same or the other participants in the play activities. Thus it becomes an utterance which can be classified unequivocally as belonging to one of the various levels of reality. The following sequence presents an example for such a retroactive disambiguation:

Sequence 13: What is one plus ten?

Li 2:	Well, what is one plus ten?	3 c
Be:	Eleven!	3 c
Sa:	Here, mister, I know it too, I know it!	3 c
Be:	Eleven!	3 c
Li 2:	What? You? ((obviously addressing Sa))	3 c
Sa:	Well — that makes — three. (('thinking' for a long time))	3 c
Li 2:	Oh! God!	3 c
Be:	I know it, I know it! ((rhythmically))	3 c
Li 2:	What *is* it?	3 c
Be:	It's eleven.	3 c
Li 2:	Yes! Fine! ((praising in an exaggerated way))	3 c

Up to this point in the play, Linne and Berna both were teachers and Sarah was the only pupil. It is possible that Berna's 'eleven' was told on level '1 a' to show the older girls that she knows the right answer in normal reality. Of course she is not allowed to answer the question as a 'teacher'. And now, Sarah with her first answer, especially by using the word 'too', transforms Berna's answer into a pupil's answer and Berna into a fellow pupil. Since

Berna does not protest against this shift, her utterance has retroactively been defined as a fictional utterance.

These coding conventions have without any doubt the effect of supplying some children whose communicative acts would otherwise have been assigned to the 'simpler' levels 2 a or 3 b, with communicative acts of the more complex or less probable levels 3 c, 2 c, and 2 b. For this reason all such indirectly derived codings were marked separately. But when analyzing the frequency of all codings, I found that the 'derived codings' comprise only 4.8% of the total, and that even with the children below the age of 4 years they comprise only 6.1% of their communicative acts. For that reason they were, without any special marking, subsumed under the 'normal codings' of the different levels, at least for the present purposes.

In a number of cases (9.7% of all communicative acts), the reality level of a communicative act could not be decided on the basis of objective linguistic markers — although normally even in these cases five or six of the possible levels could be excluded. In the main, these were cases of systematic ambiguity between the levels 1 a and 3 c (49.8%) and between the levels 1 a − 2 a and 2 c − 3 c. On the one hand, these utterances had multiple codings as not unequivocally classifiable communicative acts, e. g. as '(1 a − 3 c)'; on the other hand I decided upon one of the possible readings, following criteria of plausibility, to simplify the presentation of the results for the present paper.

It is of some interest that such cases of systematic ambiguity between two (or, very seldom, three) levels show up more frequently with the younger children than with the older ones. In group 2 (cf. Table 2) the proportions of communicative acts which cannot be associated with a specific level on the basis of objective, formal criteria is 11.0% of all communicative acts, in group 4 it is only 4.8%.

In the relatively rare cases where even criteria of plausibility did not work, the coding was done in favor of the 'simpler' categories, i. e. in favor of the levels 1 a, 2 a or 3 b and to the debit of the levels 2 b, 2 c, 1 b or 3 c. Such cases of systematic ambiguity with respect to the level to which a communicative act can be assigned, are important since this ambiguity should not only exist for the researcher, but also for the other participants in the play activities. It is left to them to decide upon the reading, and thus upon the communicative function of the communicative acts of their playmate. (Or possibly, these communicative acts are not ambiguous for them, or they do not care about their ambiguity. All communicative proccesses, especially such processes between more than two children will involve a large amount of imprecision, ambiguity, or incomprehensibility anyhow. One of the reasons seems to be that ambiguity or imprecision are not the only interactive problems which have to be mastered in real time).

The two sub-categories of communicative acts on level 3 b were separately coded and counted, i. e. the cases of narrative fiction ("now, father climbs a mountain") and the onomatopoeias which represent some action symbolically ("bang!"). But since they are equally distributed across all children, roughly one third of all 3 b's consisting of onomatopoeias, both sub-categories were combined in the presentation of the data.

6. Results

The hand-puppet play sequences which were analyzed for this paper are part of a more extended research project on the development of communicative and interactive abilities. But only the data concerning the cognitive development of the children will be taken into account here in addition to the play data. More specifically, the cognitive development of the children, measured in terms of their acquisition of concrete operational cognitive functions (by applying the standardized tests of Goldschmid and Bentler, 1968), was used to improve the grading of the children, which otherwise would have been made only on the basis of chronological age.

In the tables that follow, the children are graded according to their cognitive test scores (which range from 0, where there is no evidence for concrete-operational functions, to a maximum of 12), and only those children having the same cognitive test scores are graded according to their age. This is done because chronological age seems to be a relatively weak indicator for the cognitive, social, or communicative development of a child and should be replaced, or, at least, supplemented by other indicators.

6.1. Comments on the Data

In the data shown in Table 4 there is a clear tendency for the proportion of communicative acts located on level 1 a to decrease with rising age (or higher cognitive abilities) of the children, whereas

Table 4 Categories of communicative acts during children's hand-puppet play; the children Sl, Ka, Ss and Li are represented more than once, at different ages, as Sl1, Sl2 etc.; the children are graded according to their cognitive test scores and their age; percentages, total quantities in the last column.

Name	Age	Cognition	1a	1b	1c	2a	2b	2c	3a	3b	3c	Total
							Levels of Reality					
Sl1	3;1	0	76.9	–	–	3.8	–	–	–	3.8	15.4	26
Te	3;1	0	69.8	2.3	–	2.3	–	–	9.3	9.3	7.0	43
Kt	3;8	0	75.0	6.2	–	6.2	–	–	–	–	12.5	16
Ka1	3;9	0	48.1	2.5	–	8.0	3.1	4.9	1.8	8.1	23.6	162
Ss1	3;10	0	43.4	11.7	2.1	3.4	1.4	2.1	–	4.8	31.0	145
Ba	4;3	0	26.2	10.7	–	7.7	15.4	6.2	–	–	33.8	65
Ka2	4;9	0	28.6	6.1	–	14.3	20.4	10.2	–	6.1	14.3	49
Ss2	4;10	0	33.6	11.4	–	4.3	20.7	7.1	–	2.8	20.0	140
Sl2	4;11	0	26.3	3.0	–	6.4	3.0	6.4	–	6.8	48.1	266
Mi	5;7	0	25.5	21.6	–	–	2.0	2.0	–	3.9	45.1	51
Li1	5;9	0	13.3	2.1	–	4.9	14.0	14.4	–	14.1	37.2	285
Si	4;10	2	16.7	1.0	–	2.1	14.6	9.4	–	20.8	35.4	96
Sl3	5;11	2	29.0	8.7	–	10.1	24.6	9.2	–	3.9	14.5	207
Da	6;2	4	26.8	2.1	–	9.3	8.2	3.1	–	11.4	39.2	97
Na	4;3	7	14.1	1.2	–	1.8	17.1	10.0	–	13.5	42.4	170
Be	7;8	12	9.0	–	–	–	7.7	–	–	7.7	75.6	78
Li2	8;6	12	1.6	0.8	–	–	3.1	–	–	4.7	89.8	127
Sa	10;0	12	1.5	0.8	–	0.8	2.3	–	–	2.3	92.4	131

the proportion of the communicative acts on level 3 c, the level of completely staged fiction, increases with age and cognitive test scores. The utterances by which the fictional stage is built up or prepared in an explicit, verbal way, i. e. utterances on the levels 2 a, 2 b, and 2 c, do not seem to follow a specific pattern with regard to age or cognition scores of the children.

Table 5 Summarized communicative acts occurring during children's hand-puppet play; the children are graded according to their cognitive test scores and their age; percentages.

Name	Age	Cognition	Level '1'	Level '2'	Level '3'
Sl 1	3; 1	0	76.9	3.8	15.4
Te	3; 1	0	72.1	2.3	25.6
Kt	3; 8	0	81.2	6.2	12.5
Ka 1	3; 9	0	50.6	16.0	33.3
Ss 1	3; 10	0	57.2	6.9	35.9
Ba	4; 3	0	36.9	29.3	33.8
Ka 2	4; 9	0	34.7	44.9	20.4
Ss 2	4; 10	0	45.0	32.1	22.8
Sl 2	4; 11	0	29.3	15.8	54.9
Mi	5; 7	0	47.1	3.9	49.0
Li 1	5; 9	0	15.4	33.3	51.2
Si	4; 10	2	17.7	26.1	56.2
Sl 3	5; 11	2	37.7	43.9	18.4
Da	6; 2	4	28.9	20.6	50.6
Na	4; 3	7	15.3	28.9	55.9
Be	7; 8	12	9.0	7.7	83.3
Li 2	8; 6	12	2.4	3.1	94.5
Sa	10; 0	12	2.3	3.1	94.7

But if we simplify the data, by grouping them into only three categories, we get a more clear-cut impression of the distribution of these '2'-utterances. In Table 5, I group the children's utterances into (1) communicative units which have only relevance in the normal, everyday reality (1 a, 1 b, and 1 c), (2) those which have relevance in a fictional play reality (3 a, 3 b, and 3 c), and those whose function is to build up this fictional reality (2 a, 2 b, and 2 c).

The above mentioned tendencies of a decrease on level 1 a and an increase on level 3 c can be shown for the aggregated levels '1' and '3'. In addition there can be seen a clear preponderance of communicative acts on level '2' in the medium age group of 4 to 6 years old children — with the remarkable exception of Mi.

The tendencies mentioned — a decrease of the proportion of communicative acts on level '1', an increase of the proportion on level '3', and an U-shaped course of the proportions on level '2' also hold true if we look at the development of the children represented more than once in our sample, i. e. if we compare Sl 1 with Sl 2, etc. This is important because of the greater explanatory power attached to longitudinal data in comparison to cross-sectional data.

In the medium age group of 4 to 6 year old children, the proportion of communicative acts which prepare and build up fictional reality is extremely high, up to 44% of all communicative acts used, with a clear peak in the age group of about 5 years. In this group the number of utterances building up fictional reality exceeds the number of utterances really produced on an established fictional level. It seems as if this building-up of fiction, a process which allows the children to play with a variety of parameters of possible realities and with different plots or story lines, is, in itself, the pleasure these children draw from the hand-puppet play and not so much the acting on a finally established fictional play level.

The oldest group analyzed — Be, Li 2 and Sa (cf. Table 5) — not only shows the decline of utterances on level '1' having practically reached a final point but also shows the proportion of utterances on level '2' having decreased dramatically. These children do not need to build fictional reality explicitly or they do not deem it necessary.

My explanation is that in this age group the mode of construction of fictional reality has changed. These older children generate fictional reality by jumping to the fictional level immediately, without any preparing steps. They do not define or explicate the parameters but they simply presuppose them. It is by this presupposing that they generate them, make them referable and accountable. The children do no longer say 'now you should be a pupil', but they treat their playmate, as in sequence 13, as a pupil and thus transform her into a pupil.

Examples can be seen in the following sequence which shows the older girls as hand-puppet players:

Sequence 14: It is always him!

Sa: Mama, I'm getting sick.

Be: Wait a second- no! ((as mother))
Sa: Oh my god, I have to call the nurse again! ((as mother)
        Ding-a-ling, ding-a-ling.
        This is Doctor Netzer's office ((in a formal tone, as receptionist or
        doctor))
Li 2:   My son, he is- he isn't feeling well, it is always *him*!
Sa: Again! Fainting spells! I have to take him to the hospital again!
Be: Mama! = ((as child))
Sa: Goodbye! ((as doctor, on the phone))
Be: = I have a huge belly ache!
Li 2:   No, she is fainting. ((low, giving directions))
Be: Well, m- my daughter, she has a terrible belly ache. ((again as
        mother talking on the phone))

The children had not talked about playing this sickness sequence before they started it. Berna is a mother, a sick child and again a mother without even announcing these transformations. She makes the adequate communicative acts and creates, by doing this, the fitting context for her communicative acts. Similarly, Sarah is in succession first a child, then a mother and then a doctor.

The hypothesis that the mode of generation of fictional reality changes during the course of child development is supported by an analysis of the distribution of the three subcategories of level '2' (cf. Table 4). The youngest children only use utterances on level 2 a, their contributions to the construction of fictional reality are confined to uttering wishes to play some specific roles ("I will be a mother"). The proportion of 2 a-utterances decreases with the rising age of the children clearly in favor of level 2 b, a level on which the proposals for the construction of fictional reality no longer have the form of quasi-idiosyncratic wishes but of impersonal suggestions which refer to normative or factual necessities. Level 2 c, on which fictional reality is built up from the position of an already enacted fictional role, obtains a large share of all level '2'-utterances by the medium-aged group of our sample (by Ka 2, Li 1 and Na), but decreases with increasing age of the children. Communicative acts on this level may be considered as direct antecedents of the method of creating fictional reality by merely presupposing it: Fictional reality is already generated from the position of a fictional character, but it is still generated by using explicit utterances and not yet by creating what should be the context for one's fictional utterances by mere presupposition.

Without doubt, the generation of fictional reality by mere presupposition presumes a high degree of social script knowledge (Schank & Abelson, 1977), of shared social schemata and of shared normative and factual knowledge. Young children do not have this knowledge, or they have it only in very restricted domains. You can only generate a doctor-patient situation by merely talking like a patient if all participants in the play share schemata about how such situations are alike.

However, there are more factors to be taken into account. If children generate fictional reality by using level 2 b-utterances, they try to make their social background knowledge explicit, thereby displaying specific structural features of their social schemata. Finally, if they generate fiction from the level of 3 c-utterances by mere presupposition, they (1) display their mastery of a new communicative form, and they (2) show that they now think they can rely on the normative and factual knowledge of the other play participants.

7. Summary

If we categorize children's utterances during their sociodramatic role play according to the parameters of the identity the speaker adopts and the scope of validity (fictionality) he claims, we can show that the categories so defined have some linguistic correlates, and we can find clear developmental effects in the distribution of the categories so defined: The mode according to which older children construct fiction during their role play differs from the mode younger children show, or, put more generally, compared with younger children, older children show a structurally different mode of constructing the context for utterances deemed to be located on a fictional level.

Appendix

Transcript conventions

(word)	items enclosed in doubt,
((word))	contextual information, prosodic features of the preceding utterance,
.,?! –	punctuation marks are used to approximate intonation contours,

1 a − 3 c	classification of utterances, following Table 2,
(1 a)	classification enclosed in doubt,
word	parts of utterances separated for transcript design
= word	reasons,
⌈word⌊word	overlapping utterances.

References

Auwärter, Manfred, and Edit Kirsch
  1982   "Die Generierung fiktionaler Realität im kindlichen Handpuppenspiel", *Beiträge zu einer empirischen Sprachsoziologie*, edited by Hans-Georg Soeffner (Tübingen: G. Narr), 91−114.
Bates, Elizabeth
  1976   *Language and context: The acquisition of pragmatics* (New York: Academic Press).
Bateson, Gregory
  1955   "A theory of play and fantasy", *Psychiatric Research Reports* 2: 39−51.
Berger, Charles R., and Michael E. Roloff
  1980   "Social cognition, self-awareness, and interpersonal communication", *Progress in communication sciences* Vol. 2, edited by Brenda Dervin and Melvin J. Voigt (Norwood, N. J.: Ablex), 1−49.
Cook-Gumperz, Jenny, and John J. Gumperz
  1976   "Context in children's speech", *Working Papers of the Language Behavior Research Laboratory*, No. 46 (Berkeley, Cal.: University of California, Language Behavior Research Laboratory).
Cronen, Vernon E., W. Barnett Pearce, and Linda M. Harris
  1979   "The logic of the coordinated management of meaning: A rule-based approach to the first course in interpersonal communication", *Communication Education* 28: 22−38.
Erickson, Frederick, and Jeffrey Shultz
  1981   "When is a context? Some issues and methods in the analysis of social competence", *Ethnography and language in educational settings*, edited by Judith Green and Cynthia Wallat (Norwood, N. J.: Ablex), 147−160.
Fillmore, Charles J.
  1972   "A grammarian looks to sociolinguistics", *Report of the 23rd*

230   *Auwärter*

annual round table meeting on linguistics and language studies.
Monograph series on languages and linguistics No. 25, edited
by Roger W. Shuy (Washington, D. C.: Georgetown University
Press), 273 — 287.
Garvey, Catherine
1977   *Play* (London: Open books).
Garvey, Catherine, and Rita Berndt
1975   "The organization of pretend play" (Chicago/Ill.: Paper presented at the Annual Convention of the American Psychologi-
cal Association).
Goffman, Erving
1974   *Frame analysis* (New York: Harper & Row).
Goldschmid, Marcel L., and Peter M. Bentler
1968   *Concept assessment kit — conservation* (San Diego, Cal.:
EdJTS).
Hymes, Dell
1972   "Models of the interaction of language and social life", *Directions in sociolinguistics,* edited by John J. Gumperz and Dell
Hymes (New York: Holt, Rinehart & Winston), 35 — 71.
Lakoff, Robin
1972   "Language in context", *Language* 48: 907 — 927.
Ochs, Elinor, and Bambi B. Schieffelin (eds.)
1979   *Developmental pragmatics* (New York: Academic Press).
Rubin, Kenneth H., and Debra J. Peppler
1980   "The relationship of child's play to social-cognitive growth
and development", *Friendship and social relations in children,*
edited by Hugh C. Foot, Antony J. Chapman and Jean R.
Smith (New York: Wiley), 209 — 233.
Sacks, Harvey
1978   "Some technical considerations of a dirty joke", *Studies in
the organization of conversational interaction,* edited by Jim
Schenkein (New York: Academic Press), 249 — 269.
Sacks, Harvey, Emanuel Schegloff, and Gail Jefferson
1974   "A simplest systematics for the analysis of turn taking in
conversations", *Language* 50: 696 — 735.
Sanches, Mary, and Ben G. Blount (eds.)
1975   *Sociocultural dimensions of language use* (New York: Academic
Presss).
Schank, Roger C., and Robert P. Abelson
1977   *Scripts, plans, goals, and understanding. An inquiry into human
knowledge structures* (Hillsdale, N. J.: Lawrence Erlbaum).
Schenkein, Jim
1978   "An introduction to the study of 'socialization' through analyses of conversational interaction", *Semiotica* 24: 277 — 304.

Routines in Peer Culture

William A. Corsaro

1. Introduction

As I sat watching the children in the scuola màterna I was struck
by how often I had witnessed the ongoing peer activity in my ten
years of observing the play of young children. The children were,
to put it simply, "running around in circles". I have continually had
difficulty in gaining the children's perspective while they engage in
this type of play. For one thing my only attempt to participate in
this play while doing research in a nursery school in the United
States was, to put it mildly, not very successful.

The major problem was that I am physically too big to do it
right. I found it difficult to run after the child in front of me without
running into her. My steps forward were too long even when I
attempted to shorten them. So I often had to stop altogether and
let her increase the gap between us. This strategy soon led to another
difficulty. The boy behind me kept bumping into me and yelling,
Go! Go!. So I went. But then, almost immediately, I was too close
to the girl in front of me again. This problem was soon accompanied
by two others. Before long I got dizzy from the movement in circles
and then I started to feel self-conscious. This last problem was a
bit unusual because I have, over the years, been able, more or less,
to get over the self-consciousness of being an adult doing child-like
things. But in this case I was an adult who could not do the child-
like thing correctly or even credibly. So I decided to stop. Although
I often participate in more-loosely structured running and chasing
games, I have never again attempted to join this particular activity.
It sounds absurd on the surface, but in truth I was unable to run
around in circles competently.

So as I watched the Italian children I remembered my earlier
experience and I had no intention of attempting to join in the play.
However, when the teachers ended the activity by calling the children

upstairs for lunch, I remained behind and carefully reconstructed the activity in field notes. Here is what I wrote.

Example 1
2/20/84   Episode 3
Running and Chasing Routine
Scene: Downstairs
Participants: Antonia, Paolo, Renata and Pietro

One of the teachers calls for the girls to come together as a group to go upstairs and wash up for lunch. As the girls gather the teacher learns that the food is late in arriving from the kitchen and so it is too early for the girls to go upstairs. The teacher decides to let the girls wait in a group for a few minutes, but the children soon begin to leave the group and the teacher does not object. Antonia and Renata had been standing together and Paolo now comes up to them. As soon as he arrives Antonia runs off looking back at Renata and laughing. Renata now runs after Antonia and Paolo runs after Renata. The three run in a circle, keeping a certain distance while constantly watching each other and laughing. After a few minutes Pietro enters the play by running after Antonia, placing himself between her and Renata. The pace now picks up and the laughing grows louder. Eventually, Renata flops to the ground laughing loudly. Paolo falls on top of her and then Antonia and Pietro pile on. At this point, the teacher calls for the girls to reassemble, but Antonia and Renata ignore her and roll on the floor with Paolo and Pietro. Then Renata jumps up and begins running again and the other three children chase after her. The children are again running in circles. After several revolutions a teacher takes Antonia and Renata by the hand and directs them toward the stairs saying *Dai!* *Dai!*. The girls reluctantly move upstairs at the end of the group of girls on their way to wash up for lunch. On the way up Antonia and Renata look back down and wave at Paolo and Pietro who are are still running in circles and who have now been joined by three other boys. A few minutes later the boys are told to gather and go upstairs for lunch.

There are several things to note about the activity described in Example 1. First, it is enacted jointly or communally. While running the children were constantly watching each other and displaying their mutual enjoyment of the activity through laughter. Second, the structure of the activity is highly predictable, and, therefore, the activity is easily initiated. There is no need for prior negotiation. The beginning of the activity is signalled by one child's running from and looking back at the others. Third, the activity is adaptable.

It can be produced in almost any social situation. All that is needed is a little open space. So this activity is composed of three basic features: it is communal, predictable and adaptable. It is the presence of these three features which leads me to classify this activity as a *routine*, and it is the functions this activity performs in peer interaction which leads me to argue that it is a routine of peer culture.

Let us return to the description of the activity in Example 1. The activity or routine primarily involves orchestrated physical movement. The running can be seen as a physical release which the children share. Children like to run, they like to move around. For young children running, jumping and laughing are in many ways equivalent to talk (or conversation) among older children and adults. When a parent and young child meet another parent und young child whom they know on the street, the adults will stop to talk while the young children often end up running around. At times this upsets the adults who worry about the children's safety. But running for the children is a shared activity just as talk (or 'having a chat') is for the adults. It is a social activity, a shared routine, the children enjoy performing together. So the first function of the routine is that it enables children to do something they like to do together.

Another thing to notice about the description of the routine in Example 1 is when it occurs. It occurs at a time when children are asked by adults "to wait". It is, thus, an occasion where there is nothing specific to do, where there is time to fill. It should be noted that such occasions are often imposed upon children by adults. In institutional settings like the nursery school (scuola materna) there are transition periods between scheduled events. Such transition periods, and the waiting demanded, often seem arbitrary to children and they grow inpatient. Sometimes like adults children fill transition periods with talk. But in my research I have found that children most often opt for peer routines much like the one enacted in Example 1. In such cases the routines perform a second function. They break down the control of adults. In the performance of such routines children feel they have some control over their lives by doing something they like to do together.

Given the above two functions, it can be argued that 'running in circles' is a routine of peer culture among nursery school children. It is my belief that it is in such routines that peer culture is produced and shared and that a great deal of social development occurs. But before turning to a discussion of this claim and analyses of several routines of peer culture, it is useful to consider the general importance of routines in everyday life.

2. Making the Unfamiliar Familiar: Social Representations in Everyday Life

Within social psychology there has been a growing recognition of the importance of the activities of everyday life for understanding social behavior and interaction. This trend is seen throughout the work of Goffman (1959, 1983) and in both the early work in ethnomethodology (see Garfinkel, 1967) and more recently in conversational analysis (cf. Sacks, Schegloff, and Jefferson, 1974; and Schenkein, 1978). In fact, one could argue that Bordieu's (1977) recent emphasis on the importance of habitual action for the production and reproduction of social order is directly in line with Cicourel's (1974) earlier critique of traditional sociological concepts like 'status' and 'role'. Cicourel saw such concepts as "being convenient for the observer as a kind of intellectual shorthand for describing complex arrangements and activities in social life, but of limited utility for specifying how the actor or observer negotiates everyday behavior" (1974: 11).

My ideas regarding the importance of routines in peer culture for childhood socialization have been influenced by all of these theorists, but probably more so by the recent work of the French social psychologist Moscovici on social representations. For Moscovici social representations are a "set of concepts, statements and explanations orginating in daily life in the course of inter-individual communications" (1981: 181). In simpler terms Moscovici refers to social representations as the "contemporary version of common sense". Moscovici and his colleagues are interested in both the content of social representations and in how they arise and are maintained in social interaction. It is what Moscovici has to say about the latter which is most useful for understanding the importance of children's play routine in the socialization process.

In discussing Moscovici's views regarding how social representations arise and are maintained, it is necessary to consider his distinction between consensual and reified universes. In consensual universes "society recognizes itself as a visible, continuous creation which is imbued with meaning and aims; it speaks with a human voice, is part and parcel of our lives and acts and reacts like a human being" (1981: 186). In reified universes, on the other hand, "which comprise solid, fundamental, immutable entities and where particularities and individual identities are disregarded, society fails to recognize itself and its works, which appear to it under the guise of isolated objects" (1981: 186). According to Moscovici where scientific disciplines are linked to these objects, scientific authority imposes this way of thinking and experience on each of us, prescribing what is true or not true. In short, in consensual universes man is the measure of things, while in reified universes the converse is true.

It is important to consider the place of interaction and discourse in these universes. Moscovici argues that in consensual universes "society views itself as a group made up of individuals who are of equal worth and are irreducible" (1981: 186). Therefore, individuals are free to behave as "amateurs" or "curious onlookers" and through their everyday discourses on the street, in clubs, in cafes, over meals, they gradually "create nuclei of stability and habitual ways of doing things, a community of meanings among those who participate in it" (1981: 187). Conversely in reified universes, society sees itself as a system with different roles and categories, whose members are not equally entitled to represent it. "There is in reified universes", argues Moscovici, "a proper behavior for each circumstance, a proper style for making statements for each occasion, and of course, information suitable to given contexts." In this sense argues Moscovici society "depends on a sort of global environment and not on reciprocal agreements, on a set of rules and not a series of conventions" (1981: 187).

It is clear, then, that Moscovici sees science as the mode of knowledge corresponding to reified universes and social representations as corresponding to consensual universes. While science "attempts to construct a map of the forces, objects and events unaffected by our desires and consciousness", social representations "stimulate and shape our collective consciousness, explaining things and events so as to be accessible to each of us and relevant to our immediate concerns" (1981: 187). It is Moscovici's main contention that social psychology must become a science of consensual universes. I would agree and argue further that theorists of socialization must come to understand children's participation and membership in the consensual universes which they create throughout the developmental process.

But why do individuals develop social representations? According to Moscovici in consensual universes each of us wants to feel at home, to be on familiar ground. Novelty is accepted, but only to the extent that it maintains liveliness and prevents discourse from being dominated by repetition. In line with these assumptions Moscovici proposes a basic principle of social life: "every representation tends to turn an unfamiliar thing, or the unfamiliar in general, into something familiar". As a result, "objects, individuals and events are recognized and understood on the basis of prior encounters or models". In this process "memory tends to predominate over logic, the past over the present, the response over the stimulus and the image over the reality. To accept and learn the familiar, to become accustomed to it and turn it into a routine, these are ubiquitous occurrences" (1981: 188 – 189).

Moscovici's idea of turning the unfamiliar into the familiar is similar to the notion of "normal forms" as described in the work of Garfinkel (1976) and Cicourel (1974). It is a powerful idea especially when stated as a basic feature of social action. The tendency to change the unfamiliar to the familiar goes beyond general assumptions about psychological or cognitive disequilibrium or dissonance to suggest the importance of everyday social interaction for the production of social order. The notion of cognitive balance is used to predict why an individual may act one way or another, while Moscovici's conceptions of familiarization suggests "how groups or individuals faced with the apparent diversity of behaviours and phenomena that they view as unfamiliar or unpredictable, create a relatively stable order in which these become familiar and predictable" (1981: 204).

Moscovici's notion of familiarization overlaps nicely with basic features of the interpretive view of socialization we proposed in the introduction to this volume and my views of childhood socialization presented in earlier work (Corsaro, 1985). As I have noted a frequent pattern in childhood socialization involves the child's exposure to social knowledge and communicative demands in everyday activities with adults which raise problems, confusions and uncertainties which are later reproduced and readdressed in the activities and routines of peer culture. In these routines children attempt to make the unfamiliar familiar, to transform confusions and ambiguities from the adult world into the familiar and shared routines of peer culture. It is to an analysis of such routines that I now turn.

3. Social Development Through Peer Routines

3.1. Data and Method

The data for the following analysis of peer routines were collected in two long term micro-ethnographic studies of peer interaction in nursery schools. The first study was conducted in a nursery school in the United States which is part of a child study center staffed and operated by a state university for education and research. The school is located in a large metropolitan city near the university campus. There were two groups of children at the school, with approximately 25 children in each group. One group attended morning sessions and ranged in age from 2.10 to 3.10 years. The second group (which had been at the school the year before) attended afternoon sessions and ranged in age from 3.10 to 4.10 years at the start of the school term. The occupational and educational background of parents of the children ranged from blue-collar workers to professionals, with the majority of the children coming from middle and upper class families. I have presented a detailed discussion of field entry and data collection procedures for this study elsewhere (see Corsaro, 1981 b, 1985). The videotaped episodes of children's peer routines selected for analysis here are representative of the range of typical routines which occurred in the nursery school (see Corsaro, 1985 for a detailed analysis of the importance of play routines in children's peer culture).

The second study, in which data collection was only recently completed, was conducted in a scuola materna in a large urban area in nothern Italy. The scuola materna is a preschool educational program which exists throughout Italy and is administered by local governments. The scuola materna provides child care and educational programs for children from the ages of 3 to 6 years. The scuola materna which I studied was staffed by five teachers and there were 35 children who attended for approximately 7 hours (9:30 until 5:00; some children returned home at 1:00) each weekday.

The general methodological procedures, which involved participant observation, audio and video recording and microanalysis of peer interaction, were similar to those employed in the American study and described in Corsaro (1985). The data used for this report involve the preliminary analysis of peer play routines recorded in field notes and on audiotape. A more detailed analysis involving a comparison of the American and Italian data sets is presently in progress.

3.2. The Protection of Interactive Space: Children's Representations of Ownership and Friendship

In previous work (Corsaro, 1981 a, 1985) I have noted the tendency of nursery school children to claim ownership over play areas in which interactive events are emerging and to attempt to protect the activity and interactive space from the access attempts of other children. In simple terms, we can see this behavior as a peer routine — in that it is recurrent and predictable — in which children attempt to protect interactive space. The routine normally involves two phases. First, the children discuss and eventually make a joint claim on a specific area of play. The claim often involves the physical movement of objects as well as verbal descriptions of activities. In some cases the first phase may also include discussion of anticipated access attempts of other children. The second phase of the routine involves active attempts to protect the play area and ongoing interaction from the intrusion of other children. Consider the following example from the American nursery school.

Example 2
Teaching Kids to Write
Participants: Barbara (B, age 3.4),
                 Nancy (N, age 3.5), and
                 Jack (J, age 4.2)

In this videotaped episode B and N have begun to play at a table which has been moved from its normal place in the school near two other work tables to an area some distance away near the playhouse area. Another child, Bill, had earlier brought paper, pens, and a pair of scissors to the area. When B and N arrive they begin to negotiate a play activity in which they pretend to be teachers who are teaching "kids to write" (an activity which normally occurs at the work tables with the real teachers in charge). We pick up the interaction after the children have a brief exchange with a teacher (T) who comes over to pick up a pair of scissors from the floor. Soon after the teacher leaves Jack appears.

Transcription		Description
1. T-BN:	That's good you have your own desk over here for working at.	T leaves after this utterance. A boy, J, now approaches table and then moves away into the playhouse. B leaves briefly, then returns with a sheet of paper.
2. B-M:	This is our desk. Nobody can come in our office!	Immediately after this utterance J pulls out a chair and sits down at the table. B and N do not respond to J's entrance.
3. N-B:	No. We show the kids, right?	N moves off-camera after this utterance, then returns with tape. Both B and N continue to ignore J who sits at the table.
4. B-N:	We working.	
5. N-B:	Yeah.	
6. B-N:	Nobody can come in!	J is in but ignored.
7. N-B:	No.	Meaning that nobody can come in. B and N are looking at each other as they speak in these exchanges.
8. B-N:	Then we teaching.	
9. N-B:	Right.	
10. B-JN:	No. He not-can't come in.	B's utterance is in response to J's reaching for a stapler.
11. N-J:	No, no! We're teachers.	N slaps at J's hand as she says no. J grabs stapler and N pulls it away.
12. N-J:	No!	As she takes stapler from J.
13. N-B:	We don't-we're the class-students, right? We're the students, right, B?	J now reaches over and takes B's stapler. B does not notice this.
14. B-N:	We the —	All three work: J staples, B cuts, and N draws.

15. N-B:	What's J doing — he took your stapler. Here.	N notices that J has B's stapler. N picks up the stapler and gives it back to B. Saying 'here' as she places it in front of B.
16. N-B:	B?	B now picks up the stapler.
17. N-B:	J, we don't like that child, right?	N uses J as a sort of topic-comment, identifying then commenting upon him.
18. B-N:	Right.	
19. B-N:	We getting all this mess up.	B picks up papers from table and moves toward waste basket.
20. N-B:	Yeah, we (inaudible).	

In this sequence we see both phases of the routine involving the protection of interactive space. First, B picks up on the teacher's designation of the desk as "their own" by repeating the claim and then proposing the exclusion of all others except herself and N. The phrase *nobody can come in* was frequently produced by the children in the first phase of negotiating a claim on an area of play. At line 3, N confirms B's statement (*No* meaning "Yes, nobody can come in"), and then goes on to tie B's claim back to an earlier discussion regarding teaching kids to write (earlier talk not included in this sequence). Note how B and N (utterances 4 − 9) continue to work toward a shared meaning of "what they are doing," while at the same time tying this meaning into a concern with the solidarity of the dyad and the exclusion of others. J's entry is interesting because he arrives on the scene before the girls are really ready to enter the second phase of the routine. J's presence is ignored at first (the fact that he is ignored is clear on the videotape), because at this point B and N are more concerned with the negotiation of a shared meaning than his entry. Here the speech act *nobody can come in* (2) is not a warning to possible intruders, but rather a signal to the dyadic partner that the activity is theirs and should be protected. This interpretation is further supported given that J's entry is reacted to only when it directly impinges upon the ongoing activity (10 − 11), whereupon the second phase of the routine is enacted. Again this sequence is especially interesting because N not only resists the entry of J, but also ties his access attempt to the nature of the developing play ("being teachers") and assigns J the role of the bad child or student.

Before turning to a more general discussion of the protection of interactive space as a routine in peer culture, it is useful to examine briefly an example of this routine from the Italian data. Consider the following example recorded in field notes which is one of many instances of the protection of interactive space which occurred in the scuola materna.

Example 3
2/28/84   Episode 1
Participants: Bruna (3.0),
                Cinzia (4.0),
                and Gina (5.0)

Bruna and Cinzia have built a house with Lego and have attached several toy animals to it. They then move from near the center of the large open room to two of the 20 chairs which set against the wall. The chairs are wooden and box-shaped with equal space above and below the seat. When they reach the chairs, the girls place their construction under one chair and sit in front of it hiding their house and their play from the direct view of other children. After they arrive B says: *Giociamo qui* ("We're playing here") and C says: *Nessuno viene qui* ("Nobody comes here"). After they play for several minutes G approaches and sits in the chair next to the one under which the girls are playing. G is ignored at first, but when she attempts to sit on the floor and play she is pushed away by C who says: *Via! Via!* ("Away!" "Away!"). This leads to a number of disputes between Gina and the other girls. G insists she can play and C and B say she can not. Interspersed between these discussions B and C continue to play with the animals, placing them in several locations on the house. On several occasions C whispers to B about G, who they still keep at some distance from their play. Eventually, however, G's persistence to join in breaks down the play and B and C abandon their construction and move to another area of the school. G follows after them and she is later corrected by a teacher for fighting with C.

We see in this example the same phases in the protection of interactive space which appeared among the American children. The children first agree that they are playing together and then go on to mark verbally the need to protect their play from the intrusions of others ("Nobody comes here!"). The second phase of resisting the intrusions of others occurs when another child actively attempts to enter into the play. However, this child, Gina, is persistent and the other two girls develop elaborate strategies to keep her at bay, so to speak, while they continue to play. Eventually, Gina's persistence leads to the termination of the activity and Bruna and Cinzia's movement to another area of the scuola materna.

Another interesting thing to note here is that the ecology of this playroom in the scuola materna made the protection of interactive space somewhat problematic for the children. Unlike the American nursery school where the playrooms were all divided into smaller subareas by partitions (e. g., bookshelfs, cupboards, etc.), this particular playroom in the scuola materna has one large area of open space surrounded by the chairs which sit against the walls. However, these ecological features of the scuola materna did not stop the children from attempting to protect interactive space. On the contrary, the children instead adapted their play and the use of space to meet their needs. In this example, the children created a somewhat secure location by transforming the area under the chairs into play space. In other instances children moved the chairs or arranged play materials in such a way to create more private play areas.

So we see that the routine of protecting interactive space appeared in the peer play of children from both cultures. But why does this routine occur and what is its significance for children's social development? In earlier work (Corsaro, 1981 a, 1985) I have argued that children's protection of interactive space is related both to the social contextual demands of the nursery school and to the children's developing communicative abilities. Establishing and maintaining peer interaction is not an easy task for young children since they are in the process of developing the linguistic and cognitive skills necessary for communication and discourse. The nursery school is an ideal setting for facilitating children's development of social skills. It is a setting in which children not only learn to initiate and construct interactive events with peers, but also one in which they attempt to maintain these events amidst a wide range of possible disruptions. In short, the desire on the part of the children to maintain peer activities in spite of frequent disruptions from multiple sources is the basis of their tendency to protect interactive space.

On the surface the children's protection of interactive space may seem uncooperative or selfish to adults. But it is not that the children are refusing to cooperate or resisting the idea of sharing. On the contrary, the children wish to continue to share the interactive experience already underway *with each other*. This interpretation is based on viewing the behavior from the children's perspectives, from their social representations of their shared peer culture.

But what are children learning in their participation in this routine? Does the children's protection of interactive space have a positive impact on their social development? I believe that it does. In the protection of interactive space children develop and use elaborate communicative strategies: (1) to claim ownership of objects, play areas, and the unfolding events themselves; (2) to resist the access attempts of others; and (3) if not an original participant to attempt to gain access into ongoing play (see Corsaro, 1979). In this sense the nursery school sets up important communicative challenges which children actively confront through their creation and participation in routines like the protection of interactive space.

The protection of interactive space can also be seen as having important effects on children's development of social knowledge. When children first arrive at the nursery school they discover that their conceptions of ownership, possession, and sharing, which are based on their earlier experiences within the family, are not compatible with the interactive demands of this new setting (also see Newman, 1978). In the home ownership is more tangible. For example, some things (toys, clothing, etc.) belong to the young children, other things to siblings, and still others to parents. Although some things must be shared in common (e. g., the television), it is adults who control their use. The problem of sharing possessions, most especially in families with one or two children, usually occurs when a young child has a visitor. On these occasions the child is asked to share his possessions with playmates. But this sharing is always temporary and actual ownership of the objects is never challenged.

At the nursery school things are different. All the toys and educational materials are communally owned. These objects belong to the school, or more specifically as the teachers say in the scuola materna to "i bimbi della scuola materna" (the children of the school). Since ownership of materials is communal, their use depends on negotiations for temporary possession during which the materials are shared, normally by two or more children. It is during the course of such negotiations that we often see the children attempt to protect interactive space. In this routine children attempt to establish joint ownership of objects and the play itself within a small group, and to protect the play against the intrusions of others.

What then may be happening here specifically regarding the children's conceptions of ownership and possession? From experience in the family children tend to equate ownership with individual possessions, that is, objects are matched with people (e. g., mommy's sewing machine, Johnny's bicycle, etc.). In dealing with the new demands of the nursery school the children seem to equate ownership with the temporary control of the ecological space and interaction in which materials are used. This process is in line with Moscovici's notion of "anchoring" social representations which he describes as "bringing them back to everyday categories and images, and attaching them to recognizeable reference points" (1981: 192). For the children the point of reference has changed from the home to the school. At school the children are anchoring ownership to their and their playmates' presence in an area of play which is verbally marked as shared and protected in the course of this peer routine. The result is a more advanced notion of ownership, one which goes beyond matching objects to individuals. Now children begin to see that some objects can be owned in common and shared with others in specific interactive events.

There is a second process in the routine of protecting interactive space which is related to children's conceptions or representations of sharing and friendship. From experience in the home, children come to see friends as other children with whom they come into contact. More importantly, friends are often children designated as such by adults. Adults often tend to associate friendship and sharing for children (e. g., "Jenny is your friend who has come to visit and you must share your toys with her"). As a result, children's early conception of "friend" is primarily a label for certain other children they know and who have been designated as friends by parents. In the nursery school sharing and friendship are often tied to children's attempts to generate and protect shared interactive events. The concept of friendship is no longer seen simply as a label applied to specific children. Now it is "objectified" (see Moscovici, 1981: 192) in a different way. The concept is transformed into *observable shared activities* — playing together in a specific area and protecting the play from the intrusions of others. In fact, I have found that children most often use the term "friend" to mark this shared experience and at the same time protect interactive space and label intruders as "not being friends" (see Corsaro, 1979, 1981 a, 1985). As a result of experiences in the school and participation in this particular peer routine, the children have begun to see that friendship is more than just a label. Friendship has to do with sharing interactive experiences and protecting what is shared from others.

3.3. Approach-Avoidance Routines

As I saw Martin, Jack and Joseph climbing the stairs to the upstairs playhouse I decided to observe and later to record their activities into field notes. Although boys did participate in family role play in this area of the nursery school, such play usually occurred in mixed gender groups with the boys insisting on a strict adherance to gender appropriate roles (i. e., husband, father, big brother, etc.). Therefore, I was curious about what type of role play might emerge among the four boys. As it turned out there was no family role play. Instead the boys roamed throughout the upstairs apartment, opening and closing cupboards and drawers. After a while they began jumping on the beds and each other. At this point I expected that a teacher might put an end to what is seen as inappropriate play in this area of the school. But then something interesting happened. Suddenly Joseph jumped up from the bed, pointed at Martin, and yelled: *Watch out for the monster!* Denny and Jack then also jumped up and responded *Oh, yeah, watch out!* The three boys then ran downstairs pretending to flee from Martin.

Martin was, at first, a bit bewildered by what was happening. He moved to the stairway to see where the others had gone, and, not seeing them, he returned near the bed and looked down into the school. Meanwhile, the other boys huddled together in the downstairs playhouse and pretended to be afraid. Denny suggested *Jack, go see where the monster is.* Jack cautiously moved out of the playhouse, looked up, saw Martin, and then ran back inside screeching loudly. Martin now began moving down the stairs and eventually reached the bottom, turned and saw the other boys in the playhouse. The three boys screamed and ran back upstairs. As they passed Martin, Joseph yelled *You can't get us monster!* At this point Martin began walking mechanically (somewhat like a "mummy") and followed the other boys back upstairs. This routine was then re-cycled several times with Denny becoming the monster later in the episode.

The above summary of an interactive episode collected in field notes (see Corsaro, 1985) is an example of a play routine that occurred consistently in both the American and Italian nursery schools. In the routine there was always a *threatening agent* (monster, wild animal, etc.) who was *both approached and avoided.* The routine was normally composed of three distinct phases: identification, approach and avoidance. The identification phase involved the children's discovery (or creation) and their mutual signalling of a threat or danger. This phase was important because it served as an interpretive frame for the activities which followed. That is, identification of a shared threat was a signal that the approach-avoidance routine was now underway and that emerging activities should be interpreted in line with this particular play theme. In some cases one or more children would adopt the role of threatening agent, while in others (e. g., the routine described above) children were literally thrust into the role. The latter type of identification displays the extensive control the children who are threatened have in the enactment of the routine, a point I will return to below.

The second, approach phase quite simply entailed the threatened children's careful advance toward the source of danger. There were a variety of approach strategies, but they all shared one common feature. It was essential to approach with caution. The children's behavior during the approach phase exuded caution. They would advance slowly, quietly, cautiously but with determination to confront the danger. Other children pretending to be wild animals or monsters (i. e., the source of danger) would, at first, purposely fail to notice the cautious advance of their playmates. But at some unanticipated (but predictable) moment the dangerous animal or monster would detect the approach of their counterparts; and with a shocking reaction (e. g., a growl, and evil laugh, or a diabolic threat) signal the beginning of the avoidance phase of the routine.

In the avoidance phase children in the role of threatening agent would chase after their fleeing playmates while growling, or yelling threats. The pursued children would feign fear by screeching, screaming, and attempting to hide. In most cases the threatened children would reach certain areas which served as a "home base". Less often the fleeing children would actually be captured by their pursuers and brief shoving and wrestling matches would ensue. Such activity was, however, short-lived. Eventually the attackers would move away and the danger would diminish.

At this point the play routine would end or the pursued children would initiate a new approach phase. In some cases the approach and avoidance phases were repeated several times with a large number of participants entering into and exiting from the play routine.

Although there were a wide variety of threatening agents in approach-avoidance routines, the most frequent evil villains were monsters. It was not surprising to find that children in nursery schools in the United States and Italy frequently talked about monsters. After all, monsters, goblins, and other evil characters frequently appear in fairy tales, movies, and on television. What I found most interesting is how the children incorporated monsters and other evil creatures into peer culture; that is, how the children made monsters a part of their fantasy play.

In Italy the children frequently talked about "La Strega" (The Witch). One little girl told me at one point that witches do not really exist, they are *per finta* (for pretend). But then she later pointed out to me that *la strega e il dracula sono gli amici* ("the witch and dracula are friends"). Her view of "la strega" symbolizes the children's perspective of attraction to monsters. Monsters do not *really exist*, but we can *pretend* that they do. And this pretension often has a tinge of reality. In fact, for children monsters generally represent the "unknown", and in this sense they are feared. But at the same time children have an attraction to and a curiosity about monsters. It is for this reason that monsters are often incorporated into approach- avoidance routines. Consider the following example from the Italian data.

Example 4
3/22/84   Episode 4
"La Strega"
Scene: Outside Play Area
Participants: Cristina, Luisa, and Rosa

The three girls (all around 4 years old) had been playing for some time in the outside yard near the scuola materna when Rosa pointed to Cristina and said: "She is the witch." Luisa then asks Cristina, "Will you be the witch?", and Cristina answers, "Yes, I'm the witch." At this point Cristina closes her eyes and Luisa and Rosa move closer and closer toward her, almost touching her. As they approach Cristina repeats: *Colore! Colore! Colore!* (Color! Color! Color!). Luisa and Rosa move closer with each repetition and then Cristina shouts: *Viola!* (Violet). Luisa and Rosa now run off screeching and Cristina, with her arms and hands held out in an threatening manner, chases after them. Luisa and Rosa now run in different directions and Cristina chases after Rosa. Eventually Rosa runs up to and touches a violet object (a toy on the ground), and has now reached home base. Cristina now turns to look for Luisa and sees that she also has found a violet object (the dress of another child). Cristina now again closes her eyes and repeats, *Colore! Colore! Colore!* and the other two girls begin a second approach and the routine is repeated, this time with "gray" as the announced color. Rosa and Luisa again find the correctly colored objects before Cristina can capture them. At this point, Cristina suggests that Rosa be the witch and Rosa agrees. The routine is now repeated three more times with the colors yellow, green and blue. Each time the witch chases, but does not capture the fleeing children. Finally, Cristina suggests that they go and join some other children who are playing nearby with buckets and shovels. Rosa and Luisa agree and the routine ends.

There are a number of things to note about Example 4 which illustrate the importance of approach-avoidance routines in peer culture. First, the routine allows for the personification of the feared (but fascinating) figure, "La Strega", in the person of a fellow playmate. The fact that "La Strega" is now objectified in the actions of a living person is tempered by the fact that the animator is, after all, just Cristina (i. e., another child). So the feared figure is now part of immediate reality, but this personification is both created and controlled by the children in their joint production of the routine.

A second thing to note about Example 4 is that the structure of the routine leads to both a build-up and a release of tension and excitement. In the approach phase "La Strega" relinquishes power by closing her eyes as the children draw near to her. The tension builds, however, as the witch repeats the word *colore* because she decides what the color will be and at what point it will be announced. This announcement signals the beginning of the witch's attempt to capture the children and the avoidance phase of the routine. Although the fleeing children may seem to be afraid in the avoidance phase, the fear is more feigned than real in that finding and touching of most any color can be easily accomplished. As a result, the witch seldom actually captures a fleeing child. In fact, threatened children often prolong the avoidance phase by overlooking many potential objects of the appropriate color before selecting one. We see, then, that in approach-avoidance routines the threatened children have a great deal of control because they initiate and re-cycle the routine through their approach, and they also have a reliable means of escape in the avoidance phase. Overall, this example of approach-avoidance demonstrates how children cope with real fears by incorporating them into peer routines they produce and control.

It is clear that in approach-avoidance routines children attempt to gain control over the fears, concerns and curiosities of their everyday lives. Further, in the joint production of the routine children share the building tension and excitement of the threat and the relief and joy of the avoidance or escape. In Moscovici's terms the children are attempting to make the unfamiliar (the unknown and threatening) familiar. In this sense the approach-avoidance routine nicely fits Moscovici's notion of the process of objectification. Moscovici notes that through objectification concepts which have first been "perceived in a purely intellectual and remote universe", now emerge "before our eyes in the flesh and close at hand" (1981: 198). In approach-avoidance play the children's developing social representations of evil and the unknown are, through interaction with others, becoming more firmly grasped and controlled. In addition, the children are further developing and sharpening the basic interactive skills which underlie the acquisition of all social knowledge.

4. Conclusions

In this chapter I have argued that children's participation in peer routines in settings like the nursery school have an important, positive effect on their social development. However, it is clear from other research that children's involvement in play routines begins well before they enter nursery school. In early infancy children through participation in everyday play routines with caretakers develop basic communicative skills and a sense of agency (Bruner, 1975; Halliday, 1974; Snow, 1977; Watson-Gegeo and Gegeo, this volume). Later in the infancy period children begin to initiate and take a more active role in interactive processes with adults (see Bruner, 1974; Camaioni, this volume; Ratner and Bruner, 1978). Also during this period children begin to develop interpretive skills and acquire a central categorization of the childhood period; that is children come to see themselves as "children" who are different from "adults" (see Corsaro, 1985). With this recognition children begin to note differences between the adult and child world and also begin to establish relations with peers. Attendance in nursery school, participation in organized play groups, and informal activities with peers all lead to children's joint production of an initial peer culture and launch them on a path involving participation in and the production of a series of peer cultures throughout childhood and adolescense (see Fine, this volume, for examples of adolescent peer culture).

In this chapter I have, in addition to identifying some of the routines of peer culture in the preschool period, also attempted to demonstrate how children's participation in peer routines relates to Moscovici's (1981) conception of social representations and his ideas regarding the basic process of familiarization in everyday life. Through their production of and participation in peer routines children are attempting to make the unfamiliar familiar. They are attempting to transform confusions and ambiguities from the adult world into the familiar and shared routines of peer culture. In this process, however, the children's peer world is always changed somewhat; it always becomes a bit different. What Moscovici refers to as "nuclei of stability" (1981: 187) remain, but there has been an increase in the density and a re-organization of what Jenny Cook-Gumperz and I have, in the introduction to this volume, called the "productive-reproductive complex" within children's worlds. In this sense the socialization process is viewed as children's movement toward the reproduction of the adult world through their production and sharing of their own peer culture.

References

Bordieu, Pierre
    1977   *Outline of a Theory of Practice* (New York: Cambridge University Press).
Bruner, Jerome
    1974   "The organization of early skilled action", *The Integration of a Child into a Social World*, edited by M. P. Richards (New York: Cambridge University Press), 167–184.

1975   "The ontogensis of speech acts", *Journal of Child Language* 2: 1 – 19.
Cicourel, Aaron V.
1974   *Cognitive Sociology* (New York: Free Press).
Corsaro, William A.
1979   " 'We're friends, right?': Children's use of access rituals in a nursery school", *Language in Society* 8: 315 – 336.
1981 a   "Friendship in the nursery school: Social organization in a peer environment", *The Development of Children's Friendships*, edited by S. Asher and J. Gottman (New York: Cambridge University Press), 207 – 241.
1981 b   "Entering the child's world: Research strategies for field entry and data collection in a preschool setting", *Ethnography and Language in Educational Settings*, edited by J. Green and C. Wallat (Norwood, N. J.: Ablex).
1985   *Friendship and Peer Culture in the Early Years* (Norwood, N. J.: Ablex).
Garfinkel, Harold
1967   *Studies in Ethnomethodology* (Englewood Cliffs, N. J.: Prentice-Hall).
Goffman, Erving
1959   *The Presentation of Self in Everyday Life* (New York: Doubleday).
1983   *Forms of Talk* (Philadelphia: University of Pennsylvania Press).
Halliday, M. A. K.
1974   *Learning How to Mean* (London: E. Arnold).
Moscovici, Serge
1981   "On social representations", *Social Cognition*, edited by J. Forgas (London: Academic Press), 181 – 209.
Newman, Denis
1978   "Ownership and permission among nursery school children", *The Development of Social Understanding*, edited by J. Glick and K. Clarke-Stewart (New York: Gardner Press), 86 – 101.
Ratner, Nancy and Jerome Bruner
1978   "Games, social exchange and the acquisition of language", *Journal of Child Language* 5: 391 – 401.
Sacks, Harvey, Schegloff, Emanuel and Gail Jefferson
1974   "A simplest systematics for the organization of turn-taking in conversation", *Language* 50: 696 – 735.
Schenkein, Jim (ed.)
1978   *Studies in the Organization of Conversational Interaction* (New - York: Academic Press).
Snow, Catherine
1977   "The development of conversation between mothers and babies", *Journal of Child Language* 4: 1 – 22.

A Silent World of Movements Interactional Processes among Deaf Children

Herman Coenen

> "It is not easy to uncover motoric intentionality in its essence: it hides behind the objective world to the constitution of which it contributes." (M. Merleau-Ponty, *Phénomenologie de la perception*, 167)

The following text describes some results of a research project that I undertook as a participant observer in a school for deaf children. It purports to draw the reader's attention to the fundamental and multiform activities of the body in the everyday interactions of these children: how these children's school-world with its communicative contents, its routines and its adventurous occurrences, is shaped through gestures, mimics and locomotions, to mention just a few aspects of the broad range of motoric behaviour. Special attention is drawn to the phenomenon of "introduction", showing how the children introduce strangers into their world, how they introduce each other into new situations within the context of that world — and, as a contrast, how they are introduced into an outside world: a school for children without hearing-loss. The contrast evoked here is analyzed through the concepts of 'incorporation' versus 'annexation', the former indicating a rather naturally flowing way of leading each other into a new environment or situation, mainly by bodily movements —, the latter indicating the more coercive style in which the children are taken up into a world not their own, mainly through express rule-enforcement. In the course of the whole analysis an important characteristic with which corporeality imbues these children's interactions, becomes visible: improvisation. Upon narrow inspection their everyday world shows itself as totally alive, full of fluidity and change; it is a world built upon 'improvised contexts'.[1]

1. Preliminaries

1.1. Corporeality, meaningful structure, interaction: theoretical considerations

In handling our daily affairs there is nothing that we take for granted so much as our own body. We know that it is there, that it works and we trust unthinkingly that it will go on working the next moment and throughout an indefinite period thereafter. It is there, at our disposal in an unproblematic way, and we often even use it as if it were an instrument, the most willing and plastic of all. This is even so where, in a new wave of attention to the body, we cultivate it and subject it to hygienic and sportive regimes. And as long as everything remains in good order, it is not difficult to hold this implicit vision upright. As the center of a well-functioning reality our body seems to affirm the obedient role that we ascribe it.

This much-practised attitude does not receive great correction from the human sciences. Mostly the body seems to be nonexistent there. The neglect of its functioning in personal and social life is only partly taken away by the recent attention directed to the body by such diverse disciplines as sociobiology or the socio-psychological experiments in non-verbal behaviour[2]. They do bring interesting and useful insights, but cannot work a radical breakthrough with respect to the attitude taken here. The special emphasis laid by these newer lines of research on the autonomous mechanics at work in the body, even represents a modern version of the separation of mind and body that is so deeply rooted in Western philosophy. Again, the body is viewed as being isolated from the higher, mental structures of human existence; and even where its own significance is acknowledged, it remains enclosed in a separate circuit. This view goes hand in hand with an equivalent isolation of mental activities: when it comes to action and its inherent production of meaning, all the elements for an explanation are taken from the sphere of consciousness with its rational and irrational aspects.

The critical leap away from the basic philosophical prejudices hidden in the modern human sciences, as it is performed by phenomenology, is generally known. Through phenomenology's methodic return towards the field of direct experiences new foundations have been laid for empirical and theoretical work in the sciences of man. In the building-process of these foundations the question of "meaning" plays a central role. Phenomenological research has made clear that meaning can no longer be treated as a separate factor in the constellation of human phenomena; it rather should be seen as a pervading quality underlying and integrating the many and various sectors of existence that traditionally have been isolated from each other by philosophical and scientific thinking. Especially the age-old distinction between subject and (outer) world turns out to be a false starting point for a realistic treatment of the dynamisms in social and psychic life. Subject and environment (in a multiple sense) are centres of gravity within one and the same world.

Parallel to this movement towards an overcoming of the theoretical borderline between subject and world, new insights into the signifance of the body within the area of subjective life and action have made their way. In the work of Buytendijk, Plessner, Schütz, and especially Merleau-Ponty the latter change of view has been brought to its consequences.[3] Here the body is acknowledged as playing more than just a subordinate role, separate from the centre of subjective activity which was traditionally supposed to reside in the individual's consciousness; rather, the body is our way of being present in the world, and the instance through which every activity comes to be realised. Therefore it is preferable, instead of speaking about "the body", to use the term "corporeality", as an expression of a basic characteristic of our field of action. Thus corporeality gains a crucial position when it comes to the question of how the subject's relations with the surrounding world are built up and structured. And therefore, corporeality now can be seen as lying at the heart of the problem where meaning comes from, how it develops, and how it influences human behaviour.

Through this rehabilitation of corporeality a less idealistic approach to the theory of meaning becomes possible. Instead of projecting it into a hidden corner of pure mind — an "ego", free of all worldly allegiance — one now has to look for it in the concrete structures of everyday affairs. And a point of special importance for social science is that, whereas meaning is embodied in everyday situations, it must from the outset be characterized as social. As corporeal beings we live in a common environment; the meanings that grow in our actions are the outcome of a common undertaking.

Theoretically, the possibility of bridging the distance between two generally congenial lines of research in modern sociological tradition comes into view here: the first based on the concept of typifications, developed by Schütz, Berger and Luckmann among others, the second based on the concept of the social act, stemming from G. H. Mead and Blumer.[4] The importance of the Schützian concept of typifications can be found in its stress on the acting subject's world of experience as a basis for the explanation of his actions and reactions in the social sphere. Its shortcomings seem to have their origin in an overaccentuation of the ego-centered acts of consciousness in the constitution of typifications; typifications thus become individually oriented mental models or schemes of interpretation.[5]

Starting from the other side, so to speak, the Meadian concept of social act reveals the meaning-productive character of social intercourse and places the conscious interpretations and acts of the individuals involved in a genetic and situational context. The latter thus come to be seen as aspects of a more encompassing interplay.[6] The acknowledgement of corporeality brings to light the relevance of both concepts and shows how they can be reformulated and knit together in the analysis of social processes.

Thus the leading question for the empirical inquiry presented here is: how corporeality, in its various aspects of perceptive and expressive functioning, can be seen at work in the development and structuring of interactive situations. This has to be specified at several points. First, my focus of interest is the interplay of gestures exchanged between the participants of the interaction. Each subject's movements take place in a corporeal field that is from the outset a shared one; in this field there is a continuous formation-process of social acts of which the individual movements are integrated parts. Second, this formation-process characterizes itself as a mutual improvisation by the participants, on the background of given themes and forms of action. In this improvisational activity situational structures come into being, which render each involved element its proper place. Third, these structures function as implicit meaning-patterns (social types) pervading the more conscious and willfull actions and interpretations of the participants on the one hand, while they are, on the other hand, constantly being restructured and reshaped by the latter.

It may be clear that through the general insights into the significance of corporeality for the sociological understanding of the dynamics in interactional processes a new field of study is opened up, in which traditional theories such as those on role and socialisation enter a state of flux. Also, the corporeal character of social events asks for another approach than intellectual reasoning and deductive logic alone. Therefore, in this project the choice was made for an exploration of concrete situations in everyday contexts that could give the hitherto global and presumptive insights a more substantive and detailed filling. The choice of deaf children's worlds was based on the additional motivation, that this context with its special accent on bodily movement and gesture might provide a privileged vantage point for observing the birth of meaning in the sphere of corporeal interplay. A practical aspect of doing the study in this particular context was that it could shed some light on the problems inherent in the discussion between the protagonists of the oral language approach and those of the use of sign language in the education of the deaf.

1.2. Setting and method of the study

The study was conducted in a school for deaf children in San Francisco's Bay Area, in the period between February and July 1980. Some criteria decisive for the selection of this particular school were: the "dual track" that was followed in this school's teaching system, implying the simultaneous training of oral language (based on lip-reading and use of speech) and sign-language (Signing Exact English, SEE); the sympathetic and open attitude of the school's teaching staff towards this researcher and his project; the fact that the children were used to the regular presence of parents and other visitors in the classrooms; the relatively easy access to the school's site.

The school was set up as a day center to which the children were brought by schoolbus every morning and from which they were taken back to their homes in the afternoon. The area from which the pupils were recruited is generally known as prosperous, its lifestyle being liberal, with a high amount of geographical mobility. The school's population (teaching staff not included) consisted of around twenty children in ages varying between three and nine. They were divided up into four classes, one for deaf-and-blind pupils, the other three classes for hearing impaired children in the successive age-groups of two and three, four and five, six to nine years. My research project did not include the deaf-and-blind children's class; it was restricted to the latter three classes whose population was medically characterized as children with severe to profound hearing loss. All of them wore hearing aids. Each class was conducted by a qualified teacher (two teachers for the two and three year olds) plus an aid. It goes without saying that in the following report all names have been changed for the sake of anonymity. For an impression of the everyday setting in wich the interactions analysed here developed, the following two schemes, the first temporal, the second spatial, may be helpful.

1. Temporal schema:
   8.a.m.: successive arrival of staff;
   8.30 a.m.: successive arrival of children;
   9. a.m.: lessons start;
   10. – 10.30 a.m.: play- and snack-time;
   11.45 a.m. – 12.45 p.m.: lunch-time;
   2. p.m.: end of school day.

2. Spatial schema (see opposite page).

Regarding method I have tried to develop an approach that suited the field to be studied as well as the questions to be asked. As noted earlier, these two dimensions were narrowly connected to each other, so that the object of the project can be thus summarized: to develop, on the basis of everyday occurrences among children in a school for the deaf, some insights into the processes of social meaning-constitution through corporeality. From phenomenological analyses of corporeality, I could assume that the field of study would be characterized by the partial implicitness of its meaning-structures, by fluidity and changeability, by a "gestalt"-like organisation and interconnectedness of behavioral elements, and by the concrete situatedness of this organisation. These and other considerations pointed in the direction of a method combining participant observation and phenomenological-interpretive analysis within the general lines of a "grounded theory"-approach. As a participant observer I was a regular visitor of the school, who sat around in the classrooms during the lessons, went out with the children and their teachers on the playground during physical education hours and playtime, etc. I remained in the background as much as possible, trying not to interfere in things that happened among children or between them and teachers. My role was known as that of a researcher, who was there with the intention of watching, noting down and trying to understand what was going on. And as such I was clearly accepted by the children and their teachers. This acceptance from the teachers' side was a great help: they provided me

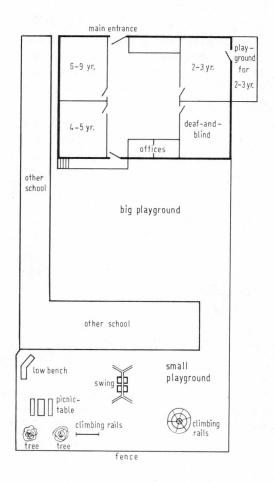

with background-information and were always willing to answer specific questions regarding the interpretation of messages in sign-language exchanged by children. Acceptance by the children was crucial, in order to be able to be part of their interactions without blocking the natural flow of these situations. Therefore, I took care to build up a friendly contact with them and not to be identified too much with the teachers. I wanted the kids to feel free — as much as possible — to act as they would have if I had not been present.

My position as an overt researcher and the specific questions I had in mind, implied the necessity of keeping a subtle balance between the role of an acquaintance and that of a stranger. In this light my decision to enter the field without a mastery of the sign-language used has to be understood. Since I was especially looking for the mostly implicit meanings of the total area of corporeal movements, I judged that it was better to refrain from concentrating on the explicit messages exchanged through the means of this codified system of standard connections of sign and signified. The intention of the study was first of all: discovery. The "grounded theory"-approach, described by Glaser and Strauss[7], seemed therefore to best fit with the general strategy that had to be followed. As an important consequence the activities of data collection and analysis had to be intimately interconnected; they were carried out alternately, at least during the period of my actual presence in the field, and thus they could reciprocally influence each other. In accordance with the general structure of the phenomenological method the analysis could be seen developing in two phases (which however were not clearly temporally distinct): The first phase consisted of elaborating some of the main features of the field's meaningful world, its routines, its specific happenings, its web of outspoken and tacit interpretations. Special attention was given to the possible crystallizations of the children's own meaning-provinces within the boundaries of the school's world at large. The second phase consisted in asking the genetic question (in a phenomenological sense): how does this world, and especially the children's own province of that world, come into being and transmit itself in the course of the everyday flow of events? This question was meant in the specific sense that was given to the problems of meaning-genesis in the first paragraph of this paper: in terms, that is, of the connection of typifications, social acts and corporeality. This led to selecting interactional sequences and scrutinizing them insofar as they showed an interplay of various manifestations of corporeal movement, perception and expression by the participants of the interaction. The ways in which this interplay produced the themes and meaningful structures of the situation at hand, were the insights that I hoped to reach through this analysis.

Before turning to an analysis of what I discovered, a last remark should be made about the activity of writing in the context of this research-project. In the exploration of a world of meaning, as was the case here, the development of texts through writing, be it in the shape of preliminary theoretical considerations, of field notes, of theoretical memos, or of a final synthetic presentation of resulting insights, takes a central place. From the beginning, these texts or text-fragments characterize themselves by a discursive form: they can be compared with textures rather than with collections of separate entities. When it comes to a final report, therefore, a reduction of the results into a set of clearly distinct propositions would be unsuitable, if ever possible. A report in the context of interpretive social research will rather follow the lines of a flowing argumentation in which, through the means of relevant citations of fieldnotes and adequate concepts built up in the analytic process, a synthetic insight is evoked pertaining to the field under study. It presents a structure that has its plausibility with respect to the world of experiences at stake. As such, however, it is merely one realisation out of a (restricted) plurality of possibilities.

2. Field Discoveries

2.1. Incorporation: receiving a stranger

The best point at which to introduce the reader to the world I explored, is the moment of my own start: a chilly, grey day, in early 1980, when I found myself passing through the rather unimposing entrance of that low wooden school building. I will show here now how that first day's feelings of estrangement were gradually overcome by the actions through which the deaf children responded to my presence. I will point out an important feature of those responses which, because of their corporeal character, may be called "incorporation".

So, I take my point of departure in those experiences of the first day: being a stranger.

If I was a stranger this was true in more than one respect. There was California, the United States, this country where I had never been before and that was so unexpectedly different in many ways, down to the most "trivial" things like doorknobs put in the *wrong* place and doors opening to the *wrong* side, or people asking me "how are you today?" without even knowing *who* I was and where I was yesterday. Then there was this school full of unknown people doing their inscrutable things, following invisible regulations and moving within surroundings full of obscure entities and functionaries in a matter of fact way that seemed as senseless as it was natural. And as if this was not enough, there were these children, with their quick, mysterious gestures, living in their own little world, impenetrable, unreachable. Was I going to do observations here? Would I ever be able to see something here? Not to speak of those nice and clear theoretical reflections about interactional context, corporeality, perception, ambiguity and temporality that I had worked out before coming here; they seemed not to work any more, and suddenly I was left without words. The children here were deaf, but I got dumb.

And in my struggle with depression and weariness, stubbornly fighting to remain sitting there in the classrooms and to get something down on my note-pad, I did not notice who it was that really helped me out of this. More than a year afterward, when that self-imposed pursuit of results was over in a way, I went through those first clumsy fragmentary notes again. And suddenly I saw: it was the kids themselves who did it and brought me in.[8] It was not me who forced my way in, it was they who, in small, inconspicuous moments took me inside. And so I gradually entered the field, quite some time after I came there. How did they do it? I think an adequate term here could be "incorporation", because it was with their bodies that they took me into their world.

First of all there were the looks. At many moments I got these open, friendly curious faces directed to me that gave the impression: "You are here, in the midst of what we are doing here; but what exactly is the part you take?". Now a distinction — although not too sharp — should be made between the two older age groups (the four and five year olds and the six to nine year olds) versus the youngest group (the two and three year olds). The impression has remained with me that in the former two groups the looks had a more express character, whereas the youngest children did not give me that sign of an outspoken awareness of and attention to my presence. For them I did not seem to exist as a separate element in their reality, until the moment when I seemed to fit into the web of practical connections that they again and again built up around themselves:

> "Charley[9] wants the little chair I am sitting on. He reaches his hand out. I get up and immediately he crawls on it. Then he points to the paper-holder (he sees that Brian sits at this table drawing on a sheet of paper from that paperholder). I give him a sheet of paper. He points out to me where I should put it: on the tray in front of him on the table. I put it on a wrong spot. He takes it up and puts it on the right spot. He starts drawing. I write his name in the margin of the sheet. He points to it. I point to the name and then on to him ...".
>
> (Somewhat later:) "Sally comes to the drawing-table, takes a piece of paper, touches me, I have to give her a pencil". (observation notes (o. n.); February 28, 1980).

Here, whith these younger children the looks seemed to be more integrated as an inconspicuous part of a practical movement of the body as a whole in which I was "asked" to do something for them. The spear-point of this total body-movement (i. e. that gestural moment which most directly caught my attention) would be: a reaching or pointing gesture of the hand, or a touch of the hand.

An important aspect, that more and more proved its relevance also in the two other classes, shows itself here: It was very difficult to distinguish sharply between an express "inviting" gesture and the movements belonging to the situation into which I was being invited. Rather, there was a sort of threshold-gesture in which I was simultaneously invited to take part in the situation *and* received as part of the situation. The invitational gesture was not just an anticipation, it was itself the start of that into which it was an invitation. This is a telling example of the equivocity of body-movements that I saw time and again during this observation-period: the movements of the body carry a diffuseness of meaning that makes it difficult to pin them down to a well defined, one-pointed "message". Even where expressly identified standard-gestures, obeying the prescribed code of sign language are used, there is an overflowing richness of (implicit) meaning conveyed by the total corporeal figure.

Let us get back to "incorporation" now. Very soon I came to see that also in the two older age-groups there was more than just the looks that took me in. It often happened on the playground, as in the following scene:

> "Little high shrieks. The six year old girl Bonny sits on the swing and wants to be pushed. I do it. Another child points up high, stands for a

while in that position reaching her arm out, until I see it: she wants to be lifted up on the swinging-rings. One of the boys is dragging another one (Martin). Martin falls to the ground, cries (without tears), his mouth wide open, with guttural sound, his face drawn. Jane (teacher) intervenes, puts him on his feet, points out[10] to the other child that he should not do that again and that he should apologize. Then they go away. Martin sees me, makes crying-like movements, draws up his trouser-leg, shows to me where he was hurt. He walks back to the scene of the accident, points to the ground. Looks at me. I pity him. He is satisfied". (o. n.; February 25, 1980).

So there are all sorts of bodily expressions in which I was asked for help: pointing with a hand, reaching out an arm, keeping a certain posture longer than normal, making demonstrating gestures (crying-like movements; drawing up one's trouser-leg). And there is even — something I did not at that time expect to find among deaf children — the use of sound.

In many of these scenes there is a mixture of explicitness and implicitness. The children often seemed to be aware that the other one's attention has to be caught by some strategy or other before the interaction will have its normal flow. So the pain following from the situation of being dragged and falling down is at that very moment made into a demonstration by an ostentative use of crying gestures, just a little more or longer than would be done by someone who "normally" cries out his pain. That is what Martin did until Jane came to help him on his feet again. In the meantime the pain seems to be over, but he seems to need something more. So the demonstrative aspect of the drawn face, the wide-open mouth is used expressly now, and directed towards me. One may say that he tries to catch my attention, but while he succeeds in doing this he elicits a reaction from me: I pity him. So, considered on the basis of their result, Martin's movements had several aspects at once: they were an express demonstration ("see what has happened to me") but implicitly they were an appeal for attention and a begging for consolation.

In the variety of bodily expressions in which my incorporation was done by the children, not only explicitness and implicitness were intermingled, but there was also a mixture of distance and nearness (speaking in a literal bodily sense): there were the looks, the shrieks, the pointings and the demonstrative showings, but the kids did not leave it at that; in every way they tried to catch the gaze, the attention and cooperation of this stranger that had entered within their horizon. In a very self-evident way they passed the borderline, experienced by so many grown-up persons, over to direct bodily contact. There were not just the little touches by the hand, there was touching in various other forms:

"Mary, Daphne and Sandra are eating at the table, outside in the sun (on the playground of a school for hearing children where they are brought once a week to attend some lessons). They are alone, I walk up to them and say "hi" (in sign language: one of the very few signs I learned). Sandra repeats the little game that she was doing together with the others a little while ago at their own school when we were going back from the playground into the school-building: she slaps me on the buttocks" . . . (o. n.; April 16, 1980).
"While we were walking to the playground Anny suddenly grasped my hand and did not let it go again. Sign of friendship. Mabel (the new help, replacing Jane who is ill) comes in her direction but is turned down: Anny gruffly bows her head, does not look at her" (o. n.; April 22, 1980).
"Bonny comes to me and tries to pull herself up on me and to climb on me. The Friday before, when I was going to leave from here, she also did that. Then she hung on my neck before I knew it. This time I say to her: "no, no; no, no", but she goes on for quite a while, until Lenny (teacher) comes and tells her to leave me alone" (o. n.; April 29, 1980).

I present this series of observational notes in their chronological order. They seem to reveal a certain development. Gradually the touches spread out over wider areas of the body and as in the last scene, they become a more total body-contact. This development accompanies my own growing feeling of acquaintance and being-at-ease. I was becoming looser, more playful and expressive towards the children. On both sides there were reactions of trust; that stranger without confidence, withdrawn and impenetrable, was now woven into their world, integrated into their field of corporeal possibilities: they could do something with me now and trusted that I would answer. At moments I was even treated as an ally who had the right of entry into their world of feelings, whereas others were kept outside. Sometimes I became embarrassed by their very direct expressions of friendship, but quite often I did answer them. And I began to understand more and more of what they did.

2.2. Incorporation: helping a new one enter

In this part the insight into the phenomenon of incorporation is extended: incorporation turned out to be practised by the children in various situations. Here I will concentrate on the situation in which a peer and possible future member of the group enters the field. Incorporation now gets some different aspects compared to the situation where I, as a grown-up visitor, was introduced into the children's world. The movements and gestures involved now become underlined by an ostentatively didactical tinge.

Incorporation work was not done to me only. Somewhat later in my observation-period I saw the children also doing it to a newcomer, Emmy, a little girl who was brought to this school for a trial period on three consecutive Wednesdays. I made some observations during her second visit to the school.

"(Physical education, on the playground:) All children are fascinated and very careful, wanting to help Emmy. At this moment they are standing in line, next to each other. Daphne is standing in front of them and throws the ball to each of them by turns. She now throws it to Emmy (who is the first one of the line), and she does this while going down on her knees; she laughs and claps her hands in a very demonstrative gesture towards Emmy, as soon as the little one has caught the ball ... Then, very demonstratively again, she reaches out her hands, indicating that Emmy should throw back" ... (o. n.; May 14, 1980).

Here the incorporating activity has a much more expressive character than in my case. The whole group is watching Emmy very attentively, every movement she makes is registered by the other children. And whereas most of the time my incorporation was done by asking me for help, it was now they who, very ostentatiously, offered help to the newcomer. Emmy was treated as a very helpless child, without any orientation in this strange setting, who literally had to be led by the hand:

"The children are going back inside. Daphne and Bonny take Emmy between themselves. As they go up the stairs Daphne very carefully bends forward, keeping her left hand in front of Emmy, who is to her right, looking at Emmy, at the stairs and then at Emmy again, saying "tap, tap, tap, tap ..."" (o. n.; May 14, 1980).

All activities in this physical-education hour, which is normally a time for the children to be very spontaneous, are now centered around this newcomer and her introduction. Especially Daphne, who is the eldest child in this class, takes this task very seriously. It is not so much that the normal activities were stopped and replaced by another, "special program"; on the contrary, many things are done as usual, but they get a special didactical tinge. All gestures are now done in a self-conscious, demonstrative way, and are executed such that they are visible for the newcomer. The normally inconspicuous and fluid development of the situation is now superseded by an accentuation and modeling of the movements forming part of it. The situation and the movements integrated in it thus take on a double meaning. On the one hand they are what they would usually be: doing games in the physical education lesson, or: going back inside the school building. Simultaneously, however, everything that is done is not done purely for its own sake, but is centered around the new child who has to be given entrance to this world over against which she must feel so helpless. Incorporation here has several aspects that did not show up as much when carried out on my behalf:

— it is done by expressly offering to the new one the possibility of taking part in the usual activities of the group;
— the new one is considered as being in need of help in this situation and is expected to remain passive;
— the task of entering this world with which the new one is confronted, is considered "difficult";
— there is an awareness of the specificity of the group's own world into which the new one is being introduced; therefore it has to be didactically underlined;
— implicity it is supposed that "in the end the new one will be one of us and know how to do everything we do here".

So incorporation here gets its full sense of extending the area of the group's normal activities over the potential new member. Emmy's integration is sought after by making use of the implicit invitational or seducing effect of situationally meaningful movements: "Just let her take part in what we do, then she will automatically do it herself and so learn what it is all about". That all of this, nevertheless, is carried out in such an expressive way shows that simultaneously the children must also be aware of the risks of failure of the undertaking: after all there is a borderline that has to be crossed by the stranger. The invitation implicit in the situational movements does not work with a mechanical necessity; it may not be picked up. Movements are opaque, their meanings are ambiguous, their suction power always remains precarious.

2.3. Improvisation: transforming prescribed tasks

Now, in tackling the phenomenon of improvisation, we seem to approach a core concept for the analysis of the children's activities. I will describe two situational types in which improvisation specifically manifests itself; first the situation where children deal with tasks that were imposed on them, second the enclosure of freedom within a schoolday represented by "play-time". In both instances the children cooperate in opening up and exploring together new spaces of fantasy. Again, as in earlier parts, our focus is directed on the way this process takes shape through the meaningful dynamics of the whole body.

The careful gestures by which Emmy was led into the group's world and the didactic modeling in which the activities of the group were presented to her produced the suggestion that it would not be easy for her to enter this world and act as a normal part of it: the implicit impression was given that this world had its fixed routines and rules with a definite but rather impenetrable special logic hidden behind them. A long effort of learning how to adapt to these patterns and how to function actively in accordance with them would be necessary after the initial incorporation was accomplished. This impression of a fixed world was also the one with which I was confronted during my own period of approach to these children's world and of incorporation in it. An important experience, however, that I underwent while this incorporation progressed was the gradual dissolving of the initial image of a massive and completed reality. As I became acquainted and began to move more smoothly within the daily school-context, not just sitting there as an immobile observer but responding by gestures, smiles, practical help, talk, etc., my understanding of the invisible network of meaning that was at work here grew. And with it grew my awareness that this "network" was only present as a horizon of which no more than some glimpses are visible now and then, a horizon that recedes for whomever tries to catch it and that changes with every movement he makes. That which happened on the foreground turned out to be anything but fixed; I saw a constant succession of situations improvised by the children. Sometimes there was a vague indication of recurring themes, but my main experience was that of surprise at the new course things could take at every instance. So after my entering the thick surrounding walls that sent out their message of stability and regular order, the world behind them opened up. I was confronted with children who were at work in many momentary undertakings, of which neither the course nor the outcome could be determined beforehand. What they did during recess-time on the playground where they were relatively free to manage their own dealings, as well as what happened in the classroom where they had to deal with imposed activities and regulations, was in an important respect characterized by improvisation. This is how I came across it in the classroom:

> "Lilian draws a heart in several concentric lines, each of a different colour. Rachel imitates it on her own piece of paper, starting with the outer line. She bends over the little box that stands between them and looks at Lilian's work. She points with her finger and wrinkles her eyebrows. Lilian answers the question, saying "yellow". Rachel shakes her head, says "red" and takes a red chalk. The two sit leaning against each other, arm against arm. Now Rachel draws a face into the heart. Lilian does it too and then colours the eyes red. Rachel bends over Lilian's drawing and makes them blue (the eyes in Rachel's own drawing are also blue); then she colours a blue mouth in Lilian's drawing. The mouth is wry. Lilian scratches the blue out with her forefinger, draws a new mouth. In the meantime Rachel has drawn a garland around the heart on her own paper. Lilian looks at Rachel's drawing, attentively, hanging over it. Then she bends over her own paper, simultaneously directing her gaze at it, and draws again. She feels her cheeks with both forefingers and then draws two red circles on the cheeks of the face on her paper. Suzie (their teacher) says it's time for fruit. Rachel was already standing near Suzie for a few moments, watching her prepare the oranges". (o. n.; April 16, 1980).

It began very simply: Suzie, the teacher, asked Lilian and Rachel to sit at the table, gave them a box full of chalks and a piece of paper each, and instructed them to draw a heart for someone they love. (Valentine's day was coming up soon.) So the theme is set, the material for realizing it is given. But then a complicated interplay between the girls develops, which move after move follows a new and unexpected course. They take up the task handed to them by the teacher and while executing it they give it a specific corporeal translation of their own.

Here another aspect of incorporation can be seen. Not only are new persons emerging in the children's environment subject to it, but given tasks and imposed regulations are being incorporated by them as well. In a subtle, and certainly little noticed way, the children transform the context in which they are placed by the school and their teachers, into a creation of their own. A first important moment in this process of transformation is this: that which was presented to them as two individual activities (each child should make her own drawing) becomes a common undertaking from the very start; the children sit very close to each other, shoulder against shoulder, the one's right arm pressed against the other's left arm — and Lilian's first move (drawing concentric lines) is immediately copied by Rachel.

Thus a chain of action is created in which every move of one child is hooked in by a move of the other child, in which the first one's move is taken over and enriched with some new element. "Hooking in" is not only a metaphorical way of speaking here, it is also done in a literal corporeal sense by the children, e. g. when Rachel and Lilian alternately lean over each other's work, gaze at it, etc.

So two developments are taking place simultaneously: every move that is done knits the two children more closely together as a "team" working on the common undertaking, — and at the same time it is a further step in the creative transformation of the given task. How central the touches, looks, pointings, etc., are in this process may be clear from the earlier observation-scene.

2.4. Improvisation: creating a fantasy chain

In describing the second situational type manifesting improvisation — the occurrences during play-time — the insight into this phenomenon is deepened. Especially I will try to analyze some of the "mechanics" at work in the corporeal sphere, by which improvisation leads to a structured and comprehensible, but quickly changing situation of play. This insight into the functioning of corporeality in the heart of the improvisational process — and, indeed, into the narrow connection of the two — makes it possible to better understand the overall improvisational aspect of these children's activities.

The phenomenon of improvisation and the corporeal basis on which it took place struck me most at those moments and locations where the children were left relatively free to develop their own play, especially on the playground during recess-time. Three interesting points were to be seen here. Firstly, the implicit way in which invitations to enter and fill out a new imaginary space were given; secondly, the quick spreading out of the new fantasy-scene over large parts of the group and of the playground; thirdly, the quick changes that the theme of fantasy underwent and the way these changes were anchored in the motoric sphere.

Here is an example of the sort of scenes that occurred on the playground quite often;

"We are walking to the playground, it's recess-time. Chris, one of the boys, is gesturing to Leigh, the teacher, partly by using his hands for sign-language, partly by using his arms and face in a theatrical fashion. I ask her what he "said" and Leigh explains: "Chris said that he is big and strong and green". And then she tells me about the T.V.show "The Incredible Hulk" in which a man is poisoned and thereby becomes big, strong and green. The actor who plays the role is deaf; the deaf children often watch it and like it very much".

Some instants later, on the playground:

"Sitting at the picnic table the children quietly eat their piece of orange. Then Anny puts the orange peel in her mouth, in front of her teeth, so that it shows between her lips. Martin, in front of her, also does it. They look at each other with big eyes. Then Martin makes clawing gestures. Leigh asks: "Are you the big hulk?". He nods slightly. Now Anny also does it and then I see a whole bunch of children doing it. They are running after each other, throwing each other down on the ground. Chris and Anny are dragging Bonny with them. Bonny gets hold of my sleeve. The two others draw her loose, throw her on the ground. Children running, cooing sounds everywhere. Then suddenly, five of them in the coneshaped climbing rails" (o.n.; April 16, 1980).

Taking the quiet scene at the picnic table as the point of departure one can see that the fantasy chain starts in a very simple manner: one of them puts an orange peel in her mouth (who among us never did this?). This move, seen by the child that is in front of her, functions as an invitation, although it may never have been so intended. Martin imitates Anny. But it does not remain at that; while looking at each other their eyes widen, get big. And thereupon Martin adds a new element: the clawing gesture. From that point on the whole thing quickly spreads to the others.

So the start is an ordinary practical situation: sitting together at the picnic-table eating oranges. Ordinary things, oranges, are the material around which the actions of the children are centered. What remains after eating is orange-peels; normally these are gathered and thrown away. But one child starts playing with its peel and the mere aspect of this induces one of the others to follow the example. As we saw before: just the doing of it implies a question. Something like: "Why don't you also do it?" And to see the first one do it is enough for the other one to pick up the question. Taking over the perceived gesture is the answer he gives. This answer is not just a declaration of some conscious intention, like: "Yes, I am going to join you in this thing", but it is the act of joining itself. The threshold to the fantasy-situation and its capricious development has been passed already.

To resume my point, the invitation is implicit, already a first presentation of the situation into which it invites the other child. And in this particular case the invitation consists of a playful manipulation of an element of a practical situation. A more or less unusual handling of ordinary utensils is the first move. It is important to acknowledge that these ordinary things and the practical setting in which they figure form the "launching-site" for the imagination that comes into being. And in the further course they remain present as the indispensable soil for intermediate landings.

Anny and Martin have opened up the imaginary scene. For me their interaction is a nicely circumscribed interplay of gestures, easy to observe in the way it progresses. The gesture by one is taken over by the other, with a small addition that slightly changes the total expression. And so on, back and forth. But then, suddenly I lose my overview: it seems that all children are running around with terrifying claws and dreadful faces, and in every corner of the playground something is happening that has to do with it. Everyone and every spot is taken up into the scene of fantasy, like an infection that has contaminated everything. The children get very excited, they move around wildly and a broad range of bodily aspects of expression, even guttural sounds, comes into play. The "infection" carries something magical: it is not just that gestures are reciprocally imitated and enriched, but through this channel that has its kernel in the very tangible sphere of the senses, a common imaginative world is being conjured up, transmitted and transformed. Here we see how far the ability of gestures to carry implicit loads — as was also the case in the instances of invitation — can reach. The interplay of gestures being performed, perceived and taken over is the corporeal story of an enchantment that is as inscrutable as it is commonplace.

Another aspect that made me lose my comfortable feeling of overview was the fluidity of the scene. As the fantasy chain unrolled itself the gestures through which it was built up were in a permanent and quick process of remodeling. And at no moment did the theme played out by the children seem to be fixed. Now it must be said that although this fluidity was at its strongest in situations of fantasy play, I had already been plagued by its manifestations since my first visit to the deaf children's school. In the most diverse situations I was confronted with it, and it was a constant threat to my self-confidence as an observer, especially in the beginning. Gradually however, I learned to see it as part of this setting and maybe even as one of its central characteristics. Only then did it become possible to get some insight into the "mechanics" of this fluidity, and to become more attentive to the perceptible forms in which the transformations of the scene took place. In the imaginative play-situations I learned much about this. An interesting discovery however came up in the following learning situation:

> "Madeleine (teacher) is doing speech-exercises with two of the children in her class, Barbara and Daphne ... Daphne talks about a boxer; she imitates the face of that race of dogs by drawing the corners of her mouth down with her fingers and dropping her eyelids. But then she says (orally): *Blee(d), blee(d), blee(d)*, in the meanwhile tapping with two fingers on her mouth-corner and cheek. Daphne is very expressive. She shows how a boxer goes k.o. She drops backwards, with her eyes closed." (o. n.; April 22, 1980).

Without giving any notice or making a halt Daphne changed the theme of her conversation. Only afterwards, when going over my notes, I realized that she had done this: so smoothly and inconspicuously did the transition take place. How did this come about?

The first and most plausible interpretation would seem to be that the double meaning of the word "boxer" was responsible for the change. This would leave to the gestures the role of a secondary expression of an association which already had been brought about in Daphne's mind through the verbal image "boxer". But if this were so, why wouldn't Daphne, when giving her demonstration of

the sportsman boxer, just have made use of the ready-made stereo-
type "head tucked away behind two fists"?

If we watch attentively what happens perceptibly, it becomes
clear that the gestural activity plays a far more important part than
it was granted in the foregoing interpretation. The story about the
sportsman boxer starts at the moment when the gesture "drawing
the corners of the mouth down with her fingers" undergoes that
very slight change by which it becomes "tapping with two fingers
on her mouth-corner and cheek". And what she further demonstrates about this unlucky sportsman is a consequent elaboration
of the thing that was said about him in the first gesture ("the poor
guy, he is bleeding terribly"). So it seems to me that the association
really takes place in the motoric sphere: carrying out gestural
movement A spontaneously fades into gestural movement A' etc.
There is an improvisational fantasy at work in the gestures, and all
possible parts of the body are involved. It is this gestural improvisation that produces an associative chain of movements in which the
transition from one imaginative theme to another becomes possible.
One could speak here of "pantomimic association".

This phenomenon of "pantomimic association" shows at several
moments in the fantasy-scene on the playground, cited above (o. n.;
April 16, 1980). Each new phase in the unfolding of the scene is
opened up by a gestural turning-point, where the association takes
place: 1. Eating out the piece of orange fades into putting the peel
in the mouth and showing it demonstratively to another child; 2.
showing the mouth with the peel in it fades into drawing a threatening face with big eyes; 3. the threatening gesture expands over wider
areas of the body, implying the clawing movement of the hands and
the corresponding lifting of the arms; 4. the threatening gestures,
after the teacher's offer of a well known interpretation ("are you
the big hulk?"), fade into more straightforward aggression consisting
of running after each other and throwing each other down; 5. for five
of them running around as threatening beings fades into climbing up
in the cone-shaped climbing rails (where I have often seen them
play "savage animals").

An important aspect of the chain of gestures fading into each
other that I saw thus develop, is that it was built up as a common
undertaking of the children present on the play-ground at that
moment; it started between two of them and by and by the whole
group was affected. Carrying out a certain movement formed the

basis for the "pantomimic association", but reciprocal perception (to see the others do it) was the condition by which everyone on the site could contribute to the further development of the chain. The mysterious side of this partaking in the common chain of gestures has already been mentioned above, when I spoke of the "magical infection" that was implied here.

2.5. Annexation into a hearing environment

At this point I propose to turn the reader's attention to a situation rather different from those described up to here: the interactions that developed when some of the children were exposed to the environment of a school not their own; this was a school for hearing children, where they were brought for a gradual integration into an open, non-deaf education process. An important discovery here was that the phenomenon of incorporation showed up again, especially between the deaf and the hearing children; but this phenomenon now became superseded by another specimen of introductional activity, which was especially present in some of the local teacher's actions: I purport to call it "annexation". In going through scenes from the observation notes I will elaborate some of the differences between "incorporation" and "annexation".

Up to here I have described the deaf children's interactions as these unfolded in this school for the deaf. Their behaviour in this place had something unproblematic, an experience that was quite unexpected and even in some way disconcerting for me: whereas I was prepared to be confronted with handicapped children I rather saw children who were very able to do their things and who at many moments were so intensively engaged in their interactions that it became very difficult for me to get some observational grip on the situation. It was not so much they who were handicapped here, as it was I who felt myself to be in that role.

We have seen how the children incorporated this visiting stranger into their own world, how they took the first steps toward incorporation of a potential new member of their world, and how they, within the trustworthy spatial, temporal and social coordinates of that world, opened up new situations and lured each other into a creative partaking in the building up of these situations.

I only came to realize how much this environment really was their "home-world", trustworthy and relatively unproblematic, when I eventually accompanied some of the older children on their regular visit to the school for "ordinary", hearing pupils. Here everything that I had learned to see as their normal context of living was turned inside out. It was a very painful and at moments angering experience. Here suddenly they were the strangers, and many times more helpless than I as a hearing person had been when I entered their world. And there were several circumstances that seemed to counteract or even prevent the incorporation-tendency that one would now have expected to start working from the other side.

This is not to say that there were no attempts at integration of the deaf children by the staff of this school. Indeed integration was the main goal of these organized visits. And the fact that one of the deaf-school's teachers was allowed to accompany the children in the classroom and, when needed, to act as an interpreter, gave this project a very tolerant aspect. Nevertheless, what I saw was such a peculiar mixture of inclusion and exclusion that a special term does not seem to be out of place to indicate the way integration took shape here. Over against "incorporation" I would rather speak of "annexation" in this context.

The contrast with what happened at the school for the deaf now makes it possible, and necessary, to give a sharper and more specified definition of what was implied by "incorporation". "Incorporation" then, is the process in which intersubjective contact, initiated by one of two parties, develops through a reciprocal partaking of corporeal expressivity and perceptivity as a common field. This process has a relatively spontaneous character on the part of those who are engaged in it; one could say that the activity implied here bears the heavy mark of the passivity[11] that forms its ground. The contact that grows here therefore has an important practical, sensorial and motoric aspect: it consists of looking at or walking toward each other, touching each other, pointing at something, manipulating things together or in front of one another, etc.

Here the participants are moving within a medium that is in principle accessible for each; because of its plasticity and lack of sharp boundaries or fixed forms it leaves room for creative fantasy that can be filled in in accordance with contextual and personal possibilities.

"Annexation", on the other hand, implies a certain constraint for one of the two parties involved. This "weaker" party is forced to accept the specialized and standardized form of communication that is guarded by the dominant party. The form of communication is specialized insofar it rests upon an overaccentuation of certain aspects of the total range of corporeal expression; it is standardized insofar as it is fixed into an institutionalized or conventional sign-system that requires a cognitive, expressive learning-process in order to be subjectively mastered.

Annexation as an activity of coercive inclusion was visible especially in the behaviour of the hearing-school's teachers toward the visiting deaf children. It was accompanied by an activity of exclusion in which the children were set apart and by which the spontaneous tendency of mutual incorporation especially at work between the deaf and the hearing children was interrupted. Thus the deaf children were deprived of their natural access to contact with the hearing ones through an expressive dimension in which both are competent. This interruption of the spontaneously developing intercorporeal communication left the children puzzled, disoriented and uncertain. It seemed to make them more ready to be subdued.

A first example of this mixture of exclusion and inclusion could be seen on the playground of the hearing-school during lunch-time:

"Daphne and Sandra are sitting on the bench. Alone, quiet. Daphne, like a grown-up lady, starts to read a book. Now and then she looks around, at what's happening on the playground. Staring a bit. Sandra sits quietly looking in the same direction ... On the other side of the bench some hearing children are sitting. One of them taps Daphne on the hand, and shows a small piece of fruit between thumb and forefinger. The hearing children see Daphne's book and one of them says (accentuating her lipmovements and pointing at another child): *She likes horses*. (Daphne's book is about horses). Then, after a short conversation with Daphne (in which Daphne remains rather passive), they walk away from the bench, discussing among them what they will do next. Daphne and Sandra are sitting alone again. All the other children are gone now and they are looking glum. After a while the teacher (one of the hearing-school's teachers who is supervising the playground) comes walking up to them and starts to talk: *Do you know why you are benched here?* The children don't react. The question is repeated. Again there is no reaction. The teacher speaks slowly and with clear lip-movements. She sits down on her heels before them. Asks: *Where are you supposed to eat your lunch?* Sandra points with her finger, timidly, at the bench. *Where were you?* Sandra answers (orally): *To the washroom*. The teacher says: *But you didn't come back here, you stayed over there*. Sandra's face gives the impression to me that she thinks it unfair. Then they are allowed to go playing. The teacher comes to me and explains that they do know the rules, but that it is difficult to make it clear to them why they are being punished". (o. n.; April 16, 1980).

In this scene the complicated role played by the "rules" in the exclusion-inclusion-process comes to light. The deaf children do not seem to be granted a say in the interpretation of the rules. The teacher supposes them to be unmistakably clear and acts upon this without giving attention to the corporeal signs sent out by the children indicating that they do not share the teacher's view. Her higher competence at the level of oral speech in relation to the children's ability at that point puts her in a position to impose her interpretation of the rules and simultaneously it is the rules — in the interpretation she gives them — that legitimize her to act as she does. This way the interpretation of the rules becomes a privilege of the hearing and orally speaking party. While being based upon elements of exclusion and inclusion in regard of the deaf children this rule-interpretation can now function as a further contribution to this very exclusion and inclusion. Trespassing the "rules" leads to isolation ("do you know why you are benched here?") and this will probably motivate the children in the future to listen more attentively to the orally proclaimed official meaning of these rules.

Annexation in its double aspect of exclusion and inclusion overtly applied in the subsequent scene in the classroom:

"Big class, about thirty children. The teacher is reading a story from a book, very quickly. Daphne sits at the back. She does not follow the story. Stares in front of her, fumbles at her desk. Madeleine (the accompanying teacher from the deaf-school) sits next to her and translates the story into sign-language for her, but Daphne pays no attention to it. The classroom teacher stops reading, stands up and walks through the whole classroom to Daphne. She asks: *What is it, Daphne?* No answer. Then Daphne gets a sermon: *You are a member of this class, you have no choice.* All other children look backwards. Madeleine translates in sign-language what the teacher says. Daphne sits there, her eyes filled with tears. Then the reading is continued, without any special attention for Daphne; the teacher does not read a bit slower, she reads without any gestural or mimic expressivity, or even a clearer accentuation of her lip-movements. Madeleine translates in sign-language. Daphne stares stiffly in front of herself, squinting. Madeleine takes Daphne's face in her hands and turns it towards her. Daphne stubbornly looks in front of herself again. After a while she starts to watch Madeleine".

After the story-reading there follows an episode in which the teacher talks to the children about an outing that is being planned and the children are asked for the reactions of their parents. Then they do a writing-exercise.

"The exercise is finished, the children hand in their papers. There is some disorder in the class. Daphne too gets up and brings her paper to the teacher's desk. On her way she tickles a boy in his neck. He accepts it without protest. When she is back at her place other children come to her and show her a football-trophy. She reacts with full interest and enthusiasm. Points at it with a questioning expression on her face. I understand that she means to say: "Is that yours?"
Then the school-bell rings. Time for going to the music-class. But the teacher orders all children to sit and bow their heads down on the desks, explaining: *This is an army-routine because of your casualness today.* After a while she orders them to get up and go to the door in row-formation" (o. n.; April 16, 1980).

An interesting aspect of the two scenes cited here is that they show the deaf child in two strikingly different moods. In the first scene she sits in the rear of the classroom, seeing only the backs of the other children, and at the farthest possible point from the teacher. Exclusion is clearly functioning. Inclusion too: everything has its way in this class as if Daphne were not there. Especially the corporeal style in which the reading is done renders this impression. Daphne simply has to resign herself to it and adapt, and she is told so. One can read from her visible reactions how unhappy she feels in the midst of all this. Her normally quite vivid movements are stopped now, her eyes look "nowhere". Her own teacher's attempt at catching her gaze by physical force (taking the child's face in her hands) is met with stiff, passive resistance.

But then the imposed, rigid order relaxes a bit. The whole class comes to life, and we see some glimpse of a different Daphne. Now she is more like the Daphne I know from the deaf-school. The first thing she does is to use her hands for making contact with another child: she tickles a boy in his neck. And now she is not being let down. The boy lets her have her way. A few moments later some children initiate an interaction with her, by walking to her and showing her something that seems to have personal value for them.

And Daphne reacts with lively and eloquent gestures. Thus an important element of the "disorder" that develops during some minutes (and that will be punished immediately thereafter) is the mutual incorporation-process being set in motion (or rather: restored) between the deaf child and her hearing "class-mates". Spontaneously the children, the hearing ones as much as the deaf ones, switch over to improvised gestural expressions which in their mutual interplay form a meaningful context outside the standards of any official system, be it oral or sign-language.

3. Conclusion: The Eloquent Body

This point brings me back to the insights that resulted from the first observations presented in this paper. The annexation episode as a contrast brings out the centrality of incorporation in these deaf children's dealings with their surroundings. It has a recurrent although not continuous character, in a social as well as in a temporal sense: it appears in various forms, according to the various social situations that come up for the children; and even forceful interruptions do not prevent the spontaneous tendency at incorporation from redressing itself time and again. It is important to note that the deaf children do not seem to be alone in this tendency. With the hearing children (at least) a common plane of exchange immediately opens itself up here, which fits in with observations that can be made at places where children of different national languages get in contact with each other.

It seems good to sum up our main conclusions as to the structural forms and conditions of the two phenomena, annexation and incorporation.

Annexation in this study manifested itself in a social environment where the children's hearing loss was explicitly treated as a handicap, and where this handicap was the problem of a minority. Solutions for this problem were sought in organizational measures directed to an adaptation — as far as possible — of the deaf minority to the everyday rules and routines of the non-deaf environment.

A strong indication for the existence of this phenomenon of annexation were the negative reactions (madness, resistance) of the deaf children to the actual situation in which they found themselves. They were taken up into a rigid order which did not take into account the special behavioral restrictions connected to their deafness. Their lack of adaptedness to the normal functioning of this order was responded to by the adults (teachers) with reprisal and punishment. An explicit reference to the normativity of this order was part of the adults' actions. The adults' intervention implied therefore that the normal flow of events was suddenly held up. In this intervention the interactional contact with the deaf child was also narrowed down to the explicit use of spoken language: the child's possibilities of reacting and defending herself were thus largely reduced. Her deafness was then clearly functioning as a handicap.

Incorporation, on the other hand, was in the first place visible in an environment where the deaf children were able to develop such forms of interaction as were adapted to their specific style of corporeal functioning. Their hearing loss was embedded as an element within their total range of expressive abilities. The social situation left them free to develop the practical and communicative skills based on these abilities. Thus incorporation was characterized by a rather smooth and uninterrupted flow of interactional events. Here things took a more or less improvised, spontaneous course. The observed sequences formed a unity, following an inner consequence in which all mutual actions were integrated. At these moments the deaf children seemed to be at ease, playful and inventive, naturally concentrated upon the things with which they happened to be busy.

In each of the instances in which incorporation was at stake the interactional order was rather implicit, no fixed rules were being followed, nor were they explicitly mentioned at special moments.

We have seen incorporation in several forms: as the way the children introduced me as an adult stranger into their web of actions, as the way they did this to a new child, as the way they introduced each other into common undertakings in or outside the classroom. We even saw it at work at the school for hearing children, at those moments when deaf and non-deaf children took their chance to communicate in the margins of the imposed order. These varied instances show the perseverance of the phenomenon in these children's world. What it brings to light is the manifold and versatile power of corporeality in the knitting and weaving of interactional patterns. This power is for the large part uncontrolled, spontaneous — and therefore, it is omnipresent. In the life of the deaf children observed here, corporeality is far more than a special instrument for a specialized form of communication, a means that is, for using sign language as a substitute and imitation of the missing oral language. At many moments, on every ordinary schoolday it becomes clear that sign language in itself is no more than a small particle in the totality of the body's social functioning — and apart from the latter it could neither be carried out nor understood. Blind spots in the grammatic and syntactic knowledge of sign-language on either side of the communicating parties are partly filled up, partly rendered harmless by that which is simultaneously happening on the more-embracing plane of total corporeal activity. Also the children were constantly engaged in inventing new gestures for specific situations: the official and standardized sign-language was permanently enriched by a very flexible and indexical idiom. This idiom was more than simple language, designed for the mere goal of conveying explicit messages: it rather formed an integrated part of the practical history of the children's interactive situations and naturally arose out of these situations more or less as an expressive by-product.

So incorporation refers us to the wider social functioning of corporeality. What is meant by this "wider social functioning"? It could be verbalized like this: through corporeal activity situations become structured into meaningful contexts. This structuring has a very direct and momentary character; it is implied in corporeal functioning itself, in the movements carried out and in perceptions undergone; it bears the mark of the concrete moment at which it takes place. Thus the aspect of improvisation that already emerged in the foregoing descriptions, turns out to be of essential importance. The structuring meant here does not consist of express "talk" or acts of "communication" apart from practical action, but rather is integrated as an aspect of the latter. It comes about in gestures that most of the time are immediately tuned in to and form part of what the children are doing at that moment: building a tower of blocks, creating a fantasy-play, etc.

The observation-scenes described here further suggest that this activity of the body should be taken in a broad sense: on the one hand it consists of a very wide range of expressive and perceptive aspects and forms, on the other hand it is not confined within the boundaries of the individual subject but rather is experienced as a common field in which a plurality of subjects is involved.

At many moments during my observations I got in touch with this structuring function of corporeality. It was the basis on which my practical participation in and my understanding of the situations created by the deaf children became possible, even without a mastery of sign-language. It was the eloquence of their gestures as they were situationally improvised and directly tuned in to the practical needs of the moment, that made me understand.

There may well be some important consequences to all this. These consequences not only affect the position of standardized sign-language (which seems to have been designed and interpreted too much as an imitation of oral language) but also the position of verbal language on the whole. All too often in the study of interaction and communication, the dominant role is granted to verbal language as a theme and as an explanatory model. Gestures and non-verbal behaviour in general are then understood as epiphenomena of the verbally spoken; and even their internal structure is conceived of as built up along the lines of that semiotic model of verbal language.

The foregoing however suggests that this line of reasoning should be reversed. As in the case of the deaf children's sign-language, verbal language could be better understood if it were seen as one specific form of corporeal expression, embedded in and functioning as an aspect of a far wider range of expressive forms.

An important practical implication of these reflections would be that the road to the development of workable systems of communication between the hearing-impaired and the hearing does not lead through the exclusive adaptation of the hearing-impaired (by training their capacity at lipreading and oral speaking) to the language of the hearing. But equally it may not be found in merely propagating standardized language, which would require the adaptation of the hearing to the institutionalized language-code of the hearing-impaired. Neither of these measures seems to have a practical chance without the mutual development by deaf and hearing people alike, of their at least potentially present capacity for improvisational movement, and of their corporeally based sensitivity for the immediate perception of movement and its inherent meaning. This, by the way, could also have considerable beneficial consequences for the interactions in the hearing world as such.

Notes

1. For more systematic and extensive discussions of these theoretical lines see Coenen (1979 a, 1979 b, 1981 b, 1985).
2. See for example Argyle (1967), Gregory, Silver and Dutch (1978), Kendon (1981) and Morris et al. (1979).
3. See Buytendijk (1964), Buytendijk and Plessner (1935), Merleau-Ponty (1942, 1945, 1948, 1958), Plessner (1923, 1941), Schütz (1932, 1970).
4. See Coenen (1979 a).
5. See Coenen (1979 b, 1985).
6. See Coenen (1979 a).
7. See Glaser and Strauss (1967), Glaser (1978).
8. At this point I must expressly mention another influence from outside this research-setting, that was a decisive help to keep me on the track and to get the attitude in which I could expose myself to the happenings described here. This influence was Anselm Strauss who week after week taught me something of the humane patience that he so visibly embodies, telling me: "Don't push too hard". Of the many things I learned from him in the domain of field research, I guess this is the one I am most grateful for.
9. For the sake of anonymity the names of children and teachers have been changed in this paper.
10. As the teachers in this school mostly do, she uses oral speech and sign language simultaneously.
11. In Merleau-Ponty's "Phenomenology of Perception" the concept of passive intentionality takes an important place. It indicates those processes in subjective life in which meaningful structures come into being without express conscious and willfull activity of the ego involved.

Bibliography

Argyle, Michael
    1967   "Verbal and Non-Verbal Communication" and "Eye-Contact and the Direction of Gaze" in: *The Psychology of interpersonal behaviour* (Harmondsworth: Penguin): 36—58 and 80—93.
Buytendijk, F. J. J.
    1964   *Algemene Theorie der Menselijke Houding en Beweging* (Utrecht, Antwerpen: Spectrum).
Buytendijk, F. J. J. and Plessner, Helmuth
    1935   "Die physiologische Erklärung des Verhaltens: eine Kritik an

der Theorie Pavlovs", *Acta Biotheoretica*, Series A, Vol. I, Pars III: 160−170.

Coenen, Herman
1979 a "Leiblichkeit und Sozialität. Ein Grundproblem der phänomenologischen Soziologie", *Philosophisches Jahrbuch*, 86, 2. Halbband: 239−261.
1979 b "Types, Corporeality, and the Immediacy of Interaction", *Man and World*, vol. 12, no. 3: 339−359.
1981 a "Wijsgerige Sociologie", in L. Rademaker (red.) *Toegepaste Sociologie*, vol. 2, (Utrecht-Antwerpen: Het Spectrum): 312−328.
1981 b "Developments in the Phenomenological Reading of Durkheim's Work", *Social Forces*, vol. 59, nr. 4, June: 951−965.
1983 "Phänomenologie und Sozialwissenschaft in den Niederlanden; eine Skizze der aktuellen Lage", in R. Grathoff und B. Waldenfels (ed.), *Sozialität und Intersubjektivität, Phänomenologische Perspektiven in den Sozialwissenschaften in Umfeld von Aron Gurwitsch und Alfred Schütz* (München: Fink).
1985 *Diesseits von subjektivem Sinn und kollektivem Zwang. Phänomenologische Soziologie im Feld des zwischenleiblichen Verhaltens* (München: Fink).

Garfinkel, Harold
1967 *Studies in Ethnomethodology*, (Englewood Cliffs, N. J.: Prentice-Hall).

Glaser, Barney
1978 *Theoretical Sensivity*, (Mill Valley, Cal.; The Sociology Press).

Glaser, Barney and Strauss, Anselm
1967 *The Discovery of Grounded Theory; Strategies for Qualitative Research*, (Chicago: Aldine).

Grams, Lilianne
1978 *Sprache als leibliche Gebärde; zur Sprachtheorie von Merleau-Ponty*, (Frankfurt, Ph. D. Thesis).

Grathoff, Richard
1976 "Grenze und Uebergang: Frage nach den Bestimmungen einer cartesianischen Sozialwissenschaft", in: R. Grathoff, W. Sprondel, *Maurice Merleau-Ponty und das Problem der Struktur in den Sozialwissenschaften*, (Stuttgart: Enke): 108−126.
1979 "Ueber Typik und Normalität im alltäglichen Milieu", in: W. Sprondel und R. Grathoff, ed. *Alfred Schütz und die Idee des Alltags in den Sozialwissenschaften*, (Stuttgart: Enke): 89−107.

Gregory, M., Silvers, A., Dutch, D.
1978 *Sociology and Human Nature: an interdisciplinary critique and defense* (San Francisco, London: Josey Bass).

Gurwitsch, Aron
1977   *Die mitmenschlichen Begegnungen in der Milieuwelt* (Berlin, New York: De Gruyter).
Kendon, Adam (ed.)
1981   *Nonverbal Communication, Interaction and Gesture* (The Hague, Paris, New York: Mouton).
Mead, George Herbert
1934   *Mind, Self and Society; from the standpoint of a social behaviorist*, ed. by C. W. Morris (Chicago and London: The University of Chicago Press).
Merleau-Ponty, Maurice
1942   *La Structure du Comportement* (Paris: Presses Universitaires de France).
1945   *Phénomenologie de la Perception* (Paris: Gallimard).
1948   *Sens et Non-sens* (Pars: Nagel).
1958   *Les Sciences de l'Homme et la Phénomenologie* (Paris: Centre de Documentation Universitaire).
Métraux, Alexandre
1976   "Über Leiblichkeit und Geschichtlichkeit als Konstituentien der Sozialphilosophie Merleau-Pontys", in: R. Grathoff, W. Sprondel, ed., *Maurice Merleau-Ponty und das Problem der Struktur in den Sozialwissenschaften* (Stuttgart: Enke): 139—152.
Morris, D., P. Collett, P. Marsh, M. O'Shaughnessy
1979   *Gestures, their origins and distribution* (London: Jonathan Cape).
Psathas, George
1968   "Ethnomethods and Phenomenology", *Social Research*, 35: 500—520.
O'Neill, John
1975   *Making Sense Together. An Introduction to Wild Sociology* (London: Heinemann).
Plessner, Helmuth
1923   *Die Einheit der Sinne, Grundlinien einer Aesthesiologie des Geistes*, (Bonn: Bouvier).
1941   *Lachen und Weinen, eine Untersuchung nach den Grenzen menschlichen Verhaltens*, (München).
Sartre, Jean-Paul
1936/7 "La Transcendance de l'ego; esquisse d'une description phénoménologique" *Recherches Philosophiques*, 6. English: *The Transdescendence of the Ego*, (New York: Farrar, Straus and Giroux, 1957).
Schütz, Alfred
1932   *"Der sinnhafte Aufbau der sozialen Welt"* (Wien Springer, 1932).

1970   *Collected Papers I – III* (The Hague: Nijhoff).

Schatzman, Leonard and Strauss, Anselm
1973   *Field Research; Strategies for a Natural Sociology* (Englewood Cliffs, N. J.: Prentice Hall).

Waldenfels, Bernhard
1967/8 "Das Problem der Leiblichkeit bei Merleau-Ponty". *Philosophisches Jahrbuch*, 75: 345 – 365.
1971   *Das Zwischenreich des Dialogs; sozialphilosophische Untersuchungen im Anschluß an Edmund Husserl* (Den Haag: Nijhoff).
1976   "Die Offenheit sprachlicher Strukturen bei Merleau-Ponty", in: R. Grathoff und W. Sprondel, ed. *Maurice Merleau-Ponty und das Problem der Struktur in den Sozialwissenschaften* (Stuttgart: Enke): 17 – 28.
1976 a "Vorwort des Übersetzers", in M. Merleau-Ponty, *Die Struktur des Verhaltens*, (Berlin, New York: De Gruyter): V – XXI.
1979 b "Die Verschränkung von Innen und Aussen im Verhalten; phänomenologische Ansatzpunkte zu einer nicht-behavioristischen Verhaltenstheorie", *Phänomenologische Forschungen*, 2 (Freiburg, München: Alber): 102 – 129.
1977   "Verhaltensnorm und Verhaltenskontext", in: B. Waldenfels, J. Broekman and A. Pazanin, Hrsg., *Phänomenologie und Marxismus, Bd. 2, Praktische Philosophie*, (Frankfurt a/M: Suhrkamp): 134 – 157.

Middle Childhood and Adolescence

The papers in this last section of the book examine children's language, social cognition and interactive skills from pre- to late adolescence. While the chapter by Fine focuses on interactive processes among adolescents, the remainder of the chapters covers the period commonly labelled 'middle childhood'.

In chapter 12 Streeck uses the notion of 'politics' to account for a variety of negotiations of conflict in a group of school-children that lead up to and secure a system of interpersonal relations based on reciprocity. He argues that socio-cognitive concepts as well as moral norms are achieved through the ways in which children coordinate their activities in peer contexts; they are agreed-upon structuring principles of interaction rather than concepts acquired and possessed by the individual mind. Streeck's method is a micro-ethnographic analysis of both verbal and 'embodied' behaviors in a 'natural experiment' in which a child was asked to teach an academic task to a group of peers. Streeck demonstrates that the children's concern for symmetry in their relations overrides the task's demands: collectively they defend their egalitarian peer-relations against the peer-teacher's attempts to use his/her assigned role as a means of gaining control over others. However, Streeck also shows that there is no fixity about the children's social system: depending upon locally foregrounded relevances, a variety of inter-action patterns is set up, and the role of social categories such as gender and relative rank varies accordingly.

Ervin-Tripp's paper (chapter 13) fits nicely into the theme of this volume in that she argues that children's second language learning is often embedded in play activities which make up the interactive worlds of young children. Ervin-Tripp begins with the common observation that "elementary school children learn second language fast from their friends. And while their parents struggle with phrase books, children are out on the playground rapidly coming to sound like natives." According to Ervin-Tripp school children's play has specific features which facilitate second language acquisition. First, play tends to refer to the here and now, making it easier for the learner to identify references. Second, play often involves physical activity or construction. Third, partners in play do a lot of "scaffold-ing," supplying questions and relevant comments, staying within the topic and with what is understandable from the context and providing model utterances. In her article Ervin-Tripp examines several types of play and specifies the second language learner's strategies of participation and how these strategies positively affect second language learning.

The paper by Siegert (chapter 14) is primarily methodological. In recent years the growing interest in children's social cognition has led to numerous studies involving clinical interviewing of children of different age groups. Although the clinical interview method has generated important information regarding the nature of children's social concepts at different ages, there are several inherent problems with the procedure. First, in clinical interviews children are often asked to make judgements about hypothetical dilemmas. It may be that children's social cognition in dealing with such dilemmas is quite different than how they cope with similar problems in their everyday life-worlds (see Corsaro and Streeck, this volume). A second problem with clinical interviewing is directly addressed in the chapter by Siegert. Siegert argues that there is an inherent paradox in research on children's social development that is based on clinical interviews. The paradox is that children are often asked to give information about behavior in egalitarian contexts (e. g., friendship and communicative processes with peers) in a setting which is itself highly asymmetrical (i. e., the adult-child interview).

Siegert's paper is based on micro-analyses of interviews with 7-year-old children in the course of a study of the children's socio-cognitive competencies. The interviews involved how the children would deal with hypothetical interpersonal problems (i. e., "friend-ship dilemmas"; see Kohlberg, 1969; 1971; Selman and Jacquette, 1977) in peer interaction. Siegert demonstrates the asymmetrical nature of the situation. He shows how the very structure of the communicative context leads the adult interviewer to control the initiation and termination of the event, the budgeting of time, and the selection and persual of specific topics. Siegert concludes that the children apparently define the interview according to the model of classroom interaction. But the analysis also reveals the children's strategies for coping with the interactive demands of this asymmet-rical situation. Siegert concludes that judgments and reasoning are always a joint production by all participants and, therefore, cannot be treated by researchers as products of a monologue. Siegert argues that instead of locating judgments in the minds of subjects, we must account for them in terms of the interactional contexts in which they were originally generated.

Chapters 15 and 17 by Weissenborn and Miller both focus on the development of social cognition in pre-adolescence, employing quasi-experimental and clinical interviewing methods as well as group discussions to specify stages in the developmental process. Both authors argue that social concepts or knowledge and the communicative abilities necessary to employ such knowledge should be studied as interrelated phenomena.

Chapter 15 by Weissenborn is a report of a study of children's development of communicative competence. Specifically, Weissenborn is interested in children's development of the ability to negotiate common frames of reference in dyadic communication. Weissenborn refers to this process as children's "learning to become interlocuters". He argues that the contradictory results of previous studies of the development of communicative competence (i. e., that children as young as four are able to adapt to the needs of their interlocuters in naturalistic, sociolinguistic studies, while children of eight and older have serious difficulties coping with decentering tasks in experimental, referential studies) are not due simply to differences in the research task. He argues that both traditions must recognize that the acquisition of communicative competence is a process that develops much beyond the age range that has been studied and that communicative competence has to be seen as composed of a variety of subskills which are best viewed as a complex (see Flavell, 1977). Weissenborn maintains that one should look at a larger age range and concentrate on the development of the subskills and their progressive coordination.

In Weissenborn's research, dyads of children ranging in age from 4 to 14 and adults participate in a communicative task involving direction-giving and the movement of toy cars across various experimental situations in which the spatial characteristics and landmarks of the model and the nature of communicative strategies available were manipulated. The tasks in every condition required the subjects' development of mutual frames of reference for successful performance. Weissenborn found that on the cognitive level there is a development from contradictory, context-dependent local reference frames to systematic integration of different context-independent reference frames. On the interactive level there was a change from dysfunctional interaction to meta-communicative agreement. The study makes clear that the different components of the task have different meanings for the children at different moments of development. Weissenborn's main conclusion is that communicative competence is not a homogeneous capacity that can be investigated independently of the goals of communication.

In chapter 17 Miller presents an analysis of the stages of moral development through an investigation of the acquisition of the linguistic skills for *moral argumentation*. Miller defines moral argumentation as a complex type of verbal activity which typically arises when two or more parties have contradictory views regarding what "is right or wrong". A property of moral (as opposed to factual) argumentation is that, to reach an agreement regarding the truth of normative statements, participants must shift to a higher perspective "in which it becomes visible for them what determines their opposition" so that a well-grounded decision between their mutually exclusive positions can be reached. The question regarding development then becomes how children learn to accomplish this shift.

Miller sees a parallel between four increasingly complex logical "problem spaces" in moral argumentation on the one hand and four stages in the development of morality in children on the other — the problems of justification, coherency, circularity and language. The "problem of justification" is solved if the parties collectively agree on the validity of a judgment regarding the morality of an action. The "problem of coherency" arises where the parties agree on the validity of a proposition, but assign a different argumentative value to it with respect to the quaestio. The "problem of circularity" relates to the distinction between the relevance of a normative statement for a given action and the validity of factual descriptions of the action. The "problem of language" is that of defining the meaning of "morally justified." Its solution requires that the parties reconstruct the entire logic of their moral argumentation and thereby explicate their respective uses of the term "morally justified". In so doing they also ascertain how they have solved — or could possibly solve — the problems of justification, coherency and circularity. A moral consensus is thus identical with a convergence of the cognitive tools for moral reasoning.

In his research Miller confronted three groups of children (5, 7 to 8, and 10 year-olds) with Kohlberg's "Heinz and the Druggist" dilemma. Miller found that the youngest group was able to solve the problem of justification, but not that of coherency, the middle group that of coherency but not the problem of circularity, while the 10 year-old children were capable of solving all three problems except that of language. In his conclusion, Miller points out that his "conception of moral argumentation tries to combine a universalistic position (related to the form of argumentation) and a relativistic position (related to the content of descriptive and normative premises)".

Fine's rhetorical analysis of adolescent gossip in Chapter 16 also examines interpersonal norms and morals. Fine's data consist of a tape-recorded conversation among three teenage-girls during an automobile ride in a small town in Minnesota. The girls are "shooting the breeze" and talk about a variety of topics including: concert-going, vandalism, death from cancer, parties, drugs, sex, watching TV, etc. A large part of their conversation is gossip. Morality and interactional norms are not an explicit topic of the talk, but nevertheless are an undercurrent theme of great importance. The implicit character of the topic, Fine points out, enables the girls to sustain different views of morality while at the same time maintaining a friendly conversation; the girls are able to blame others for activities which they do not consider blameworthy in their own cases.

According to Fine, gossip serves to promote a group consensus on shared values; at the same time, it may serve as a device for the speaker to reach individual strategic goals of status manipulation (see Gluckman, 1963; Paine, 1967). Adolescence on the other hand, is a period of developing moral standards. In his analysis Fine points out that adolescent gossip shows a strong tendency toward consensus but also a relative variability of moral standards, which Fine attributes to the fact that the standards are not yet fully internalized. Fine notes that teenage gossip involves a continual thematic variation of blame, justifications, excuses and refutations. This combination of verbal activities in gossiping enables teenagers and others to enforce conformity and to differentiate between groups.

References

Flavell, John
   1977   *Cognitive Development* (Englewood Cliffs, N. J.: Prentice Hall).
Gluckman, Max
   1963   "Gossip and Scandal", *Current Anthropology*, *4*, 307–316.
Kohlberg, Lawrence
   1969   "Stage and Sequence: The Cognitive-Developmental Approach to Socialization". In David Goslin (Ed.), *Handbook of Socialization Theory and Research* (New York: Rand McNally), 347–480.
Kohlberg, Lawrence
   1971   "From Is to Ought". In Theodore Mischel (Ed.), *Cognitive Development and Epistemology* (New York: Academic Press), 151–235.
Paine, Robert
   1967   "What is Gossip About?: An Alternative Hypothesis", *Man*, 2, 278–285.
Selman, Robert and Jaquette, Dan
   1977   "Interpersonal Awareness in Children", *American Journal of Orthopsychiatry* 42 (2), 264–274.

Towards Reciprocity
Politics, Rank and Gender in the Interaction of a Group of Schoolchildren[1]

Jürgen Streeck

1. Introduction

Peer-interaction involves politics. Children (especially schoolchildren) like to fight over political issues such as ownership, alliances, status and power, social norms, prior agreements, and broken promises. But they also like to "travel in packs" (Sacks, 1978): group-life is the most important arena for their political activities. Peer-groups are beginning to be formed during middle childhood and operate independently of adult support and intervention; they are social aggregates controlled almost entirely by their members (Krappmann, 1980; Siegert, 1980), and there are few external resources to gain power and control over other children.

Researchers opting for the "process approach" to social cognition have emphasized the importance of peer-relations for children's acquisition of socio-cognitive skills (Damon, 1982) and their internalization of moral standards (Younniss, 1984). "Social cognition" in this approach is defined as a "method to engage in communication with others" (Damon 1982: 113). Creating and caring for groups that can survive requires that children find ways of interacting with one another which enable them to keep the "steady state" (Bateson, 1949) of their relations balanced. In contrast to adult-child relations children's group-relations lack predefined formal statuses, and the procedures for setting up and holding a social system are therefore intrinsically democratic. The status quo of a group is based on public consensus; this entails, methodologically, that it is an observable outcome of interactional activities.

My aim in this paper is to show that in order to study children's conceptions of morality, reciprocity and status it is not necessary to make claims about detached thought processes; it is possible, instead, to observe their political struggles in the arena of group activities. "Interaction is an essential part of the developmental process" (Auwärter and Kirsch 1984: 167); children's democratic norms of reciprocity originate and surface in their practical negotiations with each other. Before reciprocity is internalized as a mental concept, it is achieved as a solution to conflicts of interest.

This paper presents a microanalysis of a few interactional sequences in which a group of schoolchildren negotiate and calibrate the status quo of their relations under apparently irritating circumstances. The data come from a series of 'peer-teaching' experiments in which a child in a classroom was asked to teach a group. Boys and girls had to cooperate without being very eager to do so: gender becomes a core issue in the distribution of information and the allocation of blame. The assignment of a 'peer-teacher' role to a single child appears to present problems for the others; it requires the shifting of established attention patterns and introduces a formal status and an element of power into a network of interpersonal relations which are partly antagonistic and involve a delicate balance of resources. The 'peer-teacher' role also irritates existing friendship bonds because it necessitates a redistribution of support according to extrinsic criteria. Differences in the children's academic standing, finally, imply problems for the group's cohesion.

The purpose of the following analysis, then, is to exhibit some of the social concepts that the children bring to bear upon their interaction during 'peer-teaching', and to show how versions of the principle of reciprocity emerge as practical outcomes of complex, often antagonistic negotiations.

2. Data and Methods

The 'peer-teaching' episodes were designed by Courtney B. Cazden and Hugh Mehan as a part of a larger study of children's communicative skills in a variety of classroom-situations (Mehan, 1975, 1979; Cazden et al., 1979; Cazden, 1979). The study was conducted in a combined first, second, and third-grade classroom of an elementary school in the poorest neighborhood of the otherwise booming city of San Diego, California. The classroom was evenly divided between Black and Mexican-American children. The researchers were particularly interested in revealing modes of children's communication and instruction which normally remain hidden behind the teacher-centered participation structure of the classroom. One part of the corpus of video-tapes was therefore designed to include 'hour-in-the-life' tapes of individual children: a wireless microphone was placed on the target child, and the camera followed the child throughout the first hour of the school-day which was designed as 'choosing time'; the children listened to tapes from a tape-recorder, read books in the library corner of the classroom, engaged in group-work or completed unfinished projects. The classroom was an 'open classroom', giving the children a considerably greater amount of freedom to exercise variable interactional skills than teacher-centered classrooms. The peer-teaching episodes were arranged toward the end of 'choosing time': the teacher called on the target child and explained the task, and the 'peer-teacher' then assembled the group and began the instructions (the peer-teachers also had to complete the task). My study is based on three episodes in a previously established reading group (cf. also Streeck, 1983). Its members are Leola (9; 5), Wallace (8; 9), Ernesto (8; 8), Carolyn (8; 4), and Regina (7; 7).

The methodological framework for the analysis of the materials is adapted from a paradigm of interaction analysis labelled "micro-ethnography" (Erickson and Schultz, 1982), "context analysis" (Scheflen, 1973), or "structural approach to the understanding of interaction" (Kendon, 1977). The aim of this approach to human interaction is to account for the ways in which the "ultimate behavioral materials" (Goffman, 1967) "are organized and how they function in the creation of interactional events" (Kendon 1977: 40). "The starting point ... is the interdependency of the behavior of individuals that obtains whenever they are in one another's presence. The endeavor ... is to understand how *occasions of interaction* are organized" (Kendon 1979: 5).

My analysis addresses features of the children's talk that relate to their definition of the encounter, their joint activities, and their respective roles within these activities; it also focuses on features of the children's 'embodied' relationships: whereas the different postural configurations adopted during the encounters reveal, among other things, a network of affiliations and disaffiliations (cf. Scheflen, 1972, 1974), patterns of gazing at one another are involved in the administration of attention structures forming the behavioral basis of the group's rank-order (cf. Chance and Larsen, 1976). In this paper I incorporate information from these modalities to exhibit some of the political issues negotiated in fleeting moments of interaction. My general concern is how the children structure their activities so as to meet both the requirements of the classroom *and* egalitarian reciprocity norms obtaining in their own social world. I assume that a number of the interactional competencies which children develop in middle childhood originate in the interface between the adult world and the world of peer-group interaction. Where these worlds overlap, children often have to interact under contradictory demands. They must confirm to adult standards, but in ways which also reaffirm the moral order of their peer-world. The emerging structure of the interaction in the peer-teaching-episodes can be regarded as a reconciliation of these contradictions, reached through frequently antagonistic interaction processes.

3. Official and Inofficial Identities: Negotiating Affiliation and Rank

Usually during the initial phase of an encounter participants negotiate the identities they adopt and ascribe to each other for the purposes of the situation at hand. Official identities, defined by categorical attributes, are often replaced by, or blended with, particularistically defined identities derived from the previous history of their interaction with each other (cf. Erickson and Shultz, 1982; Schenkein, 1978). Neither official nor informal identities necessarily surface in the talk's overt content; but they may be presupposed in the selection of descriptive terms and accounts.[2]

For example, while Leola and Carolyn are walking to the table where Leola is going to teach the group, Carolyn suggests *Leola, help me so we can go to (the library) at the same time*. The warrant for Carolyn's request is the (particularistic) fact that she and Leola are friends; she appeals to Leola's presumable motive to sustain their long-term relationship in the situation at hand. Carolyn insinuates the situated relevance of informal identities. The interaction during the initial phase of an encounter may also be *organized* in terms of such identity-sets and thereby foreshadow and generate the system of relationships which subsequently structures the joint activity.

3.1. The Pencil Affair

The following incident took place when Leola, Carolyn, and Wallace arrived at the group's table.

(1) 1 Leola   It gonna- ha:rd, it's ha:rd.
     2 Carolyn   Leola he⌈lp me.
     3 Leola   ⌊I already *know.*
     4 Leola   This Den*i*se pencil!
     5 Wallace   · That's *mi*:ne. (Give it   ).
     6 Leola   ⌊This Den*i*se's. —
     7 Carolyn   That's m*i*ne. I — but I'm givin' it to you.
                   (0.6)
     8 Carolyn   You want it, Leola?
     9 Leola   Uh *huh.*

The children dispute the ownership of a pencil. Leola claims that the pencil in Wallace's hand is Denise's (Denise is a friend of Leola and Carolyn but not a member of the group). Wallace insists that it is his and holds on to it. Finally Carolyn moves in, claiming it is hers, offers that Leola may have it, and Leola accepts. (As a matter of fact, the pencil is Denise's. She later comes to the table to claim it, and nobody objects.)

But there is, of course, much more going on here. Examining the talk within the context of simultaneous non-vocal activities, we find that the children are beginning to pattern their relationships. The timing of talk and nonvocal activities is particularly revealing in this regard.

Wallace arrives at the table while Carolyn produces the turn at line 2; he overhears her request for special help (which is the fourth in a series), apparently noticing that his odds in a potentially competitive activity are at stake: if Leola complied with Carolyn's request, he would end up in a disadvantaged position (he is not entitled to a similar request — because he is not Leola's friend).[3] Wallace's first motion, then, is to reach out and try to take one of the work-sheets from the stack on the table — perhaps in reaction to what he just heard: getting a work-sheet first (or as soon as he can) might be a partial compensation. But his motion collides with an identical movement on Carolyn's part: both children try to get a work-sheet first. It is at this precise moment that Leola reaches for the pencil and grabs the other end of it. This move causes

Wallace to shift his gaze and attention from the papers to the pencil. Wallace and Leola now position themselves in an antagonistic face-to-face formation, pulling at the pencil. Carolyn is thereby afforded an opportunity to take a sheet — which she does.

A web of situated relationships is established in this incident. Carolyn and Leola negotiate the situational relevance of *friendship*. While Leola declines Carolyn's request to be supported in the 'official' task-domain, she does support her in the more peripheral fight with Wallace. While a granting of Carolyn's request could interfere with Leola's role-obligations as teacher of the group, this is apparently not the case where the work-sheets are concerned. Leola's engagement in the argument with Wallace concerning his right to use the pencil improves Carolyn's standing vis-à-vis the boy. Carolyn in turn supports Leola in that argument. By claiming ownership of the pencil (at line 7), but granting Leola permission to use it (at line 8), she assumes authority and uses it to Leola's benefit. The girls mutually demonstrate that they will continue to help each other as friends vis-à-vis outsiders. Official as well as informal identity sets (teacher-student, friend-friend) are reaffirmed and made relevant but also kept separate in the situation. Note that the agreement reached by the girls (at lines 8 and 9) contradicts Leola's proposition (at line 4) which initiated her struggle with Wallace. Note also that Wallace does not give up on the pencil. These are indications that, from the children's point of view, the results of the relational work are more important than the factual circumstances generating it.

3.2. Knowledge and Control

The interaction between Carolyn and Wallace in these episodes is predominantly antagonistic. They are children of approximately equal (intermediate) rank within the group (assessed by the amount of attention each child receives from other children), although Carolyn is the better student. There is accordingly a delicate balance in their relationship, an equilibrium which becomes problematic when one of them becomes the other's teacher. Both of the episodes with Carolyn and Wallace in the peer-teacher role start with brief exchanges in which issues of dominance and control are negotiated.

Carolyn makes an attempt to gain control over the boys activities by threatening that she will not explain the work to them.

(2)	1	Carolyn	Hey boys — Ok*ay*, you know how to do it.
			I ain't gonna expl*ai*n it to you.
	2	Ernesto	We don't even kn*o*w!
			(0.6)
	3	( )	No: :h.
	4	Ernesto	Don't touch *my* sheet! =
	5	Carolyn	= Well, then I ain't sh*o*w*i*n' you how.
			(0.3)
	6	Ernesto	Touch *Walla*ce paper.
	7	Wallace	I ain't gonna work.

Carolyn's initial turn (at line 1) comprises a series of four different activities: a summons (*hey boys*), an agreement token (*okay*), an attribution (*you know how to do it*), and an announcement (*I ain't gonna explain it to you*). The attribution is constructed as a warrant for the announcement. Again we must consult the context of concurrent nonvocal activities to recover the situated meaning of this turn, in particular because it appears to be so inappropriate to the situation — after all, everybody knows that at this point only Carolyn knows "how to do it" and that it is her job to tell the others.

The first constituent of the turn (the summons *hey boys*) is uttered during Carolyn's approach to the table where Ernesto and Wallace are already seated. When she arrives, Carolyn recognizes that the boys are studying the work-sheet — her attribution *you already know how to do it* refers to that posture; it formulates its situated significance. The posture, the phrase suggests, is enough evidence to attribute knowledge of the task to the boys. This attribution is, of course, not really warranted by the facts: looking at the paper is not sufficient to find out what must be done. It is not likely, either, that Carolyn assumes that her attribution is justified. However, by linking (via the attribution) the boys' behavior to her own resources and action-alternatives in this situation (to pass on vs. withhold her knowledge), Carolyn makes an attempt to gain control over the boys' doings, to extend her status as peer-teacher and achieve dominance over them. Her utterance alludes to a rank-relevant alternative between two patterns of action in the subsequent episode: either the boys acquire knowledge in whichever way *they* want, perhaps using Carolyn as a constantly accessible source of information; or Carolyn determines the appropriate way for them to receive information. Carolyn analyzes the present state of affairs in terms of the first pattern and declines her participation in it; she thereby begins to reorganize the situation in terms of the second.

Carolyn also makes strategic use of discourse sequencing rules: recipients/referents of false attributions or statements are expected to respond with a denial. The expectable response to the (false) attribution *you already know how to do it* would be *we don't know how to do it*, an utterance which, in this context, would also carry the connotation of confession of a certain inferiority. Ernesto (at line 2) reacts in this fashion and Carolyn can now move on to seek control over the more material aspects of the situation. She tries to take Ernesto's work-sheet, apparently preparing to point out to the boys how to do the work. But Ernesto objects (at line 4), not wanting to give up control over his property. Again, Carolyn asserts that she is not going to teach the boys unless they submit to her control.

But the boys do not surrender and defend the status quo. Even though Ernesto admits that the boys "don't even know", this statement serves more as a reminder for Carolyn that it is her obligation to tell them. Ernesto subsequently invites Wallace's participation in the dispute (at line 6), but Wallace (at line 7) announces that he is not going to work at all. He thereby challenges a presupposition of Carolyn's arguments, that the boys wish to work and therefore need Carolyn's help. Wallace thus alludes to the fact that, as much as the boys need Carolyn to do their work, Carolyn needs the boys to do hers. The dependency and the resulting opportunities to thwart the other's plan are mutual: Carolyn may withhold her knowledge, but Ernesto and Wallace may refuse to listen to her.

The net result of the argument is an agreement not to cooperate at all. This agreement maintains the equilibrium in the relationship among the children, which is thus given priority over offical roles. Carolyn later makes several attempts to teach the boys, but they do not listen. Somehow they manage to get part of the work done on their own. Carolyn has overextended her opportunities afforded by the role of peer-teacher.

A similar pattern is established when Wallace is given the peer-teaching job. Again the negotiation occurs before Leola and Regina come to the table; this time Ernesto uses Carolyn's announcement not to tell the boys as a warrant for turning the tables on her. The exchange begins when Wallace returns to the table with his scissors. Facing Ernesto he says:

(3)   1   W   Go get your sss — go get your scissors.
                (1.8)
      2   W   Go get your scissors.
      3   W   (   ) first.
      4   E   (   ) Wallace.
      5   W   Go get your scissors.
                (3.5)
      6   W   I already got *mi*ne.
                (0.4)
      7   C   What we need *scis*sors for.
      8   W   For *some*thing.
                (1.2)
      9   W   M-me and Ernesto will cut *our* paper up.
                (1.1)
    10   E   We ain't gonna tell you how to do it.
    11   W   "How many words-"
    12   E   ⌈Remember, remember you wouldn't tell *us*.
    13   W   Here, Ernesto.
    14   C   You guys *got* to tell us.
    15   W   No-ee-no-ee-no-ee-no.
    16   C   MISS C!
    17   E   They wouldn't tell US!
    18   C   He won't TELL us!

The patterning of relationships begins with Wallace's repeated request *go get you scissors* (at lines 1, 2 and 5) which is exclusively addressed at Ernesto — even though Carolyn is also present. Carolyn (at line 7) demands an explanation for the request; her choice of the pronoun *we* indicates that she sees herself as a co-recipient of the request and demands access to the conversation. In his response (at line 9) Wallace insists on the reference form *me and Ernesto*. This interplay of address and reference forms foreshadows the network of affiliations which is characteristic of the bulk of the subsequent episode; Carolyn proposes membership for all children, but Wallace distinguishes two categories of participants with differential access to the talk. His turn at line 8 *demonstrates* an organization of the interaction in these terms: task-related information is held back. However, it is important to pay attention also to the content of Wallace's subsequent utterances because there is a marked contrast to the relational work performed so far. Consider the turns at lines 9 and 11. *Cut paper up* is information relevant to

Carolyn's question *what we need scissors for* — it is an appropriate, though minimal, answer. Wallace's utterance at line 11, *how many words* —, is the beginning of a reading of the instructions that are printed on the work-sheet. Even though Wallace frames his talk in terms which apparently exclude Carolyn from the activity, he also provides her with the kind of information which she needs to get her work done. His responses are 'hedges' (cf. the turn at line 15 which is delivered in sing-song) and involve a splitting-up of interactive functions: information is given, but the utterances are constructed in a manner suggesting that it is not. It is left up to the recipient what to make of them: Carolyn can either work with the information she receives, or react as if her request for information has been declined. (The exchange takes place prior to the arrival of two other group members. If Wallace fully complied with Carolyn's demand, he would have to recycle his instructions for those children and he would also provide Carolyn with an opportunity for an early start.)

It is also interesting to consider how Wallace relates to Ernesto during these sequences. In contrast to Wallace's utterances, Ernesto's announcement (at line 10) *we ain't gonna tell you how to do it* is hardly ambiguous. Rather, it narrows down the action potential of Wallace's teasing remarks and formulates a determinate meaning for them.

Ernesto obviously assumes that he is entitled to such a move. Wallace's utterance *how many words*, however, is placed immediately after Ernesto's announcement, and it is the beginning of the type of activity which, according to Ernesto, will not be carried out at all. Wallace, in other words, disaffiliates from Ernesto's announcement and challenges his claim to decide on the further course of action. Wallace does comply with his role obligations. But his turn is interrupted by Ernesto (who — at line 12 — adds a reason for his announcement) and subsequently cut off; it is questionable whether Carolyn has received it. Ernesto invokes a "principle of retributive justice" (Cazden et al., 1979), saying that Carolyn did not teach the boys either (although, as we have seen, Carolyn made an attempt to teach). Carolyn reacts (at line 14) by invoking a normative rule; she frames this rule in terms of categories of gender: the boys have to teach the girls. And Wallace teases her once more (line 15).

The picture emerging here is somewhat more complicated than during the beginning of Carolyn's teaching, mainly because Wallace and Ernesto have different ways of dealing with Carolyn. At the surface the children seem to agree that, the way things are, no teaching will be done. Underneath this agreement, however, task-related information is transmitted. There is thus a contradiction between the framing of the situation and the content of the talk. Whereas the framing is in line with the children's sorting of each other into the categories *boys* and *girls*, the information conveyed conforms to the classroom teachers's normative rules for the event. Even though the situation is still open to further negotiation, Carolyn chooses to define it as an utter refusal by Wallace to teach and calls on the teacher for support (lines 16 and 18). Coming to the table, the teacher aligns with Carolyn's view of the incident which is thereby ratified as a social fact (cf. Streeck, 1984, for a detailed analysis of that intervention).

4. Gender Politics

Gender is an important categorical principle for the organization of activities which is embodied in the children's postural configuration: boys and girls form two small huddles on opposite sides of the table with a wide gap in between. Channels of communication are restricted accordingly: gaze and talk are overwhelmingly directed at co-members of the same category (cf. Streeck, 1983, for more detail). There is occasional talk between boys and girls during their joint activity, but it is antagonistic. These are insult and argument sequences.

4.1. Gender in Ritual Insults

There are several confrontations between Carolyn and Wallace in these episodes which indicate that their antagonism is in part related to gender. These are ritual insult sequences consisting in somewhat rudimentary versions of the 'dozens', an insulting game popular mainly among Black male teenagers in the U.S. (cf. Abrahams, 1970, Labov, 1972). The 'dozens' are initiated when one participant produces a sexual insult of one of his opponent's relatives, preferably his mother; B responds with a return insult. The return insult should be syntactically parallel to the opening move: it is the purpose of the game to prove one's wit and verbal skills. The 'dozens' therefore require the presence of an audience — its response determines the winner of the contest. The 'dozens' are defined as play, and insults exchanged in them are never taken literally. The 'dozens' can be played for the sake of entertainment, but — as Labov (1972) has pointed out — they can also serve as strategic moves in an antagonistic interaction. In that case the confrontation is transposed into a lighter key and also transformed into a contest: by inviting the audience's participation the player who initiates the game gets a chance to recruit allies in the confrontation (cf. Goodwin, 1982). It is in this manner that the 'dozens' are played in the peer-teaching episodes; they are initiated by Carolyn in her confrontations with Wallace.

The first instance, in Carolyn's peer-teaching, results from an argument over 'copying'.

(4)   1   E   °They're spottin'.
      2   C   Uhhhh.
              (0.6)
      3   E   Tryin' to copy.
      4   C   Copy.
      5   W   You bitch.
      6   C   Your momma.
              (0.3)
      7   W   Yours.
      8   C   You can't even do nothin' about it.
      9   W   You're a stick.
              (0.3)
     10   C   You ain't shittin' on me. You better go and shit on your
              momma.

'Copying' in this group of children is organized by category membership: while co-members of a category (boys/girls) are allowed to copy from each other, copying across categories is prohibited. Ernesto's whispering remark to Wallace (at line 1) *they're spottin'* thus proposes that a rule has been violated. Wallace does not respond. Carolyn, however, who has overheard the remark, instantaneously grabs her work-sheet and acts as if *she* has caught the *boys* in the act of copying. Wallace then calls her a *bitch*, and Carolyn reacts by initiating the 'dozens': *your momma* is a standard format for an invitation to play them. Wallace's return move (at line 7) is minimal and expresses declination of further engagement. The next two turns are not set in a ritual key, but the game is resumed when Carolyn comes back (at line 10) with another ritual insult with which she wins: *You ain't shittin' on me, you better go and shit on your momma.* This is indeed a skillful construction; while its first constituent is a literal response to the offense *you're a stick*, the second is a move in the game, and the two constituents are connected via the ambiguity of the term *shit on.* "To shit on someone" has a literal meaning, but it also carries the connotation of 'offending, insulting somebody'. A warning (i. e., "you better not offend me") is thus backed up by a gross ritual insult of the boys' mother, and Wallace is defeated.

A pun is Carolyn's main weapon in the second instance as well:

(5) 1   C   You shut *u*p you-
    2   W   You- (.) you m*a*ke me.
              (0.3)
    3   E   (. .ͺ)
    4   C   ⌊You-you're alr*ea*dy ma::de, ho::neybu:nny.
    5   C   Who's your girl? °Your m*o*mma?
    6   W   Not you.
    7   C   I know, I'm no your girl (.) 'Cuz I ain't g*o*t no ugly brother like — no ugly boyfriend like that.
    8   W   She ain't got no brother.

Following a brief confrontation Carolyn here tells Wallace to *shut up.* Wallace in return (at line 2) challenges her to *make* him shut up. In her response (at lines 4 and 5) Carolyn shifts to the ritual play-frame; the pun around the term "to make somebody" serves as pivot. Refering to the sexual act of his parents' begetting of Wallace (*you're already made*), Carolyn also calls him *honeybunny* and thereby talks to him from the perspective of a mother talking to her infant, or a woman sweet-talking to her lover. It is the blending of the two domains that is important here. While Wallace's mother is already present as a background character at line 4, explicit mention of her is made in Carolyn's next move (at line 5). By asking him *Who's your girl? Your momma?* Carolyn not only implies that Wallace is a "sissy"; she also insults his mother by raising the possibility that she might have an incestuous relationship with him, and, vice versa, she makes Wallace look like — a "motherfucker". ("Motherfucker", of course, is one of the most frequently used but also most offensive insults in Afroamerican culture.)

The "key" (cf. Goffman, 1974) of this sequence is 'play', but that does not mitigate Wallace's defeat: he loses out to a girl in a predominantly male domain. Moreover, he does not even recognize the ritualistic character of Carolyn's insult and produces an inappropriate (literal) answer to her (ritualistic) question (at line 6) — a move that would be considered "lame" by any audience. He thereby invites further attacks: Carolyn (at line 7) argues that she would never go out with *an ugly boyfriend like that*. There is an error in her utterance, however, which she is quick to repair (*brother — boyfriend*) but which is nevertheless made the topic of another contest sequence centering around the number of brothers each child has (data not shown): Carolyn purports to have five, Ernesto ten, and Wallace "more than that". The sequence is no longer a ritual; the demonstration of superior skill is replaced by mere assertions of superiority. The way the 'dozens' are played in these episodes indicates, in sum, that gender is not only used by the children to organize the group's activity but also provides them with thematic material for the construction of argument and contest sequences.

4.2. Uses of Arguments

The second type of cross-sex talk that the children engage in while they carry out their tasks are argument sequences.[4] Boys and girls align as parties in the confrontation. Arguments, in other words, are not only organized on the basis of gender, they also provide members of the different categories with opportunities to *demonstrate* their alignment.

One such sequence is produced immediately after the teacher's intervention in the group's interaction (cf. 3.2 above).

```
(6)   1   W    They could get it wrong anyway.
      2   C    No we won't.
      3   E    (              )
      4   L                  ⌈I know y-you gotta make some wo:rds out of
                   these.
      5   W    You don't.
      6   L    Yes⌈ you do.
      7   W       ⌊ You don't.
      8   L    You see, here it say-
      9   C                        ⌊It say-
```

10	L	How man-
11	L	⌈How many words can you make out of those five letters.
12	C	⌊How many words can you make out of those five letters.
13	W	You have to read it.
14	L	⌈ Try to make at least five.
15	C	⌊Try to make at least five.
16	C	Use each one in a sentence. Shut up.
17	W	You make me girl.
18	E	⌈We can't shut up because we got our mouth to talk.
19	W	God gave us a mouth to talk with.
20	C	I can make 'low' Leo.
		(1.2)
21	E	So you ⌈ do it.
22	( )	⌊ You don't know.
23	W	I'll beat you.
		(1.4)
24	C	So I got some already. I got two of 'em.
25	C	'Low'. (.) And 'be'.
26	L	'Below'.

The dialogue centers around the issue whether or not the girls will be able to complete the task on their own. (The categorical reference to *girls* is established and ratified in the first two turns, at lines 1 and 2.) The first phase of the confrontation (lines 1 to 7) is a chaining of arguments (assertions and denials); the children enter into what Bateson (1958) has called "parallel schismogenesis": they "escalate divisive interaction by building back and forth on the same kinds of aggressive behavior" (Scheflen 1972: 23). At line 8 Leola shifts to a different strategy, moving from asserting her knowledge to its demonstration. She initiates a series of turns in which she reads the instructions from the work-sheet. But she is joined by Carolyn so that the girls (at lines 11−12 and 14−15) eventually read in unison and thereby give a spectacular show of the fine tuning of their alignment.

Talk in unison does not easily come about; it is an interactional achievement requiring (1.) provision of a slot for a joint beginning within the sequential unfolding of a conversation which is otherwise governed by the rule "one at a time" (cf. Sacks, Schegloff and Jefferson, 1974), and (2.) synchronization of the activity of the vocal chords of the participants. The slot for a joint beginning in this case is staked out from the flow of conversation via the use of prefaces: at line 8 the clause *here it say* projects the type of activity that the upcoming phrase will be occupied with (i. e., reading). Before Leola reaches the point of completion of that preface, however, and can move on to deliver the projected activity, Carolyn comes in and, copying part of the preface, shows that she has recognized it as such and is gearing up to join Leola in the projected activity. Leola then begins to read (at line 10) and, noticing that Carolyn has failed to join her, relinquishes her turn. Rather than having Carolyn join her in mid-turn, she opts for the possibility of a simultaneous re-start. When she recycles the beginning of her reading-turn (at line 11), Carolyn is with her, and the two girls deliver the reading in perfect synchrony.

Wallace, then, finds himself confronted by a coalition of girls who not only know what they are talking about but are also sufficiently together to display their competence as that of a unified party. No longer able to dispute their knowledge, he backs off and challenges them (at line 23) as competitors.

Another dispute occurs several minutes later in the same episode. It has to do with the fact that the group's division into two independently interacting subgroups entails problems of information transfer: it turns out that the girls do not have, as they believe to have, all the information needed to complete the task but are not willing to focus their attention on Wallace. The task has two parts: the children have to combine five letters from their work-sheets into five different words and then make a sentence with each word. This second part has not been understood by the girls.

In order to distribute the information without changing the group's rank-order it is necessary to rearrange the network of communication channels without placing Wallace in a dominant position. This is accomplished via the establishment of an argumentative communicative frame: as in the incident just described the children rearrange their postural configuration so that two opposing parties face one another. This is done after Leola accuses Wallace of not doing his work properly.

(7) 1   L   You only 'posed to write fi:ve.
    2   W   I do. One two three four fi:ve.
            (0.5)
    3   R   You're not 'posed to write it ⌈ uh
    4   W   ⌊ You 'pose to write se:*n* tence.

5   E   Yeah. Do it over.
6   W   You guys 'posed to write-di*d*n't she say write sentence?
7   E   Ye*a*h. Those guys-dumb.
8   C   (   )
9   L   [Oh!

Leola (at line 1) argues that Wallace is doing too much; Wallace defends himself (at line 2) by pointing to and counting the number of words he has written. But the fact is that he is still writing — there is a misunderstanding. Wallace addresses this misunderstanding in his turn at line 4. He begins to recycle his statement (at line 6), cuts off, turns to Ernesto, and elicits his confirmation that the teacher had told them to write *sentences*. (Ernesto was present when the teacher explained the task to Wallace.) Ernesto (at line 7) produces a confirmation and blames the girls with being *dumb*. Leola's response token *oh* (at line 9) displays that Wallace's utterances have indeed delivered news to her and changed the state of her knowledge (cf. Heritage, 1984).

As ordinary as this brief exchange may appear, it is still interesting to note how two different activities are simultaneously accomplished. While knowledge is distributed across the entire group (after it had only been accessible to the boys), the children also maintain and reaffirm their membership in different categories and the bonding among those who are in one category (cf. the turns at lines 6 and 7). At the level of some of the talk's content (at lines 4, 6 and 9) the sequence is cooperative (the boys could very well have kept their knowledge secret); its framing, however, is antagonistic. The children frame their interaction in line with the overall agreement not to cooperate and blame each other with incompetence, but they nevertheless cooperate and share information. Leola, for example, elicits 'teaching' from Wallace (at line 1) by accusing him of not knowing how things should be done.

An argument, then, appears to be a conversational activity well suited for cooperation under competitive conditions. The competition is shifted from the task (who finishes first) to the issue who has the better arguments.

4.3. Gender — A Transitory Phenomenon

So far, we have mainly witnessed the antagonistic framing of the interaction between boys and girls in this group. However, the children have a variety of patterns of relationship, and gender is relevant as a set of organizational categories only when it is *made* relevant by the participants. In these peer-teaching events gender is foregrounded only as long as the children are working. Boys and girls position themselves in two widely separated 'withs'; talk, unless it is antagonistic, only occurs between members of the same category who also sustain virtually identical body postures throughout most parts of the events. However, in Wallace's episode an all-embracing shift in the "participation structure" (Philips 1972) of the interaction occurs after the completion of the work, and gender no longer organizes the children's participation but is made the topic of a playful conversation to which each child has immediate and equal access.

This shift is initiated by a somewhat mysterious occurrence which happens after Ernesto (the last child to do so) finishes his work and displays this fact to the others by leaning back and stretching his legs. Suddenly and without speaking a word Carolyn and Regina raise from their chairs and trade seats. Carolyn is now in Wallace's vicinity and moves her new chair even closer to him so that she is positioned inside the boys' territory. The entire group has by now altered its configuration: the children form a wide circle within which everybody is free to look at (and talk to) everybody else; the postures are relaxed.

Carolyn smiles and says *I'm touching the boys' table.* Wallace teases her by calling her a *tomboy* — a girl who wants to be and acts like a boy. Ernesto calls her a *cowboy* (he is a Chicano child and may not know the cultural meaning of the term "tomboy"). Carolyn then turns the tables on Wallace by calling *him* a *tomboy*, a girl who only desires to be a boy.

Smiles indicate that the interaction throughout this latter part of the event is regarded as play. The children *talk* gender, but their interaction is no longer *organized* by gender. In other words, the children adopt a metacommunicative stance toward the social system which they had established and maintained for their groupwork, and, in so doing, transcend its restrictions.

5. Silent Cooperation across the Border

We are now in a position to appreciate that the children's interaction is not as onedimensional as it initially appeared to be. Different sets of relevances are brought to bear upon the events and cooperation occurs. In addition to the sequences described, there is also bonding among the group of children as a whole. The children defend the territory of their interaction against intruders (see Streeck, 1984), and an interpersonal context for each child's individual activity is always maintained: the children complete their work at different times and then leave the table to go and get a book, but one other child always remains with the late-comer at the table. Despite the internal divisions the children maintain the integrity of the interaction as a group-event.

Moreover, there are a number of barely noticeable supportive interchanges between two participants on opposite sides of the border — Regina and Wallace —, despite the fact that these children never *talk* to each other in any of the episodes. Regina is the youngest child (the only second-grader), and the task seems to be quite difficult for her. There is little explicit instruction given by the peer-teachers. Close inspection of the videotapes also reveals that Regina is not as firmly integrated in the girls' coalition as my description of their 'with' has suggested: while her neighbor Carolyn gives her little support at all, Leola (who might be willing to do so) is virtually inaccessible for her. As a result Regina spends long periods of time observing the others. Frequently she focuses her gaze on Wallace and watches what is going on between the boys. Occasionally these periods of observing lead to the establishment of an interactional axis between Regina and Wallace. I will describe only two of these occurences; in both cases Wallace provides Regina with an opportunity to talk to Leola, but also reorients her to the group's 'embodied' working consensus.[5]

In order to talk to Leola Regina must leave her place and go around the table to her; she does this twice during Wallace's peer-teaching. Regina's departures from her seat constitute 'breaches' of the group's configuration, and they are attended to as such by Wallace. Both departures, though, are also initiated in silent cooperation with him. Regina's first departure begins at a time when she is excluded from the interaction among the other girls. Carolyn has turned to Leola and raises her work-sheet so that it blocks Regina's view. Carolyn says to Leola *'We', here go 'we', Leo!*. For a moment Regina remains in the position of a silent observer, unable to participate in the interaction. A moment later, the same thing happens. This time Regina sits up immediately. Ernesto also sits up, leans forward and points to Wallace's sheet: *What's that word?*.

Regina now gazes at the boys, then shifts her gaze to Leola, and says: *I know one, Leo! I know one, Leo! I know one, Leo!*. She competes with Carolyn in the delivery of proposals for the girls' concerted work. Her utterance is a 'ticket' (Sacks 1972), serving to elicit an invitation from Leola to make a suggestion; it has an unusually elaborate package which shows how much work Regina has to invest to gain Leola's attention. During the second delivery of *I know one*, Carolyn, Ernesto and Wallace shift their gaze to Regina. At the same time, Wallace scratches his nose. This gesture is a "monitor" (cf. Scheflen, 1972), a type of behavior used to 'recalibrate' an interaction which has somehow come to be perceived as 'disorderly'. For the first time, an interactional axis between Regina and Wallace is established. A second later Regina stands up. At exactly the same time Wallace bends his head down, raises his brows, shrugs his shoulders and tilts his chair (Figure 1): he moves out of a working posture simultaneously with Regina.

Figure 1

Regina walks around the table, bends over Leola's shoulder and delivers her proposal in a very quite voice:

```
(8) 1   R   °(          )
    2   L   What?
    3   L   Oh, B E L, B O L.
    4   R   Uhhuh, O!
    5   R   O. B L ⌈O W.
    6   L          ⌊  O W.
    7   R   See.
```

Meanwhile, Wallace has dropped his right hand (his writing hand) under the table and is visibly no longer working (Figure 2): he joins Regina in the suspension of the previously agreed-upon definition of the situation. He will not move back into a working posture until Regina does so as well.

Figure 2

While Regina is talking to Leola, Wallace flips his left hand three times in Regina's direction. This is a "physiographic" gesture (Efron 1941), also serving as a 'monitor'. It is a rudimentary version of an arm-movement by which Regina would have been pushed out of her current position (Figure 3).

Figure 3

But Regina does not react, and Wallace shifts to a different type of monitoring gesture, pointing his chin to Regina (Figure 4).

Figure 4

Regina raises immediately and begins her return to her place. During her return Wallace assembles his limbs to a working posture while still keeping his right arm under the table (Figure 5).

Figure 5

From this position Regina and Wallace simultaneously move back into a writing posture (on the same frame of the videotape; Figure 6).

Regina's second departure from the formation begins not unlike the first: again Carolyn turns to Leola and excludes Regina from the interaction by raising her work-sheet. A moment later Ernesto leans forward and looks at Wallace's sheet. Simultaneously Regina

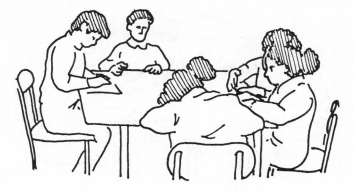

Figure 6

gets up. Within the same split-second Wallace raises his left hand from the table; the impression is created that an invisible string connects Regina's body with his hand (Figure 7).

Figure 7

While Regina walks around the table and positions herself next to Leola, Wallace initially continues to work. However, his arms are not in their normal position but withdrawn from the table by a few inches (Figure 8).

Figure 8

The girls engage in a dialogue:

(9)   1   R   We already got 'below'
            (0.4)
       2   R   Y'all got that?
       3   R   'Below'.
       4   C   'Below'.
       5   C   Leo! Wait! ⌈Lemme use your L than you can use my L.
       6   R   ⌊You got that wrong.
       7   R   Wait!
       8   C   Where's your L?
       9   R   You can't use that.
      10   L   Uhhuh.
      11   R   Uhhuh.
      12   C   Yes, you can write L.
      13   R   BOW, Leo!
      14   R   That's not a 'bowl'.
      15   R   That's not a 'bowl'.
      16   L   No, it's BOW.
      17   C   Oo, we got one two three (.) four five. We got five already.
      18   L   °One two three four five.
            (1.1)
      19   R   °Three four.
            (1.2)
      20   L   'Bow'.
      21   L   I got fi:ve.
      22   L   Here go 'bo:w'.
      23   L   You got it wro:ng.

(1.0)

24   C   You ain't got 'bow'.

During this dialogue Wallace silently produces a series of increasingly intense monitoring gestures. He begins by scratching his nose (Figure 9).

Figure 9

Then he raises his torso, looks at the girls, and scratches harder. Regina turns more toward Leola, erecting a barrier with her arm and shoulder (Figure 10).

Figure 10

Regina then leans on the table, and Wallace puts his head on his arm, simultaneously moving his elbow slightly to the left until it almost touches Regina (Figure 11).

Figure 11

Regina gets up and goes back to her place (Figure 12).

Figure 12

When she arrives at her place, she remains standing for a moment. Wallace gazes at her, gazes at Carolyn, then at Regina again.
Regina sits down and at this point Wallace puts his arm on the
table (Figure 13). Again, the two children simultaneously reassemble
the formation.

On both occasions, then, Regina's departures from the group's
configuration emerge as results of two different processes. While
she herself is temporarily excluded from the conversation on the
girls' side of the table, she witnesses that the boys also move into
a state of heightened participation. She is thus the only child

Figure 13

presently not engaged in interaction with others. When she leaves her place, Wallace also shifts to a different type of involvement: his postural shifts display that, as far as he is concerned, the activity (i.e., working) is coming to a halt. He then produces a series of monitoring gestures, increasing their intensity up to the point where Regina reacts and begins her return. Finally the two children resume their regular postures and activity simultaneously. Wallace's behavior during these incidents thus creates a 'gap' or 'slot' in the group's concerted activity which is filled by Regina's 'out-of-context'-actions. The temporal boundaries of these actions are not simply contingent upon 'brute facts' (the distance traversed, the length of her conversations with Leola) but marked in the interaction and thereby attended to as 'social facts'.

The relationship between Wallace and Regina can be regarded as a case of 'social referencing' (cf. Chance and Larsen, 1976): even though the boy does not really act, nor is he regarded by her, as her 'teacher', he nevertheless serves as her source of information for situationally appropriate behavior, while he also 'holds' her in the group.

6. Conclusion

Social cognition is "thought *in* action" (Selman 1984: 114). However, as I hope to have shown in this paper, neither the social concepts enacted by children nor the structure of their social relations are one-dimensional phenomena. Interaction is organized at "different levels of predication" (Cicourel 1975); a variety of social concepts (e. g., friendship, rank and gender) can be concurrently relevant within an encounter. Children are able to organize their interaction in different successive frames, foregrounding in one frame a concept which is given only peripheral relevance in the next. They also know how to realize different, even contradictory concepts simultaneously (e. g., by exchanging information in 'fights') and construct their talk so that it meets contrasting requirements. They come to an agreement and then they act together in ways not provided for by this agreement.

Children fight, compete and insult each other, but they keep travelling in packs, passing, as it were, through territories that are under adult control. Their interaction is skewed toward reciprocity, which thereby rises as the superior moral principle of the child's own world. "The possibility of further communication is the driving force of morality, because it covers everything that is needed for the persistence of relations with others" (Younniss 1984: 35).

Notes

1. Bud Mehan's generous support for my research at the University of California, San Diego, is greatfully acknowledged. Gisela Klann-Delius clarified for me what I wanted to say. An outline of this paper was written in a departure lounge at Los Angeles International Airport, and I am indebted to *People Express* for a ticketing policy that made me be at the airport ahead of time, as well as for the flight's delayed departure.
2. Harrie Maazeland made a number of critical observations regarding a prior analysis of the following incidents in which I employed the concept of 'plans' adopted from work in artificial intelligence (cf. Abelson, 1975). I agree that an analysis in terms of situated or conversational identities is more appropriate than the account given in Streeck (1983). My analysis is partly based on information from other parts of the corpus, and I am aware that there are considerable methodological problems in using such a strategy. A somewhat different analysis of the same data is Cazden et al. (1979).
3. The implications of Carolyn's request with respect to the relationships within the group hinge upon her selection of personal pronouns and descriptive terms: there is an underlying contrast between *me* and *us*.

The term "help" contrasts with alternative concepts such as "teach", "show" and the like: "help" entails a direct involvement of the helper in the doings of the helped. Note also that the exclusive reference of *me* has previously been established by Carolyn's appeal *Help me so we can go to (the library) at the same time*, in which *we* is used exclusively.

4. Cf. Goodwin (forthcoming) for an extensive discussion of same-sex and cross-sex arguments among children.

5. Microethnographers assume that the postural configurations adopted by participants of interactive events serve as 'embodiments' of the group's consensus regarding the current definition of the situation. By sustaining a postural configuration for phases of their concerted activity members 'cue' that definition. But they also 'hold each other responsible' to remain within that definition: 'breaches' of the configuration are usually attented and reacted to, thus displaying the normative quality of the consensus. McDermott et al. (1978: 250 — 251) write:

> Members usually hold each other accountable for proceeding in ways consistent with the context for their concerted activities. Perhaps the most compelling of the criteria for locating people's answer to the question *What's happening?* at any given moment is that the members of any group hold each other to behaving in certain contextually appropriate ways ... In order to call each other back to a particular way of behavior, the chastising members must orient to the break in the order of their behavior, formulate what has to be done, and reestablish their bodies into a positioning that signals the formulated order. And ... the people held accountable most often respond by immediately performing behavior formulated as appropriate for the context at hand. Thus, the order in their behavior becomes obvious not only in the ways they try to hold each other accountable, but in the ways they are held accountable.

References

Abelson, Robert P.
  1975   "Concepts for Representing Mundane Reality in Plans", *Representation and Understanding*, edited by Daniel G. Bobrow and Allan Collins. (New York: Academic Press), 273 – 310.
Abrahams, Roger D.
  1970   *Deep down in the Jungle* (Chicago: Aldine).
Bateson, Gregory
  1949   "Bali: The Value System of a Steady State", *Social Structure: Studies Presented to A. R. Radcliffe-Brown*, edited by Meyer Fortes. (Oxford: Clarendon Press), 35 – 53.
Bateson, Gregory
  1958   *Naven*. (Stanford: Stanford University Press).

Cazden, Courtney B.
1979   "How Knowledge about Language helps the Classroom Teacher — or Does it: A Personal Account." Paper presented at the National Language Arts Conference of the NCTE, Atlanta.

Cazden, Courtney B. et al.
1979   "Y'all gonna hafta listen. Peer Teaching in a Primary Classroom", *Children's Language and Communication*, edited by William A. Collins (Hillsboro N. J.: Lawrence Erlbaum), 183 – 231.

Chance, Michael R. A. and Ray R. Larsen
1976   "Introduction", *The Social Structure of Attention*, edited by Michael R. A. Chance and Ray R. Larsen. (London: Wiley), 1 – 10.

Cicourel, Aaron V.
1975   "Discourse and Text: Cognitive and Linguistic Processes in Studies of Social Structure". *Versus: Quaderni di Studi Semiotici*. Sept. – Dec. 1975, 33 – 84.

Damon, William
1982   "Zur Entwicklung der sozialen Kognition des Kindes. Zwei Zugänge zum Verständnis von sozialer Kognition", *Perspektivität und Interpretation*, edited by Wolfgang Edelstein and Monika Keller. (Frankfurt/Main: Suhrkamp), 110 – 145.

Efron, David
1941   *Gesture, Race and Culture* (The Hague: Mouton, 1972 new edition).

Erickson, Frederick and Jeff Shultz
1982   *The Counselor as Gatekeeper* (New York: Academic Press).

Goffman, Erving
1967   *Interaction Ritual* (New York: Anchor Books).

Goodwin, Marjorie Harness
1982   "Processes of Dispute Management among Urban Black Children", *American Ethnologist, 9*, 1, 76 – 96.

Goodwin, Marjorie Harness
forthcoming   "Children's Arguing", *Language, Sex and Gender in Comparative Perspective*, edited by Susan U. Philips, Susan Steele, and Christina M. Tanz (New York: Cambridge University Press).

Heritage, John
1984   "A Change-of-State Token and Aspects of its Sequential Placement", *Structures of Social Action, Studies in Conversation Analysis*, edited by Max Atkinson and John Heritage (Cambridge: Cambridge University Press), 299 – 345.

Kendon, Adam
 1977 *Studies in the Behavior of Social Interaction* (Lisse: Peter de Ritter Press).
Kendon, Adam
 1979 "Some Emerging Features of Face-to-Face Interaction Studies", *Sign Language Studies* 22, 7 – 22.
Krappmann, Lothar
 1980 "Sozialisation in der Gruppe der Gleichaltrigen", *Handbuch der Sozialisationsforschung*, edited by Klaus Hurrelmann and Dieter Uhlich. (Weinheim: Beltz), 443 – 468.
Labov, William
 1972 "Rules for Ritual Insults", *Studies in Social Interaction*, edited by David Sudnow (New York: The Free Press), 120 – 169.
McDermott, Ray P., Gospodinoff, Kenneth and Aron, Jeffrey
 1976 "Criteria for an Ethnographically Adequate Description of Concerted Activities and their Contexts", *Semiotica*, *24*, 3/4, 245 – 276.
Mehan, Hugh
 1975 "Students' Formulating Practices and Instructional Strategies", Paper presented at the New York Academy of Science in October 1975.
Mehan, Hugh
 1979 *Learning Lessons* (Cambridge, Mass.: Harvard University Press).
Philips, Susan
 1972 "Participant Structures and Communicative Competence", *Functions of Language in the Classroom*, edited by Courtney B. Cazden, Dell Hymes and Vera P. John (New York: Teachers College Press), 370 – 394.
Sacks, Harvey
 1972 "On the Analyzability of Stories by Children", *Directions in Sociolinguistics: The Ethnography of Communication*, edited by John J. Gumperz and Dell Hymes. (New York: Holt, Rinehart & Winston), 325 – 345.
Sacks, Harvey
 1978 "Some Technical Considerations of a Dirty Joke", *Studies in the Organization of Conversational Interaction*, edited by Jim Schenkein (New York: Academic Press), 249 – 269.
Sacks, Harvey, Emanuel A. Schegloff and Gail Jefferson
 1974 "A Simplest Systematics for the Organization of Turn-Taking for Conversation", *Language*, *50*, 4, 696 – 735.
Scheflen, Albert
 1972 *Body Language and Social Order* (Englewood Cliffs, N.J.: Prentice-Hall).

326   *Streeck*

1973   *Communicational Structure* (Bloomington: Indiana University Press).
1974   *How Behavior Means* (Garden City, N. Y.: Anchor Press).
Siegert, Michael, T.
1980   *Konfliktbearbeitungsstrategien siebenjähriger Kinder in interpersonalen Handlungssituationen*, Unpublished Manuscript (Berlin: Max-Planck-Institut für Bildungsforschung).
Streeck, Jürgen
1983   *Social Order in Child Communication*, Pragmatics and Beyond IV: 8 (Amsterdam: Benjamins B. V.).
Streeck, Jürgen
1984   "Embodied Contexts, Transcontextuals, and the Timing of Speech Acts", *Journal of Pragmatics, 8*, 113–137.
Younniss, James
1984   "Moral, kommunikative Beziehungen und die Entwicklung der Reziprozität", *Soziale Interaktion und soziales Verstehen*, edited by Wolfgang Edelstein and Jürgen Habermas (Frankfurt/Main: Suhrkamp), 34–60.

Activity Structure as Scaffolding for Children's Second Language Learning[1]

Susan M. Ervin-Tripp

It is a common observation that elementary school children learn second languages fast from their friends. While their parents struggle with phrase books, they are out on the playground rapidly coming to sound like natives. They are successful at peer play despite the lack or low level of their language knowledge. Considerable social knowledge has to underlie these transactions. Social knowledge already available at the time of initial contact is at the root of the rapid language learning process. It motivates the learning and the teaching, because language is necessary to full use of some types of successful transactions, and it provides a reference or meaning frame for acquiring new phrases.

By close observation of spontaneous play between speakers and learners of the same age it is possible to see how children manage to bring about successful play when they have minimal language in common, and how features of the play context specifically facilitate language learning.

The first focus of the paper will be on the hypothesis that children enter the second-language interaction situation with specifiable prior knowledge about social systems. In the case of peer interaction involving play and games, this knowledge involves schematic generalities of play types (e. g. that games might involve turns) as well as specifics of familiar games. The fact that children with almost no knowledge of a language can learn complex games with conditional sequences suggests that the schematic or structural generalities are important.[2]

Language and play

I have not seen any analysis of the structure of play in terms of its speech properties, or even how much speech is necessary or usual (but see Garvey 1984 for relevant comments). Play is possible with a minimum of language because children already know the schema for the type of play involved. Play is more possible without language for some games than others. Some games are almost entirely physical and can occur with no speech whatsoever. Even these games usually require verbal negotiation at the start or at certain critical junctures. These might be identifying who is to start, whose turn it is, when a violation has occurred, or to announce some accomplishment. But this talk may be so routinized as to make very limited demands on language knowledge. It may consist merely of a list of names or titles of acts. Other games are potentially entirely physical but as normally played are accompanied by so much talk that they may be seen as primarily a vehicle for social talk or for argument. Some card games are good examples. At the opposite extreme are games that depend heavily on verbal knowledge and cannot occur at all if language cannot be understood.[3]

The cooperative attitude of partners is an important feature of successful play with a minimum of language facility. Since information is not available about the wants or ideas of one partner, except minimally, the knowledgeable partner has got to be willing to guess what might be intended. We have found that the capacity to guess the trajectories of others, except in routinized cases, increases markedly after school age (Ervin-Tripp and Gordon, 1985).

Language learning

The second focus of the paper is on play as a learning vehicle. Language learning always has two prerequisites. One is the motive, exposure, and capacity to find language patterns, overt or hidden, the other is the opportunity to relate these patterns to referents, concepts, and to conditions of use. It is the second prerequisite which is most relevant here.

There are always conceptual prerequisites for language learning. For example, relatively young children learn ways of indicating transitivity and aspect. Structural signals for these features vary with language. What is clear is that the child has to understand the conceptual basis for these features in order to acquire the structural signal, whatever it is. That is, these concepts have to be present already for language learning. That seems to be true at the earliest stages. Later of course, language may also guide concepts. What I propose here is that there are social bases comparable to the conceptual bases for language learning.

Suppose children are playing a card game. One of them says "you deal". In saying this, the child is making a directive and naming an action at a certain point in the game.

The word "deal" refers to a characteristic action pattern, the same as in "he's dealing" or "he dealt me cards". But as a specific directive, it has appropriateness conditions. To say "you deal" in the middle of a hand would be heard as oddly placed, and possibly as referring to the future, or as implying the hand is over. If dealing alternates, to say "you deal" when the partner dealt the last hand would also call up special accounts for the proposed change. Thus even this simple term has a set of presuppositions relating to activity structure. These are that only one person deals, in some games that the dealer rotates, and that deals occur before hands.

A learner with prior knowledge of the activity structure within which the new language is used is advantaged. Watching language learning in the context of activities makes that prior knowledge evident.

One way to see what facilitates learning is to see what conditions make children talk best. Child-chosen topics are most productive of speech. With toddlers what we see is that talking about the here and now facilitates. Talking about the nearby but not visible is more difficult. Talking about fantasy is easier than about the past which is hardest of all. Physical activity or construction helps. Partners' talk can help, by supplying questions, relevant comments, staying with the child's topic, and with what is understandable from context, and modelling some things to say. This is commonly called scaffolding.

I think it can be argued that school children's play has all of these features. It tends to refer to the here and now. That makes it easy for the learner to identify referents. It often involves construction or activity. And partners do a lot of scaffolding, although of course it is unwitting, just as it frequently is for adults.

In sum, we can expect children will learn language from peer games when they are interested, when they share enough knowledge of the activity to know what is going on without needing explanation, and when the language used is interpretable from the context. But how does the learning occur? Observation of the process can lead us to the actual types of repairs and facilitative strategies that both teachers and learners use in their efforts to negotiate successful play.

Language is especially easy to learn when the roles permit mirroring. An example is greeting, which is often reciprocal. A learner who cannot determine what to say from a model because the roles are complementary has to have a partner willing to teach by supplying models of what to say.

We can expect children will not learn from games when they don't understand the game, when they are not interested, when you have to know too much to play, when the game depends much more on language than on action.

In the study below, having described the language demands of activities, we shall turn to the procedures for learning which were made available by the play contexts.

Data sources

The data cited below are from two studies. One is school-based with observations of Chinese- and Mexican Spanish-speaking children in California schools. The other is a study of English-speaking children playing with French friends in their homes. In both groups language exposure is less than a year. The first children were five and six, the second five through twelve.

1. Activity types

The activities which I shall discuss are of five types. They vary in activity content, importance of verbal information, and structure. These are telephone conversations, simulated soccer, card and board games, Chinese jump rope (elastic cord), and role play or fantasy games.

1.1. Play phone conversations

Telephone conversations are purely verbal, though young children sometimes act as though they were not, for instance by showing objects to a homunculus in the receiver. They can structurally be described as follows:

Greeting
Entry
Core
Farewell

The components of these exchanges vary in elaborateness. An eighteen-month old child, for example, was heard on the phone saying *Hi fine bye*. She revealed the most simple one-party structure, Greeting, reply to an Entry, and a Farewell. The easiest parts of the phone conversation to learn are the Greeting and Farewell, since they are usually mirrors. That is, the learner can just copy the partner. The Entry is not a mirror but complementary with its reply. It is usually conventionalized and may have to be taught, unless the child can overhear a model. The *fine* of the above example must have been overheard. The Core is the most structurally complex section since it contains any talk whatever. Replies to Core can, however, be conventionalized. Their learning may derive from learning formulaic replies outside of the phone context. In examples later we will see how the learning of Entries and Core begins. The telephone conversation is the extreme of a scripted entirely verbal activity which can be taught by modelling, with the exception, of course, of the conversational core.

1.2. Soccer

At the opposite extreme is a soccer game, in which the role of speech is minimal and learning is primarily from observation and action. It is not surprising that peers that do not share a language can play soccer. Those items which require language, such as calling a penalty, can be indicated by conventionalized gestures. In field conditions, language does play a role at critical junctures including identifying a goal, points, and penalties, and serving as a vehicle for emotional expression, encouragement, and advice.

There is a second type of language that goes with soccer games. That is TV announcing of games, which is a special register. It also includes the announcements of goals, points, and penalties, (but much more elaborated in syntax), and of course a lot of descriptive talk.

A third type is the commentary of observers who are not players, which is less likely to contain announcements and contains more emotional expressions, encouragement, and advice. These three types may be called the registers of players, announcers, and observers.

My data on soccer come from a board game which involved skill. The French speaking partner primarily used a TV announcer format. The learner's speech included both the normal speech used in playing the game — he was, after all, playing an exciting game at the time — and considerable observer talk, which was complementary to his partner's TV register. Both boys were twelve and experienced soccer players.

Soccer has a clear activity structure. The start is a kick. Who does it is specified by who is receiving benefits: at the start the winner of a toss, later the team scored against or the defenders when a team has kicked out the ball. The ball is kept in motion in order to achieve goals against which a goalie defends. In turn games such as card games, the participants alternate in action. In soccer, as in many sports, both teams are usually in action at once. Turns apply to large units and involve such issues as territory or role alternation. For example, if the ball leaves the field at the side it is tossed in by the team which did not kick it out, at the spot it left. If the ball leaves the field at the end, but not in the goal, it may be kicked in at the corner — a corner kick by the offensive team. Altercations are over conditions which decide who will restart, where, and how (e. g. where did the ball leave the field, who kicked the ball last) and whether some rules have been violated. Fouls occur as rule violations, such as shoving, touching the ball with the hands, or improper positions of forward players. Since the game cannot be played without agreement on these points this communication is essential.

But this essential communication is not all that occurs. In addition there is "teaching", or advice to players about what to do — kick, get rid of it, pass, shoot. And there is evaluation of what has been done — *wow, super, idiot*. All of this language in the player and observer registers is very simple structurally, easily learned by copying, and is highly contextualized so that it is obvious what it refers to. A novice player who simply watches the sequence of events could induce the rules and have a ground for understanding the words used in the altercations.

The TV announcer register, on the other hand, is structurally very complex. Although it is referentially clear, its complexity makes it much more inaccessible to novice speakers than the observer register.

1.3. Elastic jump rope

Chinese jump rope or elastics is a game two or more can play. An elastic loop is attached around either a chair or the legs of two children. The resulting parallel of elastic marks a space within which one child jumps up and down doing foot manoeuvres. The jumping in Chinese jump rope (jeu d'élastique) involves a specified number of repetitions of the manoeuvres. The difficulty increases through the game. The turn shifts when the child makes a mistake. The difficulty of the actions depends on such factors as how high the cord is on the outside children, whether around ankles, knees, or hips. The difficulty regularly increases in respect to this feature. The children may let the player choose the complexity of the jump, and each group of children develops its own set of favorite manoeuvres and terminology for them. Manoeuvres involve jumping in and out of the elastics, stepping on the cord, catching the elastic on the legs and twisting in various ways without breaking the sequence. In contrast to old-fashioned cord jump rope, there is no activity by the outside children, no rhythm to maintain relative to a turning rope, hence no verses. Outside children also have no control over rate, in fact their passive role gives them a great investment in close observation of the jumper's failures. It is the failure of the jumper that gives them their turn.

Necessary talk includes establishing turns, identifying who starts, setting height of the cord for each new child, and calling failures. Because there are disagreements about the definitions of failure and the exceptions to be permitted, the largest amount of negotiating talk surrounds failure. Some teaching talk can occur, involving describing manoeuvres. But because the moves are complicated they are not easy to describe or teach verbally. Also because jump rope is not a team game, there is less of the "observer talk" register that is found in soccer, involving directives and evaluation.

1.4. Card and board games

Card and board games played by the children have certain features in common.

a) They involve games of short duration which require repeated setting-up, or dealing of cards.

b) Dealing of cards occurs at the beginning of each game, and involves mixing the cards up, (shuffling), passing them out in a fixed order so that cards are random in distribution. Distribution continues until a fixed number of cards for a hand is received by each player.

c) Starting may occur under special conditions, such as highest card, position relative to the dealer, or highest dice toss.

d) After starting, turns have a fixed order and no player can play until the preceding player is finished.

e) In some games the events in a turn are physical, such as moving a piece on a board after tossing dice, picking a card up from the pile, discarding, arranging sets of cards such as three of a kind. Some games require verbal negotiating, such as asking for particular cards in the game of "families" (like Authors). Some games require particular announcements, e. g. "checkmate."

f) Turns rotate until a criterion of success is reached by one or more players. At this point the game may end, if there is merely a win or lose alternative. In some games points are accumulated or players are ranked by continuing to compete with survivors.

Principles a, c, d, e, and f apply also to other games such as soccer and jump rope. The talk surrounding these games turns on negotiating what game to play, who is to set up, who is to start, whose turn is next in multi-party games, announcements of intentions or results, and disputes about whether someone has won. In all games, of course, there are issues to negotiate about rules, though the complexity of the game and its flexibility can alter the likelihood of such disputes.

Some games are difficult to teach from demonstration. In these cases they are only possible if the partners already know the game. In other cases, we do see teaching by doing. Language is typically learned by copying, since roles tend to be repeated in these games.

1.5. Role playing

Role playing games were of two kinds. One type involves pre-structured roles which have fairly defined activity schemata associated with them. Examples are Teacher, which invokes a classroom scenario with content potentially extracted from whatever the child's classroom currently contains, such as math, reading aloud, and punishments. Nurse implies patients, objects, and activities like taking temperatures and wrapping bandages.

The invoking of role games of this type brings into play disputes about who will play what role, since the named role is likely to have more power, more interesting possessions, more obvious activities to undertake, and less complicated negotiations needed to get what one wants. There are often obvious complementary roles, such as pupil, baby, mother, sick people. Once the main role is pre-empted, the partners have to scramble for the most desirable remaining roles or to define what they will do in a way to make the roles interesting. This might involve creative choices among the alternative trajectories available in the main scene. For example, a pupil might refuse to comply.

In other named roles like Princess, the activities are much less clear and may have to be spelled out. If the indications for activity can be shown non-verbally, the novice speaker may be able to manage. But it seems clear that more fixed role schemata should be easier for collaboration than novel schemata — unless these are under the control of the learner.

2. Play with minimal language

When children share very little language, their play choices may be constrained. Two twelve year old boys, for example, rejected playing Monopoly since it was too hard to teach a novice player. They opted for Battleship. In this board game, all that is needed is communication about locations, then an announcement about whether a ship was sunk. Even with this simple task there were problems. Since the locations were indicated by a number-letter grid, the different pronunciations of the letters E, G, and J in French and English created confusion. The boys resolved these ambiguities by writing in the air or pointing to printed letters. Also in this setting the dominance of the French speaker was reduced and both used each other's language (letter pronunciations).

2.1. Predictable activities

Soccer

In the data were some highly successful play episodes in which the anglophone had a month or less of exposure to French. Among these was the table soccer game. It appeared that the anglophone boy knew the activity structure perfectly from his own English experience as a soccer player. He showed evidence that he knew about starting, restarting, goals, scores, and penalties as constrained in the description above. He also had been exposed to playing field soccer already at a francophone school and informally outside of school. His knowledge of the game made him a very successful partner. This success, in turn, kept the two engaged long enough for some new language learning to occur, as described below.

Role play

Seven year old Nell successfully played the teacher role despite very limited French by establishing a series of scenes which were familiar classroom activities. One was teaching to read. Pupils read passages successively, the teacher taught commutation in multiplication, and the teacher ordered the pupil to certain locations and punished her failure to comply, by whacking with a stick. All of these scenes were direct emulations of scenes from the French village school:

(1) Nell: C'est moi la maîtresse. Alors, excusez moi, tu viens ici … derrière les enfants. Tu viens ici. Et quoi, c'est quoi, toi. C'est quoi, le nom à toi?
I'M THE TEACHER. SO, PARDON ME, YOU COME HERE BEHIND THE CHILDREN. YOU COME HERE. AND WHAT, IT'S WHAT, YOU, IT'S WHAT, YOUR NAME?

F: Stéphanie … (long discussion in which a name is negotiated) …

Nell: (gets out slate): Sept. (writing on slate) Attends, attends, c'est ça, bon. Mais deux fois sept égale − − −
SEVEN. WAIT, WAIT. THAT'S IT, GOOD. TWO TIMES SEVEN EQUALS − − −

F: Quatorze. 14

Nell: ou?
Or?

F: Sept fois sept − − 7 × 7 − −

Nell: Sept fois deux égale quatorze.
7 × 2 = 14.

Nell: Mais, tu comprends, eh?
YOU UNDERSTAND, DON'T YOU?

F: Oui. (runs into corner)

Nell: Non, tu viens là! Tu, tu, tu attends là. Viens par là. Stéphanie, Stéphanie, allez vite. A toi. A toi. Non!
NO, YOU COME HERE! YOU, YOU, YOU WAIT HERE. COME BACK HERE. STEPHANIE, STEPHANIE,

HURRY UP. ITS YOUR TURN. YOUR TURN, NO! (runs
after pupil with a little stick while both giggle.)

In this classroom scene the familiar scenarios are Teaching math,
Teaching commutation, Checking, and Naughtiness punished.

Object-based fantasy

Even fantasy games could be successful if the knowledge of their
basic conventions was shared. In the following scene five year old
Kate leads a French visitor, Eric, to two cardboard cartons, and
climbs in one:

(2)   K: En bateau, viens.
           IN THE BOAT, C'MON.
      K: Bateau, bateau.
           BOAT, BOAT. (They both get in boxes and continue talking)
      E: Attention! rrrrrrrr.
           LOOK OUT! (motor roars) (K talks to herself in English)
      K: En bateau. Houp la, en bateau.
           IN THE BOAT, IN YOU GO, IN THE BOAT.
      E: J'aimerai doubler ... la route ... rrrr.
           I'D LIKE TO PASS ... THE ROAD ...
      E: Mets pas tes pieds là.
           DON'T PUT YOUR FEET HERE.
      K: Attention!
           LOOK OUT! (both tip over laughing)
      K: En bateau!
      E: En bateau! Au secours! On change de bateau.
           IN THE BOAT! HELP! WE'RE CHANGING BOATS. (They
           climb in each other's boat)

In this scene, there is a bit of parallel play in which Kate talks
to herself in English and it seems that Eric may be in a car rather
than a boat, but it may merely be two passing motorboats. The
major impression of the scene was the high degree of success in
joint play, with the francophone even emulating the novice's turns.
This success seems to come from the fact that imagining entering
and driving boats/cars, passing, possibly crashing, tipping over, and
exchanging vessels are a standard exploitation of a familiar theme.
Of course, this is a speculation. The evidence would be either the
frequency of a particular use of such materials, or the ability of
children to anticipate or recognize such schemata with minimal
cues.

2.2. Contextualized formulae

Soccer

The highly situated use of language makes new terminology or new phrases intelligible even to speakers who know relatively little. The routines of soccer were conspicuous by their repetition. The learner, despite his limited French, was very vocal. He was extremely excited by the game. He spoke on almost every move, mostly to express excitement. He already knew such vocabulary as the French for shoot, goal, get-rid-of-it (dégage), penalty (which he pronounced as a French word), and such French exclamations as *bravo* and *oo la la*, praise such as "well played" and of course counting for the score. Some turns might be verbally limited, like *Wow*, or *Ooh la la* and others were more elaborate, like *S'il te plaît, non*, "please, no". He also evaluated plays, as in *Oh, super, oh. Corner, Keegan, super, Keegan*. (Keegan is the name of a well-known player.) He named or called plays, as in:

(3)   Keegan, but. Dégage!
      GOAL. GET RID OF IT!

The learner's ability to evaluate and to name plays rested on his prior knowledge of the sequence of events, along with the vocabulary to produce a reasonable participation verbally as player and observer, though his topics were much more restricted than his partner's (the partner used TV announcer register). He talked of goals, shots, getting rid of the ball (dégage) and listed the score.

Turn exchanges

Another routinized context was negotiating turns. Turn exchange is a fundamental principle of games. The terminology of turns is essentially property or territory claiming terminology, such as "Mine", which is among the first moves learned by children in both first and second languages. For example, in the soccer and card game session of the English child in France less than a month, already there is:

(4)   Merci. A toi.
      OK. THANKS. YOUR TURN.

A more advanced exchange is a series listing for successive turns in a group as follows:

(5) E 1: C'est toi (to E 2)
IT'S YOU.
F 1: C'est moi, Rachel.
IT'S ME, RACHEL.
E 1: Et puis toi.
AND THEN YOU.
F 2: Et puis moi.
AND THEN ME.

A more complex exchange is turns in playing roles, as in this very early example:

(6) F: Qui c'est qui commence à être la maîtresse?
WHO STARTS AS THE TEACHER?
Nell: C'est quoi la maîtresse? C'est moi le maîtresse premier, et donc toi, et après, toi le maîtresse. Tu comprends?
WHAT'S THE TEACHER? I'M THE TEACHER FIRST, THEN YOU AND AFTER, YOU ARE THE TEACHER. UNDERSTAND?

Examples like these appeared in almost every game from the earliest stages.

Telephone play

Telephone play provides good examples of learning because of the predictability of routines. In our second-language data, we found a five year old with a dialog system, but as simple as "Hi fine bye" in the replies given:

(7) Greetings: ⟨Hello⟩-Hello.
Core: ⟨Question or statement⟩-Yes.
Farewell: ⟨Bye⟩-Bye.

This was a child whose knowledge of French was very simple. Her incomprehension of the questions is shown in the following:

(8) ⟨I won't stop it [cassette] if you say so.⟩ − − Yes.

In her case, structural knowledge let her participate in boundary greetings and farewells but was too primitive for her to get into a core, which called on vocabulary about topics.

Phone conversations contain scripted segments at the beginning and end. These routines are learned fast. They are similar to other encounter routines, and are modelled by the partner. The problem is going beyond the routine. In the following, a Spanish speaker after 7 months in English replied to an entry, although the routine was mismatched.

(9) Rosa: Hello.
     Emily: What's you doin?
     Rosa: Fine.
     Emily: My mommy told me to go to school.
     Rosa: Me too.
     Emily: OK bye. I'll call you back tomorrow.
     Rosa: Ok Bye.

In this conversation Rosa (Spanish-speaking) has formulae for Greeting, Entry, and Farewell. The formula for replying to an Entry doesn't differentiate between the two possible entries, "how are you" and "what you doin". In fact Emily's entry, *What you doin*, is more typical of these children. The reason for Rosa's reply is clear. *Fine* is a semantically empty routine. Replies to *What you doin?* require more productive skill. The Core requires productive skill too, but the child's formula *me too* appropriately fills the turn.

2.3. Gestural support

These examples have shown that even with very simple language knowledge, children can play successfully on the basis of their activity knowledge. A major tactic for solving the limitation in their language knowledge is to use gesture for communication and for teaching the partner.

Card games

Card games have such predictable properties that it is relatively easy to teach the common games. In the following situation the novice is trying to teach a game in which the person laying down the higher card takes the pair.

(10) A toi
      Moi
      Toi.
      Moi!
      Six, sept.
      Trois quatre. Toi.
      Neuf huit.
      Woa!
      Merci.
      A toi.

In this sequence the teaching was done entirely by naming an outcome and letting the situation teach, until a reversal on the fifth move to naming the circumstances and on the sixth to naming both. The sixth move can be glossed as "If I have three and you four, it's yours."

When the same boy (twelve) tried to teach how to play a more complex game, Snap, in which the winner is the one who says "Snap" first when the cards laid down by both players have the same number, he had to demonstrate:

(11)   Two, two, Snap, OK?
       So, Marcel, pair, OK?

Soccer

The most elaborated efforts to communicate occurred when the boy wanted to impose a penalty, and did not have enough vocabulary to explain. First, he set up the idea of what a penalty kick would look like:

(12)   Marcel! Tu (gestures) ... comme ca. Balle ... tzn! Penalty. OK?
       Marcel! YOU ... LIKE THAT. BALL ... tzn. PENALTY. OK?

The missing semantic elements, the verbs, were acted out.

Having established how to act out a penalty in the game, the boy asked for a penalty when his opponent's man bumped one of his:

(13)   Marcel! Tu ... [shoves Marcel] ... pen-al-ty. OK? Yes? OK.

Although the game was highly successful and the actions were well coordinated, there were some differences in how language was used. For example, in the second soccer session a month later the francophone continued in the third-person vein of a TV announcer, whereas the anglophone, in the interchanges involving the same scene, used first and second person pronouns as if he were an observer or player.

Role-playing

Even in role-playing games knowledge of structure can make moves intelligible, if they have enough gestural support. In role play the first moves are to identify the cast of characters and who will play what part and with what props. In the following scene, Lee, the older sister, chose the most desirable role, Nurse, with all its equipment. She sent her guest out of the room with her younger sister until the Nurse was ready to receive patients. So the other two had to negotiate the remaining roles:

(14)   Ariel: Qui va etre la maman, et puis la soeur, eh?
                  WHO WILL BE THE MOM, AND THEN THE SISTER,
                  HUNH?
        F: Moi. Moi, je suis la maman.
                  ME, ME I'LL BE MAMA.
        Lee: La soeur?
                  THE SISTER? (getting out nurse gear)
        F: C'est moi la maman.
                  I'M THE MOM.
        Lee: Oui. (continues taking out gear and arranging)
        F: C'est qui l'enfant?
                  WHO'S THE CHILD?
        Ariel: Moi.
                  ME.
        Lee: C'est Ariel.
                  IT'S ARIEL.
        F: Regarde.
                  LOOK (playing with stuffed animal)
        Lee: C'est quoi?
                  IT'S WHAT?
        Ariel: Ils sont nos bébés.
                  THEY'RE OUR BABIES.
        F: Ils sont les bébés. C'est eux qui sont malades. Viens. On va
                  à la maison. On telephone à toi. Oui. Oh, ils sont malades.
                  Il faut téléphoner a l'hôpital.
                  THEY ARE OUR BABIES. IT'S THEM WHO ARE SICK.
                  COME ON. WE ARE GOING HOME. WE'RE GONNA
                  TELEPHONE YOU. YEAH. OH, THEY'RE SICK. WE
                  HAVE TO TELEPHONE THE HOSPITAL. (They go to
                  Ariel's room to wait).
        Ariel: Non, elle est allée dans mon lit.
                  NO, SHE'S IN MY BED.

In this scene the novice participant who was younger than the other two succeeded in renegotiating the roles. Being a baby with two adults did not suit her, so she took the presence of the animals as a chance to become on a par with the older French visitor, who, herself excluded by the Nurse, was eager to cooperate. A good deal of the exchange which followed while they waited the Nurse's permission to visit was accomplished by Ariel's careful preparation of beds, culminating in her sabotage of the Nurse by bringing a mattress to the hospital and then stealing some Nurse gear. Neither her age nor linguistic handicap prevented this resistance and restructuring of the play.

The Nurse scene was a role with pre-structured complementary roles such as mothers and babies who could be patients. Linguistically unskilled anglophones also succeeded in efficient play in more unstructured roles, as in the case below where five year old Kate, 5 months in France, succeeded in directing the play of her visitors Michel, 6 and Véra, 4:

(15) Kate: Toi le petit princesse et moi le grand princesse et Michel le grand ... roi.
YOU THE LITTLE PRINCESS AND ME THE BIG PRINCESS AND MICHEL THE BIG ... KING.

         Kate: Ei, toi le Noel. Ei, no, Michel le Noel. Ei ei, toi [V] le princesse et moi le princesse.
EH, YOU SANTA CLAUS, NO, MICHEL SANTA CLAUS. HEY, YOU THE PRINCESS AND ME THE PRINCESS.

         V: On est deux princesses alors.
SO WE'RE TWO PRINCESSES. [recordings of V and M often inaudible]

         Kate: Ei toi [M] toi le Noel, Michel le Noel.
AND YOU'RE THE SANTA CLAUS, MICHEL THE SANTA CLAUS.

         V.:   Qui c'est qui est le père Noel?
WHO'S SANTA CLAUS?

         K.:   Michel.

         V.:   Où est sa barbe?
WHERE'S HIS BEARD?

         K.:   Ei, Michel allez là. Et tu − −
HEY, MICHEL, GO THERE. AND YOU − −

         K.:   Ei Michel! Tu allez, tu allez là, viens là, et et et et et Et elle et moi dors. Et et toi viens et et et et donnes le ça. [winds up music box to restart it]
HEY MICHEL! YOU GO, YOU GO THERE, COME HERE, AND AND AND AND AND AND SHE AND I ARE SLEEPING. AND AND YOU COME AND AND AND GIVE THE THAT. (pointing to music box)

         Kate: Donnes! Michel donne de de de − −
GIVE! MICHEL GIVE SOME SOME SOME − −

Véra: Non! Moi, j'ai reçu ma noel.
         NO! I'VE HAD CHRISTMAS.

Kate: Eh, tiens! Non, parce que, parce que Noel est-est le- est le
         garçon, Tiens! Toi de Noel. C'est toi le Noel.
         HEY, NO, BECAUSE, BECAUSE NOEL IS, IS THE, IS
         THE BOY. HEY YOU ARE SANTA CLAUS, IT'S YOU,
         SANTA CLAUS.

V.:   Moi, j'a ramassé mon Noel ... (   ) chemises de père
         Noel.
         [music box rewound] I'VE GOTTEN MY CHRISTMAS,
         ... (   ) SHIRTS FROM SANTA.

K: Quoi de Noel, quoi? Quoi?
         WHAT FROM SANTA? WHAT? WHAT? Ding dong,
         ding dong (K. hides her eyes).
         Ah, toi ça, toi ça, ça [music box, giggles as talks].
         YOU THAT YOU THAT.

V: (   ) Noel, et puis je dormis. (   ) NOEL, AND THEN
         I SLEEP

K.:   Oui, et et et oui, et et et toi, et toi vilain, et et comme ça,
         poop poop [spanking K and V she shows M what to do]
         vilain. Ei Michel. Ei ei toi et toi. Ei Michel. [covers her
         eyes pretending to sleep] [Michel spanks]
         YES AND AND AND YES, AND AND AND YOU,
         AND YOU NAUGHTY, AND AND LIKE THAT, POOP
         POOP NAUGHTY. HEY MICHEL, HEY HEY YOU
         AND YOU. HEY MICHEL.

K.:   Ei Ei

M.:   Quoi?
         WHAT?

K.:   Ei ei moi, moi moi, elle-vilain et et comme ça [spank] ei
         Michel, comme ça est vilain. [spanks, then covers her eyes]
         HEY HEY ME ME ME, HER — — NAUGHTY AND
         AND LIKE THIS, HEY MICHEL, LIKE THIS IS
         NAUGHTY.

Michel: Tant pis (   ) ça voilà, comme ça, ça va. [strikes V and K
         with belt chain of K's for being naughty.]
         TOO BAD. THERE IT IS, LIKE THAT, THAT'LL DO.

M: Et quand vous avez joué un tour (   ) c'est pret.
         WHEN YOU HAVE PLAYED A TURN IT'S READY.

K.:   [Takes chain and pockets it]. C'est pret.
         IT'S READY. [Michel opens K's eyes and she giggles].

V.:   C'est gentil, ah c'est gentil.
         IT'S NICE, AH, IT'S NICE.

M.:   Il y a encore pour elle.
THERE'S MORE FOR HER.

K.:   [throws chain at Michel] Et no, no, arêtes arêtez. Attends, et ça de, ça ça pour elle et ça pour moi. C'est à moi.
HEY NO, NO, STOP, STOP. WAIT, AND THAT FOR HER AND THAT FOR ME. THAT'S MINE. [K takes the helt chain and necklace and gives them to Michel, demonstrating that he is supposed to give the chain to V and the necklace to K.]

V.:   C'est à moi.
THAT'S MINE.

K.:   Oui [giggles].

V.:   Voyez.
LOOK.

M.:   Elle a rien reçu.
SHE GOT NOTHING.

K.:   [picks up a little ring from the floor and gives it to Michel] Ei, tu donnez ça et et ça, eh? C'est ça. eh? ça et ça et ...
HEY, YOU GIVE THIS AND AND THIS, HUH? IT'S THIS, HUH? THIS AND THIS AND AND ... [gestures a trade with V.] Michel? Ei ei moi, elle, et elle, moi, et elle, elle, ei Michel, elle moi et moi, elle, oui?
HEY HEY ME, HER, AND HER, ME, AND HER, HER, HEY MICHEL, HER ME AND ME, HER, YES?
[Michel takes K's necklace and puts it on V's neck]

K.:   Ding dong ding dong. Ei pour moi! Moi, moi. [gestures to Michel to return the little ring from the floor she had given him.]

K.:   Michel, moi tout ça après, moi tout ça après.
MICHEL, ME ALL THAT AFTER, ME ALL THAT AFTER.

Michel: D'accord.
OK.

V.:   Ei, attends.
WAIT.

K.:   Moi changer place [goes to little stool].
ME CHANGING PLACE.

M.:   Attends.
WAIT.

K.:   [climbs ladder to another stool] Non, ça c'est à moi.
NO, IT'S MINE.
Oui, oui, parfait. Ei, c'est fini.
YES, PERFECT. WELL IT'S FINISHED.

The remarkable success of episodes like this, which have relatively primitive language but a lot of reliance on gesture, and on prior knowledge, depends ultimately on the cooperation of partners. In this episode K has a strong notion of the roles to be allocated to different participants, and uses gesture and pronouns to identify V whom she never named. She relies heavily on attention-getting devices so that she can get gaze and use her gestures. She has a limited verb vocabulary, and used gestures to identify what *poop-poop, comme ça,* and *ça* referred to. Although she knows the verb "donner" GIVE, she did not use it when her attention was on beneficiaries, showing how fragile accessibility is.

What was most striking about these episodes was how clearly the social dynamics came through. Younger siblings sometimes succeeded, despite their more abbreviated French, in dominating the play of the older children, when there was sibling rivalry. Just as limited vocabulary restricts play only slightly, limited language does not hobble the children who want to disagree or dominate through play.

2.4. Imitation

The most obvious examples of the learning of language through play were immediate repetitions of the utterances of the other players.

Jump rope

The talk in the jump rope scenes was always about the activity. It was not formulaic however. There were a narrow range of topics, whose turn it was, where the elastic was to be set, whether a mistake had occurred, whether certain mistakes counted, how to do a particular move. Because of the narrow range of issues, the talk is relatively interpretable from context. In jump-rope a critical point is the negotiation of turn exchanges by calling mistakes. Then there can be disputes about exemptions. In the following text, a dispute develops over whether catching a heel in the cord counts as a failure or not. As in the earlier turn-taking argument, Sophie (French) and Britt (English) seem to be allied against their siblings.

(16) Ruth: Ah failli! Talons comptent pas.
                  MISTAKE! HEELS DON'T COUNT.
      Sophie: (jumper) C'est talons!
                  IT'S HEELS.
      Britt: C'est talons. Allez! IT'S HEELS.
                  GO ON!
      Georges: Failli!
                  MISTAKE!

This argument went on through twelve turns. The least experienced French speaker was Britt, who in such arguments typically copied a model. Here she picks up Sophie's phrase and adds to it the continuation formula.

In the following "Chinese jump rope" scene, there is a dispute about both who will play and who will start:

(17) Sophie: Premier!
                 FIRST!
     Georges (younger brother): Je peux jouer?
                 CAN I PLAY?
     Ruth: Si tu veux, oui.
                 IF YOU WANT TO, YES.
     Sophie (older sister): Non, non, nous trois.
                 NO, NO, US THREE.
     Britt (younger sister of Ruth): Nous trois,
                 US THREE.
     Sophie: Seulement nous trois.
                 ONLY US THREE.
     Ruth: Non, ça va mieux avec quatre.
                 NO, IT'S BETTER WITH FOUR.

In this case, the younger, anglophone (Britt) collaborated with the francophone, and merely repeated *nous trois*. Her older sister, who was much more competent in French, not only recognized the self-invitation but disputed Sophie's decision and defended her view with an argument.

Soccer

The soccer game was filled with instances of learning through immediate repetition. As the partner gave his TV commentary he produced many examples of vocabulary concerning the game which the learner picked up.

(18) Marcel: C'est un but super.
                IT'S A SUPER GOAL.
      Carl: Oui, super.
      Marcel: Le gardien dégage.
                THE GOALIE GETS IT GOING.
      Carl: Dégage, oh, non.
                GETS IT GOING. OH NO.

Board games

Predictable board game activities provide routines which can be
named and the names copied. The cycle of finishing and re-setting
the pieces of the game for a new round keeps presenting the same
categories for naming. In this scene Karla has been in France about
a month.

(19) Anne: On change de jeu, eh.
                LET'S CHANGE GAMES HUH.
      Karla: Je suis ...
                I'M ...
      Anne: Non, on change.
                NO, WE'LL CHANGE.
      Karla: Ah, oui.
      Anne: On range.
                WE'LL PUT THINGS AWAY. (begins to)
      Karla: On range.

2.5. Later copies

In addition to immediate copying, there are delayed copies, in which
the new terms were stored and used later, as in these examples.

Soccer

(20) Marcel: Voilà un tir très haut que nous ne pouvons pas suivre avec
                le caméra, un tir ... (ball, shoots)
                HERE'S A SHOT THAT'S SO HIGH THE CAMERA
                CAN'T FOLLOW IT, A SHOT ...
      Carl: Oh non.
      Marcel: Personne au centre.
                NOBODY AT CENTER.
      Carl: Un tir, ooh.
                A SHOT, OOH.

(21) Marcel: Vraiment superbe ce but.
        REALLY SUPERB, THAT GOAL.
      Carl: C'est un ... oh là là.
        IT'S A ... OH OH.
      Marcel: Bon, et voilà un attaque encore.
        GOOD, AND HERE'S ANOTHER ATTACK.
      Carl: Oh non.
      Marcel: Les rouges dégagent par leur gardien, et un rouge est à
        position sur la balle.
        THE RED GOALIE PUTS THE BALL IN MOTION,
        AND A RED IS IN POSITION WITH THE BALL.
      Carl: Oui.
      Marcel: Et il marque un but magnifique!
        HE MAKES A MAGNIFICENT GOAL!
      Carl: Keegan, superbe.

2.6. Explicit instruction

Of course, partners can teach language directly. This did not usually happen in the high-activity games since meanings mapped so readily and vividly. It does happen in phone conversations which are not scaffolded by physical redundancies. How the child Entry is learned is revealed in the following text from Fillmore (1976):

(22) Nora (Spanish-speaker): Hello. Come to my house, please.
      E: Who are you?
      Nora: Nora.
      E: Nora, you've got to say "What are you doing?".
      Nora: What are you doing?
      E: Making cookies. What are you doing?
      Nora: Making cookies, too.
      E: OK, bye.
      Nora: Bye.

In this text, the friend criticized Nora for leaping into an invitation without an appropriate entry. Invitations normally precede the farewell. In this case the friend explicitly taught the Entry form. Because the reply to the Entry is too demanding, Nora simply copied the model.

Board game

In the following card game called "Twist", the player lays down a card which must be matched either in suit or number by the next player. If that player cannot do so, a draw from the deck is in order.

(23) Anne-Marie: C'est quatre, one up.
                     IT'S FOUR, ONE-UP!
      Ruth: Un di de carreau.
                     A TEN OF DIAMONDS.
      Anne-Marie: Dix ou carreau.
                     TEN OR DIAMONDS.
      Ruth: Dix ou carreau, oui.
      Britt: Allez, Anne-Marie.
                     GO ON.
      Anne-Marie: Très bien, Ruth, je t'applaudis.
                     VERY GOOD, RUTH. I CONGRATULATE YOU.

In this text, Anne-Marie clearly plays the teacher role, correcting both the phrasing and pronunciation of Ruth, and even stops the game to evaluate, as a teacher should.

In the following game of "Jeu de familles" the learner both makes an error of pronunciation and a mistake in identifying what she wants. In this game players ask for a specific card which is identified by family (in sets of four) and by number or identity.

(24) Nell: Tu as des familles des cer?
             HAVE YOU FAMILIES OF DEER?
      F: Le quoi?
             WHAT?
      Nell: Cer.
      F: Cerf?
      Nell: Oui.
      F: Le combien?
             WHICH ONE?
      Nell: Cerf.
             DEER.
      F: Le combien.
             WHICH ONE?
      Nell: Cerf, tu comprends?
             DEER, UNDERSTAND?
      F: Oui.
      Nell: Non?
      F: Non. Le le un de la famille chevel.
             NO. THE THE ONE FROM THE HORSE FAMILY.
      Nell: Non. La famille de chien.
             NO. THE DOG FAMILY.
      F: Le combien.
             WHICH ONE?
      Nell: Chien.
             DOG.

F: Le quatre? La grand-mère?
Nell: Oh oh. Attends, le quatre.
       OH OH. WAIT, THE FOUR.
F: Le quatre?
Nell: Oui. Family, uh, le family de chat. Oh, trois, merci.
       YES. FAMILY, UH, THE FAMILY OF CATS. OH, THREE,
       THANKS.

Turn shift is so familiar (wait your turn! take turns!) that it is
a basis for learning new vocabulary. In the following scene the
anglophone knows almost no French. Although she is thirteen, her
French is so primitive that her friend speaks "foreigner style" to
her.

(25)   Anne: Tu as gagné. Tu prémier, toi, un.
               YOU WON. YOU FIRST. YOU, ONE.
       Karla: unh.
       Anne: Alors, toi go, toi. Tu commence.
               SO YOU GO. YOU. YOU START.
       Later:
       Karla: Uh je suis jaune et toi rouge, uh.
               I'M YELLOW AND YOU'RE RED.
       Anne: Tu commence, tu commence.
               YOU BEGIN. YOU BEGIN.
       Karla: Comm − − uh.
       Anne: Tu commence, oui.
               YOU START, YES.
       Later:
       Karla: Quel- quelle-couleur- couleur?
               WHAT- WHAT-COLOR- COLOR?
       Anne: Uh, ben jaune, jaune.
               WELL, YELLOW. YELLOW.
       Karla: Tu commence.
               YOU BEGIN.

In this case the referent for the word *commence* is obvious from
the activity sequence. The anglophone knows the words *tu* and *toi*
so she knows the utterance is about her. She also knows that a
restart is in order. So she infers correctly what *commence* must
mean. The speaker sees the term *tu commence* as a directive routine
located at the beginning of the game cycle. Yet the meaning of
"start" is not tangible. It refers to beginning a new game, which is

a construct based on an abstract notion of the game as a cycle. Such an inference would be impossible without an abstract notion of the game.

2.7. Problems

Language weaknesses are important to examine too. There are obviously cases where communication fails. What makes these different? Recourse to the mother tongue is one kind of evidence, recourse to the experimenter to explain, cases where the partner's speech is simply too complex to copy. We have already noted that Carl's soccer speech was much less complex than Marcel's and often had to be responsive to the game rather than to Marcel's TV announcer speech.

In the following cases, there seemed to be some defect in explanation because the complexity of idea surpassed the language resources.

(26)   (Marcel took a pair of cards, Carl thought he had won)
    Carl: *Moi!*
             ME!
    Marcel: oh.
    Carl: Whoa! (shakes finger)

(27)   Britt: Pas ça. Non, pas un carreau. Deux, c'est spécial. Est-ce ...
             si tu n'as pas un deux, alors tu, uh, deux cartes. Alors, c'est
             pas toi, c'est pas toi, c'est Ruth. Ruth, it's your turn to
             begin.
             NOT THAT. NO, NOT A DIAMOND. TWO IS
             SPECIAL. IS IT ... IF YOU DON'T HAVE A TWO,
             THEN YOU ... OH, TWO CARDS. THEN, IT'S NOT
             YOU, IT'S NOT YOU, IT'S RUTH. RUTH, IT'S YOUR
             TURN TO BEGIN.

Role assignment

In the following role playing text, the children negotiate the teacher role but in addition the anglophone adds the idea of taking turns in it.

(28)   F: C'est la maîtresse. (Nell is getting out slate and chalk)
    Nell: Toi ou moi? Quoi, la maîtresse? C'est quoi la maîtresse? Toi
          ou moi?
          YOU OR ME? WHAT'S THE TEACHER? YOU OR ME?

F: Comme tu veux.
AS YOU WISH. YOU OR ME?
Nell: C'est moi un petit peu et c'est toi un petit peu.
IT'S ME A LITTLE AND THEN IT'S YOU.
F: C'est qui qui commence?
WHO STARTS?
Nell: C'est qui qui commence?
WHO STARTS?
F: à être l'élève.
TO BE PUPIL.
Nell: Je ne comprends pas.
I DON'T UNDERSTAND.
F: Qui c'est qui commence à être maîtresse.
WHO STARTS OUT AS TEACHER?
Nell: C'est quoi la maîtresse? C'est moi le maîtresse premier ... et
donc toi le ... et aprés toi le maîtresse. Tu comprends?
WHAT'S THE TEACHER? I'M THE TEACHER FIRST,
THEN YOU. AFTER, YOU THE TEACHER. UNDER-
STAND?

Arguments

The most ultimately taxing form of language use is an argument,
when many disparate language resources may be marshalled. In the
following episode between Chinese speakers, the English argument
had a very simple structure, and finally when the repetitive idea
was inadequate the children reverted to Chinese for the more complex insult. Just a fragment is given from a longer text in Ervin-
Tripp (1981).

(29) B: My father, bigger your father.
C: You father big big big big big.
B: My father, uh, bigger you father.
C: My father my father like that! (stands, reaches high)
B: My father stronger your father.
C: My father like that! (arms wide)
B: Don't talk for — I hit you!
(In Chinese):
B: I'm gonna tell your father that you steal things!
C: When have I stolen things?
B: You, you stole Arthur's getting married thing (ring).
C: hunh-uh!
B: You stole, you stole my car and gave it to Arthur!

C: Your car! (sarcastic)
B: You, I hit you! Hit you! When we go outside, I'm gonna hit
    you! (pointing to C's forehead)
C: Well, you'll have to run very fast.
B: When you grow up and you steal, your wife isn't going to like
    you.

Arguments are entirely verbal. There is no way that the punch
line in this argument could be learned from any ritualized sequence
like the activity words in routines accompanying action or even the
script of phone conversations. This shows us the limits of the
scaffolding supplied by activity supports and scripts such as phone
conversation frames.

3. Conclusions

Our original question was how children accomplish successful play
when they share language only minimally. We hoped through studying such interaction to find what presupposed structures are present
in children's knowledge of activities, how language is used in different types of play, and how the prior knowledge scaffolds the
child's verbal interaction and language learning during play, or
failing that, what remedies a child has whose language knowledge
is too primitive for the demands of the game.

(1) We found that in different types of games children appear to
routinely *use their activity knowledge as though there were no language barrier*. Certain issues were highlighted repeatedly in the
games, namely turn taking, rules, penalties, identifying successes,
and negotiating differences. These are quite typical of monolingual
play, too.

(2) The foundation for the children's language learning in play
is their *prior knowledge of the activity structure* of the general type
or in complex games the specific game itself.

(3) *Language use differs considerably in various activities.* Yet I
am not aware of discussion of this very important issue in the
construction of social relations, and in the context for language
learning. We have differentiated between four types of talk in games:
essential, social-expressive, dispute, and secondary registers.

There could be non-verbal games in which talk is not only not
essential but interferes. In some physically organized games such as

sports, communication of some kind is *essential, or necessary to the existence of the activity*. Language or standardized gestures are used to identify major events that mark changes in activity. We found considerable ancillary talk accompanying games. While this talk did not seem logically to be essential to the conduct of the game (and in some traditions is suppressed, e. g. in traditional tournament tennis, or in chess) it is so usual as to be part of the normal characteristics of some games, or rather of certain game cultures. The expressive talk accompanying games is interpretable because it accompanies unambiguous action. Disputes occur in almost any game context. They can be hard to learn language from because they may be syntactically complex. There are some optional additional talk types or registers, like observer advice in soccer, which may have high learnability, while others, like TV register, are hard to learn.

(4) Factors which seemed to facilitate language learning in games were *redundancy* with action which made words meaningful, availability of simple *models to copy*, and *cooperative attitudes* by the partner which led to willingness to interpret the learner's tries, or to give language instruction.

(5) The language learned in games varies in complexity. The easiest to learn appear to be syntactically simple, highly repetitive formulae. These are probably the least "progressive" from the standpoint of syntactic variety and complexity. The child's social success and sense of participation through the language are benefits, however, even from formulaic language used to get launched. Fillmore (1976) has shown how a socially active child can use formulae as a basis for language elaboration.

In this study I have taken some steps towards a kind of description of language uses of children at play. Certain activities have demand characteristics with respect to language. We might, for example, find that some types of speech acts are especially common in certain kinds of play, that some kinds of syntactic elaboration are called for. I have argued here that these activities not only make possible the child's display of language knowledge, but create some conditions for the child to learn, to understand new words and new constructions, to imitate, to recall, and to try to extend what is known. Learning derives not just from speaking but from hearing language used in a context where the meaning is obvious and where the learner is interested enough in what is going on to play close attention. That is why play contexts are so much more efficient than traditional classrooms.

Notes

1. The data reported were obtained through National Science Foundation SNS-78-26 539 and National Institute of Education 6-79-9116. The analysis was supported by two periods of sabbatical leave and a workshop of the Max-Planck-Institute für Psycholinguistik in Nijmegen, Netherlands. I am indebted to the families which cooperated in the taping, to Lily Wong Fillmore and her colleagues who have provided Chinese and Spanish data, and to Amy Strage for suggestions regarding the French data.
2. I am indebted to A. J. Greimas for giving me this interpretation, and thus ultimately stimulating this project.
3. Observations of children with little communicative competence (e. g. deaf children in oralist families) suggest important limitations in types of play possible and in the ability to negotiate complex agreements in the course of play.

References

Ervin-Tripp, Susan M.
    1981   "Social Process in first and second language learning", *Native language and foreign language acquisition*, edited by H. Winitz, Annals of the New York Academy of Science.
Erwin-Tripp, Susan M. and Gordon, David
    1985   The development of requests. In Richard L. Schiefelbusch (Ed.) *Communicative competence: Assessment and intervention*. San Diego, California: College-Hill Press.
Fillmore, Lily Wong
    1976   *The second time around: cognitive and social strategies in second language acquisition*, unpublished doctoral dissertation, Stanford University, Stanford/California.

Garvey, Catherine
   1977   *Play* (Cambridge: Harvard University Press).
Labov, William
   1969   "The logic of non-standard English", *Georgetown Monographs in Language and Linguistics* 22, 1 – 22, 26 – 31.

Adult Elicited Child Behavior:
The Paradox of Measuring
Social Competence Through Interviewing

Michael T. Siegert

In recent years we have witnessed a remarkable increase of cognitive developmental research which covers a broad range of social and moral aspects of human behavior. Studies of moral judgment (Kohlberg, 1969), role-taking (Flavell, 1968; Selman and Byrne, 1974), social concepts (Turiel, 1975), and interpersonal awareness (Selman and Jaquette, 1977) are attempts to grasp central dimensions of human development through sequencing models influenced by Piaget's stage model of the development of intelligence (Inhelder and Piaget, 1958) or Kohlberg's (1969) conception of the development of moral judgment. Developmental theories of ontogenesis are, roughly, based on the assumption that overt activities (performances) of the human organism are related to "underlying" competences which themselves are not directly accessible but can only be systematically inferred. It is a well-known fact that the competence-theoretical research program faces a number of objections which on the one hand are based on the yet unclarified relationship of moral conduct and moral judgment (Blasi, 1980), and on the other hand focus on methodological problems with regard to the status of the competence paradigm as an empirically derived theory.

With this presentation I want to illustrate the argument that the competence-theoretical program is forced to deviate from its own theoretical premises once it enters the field of empirical research, data gathering, and data analysis. With respect to research practices the competence-theoretical program falls back upon models of data reduction which clearly contradict basic presuppositions of social action. I would like to argue that competence theories subscribe to an "interactive paradigm" only in the realm of theory construction but not yet in their practices of empirical research: most studies disregard the contextual determinations and the dialogical production of verbal utterances.

The data base of my paper consists of interviews conducted with 7-year old children in the course of an investigation of their socio-cognitive competences. Special emphasis was placed on the question which competences children display when they are confronted with interpersonal problems of peer-interaction (see the "friendship dilemma" in the appendix). I will use selected fragments of the interviews to illustrate the meaning and the relevance of context and of the specific interviewer-child-relationship for the shaping of children's utterances.[1]

1. The asymmetrical structure of interview communication — On the method of competence research

The principal means of competence research are open or half-standardized thematic interviews based upon Piaget's method of critical exploration (Inhelder, Sinclair and Bovet, 1975). Overall, this method aims at a production of webs of reflective reasoning (Cooney and Selman, 1978): the interviewer's task is the stimulation of subjects to give reasons and justification for preferred activities, attitudes, or evaluative judgements. Interviews involve an asymmetrical mode of communication such that adult subjects are implicitly expected to suspend their claims to an equal distribution of communicative rights. It is the interviewer himself who initiates and terminates the exchange, who is responsible for the budgeting of time, and who selects or discards topics, and in general establishes constraints on subjects' behavior. He thus holds a clearly dominant interactive position. Included in this position is the priviledged access to interview topics. With respect to their properties as socially defined areas of social interaction, interviews involve a number of contractual features which bear upon the course of the interview although they are hardly ever explicitly addressed. One of these contractual elements is the agreement on time and duration of the interview which can be only consensually exceeded. Only the interviewer can rely on the agreed-upon schedule in order to influence the course of the events. The interviewer, in contrast, is not entitled to ask his subject to speed up things because of time pressure. Also, an extension of the interview is not taken into consideration in the case of the agenda not having been fulfilled.

Time thus provides an important organizational principle for the interview, in particular when it is not up to the interviewer to reduce the agenda by himself. Another relevant contractual feature of the interview is a norm of "free will" on the part of the interviewee. The subject's decision to participate and his willingness to respond are never formally transformed into an obligation. There are no obligations for the respondent that go beyond those conversational postulates which must be fulfilled in any conversation. (Even a refusal to respond must not necessarily be justified by the interviewee.) The norm of "free will" shows clearly that the structural asymmetry of interview communication is partly compensated by contractual elements. The difference in the allocation of interactional rights is not altered by these mechanisms; however, we assume that at least in the case of adult subjects, power differences between the participants can only play a limited role.

2. Child-Interviewer-Interaction: School setting and pedagogical constellation

The interview model described above only applies to adult speakers: for various reasons, it cannot be utilized when the subjects are seven-year-old children. There are important differences with respect to the organization and arrangement of the research setting and the specific constellation between subjects and interviewers. In the case of this investigation, children could not independently decide whether or not they were going to participate. The researchers' criteria, the school's support and, finally, the parents' permission all reflect the fact that in this type of research setting children's participation is necessarily externally determined.

A very fundamental normative presupposition of the participation in research and test situations has thus been suspended: voluntary participation. There has been no explicit arrangement between researchers and children on the matter of duration which is another indication of the lack of influence on the part of the children. Nevertheless, it was clear to a number of children that a maximum time limit for the interview was implicitly given by the time schedule inherent in the school where the interview took place. If the interview is not intended to have the effect of punishment, demands placed on the children must parallel school time periods. I do not want to debate here the issue whether or not the time limit was transcended in the case at hand; rather, I want to point out the different ways in which interviewer and child make use of the objective restrictions on the course of the interview. Consider the following fragment:

(1) S: Maria, 7 years old; I: Interviewer; Sigga: main actor of the friendship dilemma; Disa: Sigga's 'old' friend
     I: Do you think Sigga will tell Disa about the trip to the movie on Sunday when she comes to her?
     S: No.
     I: Why won't she do that?
     S: I just don't know.
     I: What could you imagine?
     S: I don't know. School has been out a long time now.
     I: What kind of a girl would Disa think Sigga was if she had gone to the movie?
     S: Bad.

It may have been the case that Maria only made reference to time in order to avoid further probing for an answer she has not given; in the next instance, however, we find a reference to time in connection with an extended response.

(2) I: (confronts Maria with a schoolyard-situation planned in the manual in which the main actor of the story is being laughed at for her decision)
     S: She wouldn't care even though they were teasing her. Now school is just completely out.
     I: Let's talk a little more. What would Sigga say ...

From here on, clues become more intensive and appear during increasingly shorter time intervals:

(3) I: If you were Sigga what would you say?
     S: Just that she was unable to come.
     I: But (blank).
     S: Aren't we about finished?
     I: We're just about finished.
     S: How much is left?
     I: There is just a little. If you are quick in answering, we will be quicker with what's left. If Inga asks Sigga and says: why didn't you want to come with me ...

And during the last third of the interviews:

(4) I: Are there no exceptions?
    S: (quietly) I just can't get out if I stay any longer.
    I: Why?
    S: Hanna is gone.
    I: Is that your girlfriend?
    S: No, that's the porter, you know.
    I: I will see that you get out.
    S: The schoolbag is locked in the room.
    I: We will find it, that's alright. You remember we were talking about three girls ...

These excerpts may serve as extreme examples of the way interviewers deal with the time budget and its perception by children. The passages reveal that children rarely succeed in using objective constraints on the interaction for their own benefit. The interviewer does not recognize the contractual character of the interaction; we can assume that she would argue more to the rules when interacting with an adult. She uses two strategies: ignoring the complaint and putting the blame on the child; they both reflect the power difference between interviewer and child. The interviewer clearly demonstrates that she is capable of deciding the adequacy of the child's suggestions and complaints.

The strategy of blaming can lead the interviewed child to think that he has "done something wrong", that he has perhaps not responded quickly enough or said the wrong thing and that he himself has to deal with the consequences. We do not know what specific emotional reactions and cognitive assessments this type of constellation produces in children. We can nevertheless assume that these reactions are not amenable to the leading interest of eliciting peer-group related competences. We do not have to give any detailed interpretation of the examples above to see that we are dealing with a real conflict between interviewer and child rather than with a hypothetical conflict between fictitious characters. The way children react to the interview constellation and to the interviewer's questions is visible in the following example; here, the child imitates the style and content of the interviewer's questions.

(5) S: Maurus, 7 years; I: Interviewer; Siggi: Main actor of the friendship dilemma; Petúr: the "Newcomer"
    S: Well, I don't know.
    I: What would you say if you were Siggi?
    S: I don't know. What would you say if you were Siggi?

I: First of all I'd like to know what you would say.
S: I would just say I don't want to go to this movie. What would you say?
I: I just don't know.
S: You have to tell.
I: I'm not certain.
S: You have to.
I: It's no fun to know what I would say. Listen, you are doing very well but if Petúr started to ...

In addition to a "role reversal", we find in this instance a phenomenon that largely characterizes interview interactions: the hypothetical conflict intended by the interviewer (the friendship dilemma) is substituted by a real conflict between interviewer and child. As a result, peer group related competences are perhaps not elicited, in contrast to competences, however, which relate to the child's strategies of coping with problems between himself and an adult.

The influence of the overall present school-setting goes far beyond the mere fact that the interview takes place in a classroom; by this it is made difficult or impossible for the children to abstract from a school-like frame of interpretation. It is well known that the school-setting is defined by a number of implicit and explicit regulations; the most important of which are those which relate to the acceptability or desirability of "uncontrolled" actions. School-settings are especially characterized by their omnipresent tendency to evaluate students' behavior in terms of "right" or "wrong."

The following fragments show evaluations of children's replies as "right" or "wrong."

(6) S: Subject, 7 years; I: Interviewer; Siggi: Main actor of the friendship dilemma; Rúnar: Siggi's "old" friend; Petúr: the "Newcomer"
     I: But tell me one thing, how do you think, if you were Siggi and you had decided to go to Rúnar, how do you think Rúnar would feel if you went to a movie? If Siggi went to a movie with Petúr how do you think Rúnar would feel?
     S: Badly.
     I: Why would he feel badly?
     S: Because Petúr, Siggi didn't come.
     I: Yes, that's right. And what does Siggi think Rúnar will think about him if he had gone to a movie?

(7)   And in the case of a girl:
     I: Could it be that Siggi felt both good and bad at the movie?

S: That might be.

I: Why would she feel good and why badly.

S: Maybe because it's a good picture and badly, because she hasn't mentioned this to Disa or — I don't quite know.

I: This was an excellent answer. Has it ever happened to you that you have two types of feelings at once, perhaps both good and bad?

There are "right" or "wrong" answers even — as the interviewers' confirmations indicate — to questions regarding emotional states and consequences of action. The interviewer seems to know the solution to all these tricky problems; accordingly children feel that they must try to find out, just like in tests, what the best answer is. Furthermore: if the child wishes to please the interviewer, to receive feedback or wants to terminate the interview soon, the best strategy for him to choose is to give the "correct" answers to the interviewer's questions. A possible consequence of open or hidden evaluations of children's responses by the interviewer can be found in the following example:

(8) S: If I were him then I'd play with the new boys rather than leave him out and go to the movie.

I: Would you rather go to the movies?

S: No, I would rather go to the new boy's.

I: Petúr invited him to a movie. You just told me that Siggi would rather go to his friend Rúnar who owned the matchbox cars and the car track.

S: (Silence)

I: Are you quite certain about what Siggi would do?

S: Yes, he would ask whether he could invite him to come along to the movie also.

I: He can't do that. He has to do either one. He has to choose between whether he is going to Rúnar or to the movie with Petúr.

S: I think to a movie with Petúr.

I: Do you think he'll go to a movie with Petúr?

S: (Silence)

I: But you said differently before.

S: (Silence)

I: Why did you say that?

S: I don't know.

Instead of exploring the entire complexity of this scene we can simply point out that it centers around the child's changing of his response; this change was evidently induced by the interviewer and has an effect upon the entire ensuing dialogue and the strategy of the interviewer. The change in the child's response not only relates to a change in the course of the events in the story. Unnoticed by the interviewer, the boy gives up his attempt to find a consensual solution for all three participants in the story. There are only two "correct" solutions and the child must choose between the alternatives — so we can paraphrase the message of the interviewer's intervention. Accordingly the previous proposals and ideas must have been "false" for reasons not further explicated.

We can conclude that the children are faced with a school-like constellation: the interviewer initiates topics, discards or confirms responses, and imposes her definition of the situation, as the examples demonstrate. It is thus likely that the children define the interview according to the model of classroom interaction. They are unlikely to get beyond school as their predominant field of association; even if they do so, and do so successfully, the questioning routines of the interviewer continuously revive the school-type pattern of interactional asymmetry.

3. A Paradox of Developmental Research — The Problem of Discrepant Contexts of Interaction

The inherent difficulties of the interviewer-child constellation are supplemented by an additional problem in the logic of inquiry. Roughly, I am addressing the question if, in what way and to what extent developmental research takes into account differences in the organization of interactional contexts across different life-worlds and age-groups. Here, the general problem relates to the differences in contexts of social activity among children and adult competent speakers, respectively.

Children are hardly adequately portrayed as "little adults"; child interaction follows a logic of its own (Ausubel & Sullivan, 1970; Camaioni, 1979; Mishler, 1975; Corsaro, 1979). This insight of interactionist role-theories and pragmatics has important practical implications when research is designed to capture elements of the every-day life-world of peer-interaction by means of interviewing. Mainly, the interviews conducted on the "friendship dilemma" (which present an interpersonal conflict within a same age-group) were intended to explore children's activities outside the school and the family. The children were asked to provide information on features of their participation in an action system with an interactive organization which is fundamentally reciprocal.

Peer-interaction is to some extent withdrawn from adult influence and is, basically, interaction among equals. Here children must work out collective consensuses on joint lines of activity without relying on age differences and sex roles or rules and recipes of action which are defined by the family system. Peer-groups are without predefined warrants of certain individuals to define or decide a situation; rather, rules guiding interaction as well as material action and sanctions against violations of agreed-upon rules must be negotiated on an ad hoc basis. Even positions within a rank order must be negotiated or obtained. It is thus obvious that in the given kind of research setting, two discrepant social contexts and their related modes of interaction conflict with each other. A highly specific context of adult-child interaction, defined by a relational pattern of incomplete reciprocity, contrasts with a life-world in which there is no unquestioned dominance or submission.

The point I want to make is obviously not that adults are unable to understand the organization and meaning of children's verbal activities. The possibility of understanding the other cannot be sensibly denied (Margalit, 1976). The problem that I would like to address, rather, is the possibility that children reveal in contexts of peer-activity social competences which differ from the interviewer's "model of the competent speaker" and, therefore, remain uninterpreted or are, at worst, not even admitted as displays of social competence.

We have already seen parts of an interview where the interviewer rejected a proposed solution as not viable; in that example the child aimed at an arrangement in which none of the children in the story had to stay alone. An instance of another class of proposed solutions can be found in the following example: the child attempts to change the temporal organization of the events in the story and thus provides a possible solution which was for external reasons not provided for by the research design.

(9) I: What would you do?
  S: I would talk to this Inga and ask her whether she had bought tickets for the movie and whether we couldn't just go some other Sunday or some other day or invite Disa also.

> I: Why would you do that?
> S: I don't know.
> I: But in our story Sigga has to choose one or the other.

The girl makes an interesting suggestion for a solution of the problem. Not only does she suggest to delay the visit to the cinema to some other day, she also links this idea to the issue of "tickets" in a very realistic manner. It must be emphasized here that she proposes that the children in the story should agree on postponing the visit to the cinema. If all these proposals fail, she argues, one could always go to the movies together. This may serve as a good example for the egalitarian process of negotiation of activities that is typical of peer-group interaction. We do not have to point out that this girl exhibits remarkable social competences which are nevertheless common under conditions of equal influence.

But even this critical view of the interview is based on the assumption that child and interviewer share a common background of social experiences. We must not disregard the possibility, however, that children are reluctant to inform adults about peer-groups' social activities. This may be due to sensitivities for interactional situations that are acquired by the children primarily in teacher-child interactions.

The different organization of the respective social contexts and their definition according to opposite types of interaction point to an inherent paradox of interviewing which leads to a conflict with the overall goal of questioning, namely to elicit competences of interaction with age-mates. The children's performance — language, action, and gesture — are under contextual and interactional constraints that make it difficult to assess their underlying competences of interacting with peers. What is paradox about this constellation is the fact that the children are asked to give information about behavior in a completely egalitarian context, but to do so in a setting which is itself highly asymmetrical. Generally speaking, the possibility of a paradox in the logic of inquiry always arises when the investigation addresses competence for conduct in settings which, in terms of interactional structure, defining topics or the prevailing normative systems, contradict the structure of the research setting itself.

4. Some Aspects of the Process of Verbal Action in the Dialogue between Child and Adult Interviewer

It is the interviewer's task to induce children to reveal preferences for action that enter their day-to-day activities as well as their perception of the behavior of the characters in the story. At the same time the interviewer must probe the subjects for arguments which justify their ideas and proposals. In terms of interview technique *why-* and *what*-questions alternate, although there is a skewing towards questions asking for explications and reasons. What does the communicative order of the interviewer-child dialogue look like? How are the children's utterances generated which later form the basis of the researcher's assessments of their competences in interacting with peers?

If the children do not succeed in conforming with the preferred interpretation of the interpersonal conflict in the story upon first hearing it, they fail at the level of problem presentation. Their failure may be due to their general life circumstances, their actual frame of mind or their divergent perspective on the events.

In this case, the interviewer must in some fashion make the child familiar with the prefabricated definition of the situation as it was imposed on the story by the researcher. This task may be fulfilled by explicative specifications of the setting and the problem inherent in the story; also additional assumptions can be made and categorically fixed. The following fragment shows that a child who refuses to understand can be forced to accept a simple alternative which he himself would not subscribe to; the interviewer introduces a number of additional clauses:

(10) S: If I was this Sigga in this story, then I might go to Disa's in the morning at another time than the movie is and then maybe go to the movie. If I had time to go to her in the morning.

I: But if Disa perhaps is not home, until this particular time, she may have to go somewhere with her mother and father and then when she comes home it's precisely the same time that Sigga has to go to the movie.

S: Then I might go to her that evening, if she was at home or whenever she was at home.

I: And what would you then do?

S: I don't know whether my mother would allow me to go, whether she would let me.

I: But if your mother said, "You just have to decide for yourself"?

S: Then I would go to the movie and then perhaps the following
day, when Disa is at home, I would go to her.

I: Why do you think, would she rather go to the movies?

It is obvious that the interviewer does not fully succeed in
convincing the child that there is only one clear-cut alternative for
a solution of the interpersonal problem. Rather, she uses a "trick"
to make the girl accept the frame of the situation. In her last
question she disregards that part of the girl's answer that speaks to
the possibility of reaching an agreement and reduces it to a preference for "going to the movies".

Once a frame has been established with sufficient clarity, the
interviewer must use questioning strategies that are able to elicit
argumentations on the part of the subject. The subject's process of
"reflective reasoning" is induced by a number of elicitation practices
ranging from probing for reasons to the use of "counterevidence"
and attempts to confront the subject with inconsistencies in his
responses. The term "elicitation practices" here refers to practical
modes of generating information and data in research which em-
ploys questioning techniques. The hidden operation of these practices can be demonstrated even in those research settings in which
they are supposedly blocked out by means of standardized ways of
proceeding (Cicourel et al., 1974). The interviewer's task of eliciting
specific argumentations that are defined as relevant by a theory
presupposes she makes use of ad hoc hypotheses regarding the
supposed mental reality of the subject and his perception of social
reality. These hypotheses in turn influence the children's performance. But the children also work out hypotheses regarding the
meaning of the entire situation and the things the interviewer wants
them to do: why she keeps questioning their responses, why she
tries to criticize proposals which would be routinely accepted in
everyday settings, why she does not "listen". Especially the interviewer's insistent refusal to accept certain responses may make the
children believe that there is some yet unknown trick which they
have to find out in order to avoid the interviewer's difficult questions.

The interview may even enter into a "crisis interview" for the
child if the child is unable to share the interviewer's view of the
story or if he fails to clearly demonstrate that he accepts the given

interpretation of the conflict. No explicit acceptance is required; rather, the subject must play a language game required by the theory, be it voluntary or by induction by the interviewer. It is the language game-like character of the interview and its central problem (the friendship dilemma) that engenders additional restrictions on the interview situation. The interviewer relies on ad hoc hypotheses in order to restrict the children's options in the situation and to define for them what may count as "acceptable" or "unacceptable" argumentation.

The disturbing effect of conflicting definitions of the situation can be seen in the following fragment:

(11) I: But what would happen if Siggi did not go to Rúnar as he had promised?
      S: Then I would rather go to the movie.
      I: But if we pretend that Siggi had gone to the movie?
      S: Then I would go to a movie.
      I: But how does he then think Rúnar would feel?
      S: I don't know.
      I: Don't you think you know something about that?
      S: No.
      I: If you have a good friend and have promised to visit him but then don't come and go to a movie instead, how do you think he would feel?
      S: Badly.
      I: What?
      S: Good.
      I: Do you think so?
      S: Yes.
      I: Why?
      S: He would go to the movie himself.
      I: No, he is not going to a movie. He just waits at home with the car track and doesn't understand why you don't come.
      S: Was he fooling them?
      I: No, I was asking you: If Siggi goes to the movie with Petúr how does he then think Rúnar will feel?
      S: Badly, very badly.
      I: What does he think Rúnar will do?
      S: Go to his house and ask whether he isn't coming.

This scene may serve as an example for the conflict between discrepant assessments of possible further developments of the friendship dilemma. Differences in the perspectives of interviewer and child also have an effect on the emotional states which they respectively attribute to the characters in the story. While the interviewer stays within a limited framework as it is given by the friendship dilemma and appears to be bewildered by unforeseen alternatives, the child sees additional ways of continuing the story. The passage centers around a fallacy of the interviewer who fails to acknowledge that the interviewee identifies himself with the role of the "old friend who is left behind" (Rúnar). From this perspective the child subject develops a rather viable solution, namely "going to the movies". When the child is given a question on the emotional states of the characters, he abruptly changes his strategy of responding; apparently he noticed that the interviewer was striving for a different kind of answer. The interviewer's attempts to induce the child to give "frame-conforming" responses comes to a temporary end when the child has learned that Rúnar is only "allowed" to feel miserable and that he has to go on doing so.

The contextual restrictions imposed on subjects' responses by the language game-like character of the interview tend to produce a paradoxical situation. For example, children are instructed that there are no "right" or "wrong" solutions to the dilemma and that they ought to name only those solutions and argumentations which they themselves would opt for. This contrasts with the interviewer's task to establish the researcher's interpretive frame and to challenge subjects by questioning their assessments and judgments. The subjects' responses are far from being haphazard. Rather, subjects soon find out that, in spite of the instructions they were originally given, they are being tested for the reliability of their judgment and their willingness to play a language game that they can neither define nor influence.

5. Conclusion

In concluding, I would like to draw attention to two inferences which can be drawn from the problems outlined above; they might perhaps have some impact on a new orientation of competence research.

If we take into account that in situations of questioning all of the subjects' responses are shaped by specific features of the dialogue and its context, we must drop the assumption that properties of the competences in question surface independently of the actual dialogue. Judgments, reasoning, and justifications are always a joint production by all participants; therefore, they cannot be treated by researchers as products of a monologue or as self-contained data. Instead of locating judgments in the minds of subjects, we must account for them in terms of the interactional context in which they were originally generated. This requires a different research strategy: instead of replacing the dialogical situation of the method of critical exploration by a monologue model of the singular actor — as it is normally done in the analysis of interview data — we must take the interaction between interviewer and subject as the minimal unit of analysis.

It is especially difficult to assess children's competences by means of interview techniques if the competences we are interested in are normally displayed in peer interaction. Data from interviews which are conducted by an adult interviewer give us more insight into competences displayed by children in interactions with adults, where they must cope with the adult's definition of the situation. It is questionable, however, if these findings can be generalized to other contexts, especially to contexts of peer interaction. The childrens' verbal behavior takes place within an incompletely reciprocal action system; this system is shaped mainly by three factors: the school setting, the adult-child interactional format of the interview and, finally, by the opposed interactional logic which covers the interview constellation on the one hand and the object of investigation on the other. We are thus dealing with highly specific data whose contextual determination is impossible to disregard even if the interview arrangements are completely different. This difficulty can only be solved by investigating issues of peer relations among children within their natural contexts of occurrence. Here, a combination of data from participant observation with data from group discussions among children seem to provide a promising alternative.

Note

1. Data come from the project "Child Development and Social Structure", a longitudinal study on the relationship between socio-cultural change and child development on Iceland being conducted at the Max-Planck-

Institute for Human Development and Education, Berlin, with Dr. Wolfgang Edelstein as principle investigator (Max-Planck-Gesellschaft Jahrbuch 1980, 723—727). The interviews serve to investigate a number of aspects of subjects' social cognition with emphasis on the development of the level of moral judgement as represented in the structure of arguments employed for the justification of decisions.

Appendix

Friendship (Boys)

Siggi and Rúnar are eight years old and very good friends. They had been friends for a long time and played a lot together. Both had other friends, and did other things, but their Sundays together had become something special. Then they played together only the two of them, either at Siggi's place or Rúnar's place.

One day a new boy, Pétur, moved into the neighbourhood. Very soon he became acquainted with the two boys. Right away it seemed that Pétur and Siggi hit it off very well, but Rúnar did not like Pétur as well. Rúnar thought that Pétur was a showoff, but he also thought that Siggi and Pétur spent too much time together.

Once when Pétur left the other two alone, Rúnar told Siggi how he felt about Pétur. "What do you think of Pétur," asked Rúnar. "I thought that he was kind of pushy, butting in on us like that."

"Come on, Rúnar, he is new in town and just trying to make friends. The least we can do is to be nice to him."

"Yeah, but that does not mean we have to be friends with him, does it," replied Rúnar. "Anyway, are you coming over this Sunday? I have just got a smashing car-track and new matchbox cars, which I would like to show you. Please come, it has really been dull at home this week."

"Sure I will be over, Rúnar." With that the two boys ended the discussion.

The same evening, Pétur phoned Siggi and invited him to the cinema this coming Sunday. The picture was a good one and after the cinema Siggi was invited to Pétur's place, along with a few other boys, whom Pétur had invited as well. His mother was going to give them coca-cola and hot dogs. Now the only problem was that the cinema and the invitation happened to be at the same time Siggi had promised to go to Rúnar's. Siggi might be able to work things out with Rúnar most Sundays, but this particular Sunday, Rúnar had really wanted to have Siggi around to talk things over. Siggi did not know what to do. Go to the cinema with Pétur and leave his best friend alone when he needed him so much, or stick with his best friend and miss a good time?

Bibliography

Ausubel, David and Sullivan, Edmund
  1970   *Theory and problems of child development* (New York: Grune and Stratton).
Blasi, Augusto
  1980   "Bridging moral cognition and moral action: A critical review of the theory", *Psychological Bulletin* 88: 1—45.
Camaioni, Luisia
  1979   "Child-adult and child-child conversations: An interactional approach", *Developmental pragmatics*, edited by Elinor Ochs and Bambi Schieffelin (New York: Academic Press), 325—337.
Cicourel, Aaron, Jennings, K., Mehan, Hugh, et al.
  1974   *Language use and school performance* (New York: Academic Press).
Cooney, Ellen W. and Selman, Robert L.
  1978   "Children's use of social conceptions: Towards a dynamic model of social cognition", *New Directions for Child Development* 1: 23—44.
Corsaro, William A.
  1979   "Sociolinguistic patterns in adult-child interaction", *Developmental pragmatics*, edited by Elinor Ochs and Bambi Schieffelin (New York: Academic Press), 373—389.
Edelstein, Wolfgang, Keller, Monika and Wahlen, Karl
  1980   "Project: Child development and social structure", (Göttingen: *Max-Planck-Gesellschaft Jahrbuch*), 723—727.
Flavell, John
  1968   *The development of role-taking and communication skills in children* (New York: Wiley).
Inhelder, Baerbel and Piaget, Jean
  1950   *The growth of logical thinking* (New York: Basic Books).
Inhelder, Baerbel, Sinclair, Hermine and Bovet, Magali
  1975   *Learning and the development of cognition* (London: Routledge).
Kohlberg, Lawrence
  1969   "Stage and sequence: The cognitive-developmental approach to socialization", *Handbook of socialization theory and re-*

search, edited by David A. Goslin (Chicago: Rand McNally), 347—480.

Margalit, Avishai
  1976   "Talking with children, Piagetian style", *Language in focus: Foundations, methods, and systems*, edited by Asa Kasher (Dordrecht: Reidel Publishing Company), 457—471.

Mishler, Elliot, G.
  1975   "Studies in dialogue and discourse. II: Type of discourse initiated by and sustained through questioning", *Journal of Psycholinguistic Research* 4: 99—121.

Selman, Robert and Byrne, Diane
  1974   "A structural-developmental analysis of levels of role taking in middle childhood", *Child Development* 45: 803—806.

Selman, Robert and Jaquette, Dan
  1977   "Interpersonal awareness in children", *American Journal of Orthopsychiatry* 47 (2): 264—274.

Turiel, Elliot
  1975   "The development of social concepts: Mores, customs and conventions", *Moral development: Current theory and research*, edited by David J. DePalma and Jeanne M. Foley (Potomac, Md.: Erlbaum).

Learning How to Become an Interlocutor
The Verbal Negotiation of Common
Frames of Reference and Actions
in Dyads of 7—14 Year Old Children*

Jürgen Weissenborn

1. Introduction

One of the central functions of language is to make joint reference
and action possible in situations of social interaction where, in the
absence of a shared perceptual field, the interlocutors cannot rely
on non-verbal communicative means in order to convey information. The first utterances of the language learning child are not yet
adapted to communicative situations of this type. On the contrary,
his utterances generally can only be interpreted with reference to a
perceptual context that is common to the child and his interlocutors.
What the child has to learn then, is to successfully communicate in
the absence of a shared perceptual environment and thus to convey
by verbal means only, all the information the interlocutor needs in
order to interpret his utterances insofar as this information cannot
be presupposed to be known or at least to be perceptually available
to the listener.

I will call this information 'reference frame'. It is the set of
propositions that allows the listener to unequivocally attribute reference to the utterances of the speaker. The example in Figure 1 will
illustrate this:

If in the situation represented in Figure 1 person A asks person B
"Bring me the balloon in front of the car", the reference of "in

* I thank Regina Stralka for her help in analysing the data, Ewald Lang
  for comments on an earlier version of this paper, and Colin Brown,
  Nancy Budwig, Charlotte Koster, and especially Jane Edwards for correcting my English.

front of the car" in the presence of two balloons located as shown in the picture will stay unclear as long as the perspective underlying the use of the expression 'in front of' has not explicitly been specified. In our case there are two perspectives: the intrinsic or driver's perspective, and the deictic or speaker's perspective (Miller and Johnson-Laird, 1976). One of these perspectives constitutes the necessary minimal reference frame for the utterance "Bring me the balloon in front of the car".

Figure 1 "Bring me the balloon in front of the car"

Reference frames are, like frames (Minsky, 1975) or scripts (Schank and Abelson, 1977), knowledge structures that form the necessary background for the functioning of verbal interaction. So, in the case of a commentary on a soccer game, knowledge of the rules of the game is certainly an indispensable part of the reference frame, as is, in the case of moral argumentation, the set of moral principles that are collectively agreed upon by the participants (Miller, this volume). Thus, the ability to establish and to maintain reference frames constitutes one of the main factors for the integration of the child into the social world.

For a given communicative situation an optimal reference frame can be conceived of in terms of the goals of the interaction, independently of the interlocutors that are involved. Which elements of this reference frame have to be transmitted verbally in an actual communicative situation depends essentially on how much of it is known by the hearer.The determination of this knowledge is a task that has to be solved interactively by the interlocutors.

What has been said so far presupposes that the interlocutors are aware of the conditions that are imposed by a given communicative task on the structure of the common frame of reference. At any given point of their verbal interaction they have to monitor the establishment and the maintenance of the reference frame in accordance with the constantly changing context conditions of the ongoing communication. This monitoring constitutes a main prerequisite for sustaining coherent discourse.

Despite its central importance for goal oriented communicative activities the ontogenesis of how children establish reference frames has not yet received the systematic attention it deserves (see Nelson, 1981 on the ontogenesis of scripts for an exception). Neither work in the experimental nor in the observational approach on the development of communication has really focused on this issue. This omission may stem from the fact that the communicative situations that have been investigated so far in both paradigms were altogether too limited, so that the importance of the reference frame was not recognized.

The experimental studies were restricted in various respects: For example, they took place in the shared perceptual field of the interlocutors or the interlocutors were not really engaged in a common activity. The observational studies, on the other hand, neglected the investigation of more complex goal oriented referential situations that typically require a coherent frame of reference.

The two research paradigms led to two sets of contradictory results concerning the development of communicative competence in children: whereas studies in the observational approach showed that children as young as three to four are able to adapt in various respects to the status and the needs of their interlocutors, studies in the experimental approach showed that children of eight and older had still serious difficulties coping with the aspects of a task that asked for decentering (see Dickson, 1981; Beaudichon, 1981, 1982 for a detailed review). These diverging results allow two conclusions:

(a) they show that the acquisition of communicative competence is a process that develops far beyond the age range that has mainly been studied until now. That is, it takes a long time until the child is, in principle, able to solve the various problems he is confronted with in verbal interaction in different contexts and, related to this fact,

(b) that communicative competence is the result of a successful coordination of different abilities which themselves must be viewed as highly complex (Flavell, 1981; Shatz, 1983).

This implies firstly that one should look at a wider age range, and secondly, that one should concentrate on the development of the component abilities and their progressive coordination, whereby the latter process constitutes the main developmental task that has to be solved by the child. By studying children up to age fourteen and by concentrating on their ability to establish and maintain reference frames, which crucially relies on the coordination of sub-skills, this study tries to take these implications into account and to avoid some of the shortcomings of previous work.

The experiment carried out consisted of a direction giving task with pairs of German children of the same age, — 7, 8, 9, 10, 11, 14 years — and adults; 6 — 10 pairs of subjects were tested for each age group.

2. Organization of the Task

The participants cannot see each other. Each has an identical model of a small town in front of him and the direction giver has to specify for the other participant the route of a toy car through the town (see Figure 2).

The task material consisted of two identical 3-dimensional wooden models of towns (0,60 m × 0,70 m). The houses, with red or blue roofs and two different sizes, were organized symmetrically (mirror-image) around a central axis.

Four different paths (A, B, C and D) of equal difficulty (same number of subpaths and turning points) were defined and each was then successively described by one child to another under three different conditions:

(1) with supplementary landmarks (trees, animals, cars) destroying the symmetry of the display and with gestures (the children were allowed to use their hands freely during the description);
(2) without landmarks and with gestures;

SCREEN

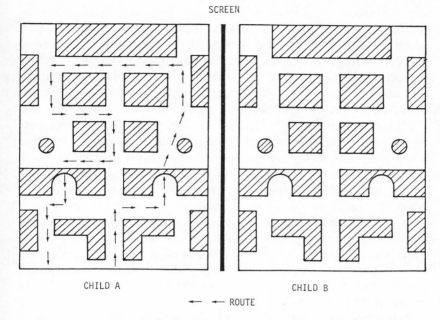

CHILD A CHILD B

◄─ ◄─ ROUTE

Figure 2 Schematic plan of the model town

(3) without landmarks and without gestures (the children were sitting on their hands).

Thus these conditions were combined with paths A to C as follows: 1 A − 2 B − 3 C; 2 B − 1 C − 3 A; etc. Path D was always described by the child to the experimenter under condition 2. The descriptions were videotaped.

The symmetrical design of the model was chosen because the referential determinacy of any path description that refers to it is only guaranteed if these descriptions are embedded in a verbal reference frame that has jointly been defined by the participants. For example a description like "You pass under the bridge" would not suffice given that there are two bridges. The same holds for every other building.

In order to resolve this indeterminacy the use of relational expressions like "left" and "right", "in front of" and "behind", etc. is required. But, as we have seen above, the reference of these terms is itself indeterminate between the deictic and the intrinsic perspective when applied to oriented objects. Thus, when applied to the toy car that the child drives along the path, "left" and "right" coincide with the describer's perspective as long as the car moves away from him; when the car moves towards him this is no longer the case so that, at least for this instance, the describer has to specify explicitly which perspective he has chosen if he wants to avoid misunderstandings.

This is only possible if these alternative perspectives are discriminated and if the ensuing necessity to coordinate the speaker's and the listener's perspective is recognized. Notice that the two perspectives or reference frames are not equivalent in terms of cognitive complexity. The deictic perspective is based on the projection of the body schema of the speaker onto the experimental display whereas in the intrinsic perspective it is first mentally transposed onto the oriented object (i. e. the toy car) and then projected onto the display thus necessitating the constant coordination between the original deictic and the transposed intrinsic use. Thus the structure of the experimental display asking for the use of these spatial terms has necessary conversational implications in that it requires the negotiation of the rules of use of these terms in order to establish a shared frame of reference and action.

What has been said so far about the consequences of the experimental design for the task solution applies in particular to condition 2.

The task requirements are obviously quite different in condition 1 where the symmetrical design is destroyed by the introduction of additional landmarks. In this condition an unambiguous description of the path could be achieved by relying mainly on the information provided by these elements without necessarily using relational terms like "left" and "right". That is, these landmarks furnish a concrete and fixed frame of reference, external to the describer.

Condition 3 was designed to study the influence of the absence of gestures on the child's descriptive abilities. This is a separate issue. I will say nothing about it here.

In order to evaluate the describer's ability to establish a coherent frame of reference a certain number of parameters have been defined that are considered to characterize each individual describer's performance, e. g. completeness of the path description defined in terms of adequate characterization of the turning points and the connections between them, prevailing perspective, perspective awareness, etc. A detailed presentation and quantitative analysis of these parameters can be found in Weissenborn and Stralka, in preparation.

3. Hypothesis

It was hypothesized that children's success in establishing common reference frames would crucially depend on the level of performance reached in development and the coordination of the particular cognitive, interactive and linguistic skills that are involved in the realization of the direction giving task. These component skills can be characterized briefly as follows.

(1) The *cognitive abilities* mainly concern the subject's analysis of the experimental display in order to devise an adequate strategy of path description under the different task conditions. The central problem that has to be solved in this respect is the choice of the properties of the display on which to base the descriptions.

It follows from the structure of the display that not all properties are equally appropriate. There is clearly a hierarchy of descriptive means. Thus the size, color, form and other properties of the buildings (number of windows, doors, floors) are the least suited to establish reference to a specific position on the path that is to be described, whereas reference to the general geometric properties of the display, i. e., its mirror-image structure (e. g. "left/right half"), and the grid of the streets (e. g. "at the intersection of the second street from above and the central street") is most efficient.

Most obviously the necessity of perspective discrimination constitutes an additional cognitive problem.

(2) As to the *interactive abilities*, they mainly concern the determination, evaluation, and taking into account of the comprehension conditions of the listener. In this study this concerns above all the fact that the interlocutors do not share a common perceptual space, and the implications this has for the speaker's descriptions.

(3) The *linguistic abilities* are concerned with the verbalisation of the object and interaction related representations under (1) and (2).

This speaker centered characterization of the different abilities has to be supplemented by the ability of the listener to construct a representation of the path on the basis of the speaker's utterances. This presupposes that the listener is able to detect speaker utterances that are inadequate with respect to the communicative aim and to improve them in cooperation with the speaker.

On the basis of findings of previous work in the development of spatial cognition and of spatial expressions (cf. Piaget and Inhelder,

1948; Liben, Patterson and Newcombe, 1981; Weissenborn, 1980, 1981, 1984) as well as of communicative competence (Dickson, 1981; Flavell, 1981), it was assumed that children's performance would go from minimal interaction and preponderance of idiosyncratic, speaker/describer-centered reference systems to increasing mutual verbal control of the common activity, including metacommunicative strategies like the coordination of lexical rules of use, e. g. deictic vs. intrinsic use of "left" and "right".

It was also assumed that the performance of the children in these particular subskills in the context of the communication game should be inferior to their performance in these subskills taken in isolation. This should then result in a later onset of adequate communicative competence than would have been predicted on the basis of the children's performance in tasks involving the subskills alone.

4. Results

The following results are based on the analysis of path $A - C$ in interactions between subjects of the same age. With respect to the strategies displayed by the children in order to establish a shared reference frame, we can roughly distinguish four types of task solutions that correspond to the successive development, integration and coordination of the different subskills involved. Each type characterizes a certain developmental level that determines the structure of interaction of a group of children. This does not mean that the individual performance of a given child coincides in every detail with a specific level. Rather than characterizing individual performances, the types are formulated in terms of the general organizing principles and representations underlying these individual performances.

In the following presentation and discussion of the results I will describe for each type, first, the structural characteristics of the reference frame employed, i. e. means used for indicating location (*landmarks*) and direction, the connection between places (*connectivity*), the extent of perspective awareness, and second, the forms of interaction.

4.1. First group: Primacy of perception-driven, indeterminate local reference frames

The first group is mainly composed of seven-, eight- and nine-year-old children.

Structure of the frame of reference

The behaviour of the children of this group shows that although they have understood the task, they are unable to satisfy the conditions that the structure of the display imposes on the verbal establishment of a shared reference frame. Consequently, in most cases the exact referent of the instructions of the describing child cannot be determined. The principal reason for this indeterminacy is that the descriptions focus on 'local' properties of the display (as opposed to 'general' ones, e. g. its geometric structure) such as the size, the color, and the number of windows of the buildings that, as we have already mentioned, do not allow the hearer to locate the referent in the absence of additional positional and directional information (see example 1).

(1) S2/7−1 A (i.e. subject: 2, age group: 7 years, treatment: 1 A, D = direction giver, R = direction receiver)
D: an einem kleineren Haus mit drei Fenstern
(at a smaller house with three windows)
R: hm
D: da fährst du dann lang darein
(there you drive along into there)
R: hm in die erste oder in die zweite?
(into the first or into the second?)
D: wie in die erste?
(what into the first?)
R: hier bei dem Haus bei dem blauen
(here at this house, at the blue one)
D: nein da in die Rille in die Rille
(no, there into the groove into the groove)
wo einmal das kleine Haus steht
(where the small house is)
mit drei schwarzen Fenstern
(with three black windows)
und das andere Haus das längliche hat
(and the other house, the longish one, has)
eins zwei drei vier fünf sechs sieben
(one two three four five six seven)

The descriptive strategies of this group are apparently based on a representation of the display that is highly perception-driven as opposed to a problem-oriented representation that rests on parameters that are functional with respect to the task.

An extreme example of this field dependency of the descriptions is the instruction "into the groove" in example 1 that indicates that the street function of the space between the buildings is not recognized.

The assumption that the verbalization strategies on this developmental level are primarily perception-driven receives additional support from the way the descriptions are influenced by the different task conditions.

Whereas under condition 1 (with supplementary landmarks) children make use in an unsystematic manner of all perceptual properties, under condition 2 and 3 (without landmarks) they develop strategies that rely only on certain context parameters. The absence of landmarks leads the child to concentrate on specific aspects of properties of the display. This yields highly schematized descriptions that are as dysfunctional as the less structured ones (see example 2 and 3).

(2)   S.3/7 − 3 C
    D: Ecke dann fährst du geradeaus
        (corner, then you go straight ahead)
    R: geradeaus
        (straight ahead)
    D: dann wieder um die Ecke
        (then again around the corner)
    R: Ecke
        (corner)
    D: geradeaus wieder um die Ecke
        (straight ahead again around the corner)
    R: geradeaus
        (straight ahead)
    D: wieder geradeaus um die Ecke ...
        (again straight ahead around the corner)

(3)   S.9/9 − 3 C
    D: an einem hm runden Turm vorbei
        (you go past a round tower)
    R: ja
        (yes)
    D: an einem langen blauen Haus
        (past a long blue house)

R: ja
   (yes)
D: an einem langen blauen Haus
   (past a long blue house)
R: ja
   (yes)
D: an einem runden Turm
   (past a round tower)
R: ja
   (yes)
etc.

The uniformity of the display constitutes a major difficulty for the establishment of a functional reference frame. One strategy chosen by the children of this group to overcome this difficulty and to impose a structure on the display can be characterized as an attempt to transform the unfamiliar space into a familiar one by relating it to their everyday environment and its prototypical elements: The children try to individualize the buildings by giving them names like "hospital", "school", "fire department", etc. As these elements can be supposed to be shared knowledge of the speaker and the hearer their use can be considered as an indication that the describer realizes the need for some path-independent common reference system (see example 4).

(4) S.12/9 – 2 C
D: da siehst du ja'n Feuerwehrhaus
   (there you see a fire department)
R: ich seh zwei Feuerwehrhäuser
   (I see two fire departments)
D: ja ich auch
   (yes, me too)
R: aber welches Feuerwehrhaus rechts oder links?
   (but which fire department, the right one or the left one?)
D: links rechts das Feuerwehrhaus
   (the left, the right one)

A further indication of the preponderance of perception-driven representations is the generally insufficient contextualization of local deictic expressions like "here" and "there", "left" and "right" that, in order to refer in the absence of a shared perceptual space, ask for the verbal introduction of reference points, e. g. *"next to the bridge* there ...", *"at the tower* you turn left" (see examples 1 and 5).

(5)   S.6/7−2 B
   D: also wir fahren jetzt bei den linken fahren wir los
       (on the left there we start)
       und da fahren wir bei der Brücke vorbei
       (and there we pass the bridge)
       da gehts ja hoch da fahren wir ein bißchen geradeaus
       (there it goes up, there we go a little bit straight)
       da haben wir wieder ne Kurve die ein bißchen nach rechts fährt
       (there is a turn that goes a little bit to the right)
       da fahren wir wieder n bißchen hoch
       (there we go up again)

"Left" and "right" are mostly employed in the deictic mode, the mode being always left implicit. The children show no awareness of the conversational implications of the use of these terms, that is, the necessity of making the chosen perspective explicit at least at that point of the path where the deictic and the intrinsic perspective are mutually exclusive.

The lack or inadequate use of positional and directional expressions results in a very low connectivity of the descriptions. The main technique is a jumping from landmark to landmark ignoring intervening crossroads and turning points. As a consequence, the symmetrical design of the experimental display dissolves into unrelated subspaces that come into focus only insofar as they are part of a particular path.

Interaction

Given the great number of inadequate descriptions of the describer one would expect frequent listener interventions requesting additional information. This is generally not the case.

The speaker's descriptions are tacitly accepted by the listener who moves his car to a certain place and then declares that he has finished. The listener is apparently ready to accept any description as long as he is able to relate it to some element of his perceptual space. That is, the listener does not distinguish between the reconstruction of a possible path and the reconstruction of the path intended by the speaker. Neither the describer nor the receiver are aware of the uncertainty of the descriptions. The children experience the identical action space as a sufficient reference frame that allows a great deal of referential indeterminacy, without loosing the illusion of mutual understanding. This only happens when the listener is unable to act out the description as in example 6:

(6)   S.5/7 – 3 C
   D: und dann fährst du ein Stück geradeaus
         (and then you go straight)
   R: ich kann nicht
         (I can't)
   D: links doch du kannst geradeaus fahren
         (to the left, you can go straight)
   R: krach ich ja fast runter
         (I will fall down [i. e. from the table])
   D: nein du krachst nicht runter
         (no, you won't)
   R: das kann nur an der rechten Brücke gewesen sein
         (this can only have been at the right hand bridge)

No joint attempt is made to recoordinate the respective positions but the receiver decides, on the basis of his own reference system, where he should be ("... at the right hand bridge").

If there are requests for additional clarification the speaker often pretends not to hear them or he simply repeats the description already given (see example 7).

(7)   S.1/8 – 3 C
   D: rechts rein bis zum kleinen roten Haus
         (you turn right, up to the small red house)
   R: welches kleine kapier ich nicht
         (which small one, I don't understand)
   D: ja das kleine hinter dem blauen
         (the small one, behind the blue one)
   R: hinter dem blauen hinter dem ... wo ist das denn?
         (behind the blue one, behind the ... but where is that then?)
   D: fährste geradeaus bis zum nächsten kleinen Haus
         (you go straight, up to the next small house)
   R: hinter dem blauen ich komm ja gar nicht mit
         (behind the blue one, I can't follow)

Thus, in the absence of perspective awareness and of mutual control of their utterances, the participants continue under an illusion of mutual understanding that is only rarely disrupted.

4.2. Second group: Primacy of perspective-driven, speaker-centered reference frames

This group consists of mainly nine-, ten- and eleven-year-old children.

Structure of the reference frame

There are two characteristics of spatial representations which distinguish this group from the preceding one. The first is the use of a hierarchical, perspective-driven representation of the task space, which can enable the establishment of a mutual reference frame by the interlocutors, in contrast to the preceding perception-driven and perspectiveless spatial representation which could not. 'Hierarchical' means that we can now observe task specific constraints on perception. This task specificity narrows the range of parameters selected by the children for indicating position. Thus, the perceptual aspects of individual landmarks become less important than relational properties such as position with respect to a fixed point or a particular path.

Consequently, and this is a second characteristic of the descriptions of this group, the children begin to focus on the connections between the turning points of the path, and make use of a new type of landmark, the 'guiding landmark', which marks intermediate positions on a particular subpath, e. g. "past the tractor", "through the tunnel".

Landmarks are still specified by enumeration of their perceptual properties (color, size, number of windows etc.) but, in addition, the landmarks take on a higher-order, relational function, serving systematically as markers of the starting or the endpoint of a subpath. This results in an increase of connectivity as compared to the first group. The change from an object-centered, local representation of the display to a representation that rests upon its general geometric properties (mirror-image design) shows up in labels like "main street" or "central street" as well as in reference to the right and left half of the play board (see example 8).

(8)   S.4/9 – 1 A
    D: du fährst nach links rein
        (you turn left into it)
    R: wo muß ich stehen?
        (where should I be?)
    D: an dem Mittelgang
        (at the path in the middle)
    R: da
        (there)
    D: und dann fährste links rein rechts dann fährst du weiter
        (and then you go left into it-right, then you go on)

da kommst du an einem Traktor vorbei fährst wieder an dem
(there you go past a tractor, you pass the)
runde Ding vorbei
(round thing again)

But the decisive change as compared to the first group consists in the appearance of perspective awareness that allows for the controlled coordination of different positions by relating them to a (verbally introduced) vantage point, e. g. "seen from above", "seen from my point of view", "there, where you are sitting".

With the introduction of perspective new descriptive devices become available to the child. The most important one for this group is the recourse to enumerations made with reference to a starting point (see example 9).

(9)   S.7/11−2 B
      [the children are trying to overcome a misunderstanding]
  R: die langen der langen Häuser
      (the long the long houses)
  D: da sind ja vier hintereinander
      (but there are four of them in a row)
  R: ja und meinst du jetzt der dritte am dritten
      (yes, and do you mean the third, at the third)
  D: was tut er am dritten? Nein ist falsch
      (what is he doing at the third? No, that's wrong,)
      das zweite von oben das zweite
      (the second from above, the second)
      blaue Haus da mußt du sein
      (blue house there you should be)
  R: wieso von oben?
      (why from above?)
  D: von oben gesehen da ist zuerst ein Hochhaus
      (seen from above there is first a tall building)
      siehst du das?
      (do you see it?)

Thus, the descriptions of this group do no longer show the referential indeterminacy due to incomplete contextualization that was characteristic of the first group.

Although it is true that in principle the interlocutors of this group have at their disposal all the prerequisites for the establishment and maintenance of a shared reference frame, the actual behaviour of the children shows that their performance is still constrained by a

number of factors. That is, children have not yet developed generalized and homogeneous strategies which they can use over the entire
path description. They use *partial* strategies, including the object
oriented strategy of the first group.

This can best be illustrated with reference to the use of orienta-
tional expressions. The choice of deictic rather than intrinsic use of
"left" and "right" and the choice of a vertical projection plane ("up"/
"down") rather than a horizontal one ("front"/"back") apparently
depend on certain contextual factors.

Thus, three contexts of use can be distinguished, based on how
the describer enters a turning point on the path.

(1) The car moves away from the describer (a) and then left or
right (b)

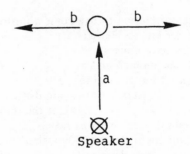

(2) The car moves sideways (a) and then left or right (b)

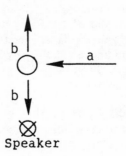

(3) The car moves towards the describer (a) and then left or right
(b)

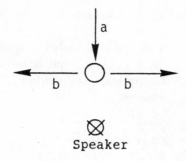

Speaker

In case (1) "left" and "right" are nearly exclusively used. In (2) three strategies can be observed:

(i) implicitly intrinsic use of "left" and "right", and equally frequently,
(ii) implicitly deictic use of "up" and "down" (vertical projection plane),
and rarely
(iii) implicitly deictic use of "front" and "back" (horizontal projection plane).

In order to appreciate correctly strategy (i) it should be mentioned that the describer makes his body axis coincide with the axis of the car before uttering those terms. That is, he is not yet in command of a mental rotation operation so that (i), strictly speaking, should be considered a deictic perspective.

In case (3) the use of "left" and "right" is unsystematic and always implicitly deictic. The absence of the intrinsic perspective may be attributed to the difficulty for the describer in making a 180° turn on his chair. This seems to indicate that the deictic perspective is still primarily represented in a proprioceptive motor format and is not yet available as an independent operational concept.

Interaction

In contrast to the first group, in this case interaction begins to play an increasing role in task solution. Especially in the case of coordination failure, a recoordination is actively searched for by the interlocutors. But the already mentioned instability of the available reference frames, which originates from constantly changing context conditions over the path, has important interactive consequences insofar as it causes misunderstandings and also difficulties in solving them.

Thus, given the fact that the describer is primarily attentive to local path properties, he is often not aware of possible alternative interpretations of his descriptions, and neither is the listener. Example 9 illustrates these problems.

(9)   S.3/11 — 3 B
D: also bin ich jetzt an dem Tor an meiner Seite
      (I am now at the gate on my side)
R: ja [*both children occupy the same position*]
      (yes)
D: und dann fährst du um das Tor herum bis zur anderen Seite
      (and then you go around the gate to the other side)
R: ja
      (yes)
D: und dann siehste doch so'n blaues Haus mit großem Dach
      (and then you see a blue house with a big roof)
      also großem blauen Dach
      (a big blue roof)
R: ja da sind viele Häuser mit'n blauen Dach draußen
      (there are many houses with blue roofs)
D: ja dat is eh direkt das dritte das dritte von dir aus gesehen
      (that is — immediately the third one, the third one seen from
      your perspective)
R: eins zwei drei von mir aus gesehen?
      (one two three, seen from my perspective?)
D: so'n großes Haus neben dem Rundbolzen
      (such a big house next to the round block)
R: ja
      (yes)
D: und da fährste zwischen dem Rundbolzen und den blauen
      (and there you pass between the round block and the blue)
      Haus fährste
      (house)
R: ja bin ich jetzt [*R occupies the mirror-image position of D*]
      (ok, here I am)

In this case a first misunderstanding results from the fact that the phrase "to the other side" is misinterpreted as having the play board, rather than the gate, as its point of reference. A second misunderstanding arises from the listener's taking into account only the blue houses instead of all of them.

This example shows that unequivocal descriptions are generally not available to this group from the outset, but rather develop gradually over the course of the task.

In contrast to the preceding group, misunderstandings are not simply ignored or passed over in favor of ongoing action. Some attempt is made to resolve them, but, since the only strategies available are local strategies, recoordination often fails and misunderstandings persist.

This seems to stem primarily from the fact that the strategy of coordinating reference frames by explicit exclusion of alternative perspectives can, at this stage, be used interactively only in certain contexts, rather than being available as a general procedure. That is, perspective awareness is mainly to be considered as a principle of implicit control for the speaker's own descriptions.

4.3. Third group: Stabilization and interactive availability of reference frames

This group includes mainly eleven- and fourteen-year-old children.

Structure of the reference frame

This group is characterized by the generalization of perspective-driven strategies for the establishment of shared reference frames. This means that perspective choice no longer shows the strong context sensitivity and the instability found in group 2.

Another consequence of greater context independence is that the child can use perspective consciously for the determination of spatial reference. The existence of diverse but functionally equivalent reference frames is no longer a source of misunderstandings but rather can now be productively exploited for alternative descriptions of the same spatial configuration in cases where this becomes necessary for the resolution of conflict situations. Context independence is also reflected in the fact that the abstract structure of the display now becomes available as a reference frame. Landmarks at turning points are conceived of as nodes in a network and it becomes clear that their disambiguation and the disambiguation of the paths entering and leaving these nodes are the central part of the reference frame construction. That is, locations (starting and end points, intermediate places) are mainly determined by relational means,

e. g. "the first street from the left", "between the second and the third from the last house to the left from my point of view".

Another important change concerns the more and more systematized and detailed descriptions of the connections between landmarks that are now frequently characterized by the combination of measure phrases and relational expressions as in "a little bit below", "more towards the center", "much more to the left", "immediately down", etc. If not otherwise specified, the deictic reference frame is now tacitly and primarily used.

Interaction

The most noticeable change in interaction concerns its recognition as a constitutive component to task solution, that is, its integration into a general problem solving strategy. The describer apparently relies on the receiver's control of his descriptions, and the possibility the latter has to react if necessary.

That is, he starts with a rather general first formulation which he is ready to change and to specify depending on the subsequent interventions of the listener. This points to the interlocutors' awareness of the importance of mutual monitoring of their utterances.

As a consequence, this leads to a quick recognition of coordination failures and, in general, to their resolution. There is a clear improvement of the description in the course of verbal exchanges between the children. Normally it is the listener who plays the most active role in this process of continuous specification (Deutsch and Pechmann, 1982).

Examples 11 and 12 show how descriptive and interactive strategies combine in the recoordination of reference frames.

(10)   S1/11 − 2 B
    D: jetzt stehe ich mit dem Kopf zu dir hin
        (now I have my head in your direction)
    R: ja
        (yes)
    D: und dann fährste vom Fahrer aus gesehen wieder links durch
        (and then you turn left again, from the driver's perspective,)
        die beiden letzten kleinen blauen Häuser dann immer
        (between the last two small blue houses, then always)
        geradeaus bis du an dieses kleine rote Haus kommst und dann
        (straight ahead until you come to this small red house and then)

R: ja
    (yes)
D: vom Fahrer aus gesehen wieder rechts
    (from the driver's perspective, right again)
R: rechts also wieder zu den Hochhäusern also eh so hoch?
    (again right towards the towers that are up there?)
D: nee da kommste runter
    (no, you come down)
R: runter muß ich?
    (I have to go down?)
D: ja guck mal da jetzt stehste
    (yes, look, now you are)
R: zwischen dem ganz großen roten und dem kleinen
    (between the very big red one and the small one)
D: nee auf der rechten Seite?
    (no, on the right?)
R: von mir aus gesehen jetzt?
    (from my position of view, now?)
D: ja
    (yes)

(11) S2/14–3 A
D: ja und dann bis zum nächsten kleinen Haus,
    (yes and then you go up to the next small house,)
    dem mit dem blauen Dach ganz rechts
    (the one with the blue roof, completely to the right,)
    hin eh nach links hin ganz
    (to the left, completely)
R: ganz
    (completely)
D: ganz nach links hin
    (completely to the left)
R: rechts meinst du wohl?
    (you mean to the right?)
D: du bist doch jetzt links eh rechts angefangen ...
    (you started on the left, the right side ...)
R: nee (...) du hast gesagt ich sollte links anfangen
    (no you told me to start on the left side)
D: oh nein du solltest aber rechts anfangen
    (no, you should have started on the right side)
R: das hab ich mir doch gleich gedacht (...)
    (that's what I imagined,)

Although perspective specification usually occurs when it is needed, it always occurs in a *post hoc* rather than in an anticipatory manner.

The basic strategy of the speaker is to assume tacitly that a consensus exists between the listener and himself with regard to the actually valid perspective that normally holds over all contexts. This finding is contrary to what we have observed for the preceding groups. And indeed the deictic perspective constitutes the default value for the listener in the absence of perspective specification.

Thus, on the whole, mutual understanding is less problematic than in the preceding group but misunderstandings still cannot be avoided as long as there is no *anticipatory* perspective or reference frame agreement.

4.4. Fourth group: Metacommunicative, anticipatory mutual control of reference frames

This group contains only adults. In contrast to the organization of the previous sections, reference frame establishment and interaction are discussed jointly here.

The main difference, compared to the problem solving strategies of the oldest children, is that the different possible reference frames have now become the object of explicit negotiation between the interlocutors, thus eliminating from the outset the most important source of misunderstandings (see example 12).

(12)　S.1/adults — 1 A
　　　R:　auf den grünen Baum zu
　　　　　(towards the green tree)
　　　D:　ja auf den grünen Baum zu
　　　　　(yes, towards the green tree)
　　　　　und dann von uns aus gesehen dann wieder soll'n wir von
　　　　　(and then seen from our perspective, you have to — shall we)
　　　　　uns aus gesehen machen oder von dem Autofahrer?
　　　　　(describe it from our perspective or from the dirver's perspective?)
　　　　　von dem Autofahrer ne ist besser
　　　　　(from the driver's perspective, that's better)
　　　R:　ja
　　　　　(yes)
　　　D:　also der Autofahrer muß jetzt rechts fahren
　　　　　(so the driver has to take a right turn)

In every situation the full range of alternative reference frames is available to the describer and can be simultaneously drawn upon

as in expressions of the type "you go up; *that is*, to the right". The
following text shows two examples of this type:

(13)   S.5/adults − 3 C
   R: jetzt fahr ich wieder auf mich zu
        (now I go towards me again)
   D: ja von dir aus gesehen nach links vom
        (yes, from your perspective to the left, from the)
        Auto aus gesehen nach rechts ...
        (perspective of the car to the right)
        ...
   D: fährst dann vom Auto aus nach links also
        (then you go left from the perspective of the car that is)
        von dir aus gesehen nach unten zu dir hin
        (from your perspective, downwards towards you)

Thus, the describer indicates that the different reference frames
are equivalent. These 'multiframe' descriptions may be distributed
over utterances by both interlocutors as shown in the next example:

(14)   S5/adults − 3 C
   D: an der Hauptstraße biegst du wieder rechts ab
        (on the mainstreet you turn right again)
   R: also Richtung zu mir hin
        (that is, towards me)

The mutual control of understanding through explicit variation
of possible reference frames constitutes the main strategy to avoid
misunderstandings. Further negotiations of descriptive strategies
like the following show that these strategies are the result of a
general interactive problem solving process that takes into account
the task configuration in its totality (see example 15).

(15)   S.3/adults − 3 C
   R: ja mach doch mal einfach mal immer mit der erste links
        (simply say 'the first to the left')
        erste rechts, das ist doch vielleicht
        (the first to the right', that is perhaps)
        einfacher für dich, verstehste
        (easier for you, you understand)
   D: ja denn fährste links
        (ok, then you go left)
   R: erste links ne?
        (the first to the left, isn't it?)
   D: erste links
        (the first to the left)

The availability of reference frames that have been established on the basis of explicit negotiation allows the interlocutors of this group to proceed in a coordinated manner so that mutual understanding can be maintained or reestablished at any moment.

5. Conclusion

The aim of this study was to investigate the development of the establishment of verbal reference frames in an interactive, goal-oriented situation and in the absence of a common perceptual field.

Adequate reference frames are considered to be a central component of successful communication, and as such serve an important function in the process of the integration of a child into the social world. In this process the differentiation and control of perspective play a crucial role.

Four levels in the development of reference frames were distinguished:

(1) Primacy of perception-driven, indeterminate local reference frames.
(2) Primacy of perspective-driven, speaker-centered reference frames.
(3) Stabilization and interactive availability of reference frames.
(4) Metacommunicative, anticipatory mutual control of reference frames.

That is, on the cognitive level we can observe a development from indeterminate, implicit, context-dependent local reference frames to systematic integration of different context-independent reference frames that are monitored by perspective awareness. On the level of spatial representation of the experimental display that underlies the reference frame, this development can be characterized as a change, in terms of Gestalt psychology, of 'figure' and 'ground'. Whereas the youngest children focus on the concrete elements and their perceptual properties ('figure'), while the abstract pattern delimited by these elements, i.e. the grid of the streets ('ground'), is largely ignored, later on the importance of the concrete elements decreases ('ground'), and the children refer more and more to the abstract pattern of paths ('figure').

On the interactive level we notice a development from uncontrolled parallel actions to metacommunicative coordination of descriptive strategies.

With regard to the linguistic aspects of the descriptions, this development can be characterized as a stepwise decrease of the influence of non-linguistic context factors (*pragmatic decontextualization*) accompanied by progressive embedding of the descriptions in a verbal context (*linguistic re-contextualization*).

These findings are in accordance with our initial hypotheses. It is remarkable that even 14 year olds have not yet reached adult performance level. This result may be explained by the constraints that the combination of various context factors (e. g. the lack of a common perceptual field, the absence of salient features in the experimental display, the need for subjects to constantly reorient themselves as their position changes) places on the child's performance.

The influence of dynamic context on spatial cognition and reference in the child would thus appear to require further investigation.

More generally, the study of dynamic contexts should help us to better understand the relationship between component abilities within complex verbal tasks.

On the whole, the development shows an increasing availability of control processes that allow the child to apply his cognitive, interactive and linguistic abilities to a specific aim under varying contextual conditions. This confirms the importance of metacognitive processes for development in late childhood that has recently been stressed by various authors (Flavell, 1981; Hickmann, 1985; Karmiloff-Smith, 1986; Tunmer and Herriman, 1984).

Throughout the study, the role of reference frame establishment that is, particularly of perspective discrimination and coordination as aspects of successful decentering, has become evident. Decentering has mainly been treated as a result of self-reflexive efforts of the child (see Youniss, 1984). But this approach leaves open how perspective awareness, awareness of its relativity, enters the child's mind (Rotman, 1977).

Thus the question of the relationship between cognitive, social and language development constitutes a central issue for developmental theory. The positive role of social interaction in the development of non-social and social cognition has been stressed by several authors (Damon, 1984; Doise and Mugny, 1979; Miller, this volume). The present study suggests that interaction is a positive factor in the development of control processes, e. g. perspective awareness. Especially the older children (age 11 and 14) improved their performance in the course of the task. This observation is compatible with an approach that explains the acquisition of control through collective (group) practice of control procedures in verbal interaction.

References

Beaudichon, Janine
  1964   "Problem-solving communication and complex information transmission in groups", *Children's oral communication skills*, edited by W. Patrick Dickson (New York: Academic Press), 357 – 374.
  1982   *La communication sociale chez l'enfant*. (Paris: Presses Universitaires de France).
Damon, William
  1984   "Struktur, Veränderlichkeit und Prozeß in der sozialkognitiven Entwicklung des Kindes", *Soziale Interaktion und soziales Verstehen*, edited by Wolfgang Edelstein & Jürgen Habermas (Frankfurt: Suhrkamp), 63 – 112.
Deutsch, Werner & Pechmann, Thomas
  1982   "Social interaction and the development of definite descriptions", *Cognition* 11: 159 – 184.
Dickson, W. Patrick
  1981   "Referential communication activities in research and in the curriculum: A metaanalysis", *Children's oral communication skills*, edited by W. Patrick Dickson (New York: Academic Press), 189 – 204.
Doise, Willem, Mugny, Gabriel & Perret-Clermont, Anne-Nelly
  1976   "Social interaction and cognitive development: Further evidence", *European Journal of Social Psychology* 6: 245 – 247.
Flavell, John H.
  1981   "Cognitive monitoring", *Children's oral communication skills*, edited by W. Patrick Dickson (New York: Academic Press), 35 – 60.
Hickmann, Maya
  1985   "Metapragmatics in child language", *Semiotic mediation. Socio-cultural and psychological perspectives*, edited by Elizabeth

Mertz & Richard J. Parmentier (New York: Academic Press), 177—201.

Karmiloff-Smith, Annette
1986   "Stage/structures vs. phase/processes in modelling linguistic and cognitive development", *Stage and structure: reopening the debate*, edited by I. Levin (Norwood, N. J.: Ablex Publishing Company), 164—219.

Liben, Lynn, Patterson, Arthur & Newcombe, Nora (eds.)
1981   *Spatial representation and behavior across the life span* (New York: Academic Press).

Miller, George & Johnson-Laird, Philip
1976   *Language and perception* (Cambridge: Cambridge U. P.).

Miller, Max
1986   "Learning how to contradict and still pursue a common end: The ontogenesis of moral argumentation", (This volume).

Minsky, Marvin
1975   "A framework for representing knowledge", *The psychology of computer vision*, edited by Patrick H. Winston (New York: McGraw-Hill), 211—277.

Nelson, Katherine
1981   "Social cognition in a script framework", *Social cognitive development*, edited by John Flavell & Lee Ross (Cambridge: Cambridge U. P.), 97—118.

Piaget, Jean & Inhelder, Bärbel
1948   *La représentation de l'espace chez l'enfant* (Paris: Presses Universitaires de France).

Rotman, Brian
1977   *Jean Piaget. Psychologist of the real* (Hassocks: The Harvester Press).

Schank, Roger & Abelson, Robert
1977   *Scripts, plans, goals and understanding* (Hillsdale, N. J.: Lawrence Erlbaum Associates).

Shatz, Marilyn
1983   "Communication", *Cognitive Development*, edited by John Flavell & Ellen Markman, *Handbook of child psychology*, 4th ed., Vol. 3, edited by Peter Mussen (New York: Wiley), 841—889.

Tunmer, William & Herriman, Michael
1984   "The development of metalinguistic awareness: A conceptual overview", *Metalinguistic awareness in children*, edited by William Tunmer, Chris Pratt & Michael Herriman (Berlin, Heidelberg, New York, Tokio: Springer Verlag), 12—35.

Weissenborn, Jürgen
1980   *Children's route directions*. Paper presented at the LSA Sum-

mer Meeting, August 1980, University of New Mexico, Albuquerque, New Mexico. MPI für Psycholinguistik, Nijmegen.

Weissenborn, Jürgen
1981   "L'acquisition des prépositions spatiales: Problèmes cognitifs et linguistiques", *Analyse des prépositions. IIIme colloque franco-allemand de linguistique théorique du 2 au 4 février 1981 à Constance.* edited by Christoph Schwarze (Tübingen: Max Niemeyer Verlag), 251–285.

Weissenborn, Jürgen
1984   "Ich weiss ja nicht von hier aus, wie weit es von dahinten aus ist." "Makroräume in der kognitiven und sprachlichen Entwicklung des Kindes", *Sprache und Raum*, edited by Harro Schweizer (Stuttgart: Metzeler), 209–244.

Weissenborn, Jürgen & Stralka, Regina
"The role of context in children's spatial descriptions", In preparation.

Youniss, James
1984   "Moral, kommunikative Beziehungen und die Entwicklung der Reziprozität", *Soziale Interaktion und soziales Verstehen*, edited by Wolfgang Edelstein & Jürgen Habermas (Frankfurt: Suhrkamp), 34–60.

The Social Organization of Adolescent Gossip:
The Rhetoric of Moral Evaluation

Gary Alan Fine

All talk is evaluative. People communicating with each other attempt to build lines of meaning that orient themselves in desirable and appropriate ways to other conversants and that shape the others' attitudes and beliefs in ways which promote identification with oneself (see Morris and Hopper, 1980; Jackson and Jacobs, 1980). This is the core of rhetorical analysis — under what circumstances and through what techniques does persuasion and identification come about. Most rhetoricians (following Aristotle) have attended to formal or carefully constructed speech — speech that is deliberately crafted for some persuasive end. However, rhetorical analysis applies not only to carefully constructed speech, but to everyday interaction as well. The world is, in all its particulars, a moral drama (Guṣfield, 1981; Lyman and Scott, 1970).

Talk, of course, is one of the most pervasive aspects of human interaction, and distinguishes humans from their colleagues in the animal kingdom. Humans are constantly talking at and with each other about matters both consequential and mundane — a great wave of babble. And, as in all things, the mundane outweighs the monumental. However, this mundane talk is not without social significance (Haviland, 1977). When people are "just talking" they are not saying nothing; rather, they are conversing about things of immediate, though evanescent, interest. Talk has as its primary goal *involvement* — to maintain the interest of those who are participating — and, as a consequence, speakers use a variety of techniques to pique and maintain their listeners' attention.

Talk, unlike speech(es), carries with it an additional implication — that it is talk among individuals. Talk is embedded in an interaction of at least two persons. This means that talk is more reactive to the situation than are monologues in which the mere presence (and attention) of an audience is the necessary requirement for speech. Lectures are but poor reflectors of conversational requirements (Goffman, 1981).

People do not just talk; rather, they manage topics — topics which have meaning to them. Yet, there have been comparatively few studies of the *content* of talk, most of which concentrate on the management of topic (e.g., Button and Casey, 1984; Covelli and Murray, 1980; Maynard, 1980). It is obvious that speakers talk about topics they know something about (at least in a surface way), and typically such topics are also known about in a general way by the audience. Thus, the objects of talk are part of a universe of discourse. The limits of talk tend to be the limitations of knowledge (actual or assumed). Further, interactants develop in their lines of talk attitudes to that which they discuss — with nouns come verbs, adverbs, and adjectives. The topicality of talk cannot avoid evaluation. Even if explicit good/bad statements are not expressed, the speaker communicates through tone. So, talk consists of content and evaluation. In interpersonal talk the speaker expects the audience to take a sympathetic perspective toward what s/he is expressing (Morris and Hopper, 1980). To this end speakers employ a set of rhetorical strategies which, when successful, leads the audience to adopt an alignment sympathetic to their own, or at least one which is not publicly critical.

This process is complicated by the fact that in conversations several individuals are involved — each proposing topics and evaluations. Each conversant must adjust the talk to each of his/her partners to make the conversation possible. The participants fit together lines of talk to structure that which we call conversations. This approach draws on Blumer's (1969) analysis of collective behavior as the fitting together of lines of action; a conversation is a quintessential example of collective behavior. Since people frequently enter conversations without planning what topics they will address and what they expect of others, a lengthy conversation is a considerable feat. How is it that several people, each with their own view of the world that may come into serious conflict, can so often carry off a conversation which appears to be filled with harmony, rather than disagreement? In other words, how do several lines of content-evaluation-persuasion mesh into a "friendly" conversation?

1. The Conversation

In order to explore the emergence of conversational consensus I will examine a conversation. I believe the examination of a single, extended conversation is fruitful for this purpose — allowing for a depth of understanding of the speakers' circumstances.

The conversation is situated in a ninety minute automobile ride taken by three teenage girls in and around a small town in southeastern Minnesota. During this time the girls were "cruising" and were "shooting the breeze." The ostensible purpose of the tape was to complete an assignment for a class which I taught on "The Sociology of Youth." One of the three girls (Laura)[1] was a student in the class; her course assignment was to talk with a high-school or elementary school student, and then write a paper based on the conversation. Although students were not required to record their conversations, Laura did. Laura did not structure the conversation, and few references are made to the tape recorder or to the use of the conversation as a college project.

The other two conversants were sixteen-year-old friends. One of them (Toni) was the sister of Laura's boyfriend and the other (Bev) was the sister of Laura's best friend. Bev and Toni consider themselves to be best friends. Laura had just graduated from the same small town high school at which Bev and Toni were then juniors.

The conversation is "typical," and yet none the less remarkable for the wide range of topics that are covered within the same interactional skein: concert-going, vandalism, death from cancer, partying, petty theft, drug use, television watching, sexual activity, and waitressing. These topics "naturally" flow into each other, as the conversation was a single extended period of talk among friends, and represent an impressive display of topic management.

2. The Value of Gossip

The examination of gossip has traditionally been part of the domain of anthropology. Gossip has proven to be a very fortunate topic in that it provides for a quick entrée into the structure and social relations of a community; a lot of evaluative information is communicated rapidly in gossip — even though the accuracy and provenance of these "facts" are open to question. Gossip provides a "map" of a social scene.

Anthropologists traditionally have taken one of two orientations toward gossip. Either they see gossip as promoting consensus (the functional perspective) or achieving an individual's strategic ends (the information management perspective). The functionalists (e. g., Gluckman, 1963) see gossip as increasing group cohesion and enforcing the community's moral evaluations by establishing normative boundaries. This social control is evidenced in Colson's study of the Makah Indians of the Northwest United States, a group under pressure to become acculturated into American society. Colson (1963: 228) maintained that only through the social control implicit in gossip could these natives maintain their cultural values. This argument, like much functional theory, ignores the individual in examining the group as a collective entity and deemphasizes the existence of intra-group conflict.

Reacting against the functionalist perspective, Paine (1967; see also Szwed, 1966) posed an alternate theory that focused on the position of gossip in "information management." Gossip is seen as purposive behavior, serving social or political ends for the tellers by managing the impressions others have of them and altercasting others. Cox (1970) proposed such a view of gossip in describing how traditionalists and progressives used gossip in a conflict on a Hopi Indian reservation to discredit the opposing group.

A third, more recent, approach examines gossip as a technical achievement. Gossip is a rule-governed linguistic phenomenon and may, in certain instances, reflect an intricate sense of linguistic understanding (Goodwin, 1980). Talk from this perspective is a cultural achievement (Haviland, 1977) and represents a profound display of linguistic competency. This approach, like the others, is not much concerned with what is being said where, but on how it is being said.

This lack of emphasis on the construction of gossip meaning is, I believe, limiting. Gossip is embedded in a conversation, and so constitutes a performance with an audience; the audience's presence and reactions shape and direct the gossip. Although I rely on dramatistic theory, as do those who conceive of gossip as information management, I do so for different ends — to see how meaning and consensus are constructed and to see how blame is parcelled out.

3. Teenage Talk

Although I could have chosen any set of interactants in order to
analyze their gossip, I selected the gossip of female adolescents. As
has been noted (e. g., Kohlberg and Gilligan, 1972; Ransohoff,
1975), the adolescent years are a period of developing moral standards, and often these standards are embraced with fervor. Teenagers frequently express hostility towards those who step outside
their moral boundaries. However, these moral boundaries are still
being constructed, defined, and changed (Fine, 1977, 1981). Unfortunately, there is not always agreement on what constitutes proper
moral behavior, and on how behaviors are to be interpreted. As a
result, two forces work at cross-purposes in teenage gossip. First,
a strong drive pushes adolescents toward consensus. This need for
social comparison seems more potent than for adult gossip — a
reaction against the fact that comparative standards have not been
fully internalized. Second, because moral standards are still being
developed these teenagers reveal a somewhat greater variability in
evaluation. The "correct" evaluation of action is not always self-
evident, and the proposed evaluation may depend more upon the
evaluation of the target of talk than on the act described. Some
teens can "do no wrong," while others can "do no right." Teenagers
must present actions which are susceptible to several possible interpretations in ways which are likely to be supported by other speakers, either through ratification utterances or by story-chaining
(Ryave, 1978; Jefferson, 1978; Kalčik, 1975). The audience members
actively or tacitly ratify the speaker's remarks, even if they disagree
with the talk in principle. Interactants have techniques by which they
can express their disagreement — through later contrary examples
(which, too, are usually not disagreed with) or by audience role
distance through joking interjections.

The argument of this paper is grounded in several approaches
to talk. First, I employ the dramatistic approach to rhetoric
pioneered by Kenneth Burke (1969 a, b), which examines how rhe-
tors promote identification between themselves and their audiences.
Persuasion for Burke is grounded in identification with the speaker.
Second, I employ performance theory from folkloristics, particularly
as related to the personal experience story or memorate (e. g.,
Kirshenblatt-Gimblett, 1975). This perspective emphasizes that performers construct their stories as a result of what has preceeded

and how the audience is reacting to the story during the telling. From this perspective talk is an emergent aesthetic property of conversationalists. Finally, I draw on the symbolic interactionist perspective on negotiated order. Participants develop a consensus based on negotiated meaning, involving accounts, alignments to action, and blame. This process is essential when one is dealing with ambiguous moral issues, as in adolescent gossip. These three approaches supplement each other in this analysis of gossip.

4. Consensual Talk

In order to examine the process by which consensus gets constructed, let us consider the following snippet of dialogue among these three women, here discussing their male peers:

Toni: [to Tom, who she sees from the car window, but who is so far away that he can't hear what is being said. Toni speaks in a sing-song voice] Tom, Tom, I love you. I love you.

Laura: Tom who?

Toni: Tom Kinney. He was going to break up with Bonny 'cause he thinks that I want to go out with him. He told Bruce that. And I said//I don't want to go out with Tom Kinney.

Laura: °Tom Kinney?

Bev: Him and Brucie got a real uh//hot thing for//me and her. Yuch.

Toni: °big deal   °us two

Bev: [to Toni] Brucie's the, wait, how did it go? Oh yeah, Tom's the summer puke and Brucie's the fall puke [Bev and Toni laugh] and they//'re so ishy.

Toni: °sooooo ishy.

Toni: Tom went around try to//

Laura: I thought he's real nice

Toni: He's ohhkh. [all three laugh] He's goin' steady with Bonny. Out to the ... oh oh [Toni and Laura laugh about something relating to the driving] out to the golf course. He um start ... um trying to kiss everybody, *all the girls.*

Bev: Really ... Made passes at Lorna, Toni, and 'bout ready to make one at me, and, and that dumb cop came up there on the golf course. We were all out there//having a party.

Toni: °Left a bag [of marijuana] out there.

Laura: Oh, was that when you threw it//in the bushes that time?

Toni: °Yeah.

For this stretch of talk to be effective as gossip all parties must accept the proposed evaluation of the targets. The two younger women, Bev and Toni, had talked about their two male *friends* previously, and in the process developed a characterization of them (as *pukes*), a symbolic evaluation which remained latent in their idioculture (Fine, 1979). The consensual validation of their opinion is seen by the unison with which these girls claim that Tom and Brucie are *so ishy*. This phrase has apparently become traditional. At first, Laura doesn't share the characterization of Tom, and comments *I thought he's real nice.* However, Laura introduces her defense of Tom with *I thought* — implying that her opinion is subject to change and that the views of her friends are more important than her previous knowledge. She does not say "I think he's really nice" or even "He's really nice." Laura does not challenge the characterization of Tom, and in effect, ratifies the attack when she laughs when Toni says of Tom: *He's ohhkh,* a guttural exclamation which refers to something distasteful or disgusting. The report of Tom's behavior at the party is a reflection of the view of Tom as *ishy.* In other parts of the transcript similarly flirtatious boys are not subject to caustic comment. The actions condemned in a stigmatized person may be acceptable in others without such stigma.

In the second selection of dialogue the girls discuss Laura's younger brother Lonny, and some of the problems he is having with girls. Lonny is the same age as Bev and Toni:

Toni: ... Homecoming at the dance and LeeAnn and Lon left together, you know.

Laura: Oh, I didn't know that.

Toni: Yeah, and then I talked to LeeAnn ... the next night ... she was gonna go with him to Belkirk [a local dance hall] ... and ... see, she's supposed to be going with Steve Carlson.

Laura: Do I know Steve Carlson?

Toni: Probably not, I don't know.

(4.0)

Toni: But anyway, then she goes [said in a mock dramatic fashion] *"I don't know why I did it."* She goes "I wanna go with Steve," and then she goes "I don't know. I just had to get it out of my system, I guess."

Laura: Oh, god.

(4.0)

Toni: Then I heard Bonny's going with ... Tom, you know, and she was talkin' about askin' Lon to the Homecoming Dance. She

wasn' gonna break up with Tom unless she knew that she had
somebody else who would ask her out.

(2.0)

Laura: Poor Lon.

Toni: Really. He's getting thrown around a little I think. [Laura
         laughs] I'd stay up there if I was him. [Toni laughs] [Lon is
         living in Minneapolis with Laura]

Laura: I know it.

(4.0)

Toni: So many *stupid* people 'roun' here.

(2.5)

Toni: Including me, you know.

Gossiping about another speaker's relative requires delicate negotiation, particularly when the talk could reflect poorly on that
relative, and, hence, on the conversant. Toni is claiming that Lon
does not have any steady girlfriends and is used by local girls as a
second choice to make a point to their "real" boyfriends. Toni must
gossip in such a way that Laura does not feel hurt by these comments. Toni structures her gossip so that both she and Laura can
identify with and feel sympathy for Lon. Toni's "*really*" ratifies
Laura's claim that the topic is Lon's poor treatment by the local
girls, as opposed to Lon's lack of attractiveness as a partner. This
gossip, which could be interpreted in at least two ways, gains a
consensual meaning, as both Laura and Toni share moral orientations to the events described.

The final two lines of this dialogue are significant in expressing
moral consensus. When Toni remarks, in defending Lonny: *So many
stupid people 'roun' here*, she receives no response to this statement
which would seem to call for immediate ratification. As a result,
she alters the focus on the statement by adding *including me, you
know*. This shifts the original statement to refer not to the quality
of the community, but to teenagers generally — that is, all people
in this class (Toni included) are *stupid* — or at least not sufficiently
concerned about the feelings of others. From attempting to identify
with the "not stupid," an approach which seems to fail, an identification is made with the "stupid." As is true in many forms of talk,
self-corrections are considered to be preferable in creating a smooth
line of talk (Schegloff, Jefferson, and Sacks, 1977).

The third example of consensus building is a rather "juicy" piece
of gossip about an acquaintance who may be a thief. Laura and

Toni are discussing an occasion on which Toni had to work as a waitress in her father's supper club when she had laryngitis:

> Toni: Dad was pissed because I had, I couldn't talk so I, and it was so busy I had to take three tables anyway, so I'm [makes a sound which is a cross between an unintelligible whisper and a squeak] yeh know ... And ... so I took only three tables ... and that ... fucking Corine [another waitress] went by and took a dollar off one of my tables and Dad watched her do it.
>
> (3.0)
>
> Laura: That doesn't sound like Corine ... I don't think.
>
> Toni: I don't know but ...

Laura is not prepared to accept Toni's moral evaluation of Corine, since the image of Corine stealing money is contrary to Laura's more positive evaluation. This would appear to be a location for disagreement, even vehement argument. However, the conversants manage successfully to gloss their disagreement by subtly backing away from their positions. Laura in saying *that doesn't sound like Corine* attempts to transform the account into something which is atypical of Corine's normal behavior, and further gives in by saying *I don't think* — as if not to dispute the legitimacy of the evaluation. This is similar to Laura's statement about Tom, cited earlier *I thought he's really nice*. "Thinking" can serve rhetorically as a provisional belief, subject to quick modification. Toni, for her part, is willing to back off from the implication that this behavior is representative of Corine's normal behavior by saying *I don't know*. The concluding *but* indicates that Toni has not retreated from her claim that the theft actually occurred. Subtly, through indirection, these girls have stated their opinions without publicly disagreeing (for a related argument see Pomerantz, 1978 a, 1984). They share a moral order, even though they may not agree about Corine's placement in it.

These three examples of talk indicate the power of gossip in establishing consensus, while at the same time managing the impressions that others have of social actors. Successful gossip rests on the assumption of mutual identification — the claim that all of the social actors inhabit the same moral universe. This consensus is significant for adolescents who may sense the moral moorings of their lives shifting underfoot — as parents and peers have different perspectives on appropriate behavior. The gossip performs in a world in which behavior is subject to disagreement, but in one in which consensus is expected. The reaction of the conversational other must continually be taken into account, and will shape the gossip and comments drawn from the gossip. As folklorists have recognized (Bauman, 1975; Georges, 1969; Abrahams, 1970) communication is artistic in that it is responsive to its context and is socially-shaped. Gossip, although not as finely developed structurally as some genres, meets the contextual constraints of folk narrative.

5. Gossip and Blame

Symbolic interactionists have examined how individuals attempt to account for themselves through excuses and justifications (Scott and Lyman, 1970). However, alignments to situations need not only refer to the speaker's discussion of his/her own action. People also categorize the actions of others, and in the process altercast them (Weinstein and Deutschberger, 1963) — that is, provide them with new identities. Gossip involves a process by which the speaker and audience align themselves to the behaviors and moral selves of others.

Personal blame can be divided into three general types, which I term moral defect, negligence, and moral blindness. The latter two categories refer to implicit, although unacceptable, ignorance by the blamed actor. These categories can further be divided into whether they represent a permanent state or whether the blamed action is defined as an aberration. Blame contrasts with excuses or justifications which gossipers use to absolve a wrong-doer — using the techniques detailed by Scott and Lyman (1970). Excuses are defined as "accounts in which one admits that the act in question is harmful, wrong, or inappropriate but denies full responsibility," while justifications "are accounts in which one accepts responsibility for the act in question, but denies the perjorative quality associated with it" (1970: 491). Blame, by contrast, involves connecting the bad, wrong, or inappropriate act with the actor's responsibility for that act (Pomerantz, 1978 b).

Moral defect

Moral defect is the most severe form of blame in that it attempts to establish the pollution of the actor's core self. Although moral defect can be a temporary aberration (as in Laura's view of Corine's action), often a moral defect is seen as characteristic of the person. For example, Bev and Toni tell Laura about a classmate whom they consider to be immoral and promiscuous:

Laura: Will you explain to me who Debby Dicklick is?
Bev: Debby Dicklick is//
Toni: °Debby Norton is the big fat one [says in an exaggerated, high pitched voice] Hi.
Bev: [Says in a deep masculine voice] Debby sucked me off. [All laugh] What a winning name.
Toni: Debby Norton.
Laura: Debby Norton.
Toni: Yeah.
Laura: That name's familiar.
Toni: She's the one//
Bev: °that was supposed to be pregnant// in sixth grade.
Toni: °By Ken Benson's dad.
Laura: Oh, that's right.

During the conversation these girls often refer to Debby Dicklick and her friends ("the Florrie-Dorries"). The Florrie-Dorries typify immoral social actors. The speakers, like the rest of us, are not paragons of conventional morality. These girls admit to drinking while driving, using drugs, engaging in theft, and having sexual experiences. However, their own deviant actions are either excused or justified, while the Florrie-Dorries are extravagently blamed for their actions. Although I cannot conclude from the data collected whether the Florrie-Dorries are "actually" less moral, they are defined as having passed through the boundary separating "good girls" (the conversants) from those who are immoral, blemishing the face of the team (of high school girls) (Goffman, 1959: 83). These characters through their contrast make the conversants appear moral. The existence of deviants allows for the fact of conformity; if the Florrie-Dorries didn't exist, they would have to be invented.

Contrast this moral defect to the way that Toni is treated in a story she chooses to tell about herself — a narrative that in another setting could carry with it different moral implications:

Toni: Oh ... an' then you know how Jim Rollins is goin' with Susie O'Dell, heavy.

Laura: OK.
Toni: Real heavy ... Oh ...
(3.0)
Toni: Well ...
Laura: Well.
Toni: No, it's not very cool or nothin', but//
Bev: [Loud, deep, mocking voice to Toni] °Second woman.
Laura: [to Toni] You?
Toni: You know it's not ... we're never really done nothin' ... you
          know, like we were at that party, and he comes up five ... or
          fifteen minutes, tells Susie he's got to piss ... comes up to talk
          to *me*. [Toni laughs]
Laura: [in a mocking, sarcastic voice] You're a real homewrecker,
          arncha Toni?
Toni: First time I've ever done that.
Bev: Heck, I'd wreck that home if I could.

This account (not strictly gossip since it is a first-person narrative) could be read as implying that Toni has attempted to disrupt a relationship. Both Bev and Laura suggest — humorously — that Toni is a *homewrecker* or a *second woman*. Yet, Toni is not blamed. Toni justifies her own action, saying that *We've never really done nothin'*, it was just *talk*. Further, she "excuses" herself by indicating that Jim lied to come up to see her. As if this were not sufficient, Toni deflects blame from her possible "moral defect" by saying that it is *the first time I've ever done that*, implying that whatever might be blameworthy in her action was an aberration. Note that Laura never learns what Toni actually did. Bev provides the coda when she justifies Toni's action by saying: *Heck, I'd wreck that home if I could* — implying that Jim is a very desirable male.

The participants work together to insure that no residue of blame sticks to Toni through a combination of rhetorical techniques grounded in the performance of moral evaluation. No one stands up for Debby Dicklick in this group of friends.

Blame can also be attributed to people who do not have a moral defect as such. The blamed actor can be negligent — in that s/he did not intend the results that transpired, or may be morally blind — in that s/he didn't realize that the actions committed were morally blameworthy. In a sense both negligence and moral blindness might be seen as moral defects (carelessness or moral ignorance), but they differ from those situations in which people attribute moral callousness or bad faith — as with promiscuity or dishonesty. In

those cases the actors are assumed to recognize that what they are
doing is wrong, but they do it anyhow, despite the moral constraints
of the (adolescent) social order.

Negligence

Some people are not considered immoral, but still do things for
which they "should have known better." They were just "stupid"
in their actions:

Bev: [while discussing her family's history of cancer] All the doctors
that she had were so close to her that they didn't really believe
that she was dying. I don't know. Did Mary [Bev's older sister]
ever tell you [Laura] about Jerry Williams? Another//

Laura: °I heard
of the name.

Bev: Well, anyways. He was one of her doctors, and ... and Mom
knew it was terminal, and you know, 'cause Tim had told her
that. My mom asked him if it was terminal or whatever and
he goes: "Nooo, nooo, it's not," and he was her, you know
... her doctor. I can't see how they can ... not know that.

Laura: He just didn't want to believe it was terminal?

Bev: Yeah ... That's really bad when your doctor doesn't want to
believe it.

This doctor doesn't have a moral defect — possibly too much
compassion — but his actions are still blameworthy for their impro-
priety and their ignorance. Moral issues do not really come into
play in negligence, rather the condemnation is based on a technical
failure — here, the inability to read medical signs properly. Just as
an excuse provides a claim that the motivation of the error was
acceptable — blame by reason of negligence does the same. But
negligence is the attribution to an excuse which has failed to convince: it's an excuse which ultimately does not excuse; a reasonable
person would have known better.

Moral blindness

The third type of blame is directed to those who do not realize that
what they are doing is wrong. If negligence is an excuse that has
failed, moral blindness is related to a justification that has failed
and has not justified the action. Of course, moral blindness can be
seen as a moral defect, but at least it is not a directly manipulative

form of "immorality." Moral blindness applies to those who are blameworthy, but "don't know any better," as in the following examples:

Laura: [about two friends] I think that Boyd lives with Gretchen ... They are divorced you know.

(2.0)

Laura: I have given up on her.

(4.0)

Toni: I couldn't even catch up with her ... or keep up with myself, if I was//her.

Laura: °Really.

(4.5)

Laura: I haven't seen her ... she went to Seattle for a couple of weeks.

Toni: Really?

Laura: Yeah.

(10.0)

Laura: It must not have done any good, but absence makes the heart grow fonder, you know.

***

[Toni's mother is angry at Toni's father, and has threatened to take the car that night and leave their house]

Toni: I wonder where my mom's gonna go tonight. I hope she just goes ... somewhere and then she gives me the car ... I was really depressed ... She ... she ...

Laura: She's just gonna take off? That doesn't sound like your mom.

Toni: Well, she won't; she just says that to scare everyone. She goes in the bathroom; turns on the water, you know, like she like she's gonna drown herself [All laugh]. Everyone else just sits there, Dad stands outside the door waiting for her to be done, you know.

Bev: My mom quit that shit. Now she just goes to sleep. She lets my dad do all the talking; she just gets hyped for about five minutes. She runs around the floor "Aww! Aww!" [said in nasal voice]

Toni: I wish my mom would go away for a while, but she's so dumb, she just won't go away.

In these two segments of talk social actors are being condemned — but not so much for their moral flaws, as for not realizing the reactions of others to their actions. These are people who are rhetorically defined as "out of it," as lacking skills in role-taking. As with justifications, the actor presumably doesn't realize that the behavior being referred to is inappropriate. However, in justifications typically the speaker is doing the justifying for him/herself whereas in gossip about moral blindness the lack of justification is noted. Life is filled with such scenes in which actors think that their actions are justified, but these actions are seen as morally blind by those who are to judge them. This is one reason why gossip tends to be more negative than self-evaluation — one knows and believes one's own justification, while for reasons social, political, and moral, the likely justifications of others are denied.

6. Teenage Gossip and Moral Evaluation

Adolescent gossip is composed of a continual thematic variation of blame, justification, excuse, and reputation. Perhaps more than any other age group adolescents are seeking standards of action and rules of morality that will guide them in a complex and increasingly differentiated world. However, objective standards do not exist, and this becomes increasingly clear as the adolescent is exposed to a wide range of behaviors and opinions. Still, the need for standards of behavior remains strong, and groups of adolescents establish moral codes of their own — grounded in their idioculture. Frequently these moral rules are not explicit, but are grounded in an emergent collective evaluation of a situation. That is, the eventual moral evaluation of an action will depend upon such things as the characterization of the actor, the status of the moral evaluator, and the context of the behavior and of the evaluation.

Gossip is an emergent, dramatistic performance, shaped through interaction. Unlike most previous studies of gossip, I have attempted to focus on the interaction context of gossip. Gossip, more than most forms of verbal interaction, is based on consensus. It assumes that all parties to the gossip share similar moral standards, and are in a relationship to each other that they will readily agree to moral perspectives which are different from their own. Adolescent gossip is particularly characterized in this way both because of the searching for moral standards and because of the importance of peer opinion in shaping behavior. Perhaps it is symbolic that the "tribe of adolescents" is similar to other anthropological tribes in their reliance on gossip to enforce conformity and in differentiating groups.

Gossip is predicated on the legitimacy of blame. Although gossip does not by definition preclude positive evaluation, most gossip is based on a critical appraisal of the behavior of another social actor. Three types of blame were depicted in this paper. First, blame may rest on the presence of some moral defect in the social actor — a trait recognized by the actor, but displayed without regard for its consequences. Second, some blame accrues to individuals who display negligence; even though they recognize the existence of moral prescriptions, they act in such a way that results in consequences that they should have known would occur. They are "careless." Finally, some actors are characterized by moral blindness. These actors do not realize their actions are seen as morally disreputable, and so persist in their behavioral affronts to the moral order. The latter two forms are the inversion of the two major subdivisions of accounts: excuses and justifications.

The content of gossip is not grounded in general moral orientations, but is the narration of particular acts and delicts; as such we must recall that gossip is specific. A moral perspective is generated from the gossip (Moerman, 1973), but is not the gossip itself, although the two are intimately connected. Gossip is, as much as any form of communication, a means of world-building, and it deserves to be considered in analyses of the structure of talk, or, for that matter, when considering how social order is possible.

Note

1. All names in this report are pseudonyms.

References

Abrahams, Roger D.
   1970   "A performance-centered approach to gossip", *Man* 5 n. s.: 290 – 301.
Atkinson, Max and John Heritage (eds.).
   1984   *Structures of social action: Studies in conversation analysis* (Cambridge: Cambridge University Press).

Bauman, Richard
  1975   "Verbal art as performance," *American anthropologist* 77:
          290 – 311.
Blumer, Herbert
  1969   *Symbolic interactionism* (Englewood Cliffs: Prentice-Hall).
Burke, Kenneth
  1969 a *A grammar of motives* (Berkeley: University of California
          Press).
  1969 b *A rhetoric of motives* (Berkeley: University of California Press).
Button, Graham and Neil Casey
  1984   "Generating topic: The use of topic initial elicitors,"
          pp. 167 – 190 in Max Atkinson and John Heritage (eds.),
          Structures of social action: Studies in conversation analysis
          (Cambridge: Cambridge University Press).
Colson, Elizabeth
  1953   *The Makah Indians* (Manchester: Manchester University
          Press).
Covelli, Lucille H. and S. O. Murray
  1980   "Accomplishing topic change," *Anthropological linguistics* 22,9:
          382 – 389.
Cox, Bruce
  1970   "What is Hopi gossip about?: Information management and
          Hopi factions," *Man* 5 n. s.: 88 – 98.
Fine, Gary Alan
  1977   "Social components of children's gossip," *Journal of communi-
          cation* 27: 181 – 185.
  1979   "Small groups and culture creation: The idioculture of Little
          League baseball teams," *American sociological review* 44:
          733 – 745.
  1981   "Rude words: Insults and narration in preadolescent obscene
          talk," *Maledicta* 5: 51 – 68.
Georges, Robert A.
  1969   "Toward an understanding of storytelling events," *Journal of
          American folklore* 82: 313 – 328.
Gluckman, Max
  1963   "Gossip and scandal," *Current anthropology* 4: 307 – 316.
Goffman, Erving
  1959   *Presentation of self in everyday life* (New York: Anchor).
Goodwin, Marjorie H.
  1980   "He-said-she-said: Formal cultural procedures for the con-
          struction of a gossip dispute activity," *American ethnologist* 7:
          674 – 695.
Gusfield, Joseph
  1981   *The culture of public problems*, (Chicago: University of Chicago
          Press).

Haviland, John B.
1977   *Gossip, reputation, and knowlege in Zinacantan*, (Chicago: University of Chicago Press).
Jackson, Sally and Scott Jacobs
1980   "Structure of conversational argument: Pragmatic bases for the enthymeme," *Quarterly journal of speech* 66: 251–265.
Jefferson, Gail
1978   "Sequential aspects of storytelling in conversation," pp. 219–248 in Jim Schenkein (ed.), *Studies in the organization of conversational interaction* (New York: Academic Press).
Kalčik, Susan
1975   "... like Ann's gynecologist or the time I was almost raped": Personal narratives in women's rap groups," pp. 3–11 in Claire R. Ferrar (ed.), *Women and folklore* (Austin, Texas: University of Texas Press).
Kirshenblatt-Gimblett, Barbara
1975   "A parable in context: A social interactional analysis of storytelling performance," pp. 105–130 in Dan Ben-Amos and Kenneth Goldstein (eds.), *Folklore performance and communication* (The Hague: Mouton).
Kohlberg, Lawrence and Carol Gilligan
1972   "The adolescent as a philosopher: The discovery of the self in a post-conventional world," pp. 144–179 in Jerome Kagan and Robert Coles (eds.), *Twelve to sixteen: Early adolescence* (New York: Norton).
Maynard, Douglas
1980   "Placement of topic change in conversation," *Semiotica* 30, 3/4: 263–290.
Moerman, Michael
1973   "The use of precedent in natural conversation: A study in practical legal reasoning," *Semiotica* 9: 193–218.
Morris, G. H. and Robert Hopper
1980   "Remediation and legislation in everyday talk: How communicators achieve consensus," *Quarterly journal of speech* 66: 266–274.
Paine, Robert
1967   "What is gossip about? An alternative hypothesis," *Man* 2 n. s.: 278–285.
Pomerantz, Anita
1984   "Agreeing and disagreeing with assessments: Some features of preferred/dispreferred turn shapes," pp. 57–101 in Max Atkinson and John Heritage (eds.), *Structures of social action: Studies in conversation analysis* (Cambridge: Cambridge University Press).

Pomerantz, Anita
  1978 a   "Compliment responses: Notes on the co-operation of multiple constraints," pp. 79 – 112 in Jim Schenkein (ed.), *Studies in the organization of conversational interaction* (New York: Academic Press).
Pomerantz, Anita
  1978 b   "Attributions of responsibility: Blamings," *Sociology* 12,1: 115 – 121.
Ransohoff, Rita
  1975   "Some observations on humor and laughter in young adolescent girls," *Journal of youth and adolescence* 4: 155 – 170.
Ryave, Alan L.
  1978   "On the achievement of a series of stories," pp. 113 – 132 in Jim Schenkein (ed.), *Studies in the organization of conversational interaction* (New York: Academic Press).
Schegloff, Emanuel A., Gail Jefferson, and Harvey Sacks
  1977   "The preference for self-correction in the organization of repair in conversation," *Language* 53: 361 – 382.
Scott, Marvin B. and Stanford M. Lyman
  1970   "Accounts," pp. 489 – 509 in Gregory Stone and Harvey Farberman (eds.), *Social psychology through symbolic interaction* (Waltham, Mass.: Xerox).
Szwed, John F.
  1966   "Gossip, drinking, and social control: Consensus and communication in a Newfoundland parish," *Ethnology* 5: 434 – 441.
Weinstein, Eugene A. and Paul Deutschberger
  1963   "Some dimensions of altercasting," *Sociometry* 26: 454 – 466.

Learning How to Contradict and Still Pursue a Common End — The Ontogenesis of Moral Argumentation

Max Miller

Nur insofern etwas in sich selbst einen Widerspruch hat, bewegt es sich, hat Trieb und Tätigkeit.

G. W. F. Hegel, Wissenschaft der Logik (1951, Vol. II: 58)

0. Introduction[1]

Is it possible that we — take for example you and me — contradict each other and that we still pursue a common end?

Suppose that out common end is to arrive at a certain refuge somewhere in the Bavarian mountains but we have lost our way. If we take mutually exclusive views of what is the right way, can we still cooperate in order to get to our common destination, the mountain lodge? Of course we could say: "Let's throw a stick and see which direction it points to!", but in all probability we had better start an argumentation. We could reciprocally attack and question our mutually exclusive views of what is the right track. In this way contradictions could be used as a method for unravelling the truth of factual statements; and to know what the relevant empirical facts are certainly is a most significant precondition for the successful pursuit of a common end (such as finding the right track somewhere in the mountains). But how can this method be successfully applied? If I contradict you and you contradict me, will our argumentation not stagnate form the very beginning?

Now, imagine that we are still wandering around in the mountains and that we have become very hungry. But unfortunately there is only one apple to eat. And the question arises how we ought to distribute the apple among us. Is it also possible in a case like this that we contradict each other and still pursue a common end? What if each of us wants to have the apple — can there at all be a common end we could strive for in dealing with our disparate interests? Obviously there is only one common end that could make sense in a conflict situation like this: to do what is *good* or *right*. And we could use our contradictions as a method for revealing to us which mode of distributing the apple is the right one in our situation. Thus, contradicting one another could be used as a method for unravelling the truth of normative statements — provided that it makes sense to talk about the "truth" of normative statements. But again, how can this method be successfully applied? If I contradict you and you contradict me, will we not starve like Buridan's donkey?

Of course you know that this is not the way contradictions necessarily work. G. W. F. Hegel even conceived of contradiction as the source of all life and movement (cf. the motto of this paper). And if I correctly understand Hegel's somewhat mysterious conception, contradictions may result in a shift to a *higher perspective* from which the sources of contradictions become visible for the opposing parties so that they can reconcile their views in the recognition of some "rational necessity".

Whatever Hegel's message may be, his conception at least suggests that in order to understand the question: how is it possible to contradict and still pursue a common end, one must ask: how can the participants of an argumentation contradict each other and, by doing so, shift to a higher perspective from which, in principle, a well-grounded decision on mutually exclusive positions can be made. But what really does it mean to shift to a higher perspective? Is there any guideline for the participants of an argumentation to find the higher perspective under consideration? Is there a plurality of higher perspectives? And if so, can they be ordered according to a hierarchy of significance? And finally, how do children learn to accomplish this shift to a higher perspective? And how do they learn this with respect to moral argumentations?

Although this paper heavily relies on an empirical case-study, its main purpose is not to provide answers but, first of all, to suggest a more precise way to ask questions about the ontogenesis of moral argumentation. The paper begins with a summary of the main points I am aiming at: I suggest a few basic distinctions related to the notion of 'moral argumentation' and I address the question how the developmental study of moral argumentation fits into the context of the social-psychological study of morality and its ontogenesis.

In Part 1 I present some basic elements of a conceptual framework for the empirical study of collective argumentations. The conceptual core of this framework is founded on the distinction between 'arguments' and 'argumentations' and, accordingly, between the 'logic of argument' and the 'logic of argumentation'. The later is conceived to comprise the principles and rules followed by the participants of a collective argumentation when they try to coordinate their individual contributions and thus to develop a joint argument that answers a disputed question. Furthermore, a distinction is made between four domains in the logic of argumentation which correspond to four 'problems spaces' in the inter-individual coordination of arguments used in an argumentation. In Part 2 it is argued that the four types of coordination problems presuppose one another in a hierarchical fashion and that the succession of stages in the ontogenesis of moral argumentation corresponds to this hierarchy of 'problem spaces'. This argument is supported by a number of findings from a case-study of developmental differences in the moral argumentation of three groups of children (5, 7−8, and 10 years of age). Although the data-base of this study is far from being representative, the analysis nevertheless enables a preliminary assessment of the approach and shows possibilities of an empirically grounded theory of the ontogenesis of moral argumentation. This is the general value of case-studies.

The paper concludes with some general comments on systematic relations between the form (structure) and the content of moral argumentations and on developmental mechanisms for learning the principles and rules of collective argumentation.

0.1. Some basic distinctions

By *argumentation* I understand a special type of complex verbal actions comparable to activities such as 'telling stories', 'giving directions', 'explaining games'. They all serve to solve a task by verbal means. The constitutive task of an argumentation is to develop an argument which gives an answer to a disputed question, the *quaestio* of the argumentation. An *argument* is, roughly speaking, an abstract structure consisting of propositions which are connected in a specific ('logical') way; it has to satisfy the '*logic of argument*'. In contrast, argumentations consist of utterances the content of which may but need not enter the argument to be developed; many of them have purely pragmatic or coordinating functions. The task of working out an argument may be carried out by one or several people; accordingly *individual* and *collective* argumentations can be distinguished. In the course of a collective argumentation the people engaged may advocate the same or different answers to the quaestio at issue; accordingly there are *unanimous* and *antagonistic* states of argumentations. An argumentation may be *private*, e. g., a spontaneous dispute during a party or a clinch between spouses, or it may be *public*, e. g., a juridical, political, or scientific dispute, all of which are governed by institutional restrictions on turn-taking, admissible quaestiones, duration, style, etc. There are different *types of quaestiones* that epistemologically delimitate different domains of knowledge. Kant's famous questions in his *Logic Lectures*: "Was kann ich wissen? Was soll ich tun? Was darf ich hoffen? Was ist der Mensch?" (Kant 1968; Vol. IX: 25) designate the empirical-theoretical, the moral-practical, the theological, and the anthropological domain of knowledge. Presumably, further domains can be identified, e. g., the aesthetic domain. All these domains and the corresponding types of argumentation seem to differ with respect to the restrictions they impose on the admissibility of candidate arguments answering a certain 'quaestio'. Finally, the participants of an argumentation frequently seem to be less interested in 'finding the truth' concerning some 'quaestio' than in achieving certain social effects such as gaining respect, humilating the other, or 'scoring' (especially in scientific argumentations). Apparently, the primary goal of an argumentation — finding a joint answer to a disputed question — is for most people in most cases nothing else but a convenient way to achieve a secondary goal. The analysis of this aspect belongs to the *pragmatics of argumentation*, whereas the principles for coming to a joint argument constitute the *logic of argumentation*. It is this concept which is in the focus of this paper.

0.2. Moral judgement and moral behavior

In the final analysis morality is a characteristic of behavior, and moral development should lead to moral behavior. What, then, is the significance of moral judgement and argumentation to morality if our deeds are so much more important than our thoughts and words? The answer is that the description of a behavior as 'moral action' necessarily implies that it is taken as a result of a moral judgement — although additional variables (intervening between judgement and behavior) may, of course, also be taken into account. Just imagine you happen to push some button which causes the whole world to explode. If there are survivors, no one could describe your behavior as immoral because you obviously did not intend to push that fatal button, i. e., you did not for some reason prefer this action and its consequences to a set of possible alternative actions and consequences, which means that you did not pass a corresponding moral-practical judgement. Speaking of "moral actions" presupposes that the action has been partly caused by a moral judgement and choice. This view of the relation between moral judgement and moral behavior is at present not controversial among most social and developmental psychologists.

0.3. Formal and interpersonal morality

However, there is a most interesting controversy about the relation between moral judgment and moral argumentation. Moral judgements are usually advanced in an interpersonal context; and to attack or to defend a moral judgement usually involves the implementation of a collective or interpersonal argumentation. Hence, the ability to pass moral judgements is not sufficiently described by referring to the monological ability to form normative premises and to derive logically correct inferences; moral judgements involve, as Habermas (1973 a: 147) points out, the ability "to convince the participants of a discourse of the validity of a claim (Geltungsanspruch), i. e., to rationally motivate them to accept such claims".

So far, however, most studies of the development of moral judgements have failed to consider it in its interpersonal context. It is true that Kohlberg (e. g., 1971, 1976) considers in his immense and currently most influential oeuvre on moral development what he calls "structures of argumentation". However, he is only interested in the reconstruction of content-bound "moral principles" which persons hold at different developmental stages. Within Kohlberg's framework, the ability to pass moral judgements is restricted to the ability to hold certain normative beliefs (premises) and to derive logically valid conclusions from them.

Norma Haan (1978) has vehemently criticized this conception of "moral judgement ability" which she (somewhat misleadingly) labels "formal morality"; and she suggests an alternative conception which she calls "interpersonal morality". According to Haan there are two basic deficiencies of the conception of 'formal morality':

(a) induction versus deduction

If a theory of morality and its ontogenesis is supposed to clarify by which basic cognitive abilities individuals solve their interpersonal conflicts, then the significant empirical phenomena for such theories are not 'private deductive inferences' but the 'inductive processes' within a moral argumentation: "Interpersonal reasoning arises within the context of moral dialogues between agents who strive to achieve balanced agreements, based on the compromises they reach or on their joint discovery of interests they hold in common." (Haan 1978: 302).

(b) contextualisation versus decontextualisation

"Because interpersonal reasoning is pervasively contextual in character, it is more likely to 'fit' a situation and thus reveal its possibilities for resolving action; formal reasoning is an attempt to match the situation to a priori, imperative, ideal rules to achieve a solution; in the process, critical details may be discarded or lost." (Haan op. cit., 303).

However, this focus on the inductive processes of context-bound (situated) interpersonal reasoning is logically not immune to an extreme kind of relativism, despite the fact that Haan herself does not at all subscribe to a relativist position. Is any 'interpersonal moral judgement' justified if it only 'fits' a situation in the eyes of the persons affected? And what about the developmental succession of 'moral principles'? Is there not, as Kohlberg claims, an increasing affinity to 'true' morality?

Evidently, both Kohlberg and Haan stress an essential aspect of 'moral reasoning'. But neither framework solves the question how a moral judgement can, at the same time, be situationally appropriate and guided by moral principles; or rather: how collective processes of moral reasoning can solve the problem of being situationally appropriate (i. e., bring about a joint definition of the conflict among the participants of an argumentation) *and* of being guided by 'true' moral principles.

If I am not totally mistaken, any (developmental) cognitive theory which can provide reasonable answers to the question how moral reasoning can be situated (contexted) and still be guided by 'true' moral principles would have to take the formal, or rather: procedural, conception of morality seriously. In my view, there is a strong congruence between the following questions:

(a) How do individuals pass an 'interpersonal moral judgement'?, and
(b) How do the participants of an argumentation proceed in order to find a jointly accepted answer to a jointly identified moral quaestio? In other words: what is the logic of moral argumentation?

And similarly between:

(a) How can the rationality or validity of a moral judgement be estimated?, and
(b) On which (ontogenetic) level of the logic of moral argumentation can a moral judgement be defended by the person who has passed it?

Does this conception of 'interpersonal morality' rule out any compatibility with Kohlberg's developmental theory of morality? I do not think so. It is conceivable that the logic of moral argumentation that is characteristic for each developmental stage is a fundamental precondition for the emergence of precisely those moral concepts which underlie Kohlberg's identification of that stage. However, in this paper I do not yet dare to spell out in detail my admittedly still somewhat vague ideas on the possible compatibility between Kohlberg's theory of morality and my own considerations of the ontogenesis of the logic of moral argumentation. If you play a game at too many frontiers, you may lose at too many places. I do not like to lose at all, and therefore I have restricted the following considerations mainly to an explication of what, in my present understanding, constitutes the logic of moral argumentation, and to an outline of a model of ontogenetic stages of the logic of moral argumentation.

0.4. Genetic analyses and metaethical problems

Can empirical analyses of given moral argumentations be of any value to the solution of metaethical problems? Metaethical problems concern the nature of moral concepts, moral arguments (e. g., can they be true?), as well as questions about what constitutes morality, i. e., what the terms "morally good" or "morally justified" ultimately mean.

Most researchers certainly would argue that, quite to the contrary, some understanding of metaethical problems is always — implicitly or even explicitly — presupposed by an empirical analysis of moral argumentations and thus significantly determines its potential result. I would not contest such an opinion; however, it would be unsatisfying if that would be *all* one could say, because then this opinion would lead to an extremely relativistic view of the significance of empirical research in moral development for our overall conception of morality.

In contrast to this, Piaget has developed a paradigm of a "genetic epistemology" which can be characterized as an attempt to clarify the possible contribution of empirical science, in this case: developmental psychology, to the solution of epistemological problems. Especially enlightening are Piaget's considerations of the relation between "empirical truth", "formal logic" and the "cooperation of individuals" (cf. Piaget 1975, Vol. III).

Piaget assumes that if there is no "external or internal absolute" which could serve as a criterion of empirical truth, we are left with the criterion of consensus between individuals. However, the consensus of individuals as a basis for empirical truth cannot be reduced to the statistical congruity of individual opinions: "It is the dynamic convergency which results from using the same tools of thinking; in other words, it is the agreement which arises on the basis of the same cognitive operations that have been used by different individuals" (Piaget op. cit., 238).

Piaget's starting point is an intuitive understanding of the notion of "truth" of an empirical statement which, in his case, is based on a 'consensus theory of truth'. What is interesting, however, about Piaget's conception is that he transforms metatheoretical problems (the question: how can consensus among individuals be a criterion of empirical truth?) into problems for an empirical science (the investigation of cognitive operations underlying basic processes of coordination among individuals).

Is it possible to transform, in analogy to this, metaethical problems regarding what it means for a normative statement to be 'true' into problems for empirical science, in this case: developmental and social psychology? At this point, I do not dare to give a definite answer to this question but only give it some brief considerations at the end of this paper.

1. A conceptual framework for the analysis of the logic of moral argumentation

1.1. Argument and argumentation

Arguments are abstract structures consisting of propositions; a set A of propositions (p) is an argument if and only if for all $p \in A$, p is either basically (or immediately) accepted or if p is derived from other elements of A by certain rules (transition rules).

The *logic of argument* deals with the question: what are the legitimate transition rules? A special class of legitimate transitions is defined by the rules of classical deductive logic. There are other kinds of legitimate transitions, i. e., those of some types of inductive logic or probabilistic transitions. Some writers tend to define the class of legitimate transitions even wider, e. g., Toulmin (1975) in his general conception of "rules of inference".

The central idea of the logic of argument, the transition from basically or immediately accepted propositions to further propositions, can be illustrated by representing arguments as tree-structures in which all non-dominating nodes represent immediately accepted propositions and all dominating nodes follow from the nodes which they dominate. In (1), p_4, p_5, p_8, p_9, and p_{10} are basically or immediately accepted; p_6 follows from p_8, p_2 from p_4, p_5, and p_6, and so on.

(1)

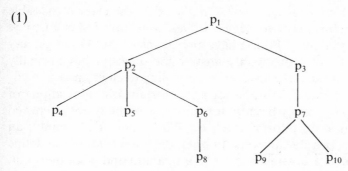

In this tree-structure model of arguments there is no fundamental difference between propositions and transitions between propositions. Transition can be transformed into propositions and represented as new nodes within the tree-structure. The nodes at the bottom of a tree-structure are liminal cases of transitions. p_1 is the *top* of the argument. An argumentation is successful if the participants succeed in building up an argument whose top is an answer to the quaestio at issue.

Real argumentations rarely proceed in terms of syllogisms or modus ponens. They usually consist of a sequence of utterances of different types: statements, questions, imperatives, etc. Even relatively autonomous discourse units such as stories and jokes can be embedded into an argumentation. In contrast to the logic of argument the *logic of argumentation* deals with the ways in which the participants coordinate their contributions so that, at least in principle, a joint argument can be developed that answers the quaestio and thus resolves the differences that caused the argumentation in the first place.

1.2. Coordination problems in moral argumentations

If there were no restrictions on the range of candidate answers to a quaestio, coordination problems could not arise in any argumentation: any answer would do. Concerning coordination problems in an argumentation, the first question to ask, therefore, is, whether there are rules defining what counts as a possible answer to a quaestio and what doesn't.

The quaestio of an argumentation defines a class of propositions, the possible answers, which are in dispute (at least partially) among the participants. For example, a quaestio of the yes-no type, i. e. "Shall you love your enemies?", implies that the class of possible answers contains only two elements, "yes" and "no". Other answers, e. g. "I don't know", "I don't have any enemies", or "Don't get any funny ideas!", do not directly answer the quaestio but normally express the fact that the speaker is not willing to enter an argumentation either because he does not share certain presuppositions of the quaestio or simply because for some reason he is not interested in it. A request for information, i. e. "What shall I do?", entails an open class of possible answers. In brief, there are rules which define what counts as a possible answer to a quaestio and what does not.

Now, the essential difficulty of any argumentation, whether moral or nonmoral, arises from the fact that the participants must coordinate their contributions in such a way that they can find and agree upon a set of immediately accepted propositions that are no longer disputed within the given context and on the grounds of which one of the possible answers to the quaestio can be converted into a collectively valid proposition, i. e. a proposition accepted by all members of the group at least for the time being. In moral argumentations this central difficulty is mostly due to the fact that an action may be good in one respect and bad in another. Predicates like "good", "bad", "better", "worse", etc. have various dimensions or parameters which must be kept apart. As a consequence, the participants may apply mutually exclusive predicates for the evaluation of one and the same action.

This central difficulty is the reason why moral argumentations frequently result in the participants simply acknowledging the fact that there are contradictory judgements; perhaps even the different parameters underlying these judgements are made explicit — but that's it! The question what is morally 'good' in the case disputed counts as undecidable, or the costs of finding out what it is are estimated as too high.

However, in cases such as the moral dilemmas of the Greek tragedy in which the hero becomes guilty no matter what he does and has to decide which guilt he chooses to take upon himself, but also in more trivial cases, e. g., the question whether I ought to help my wife with the housework or whether I may try your patience with this paper — i. e., in all cases, where at least some of the participants of an argumentation are persons directly affected by the answers given to the quaestio, there is no other way but to try to directly answer the quaestio. Simply having things take their course could perhaps produce the worst solution possible.

If an attempt is made to solve the coordination problem of an argumentation and to develop an argument as an answer to a quaestio, the pro's and con's characteristically play a fundamental role. They are the medium in which the argumentative struggle over the statements representing candidates for the set of immediately accepted propositions takes place.

As you know, during the history of philosophical ethics until the present day it has been quite contestable whether, in the case of moral argumentations, this struggle between pro and contra can be terminated other than by arbitrary decisions. If this were true, that arbitrary decisions are the 'ultima ratio', there could be no nontrivial standards of rationality for moral argumentations. But, what does it mean to say that there are standards of rationality for (moral) argumentations?

1.3. Rationality and the logic of argumentation

Does it make any difference which one of the possible answers has been ultimately and collectively accepted by the participants in their attempt to resolve the differences that have caused the argumentation? Obviously, at least in the case of theoretical-empirical argumentations (where, e. g., the quaestio is "Can you run your head against a wall and break through?"), it does make a difference which answer the participants agree upon — lest empirical experience will open their eyes. There are formal rules of theoretical-empirical argumentations which define which possible answer is *the* solution: it is the answer whose truth conditions are fulfilled. Is it equally possible to specify rules of that kind for moral-practical argumentations?

At this point I will simply assume that there are, indeed, rules of that kind for moral-practical argumentations as well. Consequently, a rational argumentation presupposes that the participants share the knowledge of what it means for a descriptive statement to be true (in the sense that it represents what is the case), and of what it means for a normative statement to be true (in the sense that it represents what is right or ought to be done). But this (implicit) knowledge of definitions of truth will not suffice; otherwise *any* set of descriptively and/or normatively true propositions would resolve the differences — given only that it is collectively accepted. Even if the participants of an argumentation agree on formal definitions of truth, they are still confronted with two fundamental problems:

(a) they must develop a joint understanding of the disputed question (the quaestio of the argumentation); i. e. they must jointly identify the differences that caused the argumentation (differences which are, in the final analysis, differences between their subjective perspectives); and

(b) they must try to *find* that set of collectively valid and mutually known propositions which converts one of the possible answers into a collectively valid answer.

Thus, in my view, an argumentation is *rational* if *in principle* it can resolve the differences that caused the argumentation. And this is the case if an argumentation conforms to the logic of argumentation the principles and rules of which supply a guideline for the processes of jointly identifying a disputed question and finding a collectively valid argument providing a true answer to that question. But, what are the principles and rules which constitute the logic of moral argumentation?

1.4. Heinz and the druggist discuss the 'Heinz-dilemma': Four possible coordination failures as illustrations of four domains of a logic of moral argumentation

I will illustrate my view of the logic of moral argumentation with a fictitious discourse. In this fictitious argumentation the main characters of Lawrence Kohlberg's famous "Heinz-dilemma" try to settle their moral conflict. The analysis of four possible coordination failures in this argumentation exposes four fundamental logical domains of moral argumentations and the corresponding rules and principles. In a slightly modified version (which is also the basis of my empirical research on children's moral argumentation; see below) the "Heinz-dilemma" reads as follows:

> "Heinz and Ingrid live in a small town. Ingrid is very ill. The doctor says that Ingrid must die if she does not undergo surgery. However, it is a difficult operation which can only be done by a famous doctor who lives in a different country. But Heinz and Ingrid do not have enough money to pay for the journey and the surgery. They try to borrow money from their friends. They even go to the mayor of the town. Perhaps he can help? But they do not get all the money they need. In his desparation Heinz breaks into a store and steals all the money that is in the cash-desk and all valuable objects. Now Heinz has all the money he needs in order to save his wife's life. But the store-owners have become poor overnight. Should Heinz have done this?"

The problem of justification

Suppose Heinz meets the owner of the store after the burglary (in Kohlberg's version he is a druggist). Heinz is convinced that the burglary was justified; the druggist is convinced that it was not.

Obviously the opponents endorse different and (at least) partially incompatible views of what is right or wrong. Their argumentation starts like this:

Heinz: Sorry. It was inevitable to break into your store.
Drug.:   Are you crazy? How can you say that!

Both Heinz and the druggist relate their utterances to the implicit question: "Should Heinz have done this (the burglary)?" (quaestio of the argumentation). However, whereas Heinz gives an affirmative answer, the druggist gives a negative one. With these contributions made none of the possible answers to the quaestio has been converted into a collectively valid proposition.

The first and basic coordination procedure to be applied now consists in a set of rules for solving the *problem of justification*. The following thesis (T_1) characterizes this procedure informally:

T_1:   The propositions (candidate solutions of a possibly joint argument which more often than not are only indirectly conveyed by the participants' utterances) have to be justified. A proposition is justified if and only if it is either collectively valid from the outset (i. e. if it is immediately accepted by all members of a group at some time t) or if it can be traced back to collectively valid propositions by means of collectively valid transitions. Every proposition advanced and every transition used in some participant's contribution may be disputed by another participant; in this case it is not collectively valid and must therefore be traced back to other propositions accepted by all participants.

What is agreed upon by the participants of an argumentation from the very beginning, of course, does not need to be decided in the argumentation; this explains why arguments in real discourse often seem to be so fragmentary or even incoherent.

The problem of coherence

Heinz continues the argumentation, but his contribution is immediately countered by the druggist:

Heinz: Well, everyone has a right to live!
Drug.:   Don't talk nonsense! Don't you think that that is true for me as well? After all I make a living selling medicine and not by having the medicine stolen.

Both accept the statement: "everyone has a right to live." But each one tries to justify his own previous contribution with this statement, i. e., each one gives this statement a different argumentative value.

A second coordination procedure has to be applied now, provided the opponents still endeavour to develop a joint argument as an answer to their (implicit) quaestio; it consists in a set of rules for solving the problem of coherence of argumentations. Like the other coordination procedures, it only represents a *special case* of the basic coordination procedure for solving the problem of justification.

T_2 is an informal characterization of the procedure for solving the problem of coherence:

> T_2: The coherence of an argumentation must be ensured. All contributions accepted must also be given the same argumentative value by the participants. Translated into the language of tree-structures outlined above, this means that the argumentation's coherence is established if and only if the participants assign an accepted proposition to the same node within the same tree-structure.

But how can the participants possibly use an abstract schema of that kind as a basis for reaching a joint conclusion before this conclusion has actually been reached and accepted?

I will try to give an answer for Heinz and the druggist. As competent conversationalists they know in principle how they have to proceed in order to find an answer to their quaestio: they have to answer subquaestiones; they also know that, in this case, there are at least five subquaestiones that must be answered:

(a) Do they endorse competing parameters for evaluating the alternative actions: 'h = committing the burglary' and '$\sim$h = not committing the burglary'?

(b) What are the relevant empirical facts concerning the alternative 'h' versus '$\sim$h'?

(c) Which values are assigned to the alternative actions 'h' and '$\sim$h' on the basis of the competing evaluation parameters?

(d) How are the alternative actions to be compared within each parameter, i. e., which comparative values can be assigned to the alternative actions as a function of each one of the competing evaluation parameters?

(e) How can a difference in comparative values (as a function of different parameters) be resolved?

If Heinz and the druggist recognize that they do, indeed, endorse two different and potentially competing evaluation parameters, then the core of a candidate joint argument can be represented with the tree-structure (2) which eventually has to be extended. If they want to secure the coherence of their discourse, Heinz and the druggist have to organize the sequence of their (verbally expressed) arguments in terms of this structure, for it represents the argumentation's abstract organizing principle.

(2)

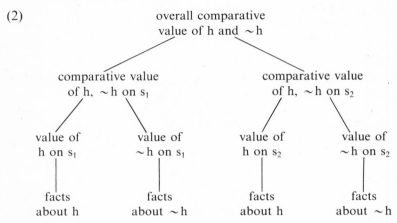

overall comparative
value of h and ∼h

comparative value
of h, ∼h on s_1

comparative value
of h, ∼h on s_2

value of
h on s_1

value of
∼h on s_1

value of
h on s_2

value of
∼h on s_2

facts
about h

facts
about ∼h

facts
about h

facts
about ∼h

(h: act of burglary; ∼h: renunciation of the burglary; s_1: parameter endorsed by Heinz; s_2: parameter endorsed by the druggist)

In real argumentations few persons will proceed in ways corresponding to the 'logical sequence' of subquaestiones as it is represented in a tree-structure. However, no matter with which subquaestio (or subsubquaestio etc.) an argumentation begins and how it continues, the 'logical sequence' of subquaestiones has to be preserved. And, to be sure, if Heinz and the druggist do not adhere to the 'logical sequence' represented in (2), they will never be able to get along. They would act like a group of people that decided to meet in one place and immediately went into different directions.

With the following contribution Heinz tries to ensure the coherence of the argumentation:

Heinz: If I hadn't broken into your store, my wife would have been condemned to die; you're only concerned with other people's respect for your property.

Heinz makes it clear that he and the druggist endorse different parameters and what these parameters are; he also expresses that, in his view, only on s_1 (value of life — parameter endorsed by Heinz) there is a legitimate transition from his previous statement "Everybody has a right to live." to his comparative evaluation of 'h' and ' ~ h' and that, consequently, the act of burglary outbalances its renunciation.

Suppose that the druggist, although he does not accept the total argument implicitly expressed by Heinz, does accept this clarification. Then not only the coherence of their argumentation is established with respect to the statement "Everybody has a right to live."; they both would also know by now that a jointly developed and accepted solution to their quaestio can be traced back to a coherent argumentation only if a jointly accepted transition from the comparative values of 'h' and ' ~ h' on 's_1' and 's_2' to an overall comparative value of both actions can be found.

The problem of circularity

Les us see how the argumentation between Heinz and the druggist goes on:

Drug.: That's exactly the point: whether or not you respect my property. If you had played Lotto, you might have won the money to save your wife's life.

Heinz: You know it's a bad joke to propose gambling. Besides that, can't you see that only because I broke into your store the situation now is good for *all* of us: you can live and my wife can live. But if I had not broken into your store only you would have had the advantage, but my wife would have died.

With these contributions Heinz and the druggist find themselves in serious trouble; not only because their opinions still lead to mutually exclusive answers to their quaestio, but above all because the development of a joint argument now requires the application of the coordination procedure for solving the *problem of circularity* of moral argumentations. However, this coordination procedure (or rather its application) is loaded with so many difficulties that, at least in everyday moral argumentations, solutions can only very rarely be realized on this level of coordination. In which sense do Heinz and the druggist argue in a circular mode?

The druggist aims at presenting the "protection (or value) of personal property" as the decisive parameter for judging the alternative actions 'h' and '∼h'. In order to demonstrate the superiority of this parameter for deciding the case at hand, he assumes a conflict situation in the context of which the competing parameter 'protection (or value) of human life' can be neutralized: both in the case of Heinz committing the burglary and in the case of Heinz refraining from it and choosing to gamble instead, it follows for the druggist that the life of Heinz' wife could have been saved. In the druggist's view of the situation the alternative actions 'h' and '∼h' receive roughly the same value on the parameter "protection (or value) of human life". And if the alternative '∼h = omission of the burglary and gambling instead' would be exposed as being unrealistic, the druggist could of course try to come up with a more realistic alternative that serves the same purpose, namely to neutralize the parameter "protection (or value) of human life". As a result, only the competing parameter "protection (or value) of personal property" would remain relevant to discriminate and decide between the alternative actions 'h' and '∼h'.

Heinz' contribution has a parallel structure. In contrast to the druggist he implicitly expresses some utilitarian maxim according to which one parameter from a set of competing parameters counts as the ultimate criterion if this parameter can be used to show that one from a set of conflicting (alternative) actions brings forth advantages for all persons affected. However, to demonstrate that only the parameter endorsed by Heinz fulfills this utilitarian condition, Heinz must suggest a corresponding definition of the situation: in case Heinz does commit the burglary all persons affected can survive and thus, on the whole, the burglary is justified.

The dispute Heinz and the druggist try to settle circumvents the question which of the competing parameters is the more important (decisive) one *per se* (the difficulty of justifying such a ranking precisely constitutes the dilemma of a moral decision); the dispute rather relates to the question whether one of the competing parameters is less decisive or can even be neutralized in the particular action conflict or its description. Of course this can be a wise strategy for solving a conflict. For example, if I held a pistol to your head and said: "Either you give me your purse or I will be condemned to starve!", you certainly would not dream of accepting this as a challenge to rank the values of human life and personal property. Perhaps you would say: "Try to get some proper work so you can support yourself!" To evaluate my armed robbery you would therefore neutralize the parameter "value of human life", no matter whether or not this parameter overrides the competing parameter "value of personal property" in my view and in yours.

This strategy may be applied for good reasons, but it inevitably results in the problem of circularity: how a given action conflict must be situated in its context, i. e., which empirical statements constitute a *relevant* description of the conflict, can only be revealed in the light of the (potentially) disparate interests involved — which can be traced back to the potentially competing parameters sustained by the conflicting parties. And conversely: which parameters are *relevant* for evaluating an action conflict cannot be decided independently of an empirical description of the alternatives constituting that action conflict. The facets of the empirically given are multifarious, and multifaceted is the manifestation of the 'morally good'. Descriptive and normative premises fulfill a mutually heuristic function in attempts to solve the *problem of relevance* in moral argumentations. But, as a matter of principle, this heuristic process leads into a vicious circle if the participants do not strictly differentiate between the criterion of relevance and the criterion of validity of statements; in the final analysis this means that the criterion of validity of descriptive statements and the criterion of validity of normative statements must be strictly kept apart.

T_3 is an informal characterization of the procedure for solving the problem of circularity:

T_3: The problem of *circularity* arises in moral argumentations because descriptive and normative premises fulfill a heuristic function for each other. The problem of circularity can only be solved if the criterion of *relevance* and the criterion of *validity* of statements are clearly distinguished; in the last analysis this requires that the descriptive and normative statements which serve as premises can vary independently of each other; i. e., descriptive and normative premises (the description of the conflict and the evaluation and weighting of competing parameters — social norms, moral maxims or principles) relate to criteria of validity which are independent of each other: in the case of descriptive statements it is the criterion of *factual truth* (truth conditions: what is the case), in the case of normative statements it is the criterion of *normative truth* (truth conditions: what ought to be done).

The problem of circularity, as I have described it, is not identical with the *naturalistic fallacy* discussed in philosophical ethics, although there are some important features which they have in common. In *Principia Ethica* (1903) G. E. Moore argued that any attempt to define goodness in terms of natural properties is a mistake and constitutes one form of the "naturalistic fallacy". (As you may know, there are some unclear aspects about this definition of the "naturalistic fallacy", but I cannot go into these problems here.). Thus the "naturalistic fallacy" is committed by anyone trying to justify generic normative statements (e. g., "One ought to do x" or "In general one ought to do x") on the basis of some empirical statement. Now, my point is not to ask whether the critique of "natural fallacies" in ethics is well taken in all respects, but what the difference is between a "naturalistic fallacy" and the potential circularity of moral argumentations as I have described it above.

Even if the participants of an argumentation would agree upon some ethos, or, to use Castaneda's (1974) term, a "moral code", and thus upon all generic normative statements advanced in an argumentation, the problem of circularity could still arise; because this circularity is related to the attempt of justifying a *particular* or *singular* normative statement. Although the participants of an argumentation may agree upon an evaluation parameter, they may disagree whether or not it is appropriate to the empirical facts at hand. So in quite a complicated way the justification of a singular normative statement ("X ought to do Y." or "X ought to do Y rather than Z.") — besides implying the justification of a generic normative statement — necessarily also implies the justification of empirical statements. And this is the source of what I have called the problem of circularity; the problem of circularity can only be solved if the criterion of the validity of descriptive statements and the criterion of the validity of normative statements are strictly distinguished. In contrast, the "naturalistic fallacy" in philosophical ethics is related to the question how, in general, the validity of normative statements can be justified.

This brings us to the final domain of the logic of moral argumentation.

The problem of language

Let us come back to Heinz and the druggist. I will assume the exceptional case that they try to solve the problem of circularity of moral argumentations.

Drug.: Are you nuts? What are you talking about? In which world do you live? My survival is not the issue here. What you say is completely besides the point.

Heinz: Well, one of our problems seems to be that we presuppose different contexts for my burglary. I maintain that I had no choice than to commit the burglary if I was willing to save my wife's life. You say, however, that there was an alternative, gambling for example. We cannot settle this question right now. But couldn't we, just to make things a bit clearer, assume for the moment that I didn't have any alternatives. Then we have to see what is more important: to save a human life or to respect somebody else's property. Let's assume we agree on this point as well and thereby come to a hypothetical judgement of my burglary — couldn't we then check whether our view really matches the situation?

Suppose, the druggist accepts this *meta-argumentative* contribution by Heinz; then still another, extremely difficult problem for their argumentation could arise. Just assume their argumentation continues like this:

Heinz: From a moral point of view I have no doubt that it is more imperative to save a human life than to respect somebody else's personal property.

Drug.: My god! What can a moral perspective mean to you, you criminal! From my point of view what is imperative from a moral perspective and what our laws say are one and the same. Our civil code definitely prohibits burglaries; and it never obliges you to commit a burglary to save someone's life.

If Heinz and the druggist still persist in their intention to develop a joint argument as an answer to their quaestio, they have no alternative but to apply the coordination procedure for solving the *problem of language*, that is, for explicating the meanings of the linguistic terms which are in dispute.

T_4 is an informal characterization of the procedure for solving this problem.

T_4: If in an argumentation the *meaning* of a *linguistic expression* becomes controversial, the participants must try to empirically reconstruct the rules of using this expression. In case the linguistic expression "moral" or "morally justified" becomes controversial, the explication of this basic predicate of moral argumentations requires, in the final analysis, the empirical reconstruction of the *logic of moral argumentation*. And conversely: if the logic of moral argumentation did not determine the rules of our use of the term "morally justified", we could never develop a joint understanding of what this linguistic expression means.

Encouraged by his reading of Rawls' *A Theory of Justice* (1971), Heinz tries to explicate the meaning of 'morally justified':

Heinz: According to my use of the English language the following condition must be fulfilled to call some action "morally justified": In an argumentation whose procedures guarantee impartiality, all persons affected by the disputed action agree upon the conclusion that the action ought to be done, i. e., that it must be preferred to all alternative actions that have been considered. From a legalistic perspective my burglary can perhaps not be justified. However, from a moral perspective, it is justified; because under the premise that I had no choice but to commit the burglary if I was willing to save my wife's life, at least in our culture — and that's, after all, where we live — my burglary would be considered "morally justified" in an impartial argumentation.

However, the druggist has always been interested in the question if there is an arbitrary residue in the way moral justifications are being advanced in moral argumentations. And he thinks that, in this precise respect, the last contribution by Heinz offers a good point to attack.

Drug.:   What can compel me to accept your explication of the meaning of the predicate 'morally justified' and not reject it as an interpretation in the light of some 'private language'?

Heinz now reconstructs the total course of their argumentation, in quite the same way as it has been done above, and he counters:

Heinz: If you accept that in moral argumentations we are forced to solve the problems of justification, coherency, circularity, and language (provided these problems arise), then you cannot stop short of accepting my explication of the meaning of the predicate "morally justified"; because the satisfaction of the empirical condition "being supported by an impartial argumentation" is nothing else but the empirical manifestation of the logic of (moral) argumentation which encompasses the principles and rules for solving the four problems stated above. In other words, an argumentation is 'impartial' if it satisfies the following two general conditions: The participants of the argumentation

> (a) have the general competence for solving the problems of justification, coherence, circularity, and language of moral argumentation; and
> (b) they are willing to use their competence for solving these problems whenever they arise.

Drug.: But why should they be willing to subscribe to the logic of moral argumentation in moral argumentations?

This replication and its implicit positivist indolence almost drive Heinz up the wall. And he feels that the following contribution is the utmost he can do in order to coordinate their understandings.

> Heinz: Look! Of course you have the freedom to subscribe to the logic of moral argumentation in moral argumentations or not to subscribe, just as you have the freedom to conform or not to conform to the rule "If you stop breathing you will die." once you have recognized its truth.
>
> Or, to say the same within an ontogenetic framework: there is a theory in social and developmental psychology which assumes that the principles and rules for solving the problems of justification, coherence, circularity, and language of moral argumentations ontogenetically develop in parallel succession. Now, suppose this theory is empirically valid; then I ask you: Obviously you don't want to crawl on all fours like a baby, why don't you as well decide to 'walk upright' in the moral domain? If you call this a case of 'decisionism', well, then this may be considered as the inevitable arbitrary residue in the way moral justifications are advanced in moral argumentations.

Does this effort by Heinz to justify the application of the logic of moral argumentation to moral argumentations amount to some higher order naturalistic fallacy? I leave you alone with this puzzle and turn to the last contribution to this fictitious argumentation.

> Drug.: Stop bothering me with your philosophical palaver. It won't bring me my property back. I will go to my lawyer now. He will certainly stop your silly fuss!

With the last somewhat speculative contributions by Heinz, and the druggist's final reaction showing him as a bad loser, I will end my effort to outline a basic conceptual framework for the analysis of the logic of moral argumentation. So far, my considerations suggest the *empirical hypothesis* that the logic of moral argumentation is constituted by the principles and rules that the participants of an argumentation follow when they try to solve the problems of justification, coherence, circularity, and language of moral argumentations.

However, the conceptual framework established so far does not say very much about the way in which the logic of moral argumentation empirically manifests itself in the use of linguistic and conversational means for coordinating the contributions of the participants of an argumentation. In the following section I therefore make a few comments about this topic before entering into the ontogenetic problems of the logic of moral argumentation.

1.5. The kinematics of contextual change

The logic of (moral) argumentation is, as I said before, essentially related to the problem how the participants of an argumentation develop the set of immediately accepted (collectively valid) descriptive and/or normative propositions supporting a joint argument which answers the disputed question and thus resolves the difference between the opposing parties that caused the argumentation. The four 'problem spaces' outlined above, and the corresponding principles and rules, describe certain aspects of this general problem of a (moral) argumentation.

But how do the participants of an argumentation proceed linguistically and conversationally when they try to coordinate their contributions in such a way that the problems of justification, coherence, circularity, and language can be solved when they arise, and that, subsequently, the set of collectively valid propositions can be found which converts the 'morally justified' answer to the quaestio into a collectively valid proposition? From the perspective of discourse analysis this very complex question implies a clarification of the basic problem of the *'kinematics of contextual change'*[2]. I will only try to say a few words about the way in which this problem manifests itself in the context of argumentations; with respect to moral argumentations I have called this basic problem the "problem of kinematics of the collectively valid" (Miller, 1980).

What is this basic problem? Let us say, at a time t of an argumentation the set of collectively valid propositions supplies the context (conversational background) for understanding the argumentative contribution made right after t by some participant. Obviously this set of collectively valid propositions may change within the time interval extending from t to t'. It may shrink or expand. However, these kinematic processes to a very large extent take place below the threshold of overtly observable linguistic/communicative behavior but are nevertheless controlled by linguistic communication. How is this possible?

The most conspicuous of all linguistic procedures used for controlling the kinematics of contextual change seems to be the procedure for ensuring that the participants can identify the intended top (conclusion) of an argument that is being advanced. The top of an argument is rarely made explicit in everyday argumentations. Even children use certain linguistic expressions to mark the argumentative 'aim' of a contribution, i. e., whether it serves as a pro- or contra-argument to a prior contribution. And by doing so, they can also clarify the implicit 'top' of the argument that is advanced with a given linguistic contribution.

Pro-arguments (as well as agreements with a prior contribution) are marked by the use of expressions such as *ja, mhm, genau, ich auch, dann, da* etc. ("yes", "mhm", "exactly", "I think so too", "then", "there" etc.) at the beginning of a contribution.

For example, five year old children argued like this:

Grischa: Ich find bißchen schlimmer, daß er (Heinz) geklaut hat.
Katja: Ich auch.
Stefan: Dann werden die anderen Leute arm.
(Grischa: I think it's a little worse that he stole something.
Katja: I do too.
Stefan: Then the other people get poor.)

Or, pro-arguments are simply marked by the fact that contributions expressing them immediately follow each other or even overlap.

Contra-arguments to previous contributions are marked by using expressions such as *nein, aber, ja aber, aber eigentlich* etc. ("no", "but", "yes but", "but really" etc.) at the beginning of a contribution.

Whereas a *pro-argument* extends the set of collectively valid propositions by adding propositions contained in the pro-argument but not yet in the 'contextual set of propositions', the kinematics of contextual change is considerably more complex in the case of contra-arguments.

When a *contra-argument* is expressed, it follows by no means that all propositions (including implicit ones) contained in the prior contribution (the one that is being countered) must be discredited as candidates for the set of collectively valid propositions. (If this were the case, there could, in principle, be no logic of argumentation: the participants of an argumentation — which, in fact, is always initiated by a contra-argument — could never develop a joint argument as an answer to their quaestio.)

But how can the participants of an argumentation ensure that their interpretations of a contra-argument converge, so that everyone knows which of the propositions conveyed (directly or indirectly) by prior contributions are denied by the contra-argument and which ones are collectively accepted and thus expand the set of collectively valid propositions?

Often the only way to remove misunderstandings is the use of *meta-argumentative statements*; for example, somebody may say: "By this (referring to his prior contribution) I didn't mean to deny everything you've said, but only ..." or "From the extremely controversial contributions of the previous speakers it nevertheless follows ...". But apparently even more subtle linguistic procedures can be used for controlling the kinematics of contextual change when contra-arguments are advanced so that basic coordination problems requiring the use of meta-argumentative statements do not arise from the outset.

All these problems point to the linguistic/communicative aspect of the general question of how it is possible to contradict and still pursue a common end. I feel unhappy myself that, within the frame of this paper, I cannot intrude more deeply into this very important aspect. On the other hand, whatever the details of the more subtle linguistic procedures may empirically turn out to be — in order for them to be successfully used for controlling the kinematics of contextual change, they presuppose that the participants of an argumentation have the conceptual apparatus for solving the problems of justification, coherence, circularity, and language of (moral) argumentations. If a participant does not know what it means to justify a contribution, to ensure the coherence of an argumentation, to avoid circularity in justifying a particular normative statement, and to explicate the meaning of disputed linguistic terms, then you will never be able to prevent a breakdown of the argumentation when a coordination problem comes up. In the following empirical analyses of moral argumentations among children I therefore try to find out, on the basis of my intuitive understanding of the transcribed texts of these argumentations, whether the four domains or problem spaces of the logic of moral argumentation manifest themselves in the data, whether solutions are collectively advanced, and what these solutions are.

2. Ontogenetic stages of the logic of moral argumentation

Do children exhibit, in their moral discussions, the logic of moral argumentation, as it was outlined in the previous chapter? Do they successively realize that logic in their group-discussions; is there a successive development in this logic parallel to their cognitive and linguistic/communicative development? Finally, does the analysis of ontogenetic data give us some empirical indication of the relation holding between the development of moral concepts (as, for example, those outlined in Kohlberg's stage model of moral development) and the ontogenesis of the logic of moral argumentation? In the following two sections an attempt is made to find at least some preliminary answers to these questions.

However, what in the first place does it mean that there could be a successive realization of the logic of moral argumentation in the group-discussions of children differing in age? Are there any plausible hypotheses that propose a model of ontogenetic stages of the logic of moral argumentation?

2.1. A model of ontogenetic stages of the logic of moral argumentation

In the fictitious argumentation between Heinz and the druggist Heinz at the end adopts the view that the principles and rules for solving the problems of justification, coherence, circularity, and language of moral argumentations presuppose each other according to the sequence in which they have been mentioned here and that they ontogenetically develop in an analogical succession. This view (which expresses the central idea of this paper) needs some explication before the developmental hypothesis it suggests will be empirically 'tested' in a case study.

Since the problems of coherence, circularity, and language represent special cases of the basic problem of justification, it makes sense that the three derived problems can only be solved if the participants understand, in principle, what it means to justify an argumentative contribution. Furthermore, a solution of the problem of language — at least where the basic term "morally justified" is disputed — presupposes that the moral domain and the factual domain can be distinguished and that children understand that normative statements and descriptive statements can vary independently of each other; i. e., participants of an argumentation must understand what it means to avoid a circularity in validating descriptive and normative statements. And finally, the solution of the problem of circularity presupposes that the participants do not miss each other's point because of merely structural reasons, i. e., that they can identify the intended argumentative place value of a contribution and thus ensure the coherence of an argumentation.

So far, at least the first part of the view adopted by Heinz seems plausible: the four 'problem spaces' of the logic of moral argumentation presuppose each other as levels within a hierarchy. But what about the second part of his view? Is there a hierarchical succession of ontogenetic stages that corresponds to the 'logical hierarchy' of these four 'problem spaces'?

First of all, at what point in their development do children understand the basic procedure of justification? Apparently already before they have completed the second year of life; this is suggested by the following example from a longitudinal study of early language acquisition (cf. Miller 1979 a; 102). In this example Simone (age: 21 months) and Meike (age: 20 months, 2 weeks) quarrel about a ball[3]:

(Context: Meike and Simone are playing in Simone's room.)

Meike:	*Simone:*	*Meike's mother:*
balla` [to Simone] (ball) [holds a ball in her hand]		
	balla⁻ [claps her hands and looks at Meike] (ball) *ball`* [softly]	
		Gibst du'n Simone? (Will you give it to Simone?)

nein [complaining]
(no) [directed to mother]

Nein.
(No.)

doch
(yes)
doch

nein [complaining]
[looks at Simone]

do-och [resentful]
(ye-es)
doch [complaining]
[reaches for the ball
and looks at Meike]
mone balla`
(Mone ball)

[brings the ball to
Simone]

Unfortunately, there are severe methodological problems concerning the interpretation of the communicative intentions children express in their one- and two-word-utterances. Nevertheless I think that this text delivers considerable empirical evidence that these children at least implicitly understand what it basically means to justify an utterance. The quaestio that seems to be at issue for Simone and Meike is: "Who may have the ball, Simone or Meike?" First, neither of the two possible and mutually exclusive answers is jointly accepted. Finally, Simone seems to trace her answer back to the statement *mone ball* which turns out to belong to the children's set of collectively valid propositions. On this basis, Simone's imperative seems to be collectively accepted. Meike brings her the ball.

Suppose that, at a first ontogenetic stage of the logic of moral argumentation, children implicitly know what it basically means to justify, i. e., that nonaccepted contributions have to be traced back to collectively valid propositions. Is there any empirical evidence for a hierarchical continuation of ontogenetic stages that corresponds, step by step, to the 'logical hierarchy' of the four 'problem spaces' of the logic of moral argumentation?

2.2. A case study

The case study reported here is based on a limited part of a corpus of data gathered for a more extensive explorative study of the ontogenesis of the logic of moral argumentation. The total data base contains both spontaneous moral argumentations in which groups of children (quite vehemently) deal with moral conflicts of their own and elicited moral argumentations based on stories told to groups of children and adolescents. The groups range in age from 3 to 18 years. Here, the argumentations about my version of Kohlberg's 'Heinz-dilemma' in three groups of children are analyzed.

Method

The three argumentations about the 'Heinz-dilemma' took place in Frankfurt in the fall of 1977. Each group consisted of four children of 5 years, 7/8 years, and 10 years, respectively.

With one exception (Birgit — group 1) all children are from middle class families (the parents are university graduates), and with one exception (Elisabeth — group 3) all children attended the same kindergarten group or school class. (Curiously enough, only Birgit and Elisabeth — although they knew the other children of their group very well — talked very little in the argumentations.) The groups gathered in my appartment.

The children were told stories that culminated in a moral dilemma. After an interview with each child the whole group was asked to take the role of parents or of a body of judges (depending on the story) and so find out whether they could give a joint answer to the quaestio — and if not, why. While the group discussed the story, I sat at a desk in a corner of the room and pretended to do some work. A friend of mine stood behind a grand piano and filmed the group discussion with a video camera.

The artificiality of this 'quasi experimental' setting was reduced because all children were close friends of my own children and my appartment was familiar to all of them; I myself was also quite familiar with all of these children. All groups produced remarkably long and lively argumentations. Only after the children considered their task (argumentation) finished did I join in the conversation, asked for a summary of the argumentation, and tried to detect contradictions in what the group said in order to see how much further the argumentation could be pushed.

The influence of this setting on the children's argumentative behavior becomes clear from a comparison with 'spontaneous' moral argumentations also included in my data base; there is little overtly aggressive behavior and the periods in which the children are seriously involved in the argumentation are quite extended. Yet, this impact of the setting is favourable to my research interests because it is closely related to only those cognitive and communicative abilities of the children which are presupposed by the logic of moral argumentation. A setting which would have given the 'subjects' broken heads would, at any rate, not have been very helpful for 'testing' first ideas about the ontogenesis of the logic of moral argumentation.

Although a case study is only a first step, it is nevertheless of high methodological significance. At least my intuitive understanding of substantial and methodological issues in the ontogenesis of the logic of argumentation was immensely enhanced by this and other case studies which cannot be presented here. On the other hand, the generalizability of information gathered from a case-study always is an open question. The only kind of evidence it supplies for the hypothetical ontogenetic model is some plausibility.

Unfortunately, hard-boiled experimental psychologists tend to only perceive these rather trivial restrictions on the empirical significance of the case study method (cf. the controversy between Miller (1976 b), Deutsch, Herrmann and Laucht (1979) and Miller (1979 b)); psychologists of this provenance often seem to forget that the development of warranted hypotheses also falls within the domain of an empirical science and constitutes a major part of scientific rationality. Moreover, concerning the significance of this case study, one should not forget the astonishing fact that, at least as far as I can see, no empirical investigation of the ontogenesis of this central aspect of social structures (the institution of moral argumentation) has so far been conducted. Therefore, this case study may also per se deserve some attention.

Argumentation analyses

In the tree-structures which are used in the argumentation analyses to represent the arguments developed by the children, the following notations are used:

$x \gg y$	x is to be preferred to y
$x \ll y$	y is to be preferred to x
$x = y$	neither x nor y is to be preferred

h   performance of the burglary
~h   omission of the burglary
h', h'', h''', etc.   substitutes for h
kons^x factual consequences of x
kons$_1^x$, kons$_2^x$, etc.   subsets of the factual consequences of x
$\langle a \rangle_K$ statement 'a' is valid for person K
$\langle a \rangle$ statement 'a' is valid for all the participants of
                        an argumentation

Group 1: 5 years old

The argumentation esentially consists of contributions made by
Katja, Grischa, and Stefan whereas Birgit remains rather silent.
Therefore, I will say that a joint argument has been developed even
if only Katja, Grischa, and Stefan have argued and found a consent.
After a short conversational phase during which none of the children
apparently wants to commit himself to an answer to the quaestio:
"Should Heinz have done this (the burglary)?", Grischa initiates a
short argumentation directly related to the task of finding an answer
to the quaestio: "I think it's a little worse that he stole something.".
Katja consents: "I do too.", and Stefan supports Grischa's statement: "Then the other people get poor.".

With this the group has developed a joint argument as a (partial)
answer to the quaestio. This can be represented as follows:

(3)

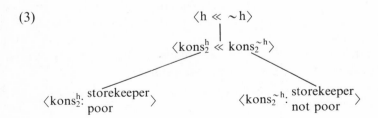

However, in the continuation of the argumentation this argument
is confronted by Katja with the following remark: "But I — I think,
that if she has to die then, I think that's also pretty bad.". Grischa
and Stefan agree. So a second joint partial answer to the quaestio
has been developed by the group:

(4)

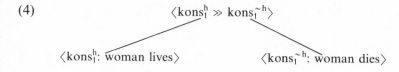

$$\langle \text{kons}_1^h \gg \text{kons}_1^{\sim h} \rangle$$

$\langle \text{kons}_1^h: \text{woman lives} \rangle$ $\langle \text{kons}_1^{\sim h}: \text{woman dies} \rangle$

The two arguments (3) and (4) do not necessarily exclude each other; in argument (4) it remains open which of the two mutually exclusive answers to the quaestio: $\langle h \gg \sim h \rangle$ or $\langle h \ll \sim h \rangle$, is to be supported by it. In spite of this not very conclusive result the group considers their task to be finished. Stefan: "Come on, let's tell him!".

In the following the group discusses the question about what and how I ought to be informed by them. As was already the case in the previous argumentations, they agree to retell the whole story. But they do not come to terms as to who should take over this task. Finally, I intervene and direct their attention to their role as a body of judges: they are expected to consider whether Heinz was right in doing what he did and whether he should be punished. And I ask them again whether they share the same opinions. The children immediately come to an agreement that Heinz should not be punished. Then Katja and Stefan essentially reproduce argument (4). Katja: "I think that ... the man must — his wife ... must not die.". Stefan: "Listen! But the man shouldn't become poor and alone. He must have money.". Thereafter Katja summarizes both contributions: "Yes. He must have money. Because he must — because I don't think it's so good if his wife must die. I don't think that's so good.". Grischa assents several times to the contributions by Katja and Stefan. The further consequences of the burglary or the omission of the burglary, namely that the storekeeper does or does not get poor, are completely ignored by the children during this phase of the argumentation:

(5)

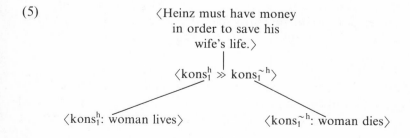

$\langle$Heinz must have money
in order to save his
wife's life.$\rangle$

$$\langle \text{kons}_1^h \gg \text{kons}_1^{\sim h} \rangle$$

$\langle \text{kons}_1^h: \text{woman lives} \rangle$ $\langle \text{kons}_1^{\sim h}: \text{woman dies} \rangle$

Although the quaestio: "Should Heinz have done this?" is not directly answered by argument (5), the children nevertheless consider their 'argumentation task' completed.

I ask the children what the result of their argumentation has been. Katja and Stefan again present the bulk of arguments (4) and (5). Grischa and, at this point, Birgit also consent. A peculiarity of the group's summary is that Stefan's contribution suggests an explicit formulation of the evaluation parameter that is implied by the arguments (4) and (5): "A — a woman must — a woman must ... have a man. And a man must have a woman.".

The argument contained in the summary with which the group tries to answer the quaestio can be represented as follows:

(6)

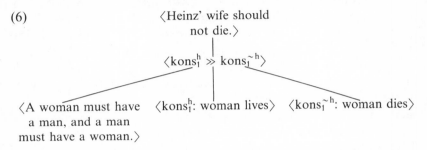

Afterwards I confront the group with the question whether their answer does not amount to the acceptance of the burglary and the consequence that the storekeeper gets poor. However, this does not follow directly from any of the arguments advanced by the group. It is therefore quite consistent when Katja and Grischa now deny that the burglary and its consequence, that the storekeeper gets poor, is right. At the same time though, they point out that it is not right either if Heinz' wife has to die. Grischa: "We don't think that's (the burglary and the consequence that the storekeeper gets poor) right. But neiter should the woman die.". For the group, both the argument (3) and the argument (6) are equally valid partial answers to the quaestio. It remains open how, on the grounds of both arguments, a coherent answer to the quaestio can be developed. But the group apparently does not even perceive this as a problem.

Group 2: 7/8 years old

Tanja, Felix, Karsten, and Tommi participate in this group. The quaestio "Should Heinz have done this?" is immediately answered with "no" by Felix and Tommi. Felix supports this with the further statement: "There is also, if you are in court, there is also the lawyer. One could try to get an advice there. From the lawyer.". Karsten and Tanja agree. Accordingly, the group has found a joint argument for answering the quaestio. But this argument with which the group tries to ignore Heinz' dilemma and which reappears in a later phase of the argumentation (where it will be analysed in detail) is not accepted by me as an answer to the quaestio. And while I once more formulate the dilemma in which Heinz finds himself, Karsten begins to make a contribution on the grounds of which he tries to support the conclusion $\langle h \gg {\sim}h \rangle$: "I think it's better — they are poor, but nevertheless they can still live. And then the woman can also still live. They (the store-owners) are just a little bit poorer now.". Karsten's argument is represented in the following tree-structure ('sto' is 'storekeeper').

(7)

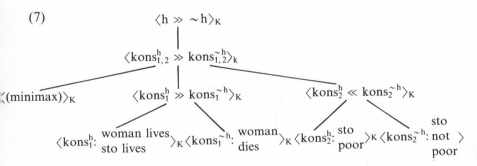

Only on the condition that Karsten implicitly endorses the higher order evaluation parameter 'minimax' does it become understandable that and how he can aggregate the competing comparative evaluations $\langle \text{kons}_1^h \gg \text{kons}_1^{\sim h} \rangle$ and $\langle \text{kons}_2^h \ll \text{kons}_2^{\sim h} \rangle$ to the overall comparative evaluations $\langle \text{kons}_{1,2}^h \gg \text{kons}_{1,2}^{\sim h} \rangle$ and $\langle h \gg {\sim}h \rangle$. What is this higher order evaluation parameter 'minimax'? A possible formulation could be: "If there are alternative actions and corresponding sets of action consequences but *only one* involves advantages for all persons affected, then this one is to be preferred to all others; and, analogically, if only one involves disadvantages for all persons affected, it is to be rejected."

But Karsten uses a 'trick' in order to make this parameter applicable at all. In his view the set of consequences 'kons_1^h' not only contains the consequence "woman lives" but also the consequence "storekeeper lives". Subsequently, the higher order evaluation parameter 'minimax' can be successfully applied; 'kons$_{1,2}^{\text{h}}$' involves advantages for all persons affected and thus 'h' is to be preferred.

Since it is unclear to what extent Karsten is aware of the higher order parameter 'minimax' implied in his own contribution, and how he would eventually phrase it, this parameter is represented within parentheses in the tree-structure (7). The more trivial parameters which obviously underlie the competing comparative evaluations ⟨kons$_1^{\text{h}}$ ≫ kons$_1^{\sim\text{h}}$⟩ and ⟨kons$_2^{\text{h}}$ ≪ kons$_2^{\sim\text{h}}$⟩, namely "value of life" and "value of personal property", are neither represented in the tree-structure (7). This also holds for all the following argument-tree-structures given that these parameters are only implicitly expressed in the corresponding linguistic contributions.

Karsten has not yet finished his contribution when Tanja contradicts him: "Well, but look! If they are poor now, and they also do not get so much money now, then the man's wife or the woman's husband must also break into a store. And then they get poor. And this goes on and on.". Tanja's contribution implies an answer, ⟨h ≪ ~h⟩, that is contrary to the top of the argument (7). Nevertheless the structure of Tanja's argument completely parallels the structure of Karsten's argument. In Tanja's argument the competing comparative evaluations ⟨kons$_1^{\text{h}}$ ≫ kons$_1^{\sim\text{h}}$⟩ and ⟨kons$_2^{\text{h}}$ ≪ kons$_2^{\sim\text{h}}$⟩ can also be aggregated to the overall comparative evaluations ⟨kons$_{1,2}^{\text{h}}$ ≪ kons$_{1,2}^{\sim\text{h}}$⟩ and ⟨h ≪ ~h⟩ on the basis of the higher order evaluation parameter 'minimax'. Only if the set of consequences 'kons$_{1,2}^{\text{h}}$' holds, in Tanja's view disadvantages arise for an infinite number of persons affected:

(8)

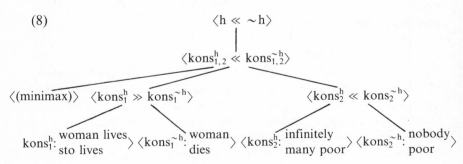

With this contribution Tanja seems to beat Karsten's argument (7). Now the whole group agrees that Heinz should not have committed the burglary. And Felix picks up his old idea that Heinz could have gone to a lawyer: "Then they can — try to get some advice.". Tanja, Karsten, and Tommi assent. And Felix continues: "Yes, go to the lawyer, he is always so good.".

Apparently the group does not want to accept $\langle kons_1^{\sim h}$: woman dies$\rangle$ as a consequence of accepting the argument (8). Felix' proposal takes this into account. The substitute for 'h', which is suggested by Felix as a way out of Heinz' dilemma, namely 'h': to get advice from a lawyer', avoids the negative consequences of both: 'h' and '$\sim$h'.

Structurally this avoidance of the 'Heinz-dilemma' implies a sharpened version of the implicit higher order evaluation parameter 'minimax'; a possible formulation could be: "If there are alternative actions and corresponding sets of action consequences, but *only one* involves *only* advantages for all persons affected, then this one is to be preferred to all other ones." But in order that this new version of the parameter 'minimax' can at all assign a preference to some action alternative for Heinz, this alternative must empirically be constituted in a way such that one of the competing parameters: "value of life" of "value of personal property", can be neutralized. In the view of the children of group 2, this condition can be fulfilled by the action alternative 'h': to get advice from a lawyer'. The neutralized parameter is "value of personal property". The argument expressed by Felix' contribution is formally represented in figure (9) (the neutralization of the implicit parameter 'value of personal property' is expressed by the node: $\langle kons_2^{h'} = kons_2^{\sim h} \rangle$:

(9)

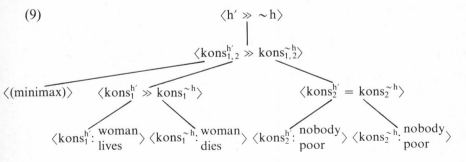

In the summary of their argumentation with which the children spontaneously begin, the group at first uses the argument (8) to support the opinion that Heinz should not have committed the burglary, or rather: that Heinz should not commit a burglary —

here the children have changed the temporal frame of reference. After this they again advance the argument (9) in order to propose the substitute 'h″' ('to get advice from a lawyer') as the solution to Heinz' dilemma.

In the following I join the group's conversation and try to pin the group down to Heinz' dilemma. I deny that in the situation in which Heinz found himself he did have any alternatives besides committing or omitting the burglary.

First Felix tries again to find a way out of the dilemma: "He ought to get a new job!". But now Karsten and Tommi reject this contribution as irrelevant. Tommi is prepared to accept the answer: $\langle h \gg \sim h \rangle$: "I would have broken into the store.". Tanja joins in his vote; however, in the following she develops — partly in cooperation with Karsten — an argument which starts out from the alternative "burglary versus non-burglary", justifies the burglary, and nevertheless tries to circumvent Heinz' dilemma in a very elegant manner: "Well, in this case I would've also broken in. But I wouldn't — I would — I would not have taken all valuable objects and all that. Only so — so one — so one can make the trip and pay for it and can live by it. Then I would take only so much that I can pay for the trip and the doctor."; and Karsten continues: "Yes. But not any more, would you? Then the people don't get poor. Then they both have the same. Then the woman can live and then both can live.".

Structurally the new argument expressed in Tanja's and Karsten's contributions completely parallels argument (9). The new argument rests on the assumption that there is an action alternative 'h‴' for Heinz which decisively changes the consequences of 'h'. 'h‴' is "to break into the store, but to take only so much that the storekeeper does not get poor". Again Heinz' dilemma is circumvented by neutralizing one of the competing evaluation parameters; like before, it is the parameter "value of personal property":

(10)

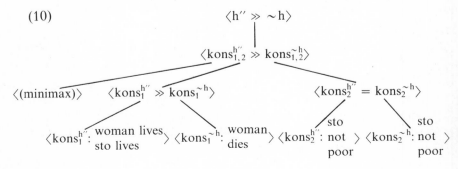

This argument is accepted by the whole group as an answer to the implicitly reformulated quaestio: "What should Heinz do?". In the following I try to block this way out of the dilemma as well. I point out that Heinz was forced to steal so much money and so many valuable objects that the storekeeper certainly would have become poor. But this objection can be overruled by the children. Tanja initiates a new argument that parallels arguments (9) and (10). The sense of what she says, briefly, is that there is a way of committing the burglary, namely 'h″″' which brings forth the desired set of consequences: 'h″″' is 'to break into more than one store'. This substitute for 'h' is subsequently specified by the whole group. What comes out as the optimal solution is expressed by Tommi: "Break into four and take a quarter each time. Then you also have the total." And Karsten continues: "That will do and they all still have enough to live on."

At this point I introduce a new point of view into the argumentation. I want to know from the group whether they think that a burglary is 'right' if the persons affected do not get poor as a result of it. That is, I indirectly convey to the group the opinion that there is a class of actions, burglaries, for all of which it holds that they are 'wrong'. The following phase of the argumentation shows that the children share this opinion. However, an argumentative situation has emerged in which the competing parameters "value of life" and "value of personal property" have to be evaluated themselves, should there still be a possibility of finding a decisive answer to the quaestio. But Karsten and Tanja refuse to continue the argumentation. It's quite obvious that they are angry about the fact that I do not accept the previous formation of a group consent concerning their elegant solution of the 'Heinz-dilemma'. Tanja: "But you shouldn't interfere all the time. When we have found something now, then — and then you say something else. And then all of us say: 'Yes, that's true. That's true.' If we — it was you who said that *we* ought to think about this.". On the other hand, the aggressiveness emerging here probably indicates that the group feels overstrained by the complexity of the argumentative task as it has now become visible.

Group 3: 10 years old

Gabriele, Oliver, Dominique, and Elisabeth are the participants. I only analyse the main line of this long and very complex argumentation. Already at the beginning of the argumentation the group sticks strikingly close to the point. For example, Oliver's contribution: "Actually the operation shouldn't cost any money." which could be used to circumvent the 'Heinz-dilemma', is bluntly rejected by Dominique: "Well, this — we don't talk about that. The point is not the costs, is it?". Concerning the context of the 'Heinz-dilemma' the group closely adheres to the story. And if diverging background information to Heinz' dilemma comes into play, even the wording of the story is cited from memory in order to settle disputed questions.

The first direct answer to the quaestio "Should Heinz have done this?" is given by Gabriele: "But I wouldn't do that if I were in his place.". After some discussion Oliver states the opposite answer: "I'd rather do it.". Gabriele's reaction is rather annoyed: "Well, if you think so.". The argumentation of the group has turned into an overtly antagonistic state.

Dominique tries to achieve a clarification: "Well, what is worse? When someone dies or when someone gets poor?". The two generic action consequences "someone dies" and "someone gets poor" give expression to the fact that in Dominique's view the point at issue is a weighting of the competing parameters "value of human life" and "value of personal property". Gabriele answers: "If someone dies.", and from this Dominique draws the conclusion $\langle h \gg \sim h \rangle$, which has already been explicitly formulated by Oliver and is now only hinted at by Dominique: "That's what you think is worse. Okay then.".

Thus the group agrees upon the following argument as a potential joint answer to the quaestio:

(11)

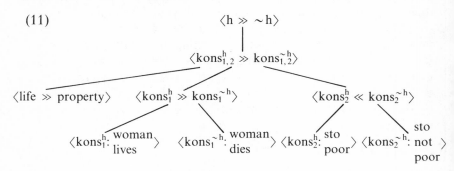

However, the group feels ill at ease with this argument. It is apparently not sufficient for the children to use the proposition $\langle$ life

$\gg$ property$\rangle$ in order to justify the burglary, that is to make the transition from $\langle \text{kons}_1^h \gg \text{kons}_1^{\sim h} \rangle$ and $\langle \text{kons}_2^h \ll \text{kons}_2^{\sim h} \rangle$ to $\langle \text{kons}_{1,2}^h \gg \text{kons}_{1,2}^{\sim h} \rangle$ and $\langle h \gg \sim h \rangle$ a legitimate one. Or to say it more simply: If the value of human life overrides the value of personal property, this is not yet sufficient warrant for saying that Heinz ought to commit a burglary. Dominique: "But actually — well, right, it wasn't really right, was it? But neiter was it — hm — exactly wrong.". Oliver agrees, and later Gabriele refers to an "uneasy feeling" with respect to argument (11).

In the following the group tries to clarify the conditions under which the proposition $\langle$life $\gg$ property$\rangle$ legitimizes the transitions to the top of argument (11). The following proposal made by Dominique seems to meet with general consent: "Well, but he is supposed to have no alternative possibilities.". With the expression "is supposed to" (in the German original it is the particle *ja*) Dominique refers to background information for the 'Heinz-di-lemma' which is binding for the whole group, namely the text of the story.

With this, argument (11) has been modified:

(12)

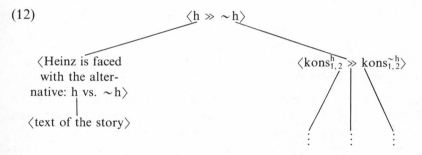

The group then submits arguments (11) and (12) to an even more fundamental critique. The children try to clarify under which conditions the proposition $\langle$life $\gg$ property$\rangle$ holds. Elisabeth: "But if she were an old — old woman, then I think I wouldn't have done it. But if she were twenty — ". Gabriele interrupts her and continues: "No. Because if she were sixty, she would die in a few years anyway.". Thus Elisabeth and Gabriele support the proposition $\langle$life $\gg$ property$\rangle$ with the proposition $\langle$a person's life is to be saved, if that person is still young$\rangle$. However, Dominique objects to this: "But nevertheless, even if she — if she is old, he may still love her. It doesn't matter who it is, his mother, wife, daughter or what". So, Dominique supports the proposition ⟨life ≫ property⟩ by tracing it back to the proposition ⟨a person's life is to be saved if you love that person⟩. Dominique's contribution is accepted by the whole group. The joint argument that is finally proposed by the group as an answer to the quaestio can be formally represented as follows:

(13)

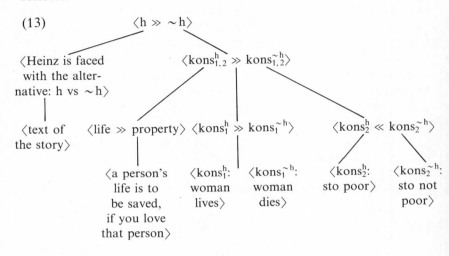

Conclusions drawn from the argumentation analyses

In spite of the fascinating subtlety of these argumentations (which could only partly be analysed here) the question could be raised whether children of 10 years of age and below already have the social background knowledge required for an understanding of the 'Heinz-dilemma'. No doubt, the 'Heinz-dilemma' was more difficult for the children than any of the other stories they also argued about. And when the argumentations analysed above are compared, for example, with the same groups' argumentations about Piaget's "stories of the broken cups" (Piaget 1932), a potential effect of the different degrees of difficulty seems to be that at least groups 1 and 2 were engaged in a much more controversial argumentation in the case of Piaget's stories (cf. Miller, 1981; Klein and Miller, 1980 b, where a case-study of the argumentations about the Piaget-stories is presented). However, on the basic structural level of argumentations, i.e., the logic of argumentation, the different argumentations of each group are very similar in spite of the different degrees of difficulty implied by the content of the different stories.

How far do the children's argumentations about the 'Heinz-dilemma' provide empirical evidence for the hypothetical model of ontogenetic stages of the logic of moral argumentation, outlined above?

Obviously the children of all groups master basic techniques of argumentation: in all of the three groups at least partial answers to the quaestio are developed, and the succession of the linguistic contributions shows that the children basically know what it means to justify a contribution. Furthermore, in all of the three groups the alternative actions 'h' and '~h' (and the corresponding sets of factual consequences) are evaluated on two competing parameters: 'value of human life' and 'value of personal property'. As far as they are made explicit in the course of the argumentation, it turns out, however, that different normative concepts presumably underlie these value orientations in the different groups (e. g., group 1: "A woman must have a man ..." and group 3: "A person's life must be saved if that person is still young or if you love that person."). Finally, there is consensus in all of the three groups that it is not right if Heinz' wife must die but that it is not right either if the storekeeper gets poor as a consequence of the burglary.

But what are the differences between the three groups? The decisive difference that is clearly expressed in the argumentations relates to the conceptual apparatus (principles and rules of the logic of moral argumentation) which the different groups apparently know in order to develop a set of immediately accepted descriptive and normative propositions for deriving a joint answer to the quaestio. To be sure, all groups develop joint answers to the quaestio. But in the process of getting there, *group 1* already fails to solve the problem of coherence; *group 2* overcomes this obstacle but fails to solve the problem of circularity; *group 3* shows first beginnings of a solution of the problem of circularity. However, when group 3 tries to develop an understanding of the higher order parameter for an evaluation and weighting of the competing parameters "value of human life" and "value of personal property", the children of this group also seem to be rather helpless. None of the groups seems to be at all aware of the language problem of moral argumentation.

Going into more detail, the argumentations of the three groups can be summarized and related to the ontogenetic model of moral argumentation (as suggested above) as follows:

Group 1:

Several phases of the argumentation of the group of the five year-old children can be distinguished. In each phase the children relate their contributions to the same subset of factual consequences resulting from 'h' and '~h'; i. e., they either focus on the consequences "woman lives versus woman dies" or on the alternative consequences "storekeeper poor versus storekeeper not poor". Thus the group can ensure that the individual argumentative contributions are, phase by phase, related to one and the same implicit evaluation parameter, and consequently the group can make sure that the participants do not miss each other's point already on a very basic level of moral argumentations. In other words, the group can ensure the coherence of the argumentation with respect to the development of partial arguments, that is, answers to subquaestiones. But the group fails in solving the problem of building up a coherent answer to the quaestio on the basis of the partial arguments that all participants have consented to; (partial) arguments $(3) - (6)$ cannot be related to the required comprehensive structure of a potential joint argument when the group is faced with the fact that two competing evaluation parameters are implicitly involved in the argumentation; and therefore this comprehensive structure cannot organize the argumentation. So the group can never get into a position where the children can envisage an overall comparative evaluation of the alternatives 'h' and '~h'. Katja's endeavour to approach an overall comparative evaluation gets stuck at the very beginning: "Well, at any rate I don't find that it's worse — well, that she — that he shouldn't —". In order to ensure the overall coherence of the argumentation the group would have to develop a higher-order parameter, i. e., a higher-order point of view from which the competing parameters can be related to each other in such a way that, in principle, a well-grounded decision can be made. Only group 2 and 3 seem to be able to adopt such a position.

Group 2:

In the really brilliant argumentation of the group of children of 7/8 years of age, the comparative evaluation of the alternatives "women lives versus woman dies" and the alternatives "storekeeper poor versus storekeeper not poor" can, without difficulty, be related as partial arguments to the required comprehensive structure of a potential joint argument.

How does the group solve the problem of coming to an overall comparative evaluation of the alternatives mentioned above — a problem that is virulent throughout the whole argumentation of this group? The group tries to find out whether one of the set of factual consequences resulting from 'h' and '~h' involves (only) advantages or disadvantages (relative to the competing parameters "value of human life" and "value of personal property") for all persons affected by the action at issue. The higher order evaluation parameter 'minimax' that underlies this utilitarian mode of aggregating different comparative evaluations of alternatives is tracitly presupposed during the whole argumentation. This higher order parameter seems to be an essential cognitive precondition for ensuring the overall coherency of this argumentation.

However, the group is not yet able to solve the problem of circularity of moral argumentation. Which of the competing parameters is the decisive one, or which advantages or disadvantages are to be preferred on the higher order parameter 'minimax', or which normative premises are to be accepted, are questions that are answered by the group depending on how the alternative sets of factual action consequences can be described, i. e., which descriptive premises have to be accepted; and vice versa, the question which descriptive premises count as valid depends for the group on how the question is settled which parameter (life vs. property) or, respectively, which advantages/disadvantages are to be accepted as decisive. (Remember that, e. g., arguments (9) and (10) with their peculiar sets of empirical propositions are developed in order to avoid the acceptance of the consequence 'woman dies' in argument (8).)

Only group 3 shows beginnings of a solution of the problem of circularity of moral argumentations.

Group 3:

Only in the argumentation of the oldest group (10 years old) descriptive and normative premises are implicitly related to criteria of validity which are independent of each other. The descriptive premises that are to be immediately accepted and partly constitute a potential joint argument must fulfill the criterion of factual truth;

this, in fact, means for the group that the premises must conform to the empirical frame established by the actual wording of the story. The normative premises that are to be immediately accepted and partly constitute a potential joint argument must fulfill the criterion of normative truth; and this, in fact, means for the group that they must conform to the normative concepts collectively valid for the group members.

Of course, the question which normative premises are *relevant* at all for answering the quaestio also depends for the group on the definition of the situation, i. e., on the descriptive premises which the participants can agree upon. Correspondingly, the alternative "life versus property" is perceived by the group as relevant only if Heinz is indeed confronted with the factual alternative 'h versus ~h'. And, vice versa, the question which descriptive premises (above all: descriptions of the set of factual consequences resulting from 'h' and '~h') are accepted as relevant for answering the quaestio depends for the group on what the 'value perspectives' are with which the participants enter Heinz' world. However, the circularity of this heuristic (which unavoidably underlies any argumentative process of finding well-grounded answers to quaestiones) does not lead the group into a fallacious circularity of justifying or, more simply, of accepting descriptive and normative premises — as the development of arguments (11)−(13) shows.

When the group tries to justify the normative premise ⟨life ≫ property⟩, however, the participants show a considerable amount of uneasiness and uncertainty. It is true that, confronted with the normative statements "A person's life is to be saved if that person is still young." and "A person's life is to be saved if you love that person.", the group unanimously prefers the latter one. But would the children indeed accept that Heinz rather has his wife die in order not to commit a burglary if he does not love his wife (any more)? If there were basic disagreements, could the children come to an understanding of the criterion of validity that has to be fulfilled by normative premises in order to count as 'morally justified'? The question, ultimately, is: could the children come to terms with an explication of the meaning of the linguistic expression "morally justified"? It is very improbable that the group is already able to solve the language problem of moral argumentations. But here, as well as at many other points of the argumentation analysis, the empirical data do not permit any definite answers.

3. Form and content: The logic of moral argumentation and the emergence of moral consciousness in children

Do not all the empirical and theoretical considerations of this paper ultimately lead to an unsatisfying formalistic theory of ethics? Is it not more important to find out what morality or even the "good" *is*, rather than to find out how we (ought to) talk about it, or how we (ought to) proceed in order to find it under any *particular* circumstances, or how children acquire these formal abilities?

Many centuries of philosophical thinking have passed without showing the slightest possibility of defining what the "good" ultimately is as such, or how the 'good' could ultimately be defined materially. Take for example the contemporary effort by the science fiction author Stanislaw Lem to propose a material definition of the "good" and the "bad" in his short story *Experimenta felicitologica* (1980): " 'Good' means nothing but 'to eat'. 'Bad' means: 'to be eaten'!". Even if Lem's statement, in a later part of his parody about theories of evolution, were true, that this definition of the "good" already holds for the first forms of life, it could still not be demonstrated that Lem's definition of the "good" is anything but a caricature of an eternal moral truth.

On the other hand, if the empirical hypothesis can be validated that there is a logic of moral argumentation and that it is universally acquired by children, adolescents, and adults (at least up to a certain ontogenetic stage which may vary individually), then a formal or procedural definition of the "morally good" can be envisaged which may claim universal validity. Even in this case nobody will ever know, once and for all, how the "morally good" has to be defined materially; but we may learn what the 'logical machinery' or cognitive apparatus is — what the competence is which is applied across cultures and thus universally in argumentations — in order to clarify which normative statements are morally justified and which ones are not.

Accordingly, given a certain socio-cultural context, i. e., a certain set of propositions that are collectively valid for some group G at some time t, any participants of a moral argumentation that belong to this group will consistently come to accept only certain possible answers to a quaestio as morally justified, given that the argumentation is controlled by the logic of moral argumentation, i. e., if it is a *rational* moral argumentation. This, by the way, is how I understand Heinz when he comes to this point in his discussion with the druggist. Heinz said that if he was indeed confronted with the alternative "life versus property", his burglary would be considered "morally justified" at least in our culture, provided that there has been an 'impartial' argumentation. I think that Heinz is right to the extent that the empirical presumption is warranted that in our culture there is a collectively valid belief that the value of life overrides the value of personal property. And I think that, on this level of the moral argumentation between Heinz and the druggist (when, as an outcome of their previous argumentation, they jointly identify the crucial difference between their standpoints as a difference concerning a weighting of the values "life" and "property") that is all that can be said.

So, my conception of the logic of moral argumentation tries to combine a universalistic position (related to the form of argumentation) and a relativistic position (related to the content of descriptive and normative premises) in such a way that each position is assigned that degree of relevance which it apparently deserves.

However, if it is neither possible to derive any material definition of the "good" from the principles and rules constituting the logic of moral argumentation, there nevertheless seems to be a definite relation between the form of a moral argumentation and the moral content it finally leads to. If a moral argumentation is started, what is at stake is which one out of a set of possible singular normative statements can be converted into a joint answer to a disputed question. However, depending on the cognitive apparatus the participants possess, i. e., depending on the degree to which they can make use of the logic of moral argumentation, there will correspondingly be certain restrictions on what can possibly be envisaged as a set of collectively valid propositions (including generic normative statements and, eventually, moral principles such as Kant's "categorical imperative") for deriving an answer to the quaestio of an argumentation. In my view, these restrictions are manifested in certain content-bound patterns of moral reasoning, that is, certain 'moral attitudes' such as an authoritarian, or an utilitarian, or a conventionalistic attitude.

Take for example a group of children whose logic of moral argumentation conforms to stage 1 (the stage of the 5 year olds analyzed above). For structural reasons they will presumably never be able to resolve a conflict by means of moral argumentation if this conflict is based on the fact that different participants adhere to different parameters (which may simply be the different interests of the participants). Then, although these children may already have internalized all kinds of moral values, only an externally motivated decision will be able to settle the conflict. In our socio-cultural context it is the authority of parents, teachers etc. which normally accounts for such an externally motivated decision. Therefore children at this stage will almost always come to endorse the false 'ontology' that the "good" can ultimately be defined as what authorities think it is. Piaget (1932) has called this a "heteronomous morality". Presumably there are analogical relations between form and content characterizing the other ontogenetic stages.

Once adolescents or adults have completely acquired the logic of moral argumentation, they will, in principle, take a universalistic moral attitude, and they will come to accept a formal or procedural definition of the "good". However, corresponding to the ontogenetic stage of the logic of moral argumentation, participants of an argumentation will endorse different 'moral attitudes' and false ontologies concerning a material definition of the "good". And that is all I am prepared to say for the time being.

4. Conclusions

Learning how to contradict and still pursue a common end involves the acquisition of the logic of argumentation. Does the same logic of argumentation shape rational resolutions of disputes in the moral and the nonmoral realms? Like many other basic questions this one cannot be dealt with here.

My major aim in this paper has been (a) to outline what, in my present understanding, constitutes the logic of moral argumentation, and (b) to deliver some preliminary empirical evidence for a model of ontogenetic stages of the logic of moral argumentation — a model which corresponds stage by stage to the 'logical hierarchy' of four domains or 'problem spaces' of the logic of moral argumentation: the problem of justification, the problem of coherence, the problem of circularity, and the problem of language of moral argumentations. Furthermore, I tried to make explicit, at least to some extent, what the 'cognitive basis' is that underlies the logic of moral argumentation at different ontogenetic stages.

Corresponding to the development of this 'cognitive machinery' children become more and more able to recognize the differences in perspective between the opposing parties of an argumentation. The explication of these differences is what 'contradictions' are generally expected to accomplish. Children may indeed become progressively able to contradict and, by doing so, get into a 'Hegelian higher perspective' from which it becomes visible what the differences objectively are that caused the argumentation; or, in other words, it becomes visible what an objective definition of a given moral conflict is.

However, this alone will not resolve any moral conflict. What is the 'true' moral point of view that has to be taken into account in order to pass a judgement on opposing arguments − a judgement that is morally justified in an emphatic or objective sense? As G. W. F. Hegel says in his *Phänomenologie des Geistes* (1948: p. 64), the "absolute" (and the morally 'good' is an "absolute entity") could never be suggested (*nähergebracht*) to us by any tool of knowledge (*Werkzeug des Erkennens*), if it were not and did not want to be with us from the outset (*nicht an und für sich schon bei uns wäre und sein sollte*).

But how can some consciousness of it arise in our minds? Obviously it is only possible on the basis of the logic of moral argumentation. Only if the participants of a moral argumentation conform to the logic of moral argumentation will they be able to recognize what, from a moral point of view, is imperative in a particular action conflict; and as a precondition of this: which idea of the morally "good" they ultimately and collectively agree upon.

To bring all this into a simple formula: In a moral argumentation an exploration of the differences between the participants sets the pace for finding those collectively valid beliefs which can rationally resolve the differences that caused the argumentation. And it is the principles and rules underlying this process of coordination that constitute the logic of moral argumentation.

How do children acquire the corresponding communicative/cognitive abilities? This paper has only scratched the surface of this problem. But perhaps it has become obvious that it will be a fascinating endeavour to explore this 'terra incognita' of developmental and social psychology.

Notes

1. This paper represents a first, preliminary and fragmentary attempt to deal with ontogenetic aspects of collective problem-solving-behavior. For the most part, it has already been written in 1980 when I tried to start an empirical research project about 'collective processes of learning' at the 'Max-Planck-Institut für Sozialwissenschaften' (Starnberg/ München). On the whole, I still maintain the theoretical and empirical theses outlined in this paper; and, so far, the case study reported still seems to represent quite a unique attempt to describe ontogenetic stages of interindividual processes of moral argumentation. In the meantime, however, I have tried to work out a more comprehensive and sophisticated conceptual framework for the empirical study of collective problem-solving-behavior and its ontogenesis. This new approach differs from the conception outlined here in three respects: (a) besides moral argumentations empirical-theoretical argumentations (especially collective argumentations about cognitive tasks of a Piagetian type) are also taken into account, and the commonalities and differences between these two types of collective reasoning and their ontogenesis are empirically investigated; (b) the conceptual framework for an empirical study of collective argumentations has been considerably enlarged and worked out in more detail; and (c) the main thrust of my present work now concerns the theoretical and empirical reconstruction of collective argumentations as an interindividual mechanism of individual development. Readers who are interested in these further questions are kindly referred to Miller (1986 b) where these questions are discussed quite extensively. Some aspects of this new approach are also summarized in Miller (1986 a).

   When, in 1980, I started to think about the ontogenesis of moral argumentation, I was mainly interested in finding some clear-cut and empirically convincing hypotheses about ontogenetic stages of individual moral reasoning as a constituent of collective moral argumentations. In this connection, my cooperation with Wolfgang Klein (Max-Planck-Institut für Psycholinguistik, Nijmegen) turned out to be a major source of inspiration and instruction for me (cf. also Miller & Klein 1981). My greatest debts, however, are to Jürgen Streeck who has carefully read this paper and has provided me with many valuable comments and criticisms.

2. Cf. the concept of a 'kinematics of conversational score' in D. Lewis (1979).

3. Expressions printed in italics represent the original German utterances. An English translation (in parentheses) is given below. The vertical order of the utterances corresponds to their temporal succession. The

nonlinguistic context and certain paralinguistic features of utterances are represented within square brackets. The symbols ⁻, ´, `, at the end of the children's utterances distinguish level, rising, and falling terminal intonation contours.

References

Castañeda, Hector N.
1974   *The Structure of Morality* (Springfield, III: Charles C. Thomas Publisher).
Deutsch, Werner, Herrmann, Theo and Laucht, M.
1979   "Die Kontroverse um eine Kontexttheorie sprachlicher Refe-renz", *Zeitschrift für Literaturwissenschaft und Linguistik* 33, 104−109.
Flavell, John H.
1977   *Cognitive Development* (Englewood Cliffs: Prentice-Hall).
Haan, Norma
1978   "Two Moralities in Action Contexts: Relationships to Thought, Ego Regulation, and Development", *Journal of Personality and Social Psychology* 3: 268−305.
Habermas, Jürgen
1973 a   *Legitimationsprobleme im Spätkapitalismus* (Frankfurt: Suhr-kamp Verlag).
1973 b   "Wahrheitstheorien", *Wirklichkeit und Reflexion*, Walter Schulz zum 60. Geburtstag, edited by Herbert Fahrenbach (Tübingen), 211−275.
Hegel, G. W. F.
1948   *Phänomenologie des Geistes* (Hamburg: Felix Meiner Verlag).
Hegel, G. W. F.
1951   *Wissenschaft der Logik* (Leipzig: Felix Meiner Verlag).
Kant, Immanuel
1968   *Logik, Psychische Geographie, Pädagogik*, Kant's Werke (Aka-demie-Textausgabe) 9, (Berlin: de Gruyter).
Klein, Wolfgang
1979   "Argumentation and Argument", *Zeitschrift für Literaturwis-senschaft und Linguistik*, 38/39, 9−57.
Kohlberg, Lawrence
1971   "From Is To Ought", *Cognitive Development and Epistemology*, edited by Theodore Mischel (New York: Academic Press), 151−235.

Kohlberg, Lawrence
1976 "Moral Stages and Moralization: The Cognitive Development Approach", *Moral Development and Behavior*, edited by Thomas Lickona (New York: Holt, Rinehart & Winston), 31−53.

Lem, Stanislaw
1980 "Experimenta Felicitologica", *Die Phantastischen Erzählungen*, edited by Stanislaw Lem (Frankfurt: Insel-Verlag), 239−294.

Lewis, David
1979 "Scorekeeping in a Language Game", *Semantics from Different Points of View*, edited by R. Bäuerle/U. Egli/A. v. Stechow (Berlin/Heidelberg/New York: Springer Verlag), 172−187.

Miller, Max
1976 "Psycholinguistische Probleme der Referenz", *Zeitschrift für Literaturwissenschaft und Linguistik* 23/24, 93−97.

1979 a "Kontext und sprachliche Referenz auf Objekte − Antworten auf eine Erwiderung von W. Deutsch, Th. Herrmann und M. Laucht", *Zeitschrift für Literaturwissenschaft und Linguistik*. *33, 110−115*.

1979 b *The Logic of Language Development in Early Childhood* (Berlin/ Heidelberg/New York: Springer-Verlag).

1980 a "Moralität und Argumentation", *Newsletter Soziale Kognition* (3rd ed.), edited by Monika Keller, Peter M. Roeder, Rainer K. Silbereisen, Technische Universität Berlin, 87−98.

1980 b "Sprachliche Sozialisation", *Handbuch der Sozialisationsforschung*, edited by Klaus Hurrelmann and Dieter Ulrich (Weinheim: Beltz Verlag), 649−668.

1980 c "Zur Ontogenese moralischer Argumentationen", *Zeitschrift für Literaturwissenschaft und Linguistik* 38/39, 58−108.

1986 a "Argumentation and Cognition", *Social and functional approaches to language and thought*, edited by Maya Hickmann (New York: Academic Press).

1986 b *Kollektive Lernprozesse, Studien zur Grundlegung einer soziologischen Lerntheorie* (Frankfurt: Suhrkamp Verlag).

Miller, Max and Klein, Wolfgang
1981 "Moral Argumentations among Children: a Case Study", *Linguistische Berichte* 74. 1−19.

Moore, G. E.
1903 *Principia Ethica* (Cambridge).

Piaget, Jean
1932 *Le Judgement Moral Chez L'Enfant* (Paris: Presses Universitaires de France).

Piaget Jean
1950 *Introduction à l'Epigstérnologie Génétique* Tome III, (Paris: Presses Universitaires de France).

478   *Miller*

Piaget, Jean, Grize, J.-B., Szeminska, A. and Vinh Bang
  1968   *Epistemologie et Psychologie de la Fonction* (Paris: Presses Universitaires de France).
Rawls, John
  1971   *A Theory of Justice* (Oxford: Oxford University Press).
Selman, Robert L.
  1976   "Toward a Structural Analysis of Developing Interpersonal Relations Concepts: Research with Normal and Disturbed Preadolescent Boys", *Minnesota Symposia on Child Psychology* 10, edited by A. D. Pick (Minneapolis).
Toulmin, Stephen
  1958   *The Uses of Argument* (Cambridge University Press).

Subject Index